The Lesser-Known Varieties of English

This is the first ever volume to compile sociolinguistic and historical information on lesser-known, and relatively ignored, native varieties of English around the world. Exploring areas as diverse as the Pacific, South America, the South Atlantic and East and Southern Africa, it shows how these varieties are as much part of the big picture as major varieties and that their analysis is essential for addressing some truly important issues in linguistic theory, such as dialect obsolescence and death, language birth, dialect typology and genetic classification, patterns of diffusion and transplantation and contact-induced language change. It also shows how close interwoven fields such as social history, contact linguistics and variationist sociolinguistics are in accounting for their formation and maintenance, providing a thorough description of the lesser-known varieties of English and their relevance for language spread and change.

DANIEL SCHREIER is Associated Professor of English Linguistics at the University of Zurich. He has taught and lectured in New Zealand, Germany and the USA. His previous publications include *Isolation and Language Change* (2003), *Consonant Change in English Worldwide* (2005) and *St Helenian English* (2008).

PETER TRUDGILL is Adjunct Professor of Sociolinguistics at the University of Agder. He has carried out research on dialects of English, Norwegian, Greek, Albanian and Spanish and has written and edited more than thirty books on sociolinguistics and dialectology including *Sociolinguistic Variation and Change* (2002), *A Glossary of Sociolinguistics* (2003) and *New-dialect Formation* (2004).

EDGAR W. SCHNEIDER is Professor and Chair of English Linguistics at the University of Regensburg. He is the editor of the scholarly journal *English World-Wide* and its associated book series, *Varieties of English Around the World*. His previous publications include *Introduction to Quantitative Analysis of Linguistic Survey Data* (1996) and *Postcolonial English* (Cambridge, 2007).

JEFFREY P. WILLIAMS is Professor of Anthropology and Chair of Sociology, Anthropology and Social Work at Texas Tech University. He previously taught at the University of Sydney and has conducted fieldwork in Papua New Guinea, the American Southwest and most recently with Montagnard refugees in North Carolina, USA. He was the co-editor of *Contact Englishes of the Eastern Caribbean* (2003).

STUDIES IN ENGLISH LANGUAGE

The aim of this series is to provide a framework for original studies of English, both present-day and past. All books are based securely on empirical research, and represent theoretical and descriptive contributions to our knowledge of national and international varieties of English, both written and spoken. The series covers a broad range of topics and approaches, including syntax, phonology, grammar, vocabulary, discourse, pragmatics and sociolinguistics, and is aimed at an international readership.

Already published in this series

Christian Mair   *Infinitival complement clauses in English: a study of syntax in discourse*

Charles F. Meyer   *Apposition in contemporary English*

Jan Firbas   *Functional sentence perspective in written and spoken communication*

Izchak M. Schlesinger   *Cognitive space and linguistic case*

Katie Wales   *Personal pronouns in present-day English*

Laura Wright   *The development of Standard English, 1300–1800: theories, descriptions, conflicts*

Charles F. Meyer   *English Corpus Linguistics: theory and practice*

Stephen J. Nagle and Sara L. Sanders (eds.)   *English in the Southern United States*

Anne Curzan   *Gender shifts in the history of English*

Kingsley Bolton   *Chinese Englishes*

Irma Taavitsainen and Päivi Pahta (eds.)   *Medical and scientific writing in Late Medieval English*

Elizabeth Gordon, Lyle Campbell, Jennifer Hay, Margaret Maclagan, Andrea Sudbury and Peter Trudgill   *New Zealand English: its origins and evolution*

Raymond Hickey (ed.)   *Legacies of colonial English*

Merja Kytö, Mats Rydén and Erik Smitterberg (eds.)   *Nineteenth century English: stability and change*

John Algeo   *British or American English? A handbook of word and grammar patterns*

Christian Mair   *Twentieth-century English: history, variation and standardization*

Evelien Keizer   *The English noun phrase: the nature of linguistic categorization*

Raymond Hickey   *Irish English: history and present-day forms*

Günter Rohdenburg and Julia Schlüter (eds.)   *One language, two grammars? Differences between British and American English*

Laurel J. Brinton   *The comment clause in English*

Lieselotte Anderwald   *The morphology of English dialects: verb formation in non-standard English*

Jonathan Culpeper and Merja Kytö   *Early Modern English dialogues: spoken interaction as writing*

The Lesser-Known Varieties of English

An Introduction

Edited by

DANIEL SCHREIER

PETER TRUDGILL

EDGAR W. SCHNEIDER

JEFFREY P. WILLIAMS

CAMBRIDGE
UNIVERSITY PRESS

CAMBRIDGE UNIVERSITY PRESS

Cambridge, New York, Melbourne, Madrid, Cape Town, Singapore,
São Paulo, Delhi

Cambridge University Press
The Edinburgh Building, Cambridge CB2 8RU, UK

Published in the United States of America by Cambridge University Press,
New York

www.cambridge.org
Information on this title: www.cambridge.org/9780521883962

© Cambridge University Press 2010

First published 2010

Printed in the United Kingdom at the University Press, Cambridge

A catalogue record for this publication is available from the British Library

Library of Congress Cataloguing in Publication data
The lesser-known varieties of English : an introduction / edited by Daniel Schreier
... [et al.].
p.   cm. – (Studies in English language)
Includes index.
ISBN 978-0-521-88396-2 (hardback) – ISBN 978-0-521-71016-9 (pbk.)
1. English language – Variation – Foreign countries.   2. English language –
Variation – English-speaking countries.   I. Schreier, Daniel, 1971–   II. Title.
III. Series.
PE2751.L47   2010
427 – dc22   2009047109

ISBN 978-0-521-88396-2 hardback
ISBN 978-0-521-71016-9 paperback

Contents

Figures

Tables

Contributors

MICHAEL ACETO is Associate Professor of Linguistics in the Department of English as well as Adjunct Associate Professor in the Department of Anthropology at East Carolina University. His published work on Caribbean Creoles and Englishes has mostly made use of primary data gathered in the field in Panama, Barbuda, St. Eustatius, and Dominica. His future work aspires to bring the discipline of linguistics in contact with the millennia of works and thought by Buddhist scholars.

DAVID BRITAIN is Senior Lecturer in Linguistics at Essex University in England. His research has mainly focused on the linguistic consequences of dialect contact, particularly in the case of a new dialect that emerged in the British Fens subsequent to the reclamation which began in the seventeenth century. He is editor of *Language in the British Isles* (CUP, 2007), co-editor of *Social Dialectology* (Benjamins, 2003, with Jenny Cheshire), and is an Associate Editor of the *Journal of Sociolinguistics*.

SANDRA CLARKE is Professor Emerita of Linguistics at Memorial University in St. John's, Newfoundland, Canada. Her research over the past twenty-five years has focused on Newfoundland and Canadian English, largely within a sociolinguistic and sociohistorical framework. She has published extensively on language variation and change in Newfoundland English, as well as in the indigenous Algonquian varieties spoken in Labrador.

SUSAN FITZMAURICE is Professor of English Language and Director of MA Programmes in English Language and Linguistics at the University of Sheffield. She has published extensively on topics in historical sociolinguistics and the history of the English language. She has recently published *Empirical and Analytical Advances in the Study of English Language Change*, co-edited with Donka Minkova (2008).

ROSS GRAHAM is a Senior Lecturer in English at Coventry University. He has published on linguistic and cultural aspects of Bay Islands English. His research interests include English in the Caribbean, sociocultural aspects of language variation, and applications of sociolinguistics to language teaching.

THOMAS HOFFMANN is Assistant Professor of English Linguistics at the University of Regensburg, Germany. His main research interests are syntactic and phonetic variation in World Englishes and Construction Grammar. His book *Preposition Placement in English: A Usage-based Approach*, based on his PhD dissertation, will appear with Cambridge University Press. He has published articles in journals including *Corpus Linguistics and Linguistic Theory* and the *Journal of English Linguistics* and is currently co-editing a volume on *World Englishes*.

JULIAN JEFFERIES graduated from the University of Massachusetts at Boston with a Master's Degree in Applied Linguistics, and is now working on a PhD in Education at Boston College. He is interested in the experiences of transnational migrants, and is currently investigating the negotiation of capital of recently arrived immigrant teenagers in the city of Boston.

MARI C. JONES is Senior Lecturer in French Linguistics at the University of Cambridge and Official Fellow in Modern and Medieval Languages at Peterhouse, Cambridge. Her research interests include all aspects of language death and revitalization, language contact and change, sociolinguistics, dialectology and questions of standardization. She has published extensively on Welsh, Breton and Channel Island French.

ELIZABETH KAY-RAINING BIRD (PhD, University of Wisconsin-Madison) is a Professor in the School of Human Communication Disorders at Dalhousie University, Nova Scotia, Canada. She has taught courses in the areas of normal processes, child language development and child language disorders. Her research areas include child language development and disorders, multiculturalism, bilingualism and Down syndrome. She is currently studying phonetic variability in dialects of Nova Scotia with Dr Michael Kiefte.

MICHAEL KIEFTE is an Associate Professor in the School of Human Communication Disorders at Dalhousie University in Halifax, Nova Scotia, Canada. He completed a BA in Linguistics at Memorial University of Newfoundland and received his PhD in Phonetics from the University of Alberta. His research interests include phonetic variation, speech perception and speech production.

LISA LIM, of the School of English, University of Hong Kong, specializes in New Englishes, especially Asian, postcolonial varieties, with particular focus on contact dynamics in multilingual ecologies. She edited *Singapore English: A Grammatical Description* (Benjamins, 2004), and is co-authoring a book on languages in contact (Cambridge University Press). Her interests also include the vernacular(s) of multilingual, minority communities, such as the Malays of the Cocos (Keeling) Islands and Sri Lanka, and the Peranakans, involving issues of identity, endangerment, shift and revitalization.

GUNNEL MELCHERS is Professor Emerita at the Department of English, Stockholm University. Nearly all her research has been devoted to regional and social variation, with special reference to the north of England and Scotland's northern isles. She has published some sixty papers and articles, e.g. chapters on phonology, morphology and syntax for the recent *Mouton Handbook of Varieties of English* (2004), co-written the textbook *World Englishes* (2004, with Philip Shaw), and co-edited *Writing in Nonstandard English* (2000, with Irma Taavitsainen and Päivi Pahta).

PETER MÜHLHÄUSLER is the Foundation Professor of Linguistics at the University of Adelaide and Supernumerary Fellow of Linacre College, Oxford. He is an active researcher in several areas of linguistics, including ecolinguistics, language planning and language policy and language contact in the Australian-Pacific area. His current research focuses on the Pitkern-Norf'k language of Norfolk Island and Aboriginal languages of the west coast of South Australia. His recent publications include (with Wurm and Tryon) *Atlas of Languages of Intercultural Communication in the Pacific, Asia and the Americas*; *Pidgin and Creole Linguistics*; *Language of Environment – Environment of Language*; and (with Foster and Monaghan) *Early Forms of Aboriginal English in South Australia*.

JEFFREY REASER is Assistant Professor of English Linguistics and Teacher Education at North Carolina State University. His research includes creation and evaluation of educational materials for dissemination of linguistic information. One such project, a multimedia, dialect awareness curriculum for North Carolina, was created for and evaluated in his dissertation (Duke University). He has also performed extensive field research on Abaco Island, Bahamas, which served as the basis for his MA thesis and a series of publications.

EDGAR W. SCHNEIDER is Full Professor of English Linguistics at the University of Regensburg, Germany, after previous appointments in Bamberg, Georgia and Berlin. He has written and edited several books (including *American Earlier Black English*, 1989; *Introduction to Quantitative Analysis of Linguistic Survey Data*, 1996; *Focus on the USA*, 1996; *Englishes Around the World*, 1997; *Degrees of Restructuring in Creole Languages*, 2000; *Handbook of Varieties of English*, 2004; *Postcolonial English*, 2007) and published widely on the dialectology, sociolinguistics, history, semantics and varieties of English. He edits the scholarly journal *English World-Wide* and the associated book series *Varieties of English Around the World*.

DANIEL SCHREIER has taught in Switzerland, New Zealand, Germany and the USA and is Associated Professor of English Linguistics at the University of Zurich, Switzerland. He is author of *Isolation and Language Change* (2003) and *Consonant Change in English Worldwide: Synchrony meets Diachrony*

(2005; both published with Palgrave Macmillan), *St Helenian English: Origins, Evolution and Variation* (2008; Benjamins), and co-author (with Karen Lavarello-Schreier) of *Tristan da Cunha: History People Language* (2003; Battlebridge). He is on the Editorial Board of *English World-Wide* and *Multilingua*.

ANDREA SUDBURY completed her MA in sociolinguistics at the University of Essex in 1996 on language attitudes of learners of Welsh. For her PhD she studied the variety of English that developed on the Falkland Islands and in particular looked at questions of dialect contact in the context of Southern Hemisphere English. From 2000 to 2002 she was a Postdoctoral Fellow at the University of Canterbury, New Zealand, and she is currently Senior Research Administrator at King's College, London.

PETER SUNDKVIST received his PhD in English Linguistics from Stockholm University in 2004, based on a thesis on the vowel system of a Shetland accent of Scottish Standard English. He was a Postdoctoral Fellow at Yale University 2005–2007, and took up a position as lecturer at Högskolan Dalarna in 2008. He teaches courses in English linguistics and phonetics, and continues to conduct research on the phonetics and phonology of Shetland speech.

PETER TRUDGILL is a theoretical dialectologist who is Adjunct Professor of Sociolinguistics at Agder University, Norway; Emeritus Professor of English Linguistics at Fribourg University, Switzerland; Honorary Professor of Sociolinguistics at UEA, Norwich; and Adjunct Professor at the Research Centre for Linguistic Typology, La Trobe University, Melbourne. His most recent monograph is *New-dialect Formation: The Inevitability of Colonial Englishes*. A collection of his essays *Investigations in Sociohistorical Linguistics* is in preparation for Cambridge University Press.

LIONEL WEE is an Associate Professor and Deputy Head in the Department of English Language and Literature, National University of Singapore. His research interests include language policy, New Englishes, metaphor and discourse, and general issues in pragmatics and sociolinguistics. His publications include articles in *Applied Linguistics*, *English World-Wide*, *Journal of Linguistic Anthropology*, *Journal of Sociolinguistics*, *Language & Communication*, *Language Policy*, and *Language in Society*.

JEFFREY P. WILLIAMS is Professor of Anthropology and Chair of the Department of Sociology, Anthropology and Social Work at Texas Tech University. His research interests lie in the area of language and culture contact. In addition to extensive fieldwork in the West Indies, he has conducted fieldwork in Papua New Guinea, Australia and the United States. His current research involves the documentation and description of the Jarai language (Chamic/Austronesian) of Montagnard refugees in North Carolina.

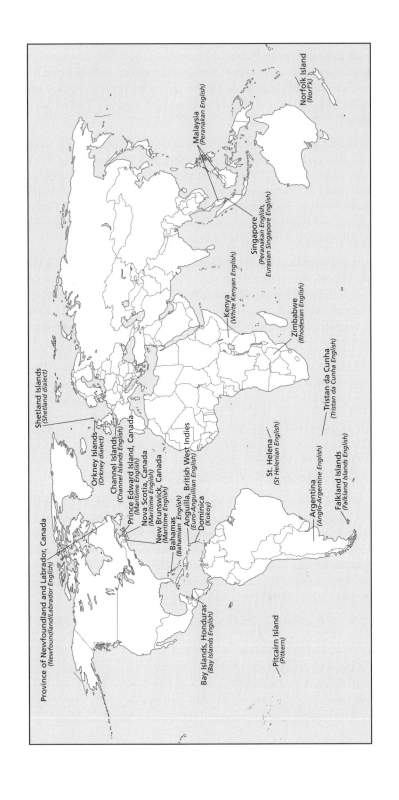

Province of Newfoundland and Labrador, Canada
(Newfoundland/Labrador English)

Shetland Islands
(Shetland dialect)

Orkney Islands
(Orkney dialect)

Channel Islands
(Channel Islands English)

Prince Edward Island, Canada
(Maritime English)

Nova Scotia, Canada
(Maritime English)

New Brunswick, Canada
(Maritime English)

Bahamas
(Bahamian English)

Anguilla, British West Indies
(Euro-Anguillian English)

Dominica
(Kokoy)

Bay Islands, Honduras
(Bay Islands English)

Pitcairn Island
(Pitkern)

St. Helena
(St Helenian English)

Argentina
(Anglo-Argentine English)

Falkland Islands
(Falkland Islands English)

Tristan da Cunha
(Tristan da Cunha English)

Kenya
(White Kenyan English)

Zimbabwe
(Rhodesian English)

Malaysia
(Peranakan English)

Singapore
(Peranakan English,
Eurasian Singapore English)

Norfolk Island
(Norf'k)

1 Introduction

DANIEL SCHREIER, PETER TRUDGILL,
EDGAR W. SCHNEIDER, AND
JEFFREY P. WILLIAMS

> The structure and use of the English language has been studied, from both
> synchronic and diachronic perspectives, since the sixteenth century. The
> result is that, today, English is probably the best researched language in the
> world.
>
> (Kytö, Rydén and Smitterberg 2006: 1)

Would anybody dare deny that English has been studied extremely thoroughly? Given the fact that hundreds if not thousands of languages around
the world are barely documented or simply not researched at all, the massive
body of research on English seems truly without parallel, so this is strong support for Kytö, Rydén and Smitterberg's (2006) claim. Indeed, so many studies
have been carried out to enhance our knowledge of all aspects of the English
language that it is impossible to attempt even a short summary here: the body
of research that has been assembled over the last four centuries is substantial
and constantly growing, from the treatises of orthoepists and grammarians
produced throughout the seventeenth and eighteenth centuries, via English
phoneticians (such as Henry Sweet) in the late nineteenth century and dialect
geography in the early twentieth century, to variationist sociolinguists in the
1970s and computational linguists in the 1980s and 1990s, at research centres
and university institutions throughout the world, on all levels of structure
and usage, phonology, syntax, lexicon and discourse, in domains as distinct
as syntactic theory, psycholinguistics, language variation and change, historical pragmatics, etc., a list that could be continued at leisure. One should
add to this the massive work on the history and development of the English
language itself (Jordan 1934; Bähr 1975; Mitchell and Robinson 1992; Barber
1994; Romaine 1998) from its origins in the fifth century to the present day,
on the extensive contact history that has shaped its evolution, and on the patterns of diffusion, out of England into Wales, Ireland and Scotland and into
the 'New' World, the Americas, the Caribbean, Africa, Asia and Australasia
(Trudgill and Hannah 1982; Wells 1982; Cheshire 1991; Graddol, Leith and
Swann 1996; Crystal 1997; Aceto and Williams 2003; Jenkins 2003; Hickey
2004; Schneider 2007). Taking all this into account, it is perhaps even an
understatement to say that 'English is probably the best researched language

1

in the world'; one should add that it is almost certainly also one of the best-*known* languages (and there is every reason to assume that this in itself is a consequence of the fact that it is the most widely *used* language in the world). How could it be any different, and why would it matter here?

From a bird's-eye perspective, it is unusual that one language should have been brought to so many locations outside its 'heartland', the British Isles, and that transplantation should have given rise to extreme diversification and the birth of countless 'new' varieties: *pidgins* and *creoles*, offspring varieties of language contact scenarios; *koinés*, varieties developing mainly through contact between mutually intelligible and structurally similar forms of one and the same language (dialects or sociolects); and more recently, varieties of English as a *Second Language* (ESL) and *Foreign Language* (EFL), which have gained in total number of speakers dramatically in the second half of the twentieth century, now representing the majority of English speakers around the world (and estimated at more than one billion; Crystal 2008). As Thomason and Kaufman (1988) point out, the 'export' of English is of great value for linguistic research, since the embedding of English into a multitude of contact settings (with countless co-existing language systems) entailed an unprecedented amount of contact-induced language change. As a consequence, the spread of English around the world went hand in hand with the development of countless offspring varieties.

Amassing knowledge is often a selective rather than a representative process, specific rather than global, and it is perhaps inevitable that some areas receive most of the attention whereas others are neglected or even ignored. This is explicitly recognized by Kytö, Rydén and Smitterberg (2006: 1) themselves, since the above quote is followed by the important qualification that 'the field [of English linguistics] is as unlimited as language itself, and therefore there will always be gaps in our knowledge of the historical development of English as well as of its time-bound, or synchronic, uses'. With regard to the study of languages (not only English, but also other world languages such as French, German, Russian, Hindi or Spanish), this means that we know a lot about some varieties but virtually nothing about others. This is stating the obvious and does not come as a surprise, given that the heterogeneity of English around the world is immense. In analogy to Orwell's well-known dictum: all languages (and language varieties) are equal, but some are more equal than others.

Our main motivation for editing a volume on lesser-known varieties of English was the following: we may know a lot about English as a world language, but just as there is a discrepancy in how much we know about English vis-à-vis other languages, there is a discrepancy in how much we know about certain varieties of English (regional or social) vis-à-vis others. Some have been documented fairly extensively (e.g. African American English or New Zealand English), whereas others are barely mentioned in the literature, let alone studied (e.g. the varieties that developed among British expatriates in

Argentina or in the whaling community on the Japanese Bonin/Ogasawara Islands). We are of course not the first to note this. The discrepancy was pointed out by Trudgill (2002: 29), who was probably the first to use the term 'lesser-known varieties of English' (henceforth LKVEs), which he used with reference to a fairly heterogeneous set of ignored varieties of English throughout the anglophone world. A volume co-edited by Richard J. Watts and Peter Trudgill, aptly titled *Alternative Histories of English*, introduced, among others, the history of some selected LKVEs in an attempt to respond to the fact that the history of English is traditionally focused on the standard variety/varieties (i.e. British and American English). Watts and Trudgill (2002: 27) claimed that

Non-standard dialects have histories too, and these histories are sometimes especially helpful because, as a result of the absence of standardisation, many of the forces of linguistic change are played out in these varieties in a much more unfettered and revealing way than in the standard dialect . . . the disregarding of varieties of English simply because the people who speak them are not White Englishmen who have for centuries been established in the southeast of England is also not only totally ethnocentric, anglocentric . . . and unjustifiable, but is also short-sighted in that it disregards an enormous mass of historical data from some of the most interesting and diachronically revealing varieties of the language in existence.

In the same volume, Mesthrie (2002) pointed out that English has always co-existed with other languages, so that non-native speakers played a more important role in the spread of English as a global language than is commonly recognized.

Our book is therefore an effort to somewhat redress the existing imbalance. We exclusively focus on varieties that have received less or no interest in the canon of English as a world language and give a long-overdue platform to those who have never made it centre stage. By doing so, we hope to demonstrate that 'lesser-known' does not equal 'of lesser interest' and that studying LKVEs can help us address some truly important issues in (socio)linguistic theory; to name but some: dialect obsolescence and death, language birth, dialect typology and genetic classification, patterns of diffusion and transplantation, contact-induced language change, conservatism vs. dynamic innovation, even the life-cycles and evolutionary paths of new varieties. Our viewpoint is that studying lesser-known varieties (of English for the present purpose, but of other languages also) is essential for gaining a more concise understanding of the mechanisms that underlie sociolinguistic diversification as well as principles of language birth and death, i.e. questions that loom large in the existing research body on English as a world language. LKVEs are as much part of the big picture as major (or standard) varieties are, and their study contributes considerably to language diffusion and spread.

A crucial point is of course how one is to assess and define the status of 'lesser-known'. Apart from the obvious criterion (simply a variety that is lesser known, at least to the outside world, and that has not received much attention in the literature), a common denominator has guided us in our selection, if only tacitly. Most LKVEs presented here share the following set of characteristics (though in varying proportions and to different extents):

1. They are spoken as first languages and not as ESL or EFL varieties, often in environments where bi- or multilingualism is restricted;
2. They are identified as distinct varieties by their respective speech communities and other groups in their social environment;
3. They are associated with stable communities or regions;
4. They are typically spoken by minorities; they are usually delimitated (not necessarily 'isolated' but socially or regionally distinct) to small communities which are embedded into a larger (regional) population ecology;
5. Many of them were originally transmitted by settler communities or adopted by newly-formed social communities that emerged early in the colonial era, so that they substantially derive from British inputs;
6. They were formed by processes of dialect and/or language contact (which makes it impossible to ascribe them genetic status, e.g. creoles or koinés, see below);
7. They frequently function as identity carriers for their respective communities;
8. They are very often endangered.

As minority varieties deeply rooted in their respective settings, the LKVEs provide model cases of natural language evolution and change 'on the ground', as it were, in the sense of the framework adopted in the *Alternative Histories of English* (Watts and Trudgill 2002), since they are for the most part fairly distant from ideologically overarching standard varieties yet often in competition with them.

What does all this mean for the status of an LKVE and for selection and possible inclusion in this volume? The most important consequence was that we placed emphasis on direct transmission by settler communities, since this meant that we had to exclude ESL and EFL varieties (though it does not of course mean that these are better known), i.e. varieties of English in multilingual contexts where English has no (or a restricted) historical role (Denmark, Japan, Israel, etc.). Second, we focused on varieties that have a time depth of several generations, i.e. that were founded or established in or before the nineteenth century. New-dialect formation is a lengthy process and the emergence and stabilization of new norms take time, so the LKVEs had to have at least some historical continuity. All in all, a total of sixteen varieties met these criteria (though to different extents) and are introduced here; these come from different parts of the English-speaking world and are spoken in the *British Isles* (Shetland and Orkney, the Channel Islands), the *Americas and the Caribbean* (the Canadian Maritimes, Newfoundland and Labrador, Honduras/Bay Islands, White Caribbean, Bahamas, Dominica and Argentina), in the *South Atlantic Ocean* (the Falkland Islands, St Helena and Tristan da Cunha), *Africa* (L1 Rhodesian English and White Kenyan English), in *Australasia and the Pacific* (Eurasian English in Singapore, Peranakan English in Malaysia and Singapore, and Norfolk Island and Pitcairn varieties).

This list is by no means meant to be exclusive and it is our hope that it both triggers an interest in these varieties and encourages work on other LKVEs that might have been included as well (and that we were not aware of). In fact, we are already envisaging a second volume in which we will build on and expand the LKVEs presented here. With this in mind, we are aware of the (somewhat ironic) fact that some of these varieties are better documented and perhaps also slightly better known than others. Whereas research has been conducted on the Channel Islands (Ramisch 1989) or Newfoundland (Clarke 1997, 2004), varieties such as Dominican Kokoy or White Zimbabwean English are documented here for the very first time. LKVEs thus do not form a homogeneous entity amongst themselves (to draw on Orwell again: all LKVEs are lesser-known, but some LKVEs are less 'lesser-known' than others), and this has consequences for selection and description, a point of criticism we have to accept and live with.

It is equally important to determine how the LKVEs should be described and summarized and how they should be grouped and presented. The contributors, all experts of the variety (indeed, in most cases the only expert), were given a template with points to bear in mind so as to ensure a coherent presentation and to facilitate comparison and analysis to the benefit of our readership. They were asked to define and contextualize the variety (by place typically), by stating why it has status as an LKVE, to detail the sociohistorical origins of the variety (inputs, etc.) and to provide sociodemographic information as well (estimated speaker numbers, status of speakers and typical settings of the variety, esp. (if applicable) in comparison with other languages or varieties spoken at that location, i.e. in multilingual countries, diglossic settings, etc.). They were also asked to describe the features of the variety as accurately as possible: *phonetics/phonology* (using the standard lexical sets and terminology as developed by Wells 1982) as well as phonotactic, prosodic and other features of pronunciation, relating the features traceable to specific input varieties, if relevant; *morphology* and *syntax* (noun plural formation and other noun forms, pronouns, verb forms (principal parts, endings), adjective comparison, adverb formation; negation, interrogatives, expressions of tense, aspect and modality, verb complementation and clause patterns, etc.); and to provide some information on the *lexicon*, if at all possible. As a conclusion, contributors were asked to assess the future of the variety as an LKVE (its vitality, stability, etc.) as well as to discuss some additional points relevant to the variety (patterns of variation, for instance). We felt that this would provide a coherent guideline and a yardstick against which the varieties, as different as they are, can be compared for subsequent research. By and large, contributors adhered to the template fairly well, though they emphasized different aspects at their own discretion, partly due to availability of data or their previous research interests (some had carried out research on phonology only, since differences in this area are more salient and diagnostic than in the domain of morphosyntax). By the same token, lexical information was not always available and remains sketchy (for instance, the chapters on Tristan da Cunha and Pitcairn/Norfolk Island provide such information, many others do not).

Finally, as far as grouping and classification is concerned, the fact that the LKVEs display considerable heterogeneity in their social and contact histories made it difficult (in fact, nearly impossible) to assign them to separate categories on typological grounds. Some of the varieties were formed mostly via dialect contact (e.g. Falkland Islands English) whereas others underwent large-scale language contact (Pitcairn). The social integration and embedding (or lack of it) into a larger section of the speech community was not a practical criterion either. Some LKVEs were spoken by expatriate communities in post-colonial settings or elsewhere (White Kenyan or Anglo-Argentine English), in sharp contrast to others that developed on islands, far away from other communities or speaker groups. Consequently, the most reasonable option was to classify the LKVEs geographically, i.e. concentrating on where they evolved and on the place where they are now spoken. This may obscure some structural similarities (e.g. due to founder-effects or direct transmission) but turned out to be a more reliable criterion than contact history or social embedding/degree of isolation. Consequently, we classified the LKVEs into five geographic areas: the British Isles, the Americas and the Caribbean, the South Atlantic Ocean, Africa, as well as Asia and the Pacific. These are now briefly introduced and discussed.

1   The British Isles

For the first thousand years of its history, English was spoken only on the island of Britain, whence it started spreading to other parts of the world only about 400 years ago, so it is perhaps hardly surprising that British varieties of English are generally rather well known and therefore do not figure prominently in this volume. It must be emphasized that during those first thousand years, large areas of Britain were not English-speaking at all: it is only during the last four centuries that English has spread into Wales, northern and western Scotland, Cornwall in the far southwest of England, and off-shore islands such as the Isle of Man. It is therefore also hardly surprising that the two lesser-known varieties of English that we do treat here are from off-shore islands that were not originally anglophone, and which have come into existence relatively recently as a result of language shift.

The northern isles, Orkney and Shetland, became politically attached to Scotland only in the fifteenth century, and as **Gunnel Melchers** and **Peter Sundkvist** explain, they had at that time been Scandinavian-speaking for many centuries as a result of Viking settlement. The rich interplay which then took place between Scots, English and Norn, as the Scandinavian variety was known, eventually leading to language shift and the ultimate language death of Norn, was a linguistically fascinating process which has given rise to a modern sociolinguistic situation, and to modern varieties of English – if indeed we agree that they are all of them English – with very characteristic phonologies, grammars and lexicons.

The English of the Channel Islands is even more recent. The original language of the inhabitants, which still survives in some areas, was a variety of Norman French. For the linguist, the linguistic and sociolinguistic developments which have led to the growth of the current varieties, as described by **Mari C. Jones**, represent an intriguing language-contact and dialect-contact puzzle involving Norman patois, Standard French, Standard English, and regional dialects from various parts of England.

2   The Americas and the Caribbean

The English of Canada is in our estimation one of the better-known varieties of the language. This applies, however, only to those relatively undifferentiated varieties which are spoken in the enormous land-mass of the country which stretches from the western borders of Quebec to the Pacific Ocean. The varieties spoken to the east of francophone Quebec have been much less studied, in spite of their considerable diversity and interest. A considerable amount of work has been carried out on the English of Newfoundland, notably by **Sandra Clarke**, who here, however, also includes a pioneering description of the origins and nature of the English of mainland Labrador. The linguistic history of this area includes the development of English varieties out of contact between the indigenous Inuit and Algonquian (Montagnais-Naskapi) inhabitants, and Europeans not only from England but also from other areas speaking lesser-known varieties of English as featured in this book, including the Orkneys and the Channel Islands. Also very clearly lesser-known are the varieties of English spoken in the Maritime provinces of Canada: New Brunswick, Prince Edward Island, and Nova Scotia. **Michael Kiefte** and **Elizabeth Kay-Raining Bird** here detail the amount of variation there is to be found across these provinces by concentrating their focus on three linguistically very different areas of Nova Scotia.

Turning our attention to the southern part of the American continent, we of course come to the areas where varieties of English are not only lesser-known but where English is also very much of a minority and indeed endangered language, since it is embedded in an overwhelmingly Spanish and Portuguese linguistic environment. By the early years of the twentieth century, there was an established community of around 30,000 anglophones in Argentina, centring on Buenos Aires, with a variety of English of their own. **Julian Jefferies** describes a community whose language is now very much under threat, and whose variety is also very little known.

The English language was transported to the West Indies with the first permanent English settlements that were established in St Kitts and Barbados in the early part of the seventeenth century. This makes the West Indian varieties of English some of the oldest in the history of the expansion of English from the island of Britain. Shaped by the sociolinguistic forces of dialect and language contact over the centuries, we find founder varieties of English which still survive in the isolated, enclave communities of Euro-Caribbeans as well as transplanted varieties whose origins are linked to emancipation. In the case of Kokoy, it was emancipated Afro-Caribbeans who carried the variety, while for Bay Islands English, it was primarily Euro-Caymanians who brought their variety of English to the Bay Islands.

English in the Caribbean, by most linguists' standards, cannot be considered lesser-known. However, that estimation is based on a monolithic view of the well-known creolized varieties of the region, such as Jamaican and Guyanese. In spite of the fact that the documentation and analysis of creolized languages of the Caribbean has dominated the literature on Caribbean linguistics, there are many undocumented and underdescribed varieties, some of which are highlighted in this volume.

The subject of **Michael Aceto's** contribution is Kokoy, a restructured variety of English on the island of Dominica. Based on fieldwork in Wesley and Marigot, Aceto provides the first documentation of this variety. Kokoy was brought to Dominica from Antigua and Montserrat following emancipation in the English-speaking possessions, making it the oldest anglophone variety on a historically francophone island.

Although the Bahamas are one of the better-known varieties of the larger circum-Caribbean region, **Jeffrey Reaser's** contribution on the English varieties of the Bahamas fills further gaps in our knowledge of this complex sociolinguistic subregion. The Bahamas are far from sociolinguistically monolithic as Reaser demonstrates through his documentation of regional, ethnic and class-based linguistic variation throughout the archipelago.

As the smallest of the eighteen departments of the Spanish-speaking country of Honduras, the Bay Islands English-speaking heritage dates to the nineteenth century, as do many of the other LKVEs represented in this volume. For the Bay Islands, it was the event of emancipation that brought English varieties spoken by settlers and freed slaves. In his chapter

Ross Graham details the English varieties spoken by both European- and African-descended Bay Islanders.

The widely scattered descendants of the early anglophone founders are the subject of **Jeffrey P. Williams'** chapter on Euro-Caribbean English varieties. These varieties of English are the oldest in the Caribbean region, dating back to the middle of the seventeenth century, and they preserve a number of archaic features not found in any other varieties in the region.

3   The South Atlantic Ocean

The South Atlantic Ocean hosts three varieties, all of which meet the criteria to be classified as LKVEs: Falkland Islands English (FIE), St Helenian English (StHE) and Tristan da Cunha English (TdCE). The three varieties are strikingly different, both on sociolinguistic and historical criteria. First of all, they differ in *time depth*: StHE is in fact the oldest variety of Southern Hemisphere English (SHemE), as St Helena was established in 1658 by the East India Company and has had a continuous native-speaker population since 1672; it predates the major varieties of SHemE by more than a century. By contrast, FIE is one of the youngest nativized varieties of post-colonial English, since it formed around the mid-nineteenth century only, so it is about the same 'age' as New Zealand English. TdCE was established just a generation or two earlier than FIE, i.e. from the 1820s onwards.

Second, each of the three varieties formed in its separate and distinctive contact setting. FIE arguably comes as close as possible to a scenario of 'pure' dialect contact as we can possibly get, with input from two major population groups from the English Southwest and northern England; StHE evolved in a population ecology characterized by considerable language contact, since slaves were imported from various locations (the (Portuguese-speaking) Cabo Verde Islands, western and southern Africa, western India and the Maldives and most of all from Madagascar). TdCE, finally, had input from (New England) American English and early South African English, as well as from distinct varieties of British English (London, Hull, Devon; the founder of the colony was from the Scottish Lowlands); a number of ESL speakers were present as well (with Dutch, Danish and Italian as first languages). In addition, perhaps the most influential settler group arrived from St Helena in 1827, which entailed that the two varieties share a number of characteristics due to direct transmission from StHE to TdCE.

In their article on FIE, **David Britain** and **Andrea Sudbury** outline the history of the colony from the early 1840s to the present day. They describe a variety that has not been studied at all until Sudbury's pioneering (2000) study, which looked into contact mechanisms and processes of new-dialect formation such as levelling, regularization and reallocation that operated when FIE formed. They detail the social history of the community from the mid-nineteenth century to the present day and describe how the Falklands war (1982) changed life on the island. They describe the phonetics and phonology of FIE and assess how it fits into the overall patterning of SHemE, yet find that its morphosyntax is not particularly distinct from other varieties.

Daniel Schreier contributes to the other two varieties of South Atlantic English and reports on findings of fieldwork on the islands of Tristan da Cunha (1999) and St Helena (2003). Both were under-researched until very recently, Zettersten (1968) being the only study of TdCE before Schreier (2002, 2003) and StHE being barely documented (the exception being two overviews on phonology and morphosyntax by Sheila Wilson and Rajend Mesthrie, included in the *Handbook of Varieties of English* edited by Kortmann et al. 2004). With a mere 280 speakers, TdCE is one of the smallest native-speaker varieties sociodemographically. St Helena has a total population of approximately 4,000, though there has been considerable emigration since full UK citizenship was returned to all Overseas Territories in 1999. Both varieties have extensive contact histories, and these both link them and set them apart. The women who cross-migrated in the mid-1820s certainly affected the development of TdCE and the two articles show that a number of features make an appearance in both varieties, an attestation to the historical links between them. St Helena shares a number of features (copula absence, zero pluralization, TMA markers) with restructured varieties elsewhere (e.g. English-derived creoles in the Caribbean), which raises important issues for independent innovation in language change (Schreier 2008). Both contributions emphasize the importance of sociolinguistic and sociodemographic factors that trigger contact-induced language change and feature selection.

4   Africa

Africa has received some attention in the study of World Englishes, and so most varieties spoken on the continent are decidedly not 'lesser-known'. The most familiar one of these is White South African English, spoken in various sociolects by descendants of settlers from Britain. Many others are second languages or increasingly moving from second to first-language status: Indian South African English has essentially completed the language-shift process; Black South African English and Cape Flats English in South Africa as well as the varieties widespread in West Africa (Nigeria, Cameroon, Ghana) and East Africa (Kenya, Tanzania, Uganda) have not. None of these varieties satisfies our criteria for inclusion in this volume, and most of them (except for Uganda) have been described fairly thoroughly anyway. In southern Africa, e.g. in Zambia, not much (though some) descriptive work has been carried out, but the L2 English spoken there fails to meet the criterion of direct transmission. In Namibia, for example, now strongly influenced by South Africa, English has gained a special status only recently, German having been more influential historically (it is estimated that some 50,000 native speakers of German still live in former German Southwest Africa, so this would actually qualify as a lesser-known variety of German). We considered Botswana but were advised that no stable group of descendants of immigrants speaking English natively exists there (Arua E. Arua, p.c. 6 September 2006). This leaves two such varieties which do exist (or did until recently) and which are covered in this volume, in Kenya and in Zimbabwe (at least until the fairly recent past). In both cases, to our knowledge these contributions are the first descriptions of these dialects ever published.

The stable colonial status of Kenya, its economic potential and the construction of the railway to Lake Victoria attracted a substantial wave of settlers of British origin to the interior highlands of the country early in the twentieth century. **Thomas Hoffmann**'s contribution tracks the history of this settlement initiative and shows that despite political turbulence during the 1950s there still exists a community of some tens of thousands of white Kenyans who by now have had African roots for roughly a century and who in the country's social setup are perceived as one more ethnic tribe, blending in with the multiethnic composition of society. Based on fieldwork in the community, Hoffmann carries out an acoustic analysis of their vowel patterns and points out some conservative features and select similarities to Southern Hemisphere Englishes (with the exception of short front vowel raising) but finds no signs of ongoing language change in an apparent time comparison.

In contrast, Zimbabwe's dictatorship and mismanagement for the last decades has resulted in a mass exodus of people of British descent, whose families, however, had also lived there for several generations. Large-scale white settlement in what was then Rhodesia, beginning in the late nineteenth century, produced a distinctive variety of English that is now, with speakers no longer forming a coherent community, vanishing. It is described here by **Susan Fitzmaurice**, herself a native speaker of this dialect. She details the history of the colony through the twentieth century, presents a case history that illustrates the present-day status of the dialect, and works out its phonological properties and some morphosyntactic and lexical characteristics.

5   Australasia and the Pacific

Similarly to the African situation, English has been thriving throughout Asia for the last half century, has made deep inroads into many countries, and has produced new and distinctive varieties (Schneider 2007), so that many linguists nowadays regard English as an Asian language in its own right. Most of these varieties, however, fail to satisfy our criteria for inclusion – either because they tend to be second languages (a categorization which is gradually changing in some locations, however, most notably in Singapore) or have been described extensively (the Englishes of India, Singapore, Malaysia, Hong Kong and the Philippines, and also, though not quite to the same extent, Pakistan and Sri Lanka) or because at present they seem to be little more than learners' varieties even if some linguists have given them variety names

(English as spoken in Japan, Thailand, Korea or China, for instance). We have identified two cases, however, where specific ethnic identities combine with the criterion of direct transmission and long-standing first-language use of English in the form of distinctly identified ethnic varieties. Again, the respective articles in this volume are the first accounts of these forms of English ever produced. Both have resulted from the long-standing British involvement on the Malay peninsula.

Lisa Lim, herself a former community member, traces the origins of Peranakan English (or Straits Chinese), mostly descendants of male Chinese traders and indigenous Malay women who constituted a culturally hybrid and economically powerful group and tended to acquire and adopt educated English very early, with their roots going back to the British Straits Settlement colony which consisted of Penang, Malacca and Singapore in the first half of the nineteenth century. Lim analyses spoken and written data of acrolectal and vernacular Peranakan English, a variety that, as she states, reflects a distinct ethnic identity but is increasingly blending with Singapore English in general, though a recent cultural revival may strengthen its vitality.

As **Lionel Wee** points out, Singapore's Eurasians, people of mixed European and Asian descent who adopted English early and typically speak it natively, constitute a distinct ethnic group but, strangely enough, are denied an official mother tongue in the state's politically projected linguistic make-up. Wee discusses the consequences of this peculiar situation and the history and status of the group, and analyses some linguistic samples and an idiolect recording, showing that except for a few peculiarities Eurasian English, although it is singled out as a distinct variety in some contexts, largely resembles acrolectal Singaporean English.

The English language in the Pacific region has undergone many contact-induced changes, which has led to a diversity of varieties, most notably Australian English, New Zealand English and Tok Pisin of Papua New Guinea. However, many of the Pacific varieties do not fulfil the criteria for inclusion in the category of LKVE. **Peter Mühlhäusler** describes two important varieties in Pitkern and Norf'k of Pitcairn and Norfolk Islands respectively. The two related varieties were the dominant languages of each community from the founding of the Pitcairn settlement in the late eighteenth century until about 1950, when English gained prominence throughout all sociocultural contexts of use. Like so many of the varieties described between the covers of this volume, Pitkern and Norf'k face threat of extinction, as Mühlhäusler makes clear. For Norf'k at least, Mühlhäusler sees hope that the language shift which is already underway can be reversed.

To conclude, our book adds to what we know about the history of English around the world by exclusively concentrating on those varieties about which we know little or next to nothing. We hope to add to the big picture by documenting the unusual heterogeneity of Englishes on a global scale, by uncovering the complicated processes that underlie the formation of these varieties and by making cross-comparisons between them as well. We strongly encourage research on these varieties since it is our firm belief that they carry immense potential for linguistic analysis. At the same time, we hope that this leads to a more serious discussion of LKVEs and a more complete documentation of English as a world language.

References

Aceto, Michael and Jeffrey K. Williams, eds. 2003. *Contact Englishes of the Eastern Caribbean.* Varieties of English Around the World G 30. Amsterdam and Philadelphia: John Benjamins.

Bähr, Dieter. 1975. *Einführung ins Mittelenglische.* Munich: Wilhelm Fink Verlag.

Barber, Charles. 1994. *The English Language: A Historical Introduction.* Cambridge: Cambridge University Press.

Cheshire, Jenny, ed. 1991. *English around the World: Sociolinguistic Perspectives.* Cambridge: Cambridge University Press.

Clarke, Sandra. 1997. 'The role of Irish English in the formation of New World Englishes: The case from Newfoundland.' In Jeffrey L. Kallen, ed. *Focus on Ireland*, 207–26.

2004. 'Verbal -s reconsidered: The Subject Type Constraint as a diagnostic of historical transatlantic relationship.' In Christian J. Kay, Simon Horobin and Jeremy J. Smith, eds. *New Perspectives on English Historical Linguistics.* Amsterdam: John Benjamins, 1–13.

Crystal, David. 1997. *The Cambridge Encyclopaedia of the English Language.* Cambridge: Cambridge University Press.

2008. 'Two thousand million? Updates on the statistics of English.' *English Today* 95, 24: 3–6.

Graddol, David, Dick Leith and Joan Swann. 1996. *English: History, Diversity and Change.* London: Open University/Routledge.

Hickey, Raymond, ed. 2004. *Legacies of Colonial English: Studies in Transported Dialects.* Cambridge: Cambridge University Press.

Jenkins, Jennifer. 2003. *World Englishes: A Resource Book for Students.* London: Routledge.

Jordan, R. 1934. *Handbuch der Mittelenglischen Grammatik* (revised by H. Ch. Matthes). Heidelberg: Carl Winter.

Kortmann, Bernd, Edgar W. Schneider, Rajend Mesthrie, Kate Burridge, and Clive Upton, eds. *A Handbook of Varieties of English: A Multimedia Reference Tool* (2 vols.). Berlin and New York: Mouton de Gruyter.

Kytö, Merja, Mats Rydén and Erik Smitterberg, eds. 2006. *Nineteenth-Century English: Stability and Change.* Cambridge: Cambridge University Press.

Mesthrie, Rajend. 2002. 'Building a new English dialect: South African Indian English and the history of Englishes.' In Watts and Trudgill, eds. *Alternative Histories of English.* London: Routledge, 111–33.

Mitchell, Bruce and Fred C. Robinson. 1992. *A Guide to Old English*, 5th edn. Oxford and New York: Basil Blackwell.

Ramisch, Heinrich. 1989. *The Variation of English in Guernsey, Channel Islands*. Frankfurt am Main: Lang.

Romaine, Suzanne, ed. 1998. *Cambridge History of the English Language*, Vol. IV: *1776 to 1997*. Cambridge: Cambridge University Press.

Schneider, Edgar W. 2007. *Postcolonial English: Varieties Around the World*. Cambridge: Cambridge University Press.

Schreier, Daniel. 2002. '*Terra incognita* in the Anglophone world: Tristan da Cunha, South Atlantic Ocean.' *English World-Wide* 23: 1–29.

   2003. *Isolation and Language Change: Sociohistorical and Contemporary Evidence from Tristan da Cunha English*. Houndmills/Basingstoke and New York: Palgrave Macmillan.

   2008. *St Helenian English: Origins, Evolution and Variation* (Varieties of English Around the World G 37). Amsterdam and Philadelphia: Benjamins.

Sudbury, A. (2000). *Dialect Contact and Koinéisation in the Falkland Islands: Development of a Southern Hemisphere Variety*. PhD dissertation, University of Essex.

Thomason, Sarah G. and Terrence Kaufman. 1988. *Language Contact, Creolization, and Genetic Linguistics*. Los Angeles: University of California Press.

Trudgill, Peter. 2002. 'The history of the lesser-known varieties of English.' In Watts and Trudgill, eds. *Alternative Histories of English*. London: Routledge, 27–44.

Trudgill, Peter and Jean Hannah. 1982. *International English: A Guide to Varieties of Standard English*. London: Edward Arnold.

Watts, Richard J. and Peter Trudgill, eds. 2002. *Alternative Histories of English*: London: Routledge.

Wells, John. 1982. *Accents of English* (3 vols.). Cambridge: Cambridge University Press.

Zettersten, A. 1969. *The English of Tristan da Cunha*. Lund Studies in English 37. Lund: Gleerup.

Part I

The British Isles

2   Orkney and Shetland

GUNNEL MELCHERS AND PETER SUNDKVIST

> Orkney and Shetland, the Northern Isles, have the satisfying quality of all islands. The sea delimits the land. It is possible to view as a mental concept the amalgam of land and sea, fields and houses and boats, cliffs and sheep holms, sea-birds and fishing boats, wind and mist, wide skies and changing clouds and lights on the water. Language adds its appeal, as well as the consciousness of the people of many nations who have come here, each contributing a little of themselves to the total picture. Others will come in the future.
>
> (Alexander Fenton, *The Northern Isles*, 1978: v)

1   Introduction

This chapter describes varieties of English as found in Britain's 'Northern Isles', i.e. the Orkney and Shetland archipelagoes, situated north of the Scottish mainland. Although separated from each other by some fifty miles (80 km) of North Sea waters, they are closely linked politically (forming one UK Parliament constituency), historically, culturally, and not least linguistically. Hence it makes sense to give a joint presentation of the varieties, yet not underestimating differences between them, ranging from ways of life to linguistic details. The most important difference is probably the fact that Orkney is much closer to the Scottish mainland (the southernmost point of South Ronaldsay is only about a mile north of Caithness). This is, among other things, reflected in language in that Orkney dialect is less distinct from mainland Scots/Scottish English.

With their relatively small land areas (Orkney 990 sq. km, Shetland 1,468) and populations (20,000 and 22,000 respectively), the Northern Isles may be minor speech communities, but their language situation is complex and the naming and definition of the language varieties is neither an easy nor an uncontroversial matter. In part, this complexity springs from the unusual history of the islands, with their still prominent and generally cherished Scandinavian heritage. The local varieties of language which we present in this chapter are unlike any other dialects of English, including Scots. They have an archaic character and abound with Nordic features at all levels of language. Yet it must be borne in mind that Orcadians and Shetlanders today are perfectly conversant with a standard variety of English, in speech as well as writing. Orkney and Shetland can, in fact, be characterized as bidialectal speech communities with access to a choice of two discrete, definable forms of speech: one a form of standard, i.e. Scottish Standard English spoken with localized accents, and the other a traditional regional dialect, partly reflecting a Norse substratum but constituting a variety of Scots. Inevitably, young speakers are increasingly losing a great deal of the traditional dialect, especially its lexicon. Since the mid 1970s, the considerable input of speakers from other parts of Britain in connection with the development of the North Sea oil industry has clearly also affected the state of the dialect.

In this presentation we generally focus on the traditional, local dialects of the Northern Isles, which truly represent unique and 'lesser-known' varieties of language. We have made an exception with regard to the description of the *accents*, which even in their more 'standardized' forms are clearly distinguishable from any other accent in Scotland, let alone World Englishes. Hence we have tried to show, for example, how Shetland vowel phonology can be described differently, depending on the form of speech referred to (Shetland dialect or a Shetland accent of Scottish Standard English).

Traditional Orkney dialect is often referred to as 'Orcadian', which appears to be a fairly neutral term. Shetland dialect, by contrast, has several names, with different users and connotations, such as 'Norn', 'Shetlandic', and simply 'Shetland' (or 'Shaetlan'); the significance of these will be discussed in the following section. 'Insular Scots', finally, is a term used by some scholars (cf. Johnston 1997; McColl Millar 2007), classifying Orkney and Shetland as a joint linguistic area, since their dialects 'share more with each other than they do with any other Scots dialects' (McColl Millar 2007: 4f.). In our presentation, however, we will use the neutral terms 'Orkney dialect' and 'Shetland dialect'.

Conceivably, some readers of this text might resent the inclusion of dialects of Scots in a book explicitly said to be devoted to 'varieties of English'. This is not the place to discuss whether Scots is a language in its own right (cf. e.g. McArthur 1998: 139) or a (very special) dialect of English. As we see it, even if its status is that of a language, it is nevertheless more closely related to English than any other language, and it is descended from Old English. We are also in good company, since a number of textbooks on 'varieties of English' include Scots, e.g. Kortmann and Upton 2008, McColl Millar 2007.

2   Sociolinguistic history and current status

2.1   *Orkney and Shetland dialects as LKVEs*

As so beautifully captured in the words of the ethnologist Alexander Fenton introducing this chapter, the very fact that Orkney and Shetland are island communities lies at the heart of their uniqueness. In addition, they are geo-graphically peripheral: Shetland, characteristically, is often excluded from maps of the British Isles, or at best randomly placed in a separate square. As language areas, they share the general characteristics of island commu-nities: they are close-knit, which makes them resistant to change, they have a clearly marked identity, and to some extent they represent low-contact situations, which tend to result in elaborate phonology, irregular morphol-ogy (Trudgill 1989: 229f.) and unique vocabulary. They also constitute little 'universes' which seem surveyable; conceivably, they lend themselves to complete descriptions of the linguistic situation.

Although the Northern Isles are probably fairly well known as geographical areas in the UK (not least from weather reports!), it is our experience that their dialects definitely represent 'lesser-known varieties'. A determining factor here is the population's bidialectal competence, meaning that few outsiders (or 'soothmoothers' as they are referred to in Shetland) get to hear the traditional dialects. Another factor is the special history of the islands, with their relatively late exposure to English. It follows that some insight into the settlement history of the Northern Isles is essential for an understanding of the language situation.

In spite of their peripheral location, Orkney and Shetland should not be viewed as isolated or backward communities, neither in the past nor today. The Northern Isles have been at the crossroads of shipping and trade, and subjected to immigration and impulses from various peoples: the Viking settlers arriving as early as the ninth century, the Scots gradually taking over from the early Middle Ages onwards, and the Dutch and German tradesmen in the Hansa period. Today, the islands are modern British societies, with excellent educational establishments, including some tertiary education, and a highly developed infrastructure. While traditional local industries live on, such as the flourishing production of cheese and whisky in Orkney and world-famous but recently somewhat less successful yarn and knitwear industry in Shetland, the last few decades have seen major changes in occupation and life styles as a result of the decline in fishing (with the exception of shellfish), the impact of the North Sea oil discoveries and exploitation, and the rapidly expanding tourism industry. Employment statistics now tell us that most jobs are classified as 'services' (cf. e.g. *Shetland in Statistics* 2006: 15), whereas traditionally Orcadians were mostly viewed as farmers and Shetlanders as fishermen.

Orcadians and Shetlanders, in fact, seem to be unusually versatile, multi-skilled and enterprising, adapting to changing conditions of life and not inhibited by social immobility. The Northern Isles have been perceived as more egalitarian than other regions in Britain (cf. Melchers 2008: 36; Tamminga 2008: 27). It is not uncommon for an individual to be employed in widely different spheres, especially on outlying islands. A case in point is Fair Isle, a small island situated between Orkney and Shetland, where the same man recently ran the local post office, was a member of the ferry crew, served as the local butcher, taught traditional fiddle music at the school and looked after hundreds of sheep. This means that it is hardly feasible for a sociolinguist collecting data in the Northern Isles to classify his/her informants according to a social stratification model (Tamminga 2008: 27f.). Not even gender appears to be a significant sociolinguistic factor, as convincingly demonstrated by recent research (Orten 1991: 65; Tamminga 2008: 28).

2.2   An outline of the islands' demographic and linguistic history

A North Germanic, West Scandinavian language first came to the Northern Isles with Norwegian Vikings as early as *c.* 800. It is not known for certain who inhabited Orkney and Shetland at the time of the Norse settlement, but a variety known as *Norn* (from the Old Norse adjective *norrænn* 'of northern origin, Norse') was definitely the first Germanic language to be spoken on the islands. As described in the Icelandic *Orkneyinga Saga* and *Landnámabok*, the settlers probably originated from northwest Norway. This is to some extent supported by place-name evidence, whereas other linguistic data point to a more southerly area (Agder, Hordaland). It is no coincidence that the Icelandic saga was named after Orkney (*Orkneyjar*), the heart of the Viking Earldom, which also included Shetland (*Hjaltland*) and parts of Caithness (*Katanes*) on the Scottish mainland. Orkney and Shetland remained all-Scandinavian and virtually monolingual until well into the fourteenth century, when the Scots began to come in, making the Scottish element in the earldom the dominant cultural influence gradually extending northwards into the islands.

In 1379 a Scotsman was appointed Earl of Orkney, which included the sovereignty of Shetland, and about a century later the Northern Isles became part of Scotland. A serious plea for reunion with Norway was put forward as late as 1905, in connection with the Sweden–Norway separation, but the islands have remained under Scottish and British rule. It should be pointed out, however, that the links with Scandinavia, especially Norway, were never broken, as so remarkably demonstrated through the support given to the Norwegian resistance movement during the Second World War ('the Shetland Bus'). A recent token of the close links was the presence of the Queen of Norway at the inauguration of Shetland's magnificent new museum and archives in the summer of 2007. Indeed, the Scandinavian heritage is an integral part of Orkney and Shetland identity, not least reflected in the traditional dialects.

Norn was the dominant language in Orkney and Shetland for at least 500 years, but a natural consequence of the political changes beginning in the late Middle Ages was a shift from Norn to Scots. Owing to the scarcity of written sources there is neither a complete documentation of the structure of the Norn language nor of the rate and character of the process of change. There is an ongoing, heated debate considering the actual demise of Norn, in which a group referred to as 'Nornomaniacs' by their adversaries (cf. Smith 1996) argue that the Scandinavian language lived on at least until the end of the nineteenth century in Shetland. What real evidence there is, however, suggests that, as a complete language, it died out no later than the second half of the eighteenth century, probably earlier in Orkney and most parts of Shetland (Barnes 1998). As demonstrated on a massive scale, however, remnants of Norn in the form of phonological features, inflectional endings, syntactic structures, and above all lexical items and phrases could still be collected by devoted philologists only about a hundred years ago. We are referring here to Hugh Marwick's *The Orkney Norn* (1929) and, above all, to Jakob Jakobsen's *Etymological Dictionary of the Norn Language in Shetland* (1928–1932).

It is worth pointing out that the extant Scandinavian element in Shetland and Orkney dialects differs from the Scandinavian linguistic heritage in other parts of Britain, not only in size but also in structure and history. The Norse invaders of Yorkshire, for example, met a native Anglo-Saxon population whom they could – at least to some degree – communicate with. They *influenced* the Anglo-Saxon language and some of this influence has survived: lexical items such as *lathe* for 'barn' and *lake* for 'play', phonological features such as plosives instead of affricates (e.g. *flick* of bacon instead of 'flitch') and possibly a specific syllabic structure. In Orkney and Shetland, on the other hand, a form of Old Norse was *the dominant language* for about 500 years. If the islands had remained under Scandinavian rule, the traditional language spoken in the Northern Isles today would probably be a variety rather like Faroese.

The language contact histories outlined above clearly represent two different linguistic scenarios, where the Scandinavian element in Shetland/Orkney dialect could be characterized as a *substratum* phenomenon, whereas Scandinavian features in Yorkshire, for example, will be examples of *borrowing*. Briefly, this implies that the Yorkshire scenario is typically characterized by lexical loans, mainly for cultural and functional reasons, whereas Shetland/Orkney, in addition to more lexical features, will include all levels of language (cf. Thomason and Kaufman 1988: 74f.). The very positive attitudes to Scandinavia and proud awareness of the linguistic heritage in Orkney and Shetland clearly also play a part in language maintenance. Where else, for example, would a monumental, etymological dictionary such as Jakobsen's be a bestseller?

2.3   *Current status and conditions of use*

To some extent the status of the traditional dialects in the Northern Isles can be illustrated by the significance of the various names of the varieties presented in our introduction. Since there is less confusion of names in Orkney and the naming seems less controversial, we will focus on Shetland. As we have seen, 'Norn' was 'the distinctive form of Scandinavian speech that developed in the Northern Isles' (Barnes 1998: 1), which is now indisputably extinct. Confusingly, in popular (including local) usage as well as scholarly publications, e.g. Jakobsen (1928–1932), Marwick (1929), the term Norn often refers to the language of the Viking settlers as well as the traditional dialect still spoken in Orkney and Shetland, or at least as spoken about a hundred years ago. Even a present-day, influential publication, *The Cambridge Encyclopedia of the English Language* (Crystal 1995: 111), presents Norn as a regional variety of English. In our opinion, anyone referring to present-day Shetland dialect as Norn is either ignorant or a romantic 'Nornomaniac'. 'Before we understand the modern Shetland dialect we have to get Norn out of the way' (Smith 1996: 31). The term 'Shetlandic', although occasionally used even by Jakobsen, now seems to be particularly favoured by certain groups working for the preservation of the traditional dialect. It appears, on the other hand, to be heartily disliked by most Shetlanders, including members of the cultural establishment. The most common word for the local variety of language, as contrasted with 'English', is 'Shetland', often spelled 'Shaetlan', signalling local affiliation through the use of eye-dialect.

No matter what the underpinnings to the various names are, they all express a very positive attitude to the local dialect. Its preservation and use is now explicitly encouraged and called for in the educational policies for all levels:

Dialect should not be condemned but regarded as a valid form of speech appropriate to certain situations. If a clearly defined policy of bilingualism is cultivated by the school, pupils should automatically know when to use dialect and when Standard English. (From an instruction given to teachers at The Anderson High School, Lerwick, by John Graham, former headmaster and also author of *The Shetland Dictionary* (1993).)

A language attitude study conducted at the above school in the mid 1980s (cf. Melchers 1985) showed that the schoolchildren subscribed to the bidialectal approach advocated by their former headmaster. Also, through personal comments, they generally expressed deep affection and concern for their native dialect. Similar attitudes have recently been reported from Orkney (Tamminga 2008). Although not mentioned in the action/policy programme, there is also a growing general interest in dialect *writing*, and many English teachers, including non-islanders, set aside a fair amount of time for such exercises. An ambitious undertaking in an Orkney primary school is reported in Flaws (1992).

In Orkney and Shetland today, there are obviously a number of 'sooth-moothers', i.e. incomers, who are only fully conversant with a standard variety of English. As for the native populations, on the other hand, it is not likely that there are monoglot speakers only in command of the traditional dialect. As evidenced, for example, in Document 1471 of the *Scottish Corpus*, some speakers may, however, still be reluctant to adapt to the situation:

(1)   I just canna change me tongue an that's it (male Shetland infor-
            mant, interviewed by a speaker of Standard English)

3   Features of the varieties

In the following brief account of linguistic features it has not been possible to include a great deal of information about the considerable regional varia-tion within the varieties. The most 'deviant' localized dialects are found on Whalsay and Out Skerries in Shetland, two close-knit fishing communities. In Orkney, the northernmost islands (Westray and North Ronaldsay) are held to be different (cf. Tamminga 2008, for a close study of Westray).

A more serious caveat, however, is the 'Shetland bias' particularly notice-able in our phonology section. There are two reasons for this imbalance: firstly, as already mentioned, Shetland dialect represents a more distinc-tive variety of English, richer in archaic features, including a more promi-nent Scandinavian element; secondly, beginning with Jakobsen's monumen-tal work around 1900, Shetland dialect has been much more and better researched and described, by professional linguists as well as local historians and interest groups.

3.1   Phonology

In Shetland phonology, the most significant differences between the two endpoints, i.e. Shetland dialect vs. Scottish Standard English (SSE) as spo-ken in Shetland, concern vowels. As often in Scotland, the greatest differ-ences concern lexical-distributional matters, but there are also significant systemic differences, perhaps more so than in many other localities in Scot-land. The vowel system of Shetland dialect has been accounted for by Catford (1957, 1958), Mather and Speitel (1986), Johnston (1997), Tait (2000), and Sundkvist (2004), and the vowel system of Shetland SSE has been investi-gated by Sundkvist (2004, 2007). The following outline of Shetland vowels is based on the model presented in Sundkvist (2004), which provides an inte-grated account of the Shetland dialect and SSE vowel systems. An integrated model is arguably ecologically more valid, since most speakers in Shetland are still bidialectal. The vowel system of Shetland speech is displayed in Figure 2.1, and the contrastive items are illustrated in Table 2.1.

Table 2.1 *Vowel table for Shetland dialect and Scottish Standard English*

Word	Shetland Dialect (Scots)		Shetland accent of SSE	
	Phoneme	Approximate realization	Phoneme	Approximate realization
beet	/i/	[i]	/i/	[i]
need	/i/	[i]	/i/	[i]
meid[1]	/iː/	[iː]		
beat	/e/	[e]	/i/	[i]
bait	/eː/	[eː, ɛː, œɪ]	/e/	[e']
met	/ɛ/	[ɛ]	/ɛ/	[ɛ]
Pam	/a/	[a, æ, ɛ]	/a/	[a, æ, ɛ]
palm[2]	/ɑ/	[aː, ɑː]	/ɑ/	[aː, ɑː]
fat	/a/	[a, æ, ɛ]	/a/	[a, æ, ɛ]
fau(l)t	/ɑ/	[aː, ɑː]	/ɔ/	[ɔ, ɔː]
pot	/ɔ/	[ɔ]	/ɔ, ɒ/	[ɔ, ɒ]
boat[3]	/o/	[o, oː]	/o/	[o, oː]
but	/ʌ/	[ʌ, ʌ̟]	/ʌ/	[ʌ, ʌ̟]
about	/u/	[u]	/ʌu, u/	[ʌu, u]
room	/u/	[u]	/u/	[u]
loumie[4]	/uː/	[uː]		
bit	/ɪ/	[ï, ë, ë̠, ɜ]	/ɪ/	[ɪ, ï, ë]
boot	/ø/	[ø, y]	/u/	[u]
böl[5]	/ø/	[ø, y]		
bröl[6]	/øː/	[øː, yː]		
try	/ai/	[ai, aɪ]	/ai/	[a'ɪ]
bite	/a'ɪ, ai, əi/	[ai, əi]	/ai/	[əi]
boy	/ɔi/	[ɔi]	/ɔi/	[ɔi]
bowl	/ʌu/	[ʌu, ɔu]	/ʌu/	[ʌu]

Notes
[1] 'landmark used for sea navigation'.
[2] The phonemic symbol was partly chosen to facilitate a bidialectal comparison. For some speakers, *palm* is a long /aː/.
[3] Cf. note 2. For some speakers, *boat* is long /oː/.
[4] 'oil slick'.
[5] 'animal's resting place'.
[6] 'bellow'.

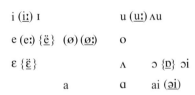

Comment:
- Items within brackets ( ): only or primarily supported in Shetland dialect
- Items within curly bracket {}: only or primarily in Scottish Standard English (SSE)
- Underlined items: marginal items, even within the variety in which they may occur

Figure 2.1 The vowel system of Shetland speech (Shetland dialect and SSE)

As may be seen in Figure 2.1, items that are not underlined or placed within brackets form a 'core system' of Shetland speech, which is common to Shetland dialect and SSE. The monophthongs within this set correspond to Catford's (1958) Basic system (/i, ɪ, e, ɛ, a, ʌ, o, u/) plus two of his four additions (A¹, A²), corresponding to /ɑ, ɔ/ respectively.

Additional items that are primarily supported in Shetland dialect are placed within brackets ( ) in Figure 2.1. Within this set, we find Catford's (1958) remaining two additions (E, Y), which correspond to /eː, ø/ respectively. Underlined vowels represent additional items reported to exist in some varieties of Shetland dialect. There are three potential additional long items /iː, øː, uː/. The most extensive account of these rather marginal items may be found in Tait (2000), and some evidence for their contrastive status is also presented by Mather and Speitel (1986) and Sundkvist (2004). It has been argued that their contrastive status, at least in part, may be accounted for with reference to the SVLR (see below) and consonant fortition (Aitken 1981).

In Scots and SSE, vowel duration varies significantly by context; vowels are typically short unless followed by /r/, a voiced fricative or a morpheme boundary, or final in an open syllable. This phenomenon is commonly referred to as 'the Scottish Vowel-Length Rule' (SVLR henceforth) or Aitken's Law (cf. Aitken 1981; Wells 1982). There is some disagreement as to the exact set of vowels that are subject to this rule however. Traditional accounts have suggested that all vowels except /ɪ, ʌ/ are subject to this rule, but more recent evidence suggests a much more limited set, at least for SSE (Scobbie, Hewlett, and Turk 1999).

The word data adduced to illustrate the additional long items often involve a word-final /d/ that represents a reflex of an earlier fricative, which may still be found in some parts of Shetland, such as Dunrossness, where *meid* is [miːθ]. In accordance with the SVLR, a long vowel was triggered in this context (*meid* [miːð]). At a later stage, the final fricative underwent fortition (*meid* [miːd]), which meant that long [iː] became contrastive with short /i/ in this context (*need* [nid] ≠ *meid* [miːd]). However, it is not clear how many cases this development accounts for, and the long items may also be contrastive in other phonetic contexts.

The vowel system of Shetland dialect is sometimes reduced, however, not only regarding the underlined items in Figure 2.1, but also items within the core system: various mergers may reduce the large system outlined by Catford (1957, 1958) to a considerably smaller one. Among front vowels, *bait* /eː/ may be merged with *beat* /e/, and even *met* /ɛ/, and for back vowels there are various potential mergers between *pot* /ɔ/, *boat* /o/, and possibly even *fault* /ɑ/ (cf. Johnston 1997; McColl Millar 2007). It is not entirely clear whether the diphthongs in *try* /ai/ and *bite* /əi/ are contrastive in Shetland speech. Recent accounts suggest that they may not be well distinguished phonetically in Shetland dialect (McColl Millar 2007: 55). As for SSE, Sundkvist (2004) found two diphthongs that were clearly phonetically separate but whose distribution was predictable in accordance with the SVLR.

Thus far we have avoided the complicated issue of regional realizational variation of the items in Figure 2.1. Two matters need to be mentioned, however: /ë:/ may be realized as [ë:] or [ɛː], or may be diphthongal, approximately [œɪ], in Whalsay (Catford 1958); the front rounded vowel (Catford's addition Y) in most localities appears to be realized around [ø ∼ œ] but may be considerably closer ([y, ʏ]) in the west of Shetland.

Turning now to Scottish Standard English, contrastive items occurring only or primarily in SSE are placed within curly brackets {} in Figure 2.1. Marginal items, which again are underlined, include two 'oncers', or particular developments in a very limited number of lexical items, in the context of a following /r/ (her /ë/ ≠ fir, fur, err /ɪ, ʌ, ɛ/; their /ë/ ≠ fair, err /e, ɛ/). Furthermore, /ɒ/ illustrates the fact that some speakers display a cot–caught contrast (Sundkvist 2004). From the perspective of Abercrombie's (1979) typology of SSE vowel systems, Lerwick people display a firm Pam–palm contrast but no pull–pool contrast. Front rounded vowels /ø, y/ are not included in the chart for SSE since they are primarily supported by Shetland dialect lexis. The Lerwick speakers in Sundkvist (2004) did not display front rounded vowels within Standard English words. However, other speakers may well incorporate such vowels to a greater extent. It may also be used variably in place names, such as The Böd [bød] of Grimista.

We may illustrate the difference between the two endpoints within the Shetland speech range from the perspective of SSE with the use of Wells' (1982) lexical sets, as in Table 2.2 below. Again, however, it must be pointed out that this table in no way captures the extensive regional variation in Shetland.

Thus far we have primarily dealt with systemic aspects of the vowel system, and we now turn to consider various linguistic features and consonantal matters. For each matter brought up, we will try to be explicit as to whether we are referring to Shetland dialect or SSE, and comment on any differences between them, to the extent that relevant information is available.

3.1.1   Vowel features

Some of the most salient characteristics of the Shetland vowel system derive from a process of vowel mutation. A subset of vowels are raised and/or fronted, and may also display an off-glide, before certain voiced consonants, as in bid [bɪ̯d], bed [bɛ̯ᶦd], bad [bæ̯ᶦd], and bud [bʌ̈d]. There is considerable regional variation regarding the phonetic realization and the set of triggering contexts. The most extensive treatment of Shetland vowel mutation is Tait (2000), and its effects have also been noted by Jakobsen (1928–1932), Catford (1957), and Johnston (1997). Vowel mutation is also displayed by Lerwick people speaking SSE (Sundkvist 2007). Furthermore, the Scottish Vowel-Length Rule applies in Shetland dialect. For Lerwick people speaking SSE,

Table 2.2 *Wells' lexical sets (Shetland speech – the view from Scottish Standard English)*

	Shetland dialect	Shetland SSE
KIT	ï ~ ë ~ ë̈ ~ ɜ ~ ɐ̥	ɪ ~ ï ~ ë
DRESS	ɛ ~ ɛ' ~ ɛⁱ	ɛ ~ ɛ' ~ ɛⁱ
TRAP	a ~ æ ~ æⁱ ~ ɐ̞ ~ ɐ̞ⁱ	a ~ æ ~ æⁱ ~ ɐ̞ ~ ɐ̞ⁱ
LOT	ɔ	ɔ, ɒ ~ ɒ̈
STRUT	ʌ ~ ʌ̞ ~ ə	ʌ ~ ʌ̞ ~ ə
FOOT	u ~ ü, ø ~ y	u ~ ü
BATH	aˑ ~ aː ~ ɑː	aˑ ~ aː ~ ɑː
CLOTH	ɔ, aˑ ~ aː ~ ɑː	ɔ, ɒ
NURSE	ɪə, ʌ, ɛ, ɜ, ɔ	ɪə, ʌ, ɛ, ë
FLEECE	i, e	i
FACE	eⁱ, ɛ, aˑ ~ aː ~ ɑː	eⁱ
PALM	aˑ ~ aː ~ ɑː	aˑ ~ aː ~ ɑː
THOUGHT	ɔ ~ ɔː, aʊ	ɔ ~ ɔː
GOAT	o ~ oː ~ oːə	o ~ oː
GOOSE	u ~ ü, ø ~ y	u ~ ü
PRICE	aˈɪ ~ ai ~ əi	aˈɪ, ai ~ əi
CHOICE	ɔi ~ ɔɪ	ɔi ~ ɔɪ
MOUTH	u ~ ü	ʌu, u ~ ü
NEAR	i	i
SQUARE	e, ɛ	e, ë
START	aˑ ~ aː ~ ɑː, ɛ	aˑ ~ aː ~ ɑː
NORTH	ɔ ~ ɔː, aː ~ ɑ	ɔ ~ ɔː
FORCE	o ~ oː, ɔ ~ ɔː	o ~ oː
CURE	u ~ ü, ø ~ y	u ~ ü

however, it only applies to /i, u, ai/, and, unlike what is commonly reported for SVLR, the set of consonants that trigger the occurrence of preceding long vowels also includes /b, g/ and, for speakers who display such an item, /dʒ/.

In 1957 Catford suggested that the syllable structure of Shetland dialect was of a Scandinavian type: in monosyllabic words, long vowels are followed by a short consonant, and short vowels are followed by a long consonant, as in *bait* [beːt] vs. *beat* [betː]. Duration measurements in van Leyden (2002) lend support to this idea. The inverse relationship between the duration of the vowel and the following consonant was found to be stronger in Shetland dialect than in Orkney or Edinburgh Scots, but not as strong as in Norwegian. It was also somewhat stronger in the local Shetland lexis than in Standard English words. However, the pattern in Shetland dialect differs from that in Scandinavian languages in certain ways. Shetland dialect of course lacks much of the structural evidence (e.g. morpho–phonemic alternations) for the complementary distribution of long and short vowels and consonants, and the V:C vs. VC: syllable structure, which may be found in e.g. Swedish (cf. Eliasson 1985). There is also an absence of some of the behavioural evidence for the presence of phonologically long consonants that may be found in Swedish, such as the ability to lengthen long segments for emphatic purposes (Sundkvist 2004, 2006). Thus, on balance, Shetland dialect appears not to have phonologically long consonants.

As shown in McColl Millar (2007: 16ff.), the Orkney vowel system is very similar to that of Shetland. Orkney phonology, however, is remarkably underresearched, especially with regard to lexical distribution. Tamminga (2008) is a very promising, detailed study, but it focuses on a limited set of vowels and deals exclusively with the island of Westray.

3.1.2 Consonant features

Shetland speech displays a number of rather salient localized consonantal features. Consonants /d, n/ and in some varieties also /ŋ, l/ undergo palatalization, commonly in contexts where vowel mutation occurs, as in *bed* [bɛ̞ᵢdʲ], *men* [mɛ̞ᵢnʲ] etc. TH-stopping, at least in initial position, is common in Shetland dialect (as in *da* and *dis*, for *the* and *this*), but was found to be variable for Lerwick people speaking SSE (Sundkvist 2007). Stops of the voiced series (/b, d, g/) are fully voiced, and those of the voiceless series (/p, t, k/) are voiceless aspirated. Speakers whose parents were born outside Shetland, however, may display voiceless unaspirated vs. voiceless aspirated series (Scobbie 2002). T-glottalling is found in the town of Lerwick.

Accounts of Shetland dialect often report the absence of a contrast between sequences spelled <wh> and <qu> (*white* = *quite*). In most localities they are both pronounced with [ʍ]. However, in the west side of Shetland and part of the central mainland, they are pronounced with [kw], and in some localities both may occur in free variation (Catford 1957). For Lerwick SSE, however, such sequences are pronounced as in mainland accents of SSE (*white* ≠ *quite*).

Traditionally, initial <kn> sequences were pronounced as /kn/ in Shetland dialect (*knee* [kniː]), which may be a Scandinavian relic feature. It is not known, however, to what extent this may still be found in natural speech. Shetland dialect typically does not have a voiced affricate, which makes *gin* and *chin* homophonous (/tʃɪn/). /tʃ/ may also merge with /ʃ/: *chop*/*shop* /ʃɔp/. For Lerwick SSE, the latter development is not found, and the majority of speakers variably display /dʒ/ (Sundkvist 2004).

As for liquids, Shetland speech is rhotic and /r/ is mostly realized as a tap, or even a short trill. In some regional varieties /l/ may undergo palatalization, and reportedly also display clear vs. dark variation (Tait 1999). In Lerwick SSE, dark /l/ occurs in all positions (Sundkvist 2007).

Orkney consonants share most of the properties described for Shetland, albeit to a lesser degree. TH-stopping is rare: the familiar form of address, for example, is represented as *thu* or *thoo* in Orkney dialect writing, but as *du* in Shetland. The relic realizations of k-clusters as described for Shetland are not found in present-day Orkney dialect. In Orkney, on the other hand, retroflex realizations of /r/ + /s/ as [ʂ] in final position are the rule rather than the exception, i.e. in words such as *nurse* or *course*.

3.1.3 Prosody

Even in popular perception, Orkney and Shetland intonation are remarkably different; in fact, the 'sing-song lilt' is probably the most salient feature of Orkney speech. In her thorough study of Northern Isles prosody, van Leyden (2004: 100) reports a difference in the alignment of the accent-lending pitch rise: in Shetland the rise is located on the stressed syllable, whereas in Orkney it is found on the post-stress syllable. There is, in fact, nothing remarkable about Shetland intonation in comparison with most mother-tongue speakers in Britain, whereas 'rise delay' is unusual, typically found in Glasgow speech but also in Celtic varieties. Van Leyden speculates that Gaelic influences may indirectly have affected the melody of Orcadian speech.

3.2 Morphosyntax

The examples given in this section are taken from various sources, in particular John Graham's dictionary, the Scottish Corpus, and our own fieldwork. The origin of the data is indicated by (O) or (S), i.e. Orkney or Shetland.

3.2.1 Nouns

The definite article (*the* in Orkney, *da* in Shetland) is used with certain nouns with which it would not be used in Standard English, such as *da gulsa* 'jaundice', *da bruntrifi* 'heartburn' (S). Another characteristic use of the article is found in expressions for 'today', 'tomorrow', 'tomorrow night' etc., where Orkney and Shetland dialect has *the/da day*, *the/da nicht*, *the/da mo(a)rn*, *the/da moarn's nicht*. 'Yesterday evening' is *the/da streen*. Irregular plural forms such as *breider* 'brothers', *een* 'eyes', *shön* 'shoes' are still often heard, at least in Shetland.

(2)   We riggat wiz athin wir Sunday suits in polished wir shön.
         'We put on our Sunday clothes and polished our shoes' (from a diary written by Alec Stout, Fair Isle)

3.2.2 Pronouns

The forms of the personal pronouns in Shetland and Orkney dialect differ considerably from Standard English, as exemplified in (2). The object form of the first person plural is *wis*, and the third person singular (neuter) is realized as *hit* (S), *hid* (O). The most interesting aspect of the personal pronouns, however, is the use of two forms of address: informal *du* (S), *thu* (O) vs. formal *you*.

(3)   You manna ('must not') 'du' your elders (S)

The maintenance of this distinction is still very much alive, and determined by subtle factors related to age, status, situation, familiarity, attitude etc. (cf. Melchers 1985). The distinction is clearly noticeable in code-switching.

Natural gender is typically found in Shetland dialect: tools, for example, tend to be viewed as masculine, whereas species of fish, *kirk*, *world*, and some time expressions are feminine:

(4)   Da millennium is comin, but shö . . .

In referring to the weather a characteristic feature of Shetland dialect is the generic use of *he*:

(5)   He's blowan ap ('the wind is rising')

3.2.3   Verbs

As in many other traditional dialects, irregular verb forms differ characteristically from Standard English, include verbs that are regular in the standard, and display considerable variation.

(6)   The nurse pat the thermometer under me oxter ('armpit') (O)

(7)   Her man was cassen awa ('lost at sea') (S)

In contrast with Standard English, a distinction in form is made between verbal adjectives/present participles on the one hand and verbal nouns on the other, as illustrated by the following Orkney examples:

(8)   Sheu's knittan

(9)   Sheu's deuan her knitteen

A remarkable and intriguing feature unique to the Northern Isles is the categorical use of *be* rather than *have* as a perfective auxiliary:

(10)   I'm been dere twartree ('a couple of') times (S)

(11)   I war paid him afore that (O)

With reference to agreement, an archaic feature of Shetland dialect is the use of an -*s* ending in the third person plural present indicative, but only if the subject is a noun or a pronoun separated from the verb:

(12)   dis (yon) horses pulls weel

(13)   dey pull weel

Der (S), *thir* (O) corresponds to 'there is' as well as 'there are':

(14)   Der a boat hoose yonder

(15)   Der folk here fae Sweden and Norway

Finally, traditional Shetland dialect may still display inverted word order and lack of *do*-support, as well as overt-subject imperatives:

(16)   Sees du yon, boy?

(17)   Geng du my boy!

3.3   Lexicon – a few notes

The most striking component of traditional Orkney and Shetland vocabulary is no doubt the Scandinavian element, which – like other levels of language – is more richly represented in Shetland. A detailed study of the vocabulary investigated by the *Linguistic Survey of Scotland* shows that Orkney retains about two-thirds of the Scandinavian-based vocabulary elicited for Shetland.

In our phonology and morphosyntax sections, traditional dialect vocabulary has been exemplified to some extent. For lack of space, it is not possible to do justice to the unique and fascinating local lexicon; it is also notoriously difficult to provide structured accounts of a 'dialect thesaurus'. We will limit ourselves to exemplifying a few areas which are particularly rich in local, nonstandard vocabulary:

> Flora and fauna: *cockaloorie* 'daisy', *shalder* 'oyster-catcher', *scarf* 'cormorant';
> Traditional tools: *tushkar* 'spade for cutting peats' (a device developed in the Faroe islands);
> Weather terminology: *dalamist* 'a special, low-lying mist';
> Colours and characteristics pertaining to sheep: *sholmet* 'wearing a helmet', *moorit* 'light brown';
> Emotive, characterizing adjectives: *debaetless* 'exhausted', *inbigget* 'stubborn'.

4   Conclusion

In answer to the question 'What would make you want to leave Shetland?', a young woman recently said 'Nothing that I can think of' (*Shetland Life*, May 2008). This attitude is symptomatic of present-day attitudes among young people in the Northern Isles (cf. Melchers 1985; Tamminga 2008). It is accompanied by an increasing interest in and commitment to the local heritage, not least the local dialect. Tangible expressions of this commitment are, for example, the recent establishment of the Orkney College, the documentation and research carried out by the Shetland and Orkney Archives, the ambitious place-name project launched by the Shetland Amenity Trust, and the publication of anthologies of dialect literature. Even the oil companies, seen by many as threats to traditional culture, have contributed by sponsoring literary competitions and the printing of a facsimile edition of Jakobsen's dictionary.

In Orkney as well as Shetland the last few years have also seen the emergence of societies concerned with the preservation of local dialect, producing popular materials such as dialect calendars and fridge magnets. As the name of one of these societies, 'Shetland ForWirds' suggests, they are mainly concerned with the lexicon.

It is likely that very localized subdialects such as Fair Isle or North Ronaldsay are subjected to dialect-levelling. Virtually all children now receive secondary education in Lerwick, and we have observed that children in Out Skerries no longer produce the characteristic consonants recorded some twenty-five years ago. As in all traditional, rural dialects, a great deal of the vocabulary relating to dated implements and activities is clearly moribund. As we see it, however, Orkney and Shetland accents and dialects will remain uniquely different and distinguishable varieties of English.

References

Abercrombie, David. 1979. 'The accents of Standard English in Scotland.' In A. Jack Aitken, Tom McArthur and Angus McIntosh, eds. *Languages of Scotland.* Edinburgh: Chambers, 68–84.

Aitken, A. Jack. 1981. 'The Scottish vowel length rule.' In Michael Benskin and M. Samuels, eds. *So Meny Peoples Longages and Tonges: Philological Essays in Scots and Mediaeval English Presented to Angus McIntosh.* Edinburgh: Middle English Dialect Project, 131–57.

Barnes, Michael. 1998. *The Norn Language of Shetland and Orkney.* Lerwick: Shetland Times.

Catford, John C. 1957. 'Shetland dialect.' *Folk Book* 3: 71–6.

——— 1958. 'Vowel-systems of Scots dialects.' *Transactions of the Philological Society* 1958: 107–17.

Crystal, David. 1995. *The Cambridge Encyclopedia of the English Language.* Cambridge: Cambridge University Press.

Eliasson, Stig. 1985. 'Stress alternations and vowel length: new evidence for an underlying nine-vowel system in Swedish.' *Nordic Journal of Linguistics* 8: 101–29.

Fenton, Alexander. 1978. *The Northern Isles: Orkney and Shetland.* Edinburgh: John Donald Publishers Ltd.

Flaws, Margaret. 1992. 'Teaching dialect in a primary school.' *The New Shetlander* 180: 16–17.

Graham, John. 1993. *The Shetland Dictionary.* 3rd edn. Lerwick: Shetland Times.

Jakobsen, Jakob. 1928–1932. *An Etymological Dictionary of the Norn Language in Shetland.* 2 vols. Copenhagen: Vilhelm Prior.

Johnston, Paul. 1997. 'Regional variation.' In Charles Jones, ed. *The Edinburgh History of the Scots Language.* Edinburgh: Edinburgh University Press, 433–513.

Kortmann, Bernd and Clive Upton, eds. 2008. *Handbook of Varieties: The British Isles*. Berlin/New York: Mouton de Gruyter. 61.17

Marwick, Hugh. 1929. *The Orkney Norn*. Oxford: Oxford University Press.

Mather, James Y. and Hans-Henning Speitel. 1986. *The Linguistic Atlas of Scotland, Scots Section*, Volume III: *Phonology*. London: Croom Helm.

McArthur, Tom. 1998. *The English Languages*. Cambridge: Cambridge University Press.

McColl Millar, Robert. 2007. *Northern and Insular Scots*. Edinburgh: Edinburgh University Press.

Melchers, Gunnel. 1985. ' "Knappin", "Proper English", "Modified Scottish": Some language attitudes in the Shetland Isles.' In Manfred Görlach, ed. *Focus on: Scotland*. Philadelphia: Benjamins, 87–100.

   2008. 'English spoken in Orkney and Shetland: phonology.' In Bernd Kortmann and Clive Upton, eds. *Varieties of English*, vol. I: *The British Isles*. Berlin: Mouton de Gruyter, 35–47.

Orten, Elise. 1991. *The Kirkwall Accent*. MA thesis. Bergen: Department of English, University of Bergen.

Scobbie, James M. 2002. 'Flexibility in the face of incompatible English VOT systems.' Paper presented at Eighth Conference on Laboratory Phonology (Labphon 8), Varieties of Phonological Competence, Yale University, 27–30 June 2002.

Scobbie, James M., Nigel Hewlett, and Alice Turk. 1999. 'Standard English in Edinburgh and Glasgow: the Scottish Vowel Length Rule revealed.' In P. Foulkes and G. Docherty, eds. *Urban Voices: Accent Studies in the British Isles*. London: Arnold, 230–45.

The Scottish Corpus. www.scottishcorpus.ac.uk.

Shetland in Statistics. 2006. Lerwick: Shetland Islands Council.

Smith, Brian. 1996. 'The development of the spoken and written Shetland dialect: a historian's view.' In Doreen Waugh, ed. *Shetland's Northern Links: Language and History*. Edinburgh: Scottish Society for Northern Studies, 30–43.

Sundkvist, Peter. 2004. *The Vowel System of a Shetland Accent of Scottish Standard English: A Segmental Analysis*. Unpublished doctoral dissertation. Stockholm: Stockholms universitet, Engelska institutionen.

   2006. 'How Scandinavian is Shetland? A comparative phonological study between the Shetland dialect, Scots, and Scandinavian.' Paper presented at the Twelfth Germanic Linguistics Annual Conference (GLAC-12), The University of Illinois at Urbana-Champagne, 28–9 April 2006.

   2007. 'The pronunciation of Scottish Standard English in Lerwick, Shetland.' *English World-Wide* 28: 1–21.

Tait, John M. 1999. *Guid unkens efter Mark, Mark's gospel in Shetlandic*. Rotherham: Fact and Fiction.

   2000. 'Some characteristics of the Shetlandic vowel system.' *Scottish Language* 19: 83–99.

Tamminga, Meredith. 2008. *Variation and Change in a Peripheral Dialect: Evidence from Westray Vowel Phonology*. Unpublished Honours Thesis. Montreal: McGill University, Department of Linguistics.

Thomason, Sarah G. and Terrence Kaufman. 1988. *Language Contact, Creolization, and Genetic Linguistics*. Berkeley: University of California Press.

Trudgill, Peter. 1989. 'Contact and isolation in linguistic change.' In Leiv Egil Breivik and Ernst Håkon Jahr, eds. *Language Change: Contributions to the Study of its Causes*. Berlin: Mouton de Gruyter, 227–38.

van Leyden, Klaske. 2002. 'The relationship between vowel and consonant duration in Orkney and Shetland dialects.' *Phonetica* 59: 1–19.

   2004. *Prosodic Characteristics of Orkney and Shetland Dialects: An Experimental Approach*. Utrecht: LOT.

Wells, John C. 1982. *Accents of English*. Cambridge: Cambridge University Press.

3   Channel Island English

MARI C. JONES

1 Introduction

The Channel Islands form an archipelago off the Cotentin peninsula of
Normandy. They are divided administratively into two Bailiwicks, each with
a non-political chief citizen known as a Bailiff, who serves as senior judge
in the Royal Courts of Jersey and Guernsey, and moderator of each of those
two islands' parliamentary assemblies, or States. The Bailiwick of Jersey
comprises the island itself, which has an area of forty-five square miles and a
population of 88,200 and two rocky reefs, the Minquiers and the Ecrehous.
The other islands in the archipelago, belonging to the Bailiwick of Guernsey,
are Guernsey (twenty-five square miles, population 65,228), Alderney
(three square miles, pop. 2,294), Sark (two square miles, pop. 610), and
five islands of under one square mile: Herm, Jethou (combined population
97), Brecqhou (estimated population no more than 40), uninhabited Burhou
off Alderney, and a tidal island called Lihou, off Guernsey's west coast,
which does not have a permanent population.

    Though situated geographically closer to France than to the UK (at its
nearest point, Alderney lies only some nine miles west of Normandy), the
Islands are dependencies of the British Crown, to which they were formally
annexed in 1254 (though never forming part of the kingdom of England).
Prior to this they formed part of the Duchy of Normandy, itself established
in the early years of the tenth century. The first tenuous link with England
came in 1066 when William, Duke of Normandy became king of England
by right of conquest. At his death, however, his domains were separated,
his eldest son, Robert, becoming Duke of Normandy and his second son,
William Rufus, becoming King of England. Relations between the duchy
and the kingdom fluctuated under succeeding rulers but strong economic,
juridical and linguistic ties were maintained with mainland Normandy even
after 1204, when King John 'Lackland' lost the duchy to Philippe II of
France. Indeed, describing the islanders during the High Middle Ages, the

I would like to thank Dr. Darryl Ogier, Archivist of Guernsey, for his invaluable help
with this chapter. Recordings of Jersey, Guernsey and Sark English may be found at:
http://www.bbc.co.uk/voices/recordings (accessed October 2009).

Guernsey-born historian John Le Patourel stated that they 'were of the same racial blend as the Normans of the Cotentin, they spoke the same dialect, with their own local variations, traded with the same money and lived under the same customary law' (1937: 35). No attempt was made to introduce English law, and Norman law and custom in many respects still forms the basis of Channel Island governance. The islands are not represented in the UK Parliament, and it is not that body but the Crown that is responsible for them only in terms of defence and diplomatic representation, while Parliament legislates for them only by Acts which are explicitly extended directly to them by Order of the Privy Council.

To all intents and purposes, Jersey, Guernsey and Alderney are self-governing, each with its own elected legislative body, known as the States. Until December 2008, when the island held its first elections, Sark was technically a feudal state, headed by a Seigneur though in practice governed by the assembly of Chief Pleas, in part appointed and in part served by tenants of the ancient manorial holdings into which the island is divided. Many laws passed by the States of Alderney, Jersey and Guernsey require Royal Sanction by Her Majesty's Privy Council, as representative of the Queen, the islands' head of state, though much other legislation is effected locally by way of ordinance or regulation. Although part of the British Islands under UK law,[1] the Channel Islands do not form part of the UK, nor part of the European Community, though they have a particular, essentially commercial, relationship with the Community under Protocol 3 of the UK's Treaty of Accession of 1972. Islanders are therefore all full British Citizens but not automatically European Citizens. The functions of the Bailiwicks in the provision of global financial services, often characterized as of a 'tax haven' character, have increasingly in recent years led to their governments voluntarily participating in direct relations with third parties internationally, in part in reaction to arising issues, and in part as a consequence of the more general development of their economies and an awareness of the necessity of regulation.

2   Sociolinguistic history and current status of the variety

The political autonomy and diverse character of the Channel Islands means that, while certain common trends can be identified, the precise details of their linguistic histories often differ. The interested reader wishing to supplement the overview given here is referred to Syvret and Stevens (1998) (Jersey), Marr (1982) (Guernsey), Ewen and de Carteret (1969) (Sark), Venne and Allez (1992) (Alderney).

The sociolinguistic history of the Channel Islands has produced a situation whereby three speech-varieties have existed alongside each other for several

---

[1] The term 'British Islands' is used to refer to the UK, the Channel Islands and the Isle of Man and should not be confused with the British Isles, which includes Ireland.

centuries: standard French, English and Norman. The variation shown by the last between the islands has led to its designation as separate dialects, Jèrriais (Jersey), Guernesiais (Guernsey), Sercquiais (Sark) and the now extinct Auregnais (Alderney). These are often referred to collectively as 'Channel Islands French'. The roles fulfilled by these three varieties in everyday island life are very different. English and Norman are in a diglossic relationship, with English assuming 'High' functions (administration, legislation, education, media, church services and so forth) and Norman 'Low' functions (familiar discourse with family and friends). Adding standard French to the equation creates a more complex picture. It, too, is functionally differentiated from the other varieties, reserved today for formulaic official and ceremonial usage, so perhaps it is not unreasonable to speak of triglossia here.[2]

No immediate anglicization followed the annexation of the Channel Islands to the English Crown. Strong trade links with France were maintained with the common activity of fishing probably representing a major source of contact with the mainland population, and the currency they used was the French standard *Tournois*. Despite such links, however, France was now, politically at least, the enemy and, during subsequent centuries, fears of a French invasion led to the progressive fortification of Alderney, Guernsey and Jersey. All of these and Sark too, notwithstanding that island's strong natural defences, were to suffer attack, the last leading to the Battle of Jersey (1781).

The sixteenth and seventeenth centuries saw considerable change on the religious front. The Channel Islands remained part of the Norman Diocese of Coutances until 1568–9, and their religion, on the whole, Catholic until the early years of Elizabeth I. The fact that a French translation of the Prayer Book, introduced by the first Act of Uniformity of 1549, was issued for use in the churches of Calais, Guisnes, Jersey and Guernsey is proof that, at this time, the islands were still strongly francophone. Although the prayer book was intended to bring the Channel Islands into the same religious fold as mainland England and Wales, it was partly for linguistic reasons that, in due course, the islands adopted the Protestant teachings favoured by the French Huguenots (Calvinism) rather than embracing the Elizabethan church settlement and that many French religious and later political refugees made their home in the islands (the former as a response to troubles in France in the sixteenth century and again in a second wave after the revocation of the Edict of Nantes in 1685, and the latter in the late eighteenth and early nineteenth centuries).

It is impossible to pinpoint the growth of English in the Channel Islands to one specific period. The number of English troops garrisoned in the Channel Islands grew steadily in the seventeenth and eighteenth centuries, with their

---

[2] Standard French has never functioned as an everyday language of the Channel Islands either in former or modern times. Its position has always been that of an official language, and from the Middle Ages (before English began to predominate), it was used exclusively for all 'High' functions.

strategic significance as military bases coming to the fore as England was increasingly involved in wars beyond its shores. During the Napoleonic Wars almost 6,000 men were garrisoned on Guernsey (de Guerin 1905: 80–1), whose population in 1800 was recorded as 16,155 (Crossan 2005a: 31), and Alderney's attraction as an outpost at this time resulted in some 400 troops being stationed there, when the native population was around 900 (Venne and Allez 1992: 43). The troops inevitably brought the tradespeople and local inhabitants into contact with English and the increased opportunities for work in London at this time also left its mark on the islands linguistically. However, it is the nineteenth century that is held by many as the start of their anglicization 'proper' as the islanders increasingly began looking towards the outside world: 'C'est à partir de cette époque, après 1815, que la langue anglaise commence à se répandre et à être couramment parlée dans les îles, ce qui n'avait pas été le cas jusque-là' (Guillot 1975: 47).

In 1815, William Berry described Guernsey as a society where 'the old Norman French' was 'generally spoken by all ranks' and the merchants of its town, St. Peter Port, co-existed with inhabitants of the rural parishes who were 'shut out from agricultural communication with the rest of the world' (1815: 284, 298–300). The situation seems to have been similar on Jersey, where Henry Inglis described an island where Jèrriais was still very much the common tongue – even among the gentry – and where knowledge of standard French and English was still quite limited: 'the universal language is still a barbarous dialect' (1834: 72).[3] Of Alderney, he stated 'there are few English residents'. Less than a century on, both the linguistic and economic picture had changed beyond all measure: 'During the present century, the English language has, both in Guernsey and Jersey, made vast strides, so that it is difficult now to find a native even in the country parishes who cannot converse fairly well in that tongue' (Ansted and Latham 1893: 387).

This century saw a steep increase in the populations of all the islands. The 1901 census indicated that 25.6 per cent of Guernsey's population was non-native-born and, at 33.1 per cent, the figure for non-natives in St. Peter Port was even higher.[4] In 1847, work began on the construction of a breakwater on Alderney. Completed in 1861 and complemented by a chain of ten forts, its aim was to make the island a 'Gibraltar of the Channel' (States of Alderney 1974: 41). Such building operations required the importation of a large labour force, and led to the population trebling within five years. In 1861, less than half the recorded population of 4,932 were of Channel Island origin. As native-born inhabitants were now outnumbered, Auregnais began to fall rapidly into disuse. English therefore became the official language

---

[3] John Stead presents a different view, describing Jèrriais as 'daily falling into disuse and discredit' (1809).

[4] A useful and informative account of migration in nineteenth-century Guernsey is given in Crossan (2005a).

of the island almost a century before this occurred in the other islands. By 1901, Marquand was commenting that 'Alderney is the least French of the Channel Islands. The local patois . . . is rarely heard' (Venne and Allez 1992: 43). Silver mining in Little Sark in the 1830s and 1840s brought a large force of Cornish miners to the island, doubling the 250-strong population (Ewen and de Carteret 1969: 100). Many of these departed after the mines closed in 1847, several accompanied by a Sark bride, thus decreasing further the pool of native speakers of Sercquiais.

Trade with England, in particular the development of the horticultural industry, extended the commercial expansion hitherto centred on the towns to the whole of Guernsey and Jersey and integrated the economies of the islands firmly with the UK, a phenomenon that in part had its origins in the establishment of a regular packet service by the end of the eighteenth century. Communication then improved further, with the sailboats being replaced by steamers. This allowed tourism to be set on a serious footing for the first time by bringing thousands of people from the UK to the Channel Islands each year and the introduction of excursion cars to take the boat passengers for tours around the islands ensured that even the most rural parishes were brought into contact with the visitors. Immigration also had a part to play, with many of those who left England towards the end of the notorious 'Hungry Forties' attracted to the Channel Islands by a number of booming industries – such as construction, ship-building and granite quarries.

By the nineteenth century, English was also having a noticeable impact on the education system and although its introduction seems to have occurred in a somewhat ad hoc way rather than as the result of explicit policy, it was certainly reinforced by practical considerations: for example, by the end of the nineteenth century, a command of English was essential for anyone running businesses in the horticultural industry due to its reliance on trade with the UK. The fact that Norman had no formal presence in the primary school meant that the effective replacement of one H variety with another is unlikely to have been a direct factor in the dialect's decline. However, as Crossan notes of Guernsey, in words equally applicable to the whole of the archipelago, the loss of yet another domain to English 'reflected developments which had already taken root in society at large and were tending over the long run to transform [the Channel Islands] from a diglossic society, where a non-native standard was used in formal contexts but not spoken at home, into a monoglot one where English was solidly ensconced in both high and low functions' (2005b: 876).

By the end of the nineteenth century, this steady language shift, most notably among the educated classes, had been coupled with a tendency to model the Channel Islands on England culturally. For example, in St. Peter Port, whole streets of Regency-style houses had been built and renaming of streets (in English) was common practice in Jersey, Guernsey and Alderney.

Islanders soon began to realize the implications of this burgeoning anglicization for their native dialects.

Les temps changent; la navigation à vapeur, après avoir été une source de prosperité pour l'archipel, pourrait bien aussi déterminer sa ruine. Ces îles sont désormais trop près de Londres; l'élément anglais s'y implante rapidement, et trop de voix interessées jasent sur ce petit monde. (N. N. 1849: 962)

Literature about Guernsey at this time hints that English borrowings were starting to appear, with a guidebook observing how amusing it was 'to wait for the English words to peep out of so different a language' (Anonymous 1847), and it was becoming clear that the repercussions of this might be severe:

Being proud of my native isle, and of much that belongs to it, I often feel sorry that our good old local tongue is practically dying out, offering but little, if any resistance to the inroads of the English language. (Bougourd 1897: 183)

and even that a variety of English was being formed that differed from that spoken on the mainland:

The language of the townspeople, from their constant intercourse with strangers, is very intelligible English, though spoken with a peculiar accent, and frequently interlarded with the mother-tongue. (Dublin University Magazine 1846: 630)

On Sark, the last twenty years of the nineteenth century brought an influx of immigrants who became permanent residents, which

transformed the character of the island community . . . from a homogeneous group of people born in the island into a diverse assemblage with a steadily shrinking proportion of island-born inhabitants. (Ewen and de Carteret 1969: 108)

This was to recur in the years following the First World War, when high taxes in the UK brought large numbers to the island.

The feeling that the encroachment of English society was leading the Channel Islands to lose grasp of both their cultural and linguistic identity became manifest in a number of different ways across the archipelago: for example, the foundation of the *Société Guernesiaise* (1867)[5] and the *Société Jersiaise* (1873) with the stated aims of preserving objects, monuments and

---

[5] This society has no link with the current society of the same name which was established in 1882 as the *Guernsey Society of Natural Science and Local Research* (its renaming as the *Société Guernesiaise* dates from 1922).

documents pertaining to the history of these islands;[6] while Frederick C. Lukis (1788–1871) excavated and strove to preserve the dolmens and menhirs of the archipelago (Sebire 2003), and its history was written (Tupper 1854; de la Croix 1858–1860 etc.). Creating an identity that was demonstrably distinct from that of the UK may have been one reason why it was this century that witnessed the first major writings in Jèrriais and Guernesiais, which influenced the renewal of interest in dialect literature in the Cotentin.

The inroads made by English in the nineteenth century continued apace in the twentieth. The Income Tax Laws of Guernsey (1920) and Jersey (1928) were the first pieces of substantial Channel Island legislation to be drafted in English and also modelled on English, rather than Norman, law.[7] On Guernsey, local currency was set at parity with the British pound sterling, in place of the joint parity with the British and French standard that had prevailed since 1870 (on Jersey this had taken place in 1877; McCammon 1984: 185) and communications with the British mainland improved further, leading to the opening of airports in Alderney (1935), Jersey (1937) and Guernsey (1939). English became an official language of Guernsey in 1926 and has been the recognized language of the States of Jersey since 1946. Jersey's last French-language newspaper ceased publication at the end of 1959. On Sark, many island families sold their properties to wealthy immigrants during the first quarter of the twentieth century, which led to a further dilution of the local community. By 1960, only half the population was island-born and, by 1967, 61 per cent of dwellings were in the hands of 'outsiders' (Ewen and de Carteret 1969: 112).

The Second World War dealt a devastating blow to the civilian population of the Channel Islands when the archipelago was demilitarized by the British in 1940 and subsequently occupied by Germany until 1945 (see Bunting 1996). One-fifth of the population of Jersey, over half that of Guernsey and all but eighteen residents of Alderney (though no-one from Sark) chose to be evacuated to the UK, mainly women and children in each case. Although therefore in the Second World War, unlike in the First, significant numbers of the Norman speech community were not killed, their evacuation meant that, for the best part of five years, many of the archipelago's children were denied the opportunity of growing up in a Norman-speaking environment and grew up instead with English as their mother tongue. On their return, many older evacuees preferred to continue using English, which they saw as the key to social advancement and the outside world. Despite the fact that anglicization was already well advanced before the war, this unprecedented population movement and its repercussions for the islanders' ability in, and their attitude towards, the dialect was undoubtedly a pivotal point in

---

[6] Although the societies initially showed some activity with respect to language, this subsequently faltered. The *Société Jersiaise*'s *Section de la langue Jèrriaise* dates from 1995.

[7] The modern law of the Channel Islands remains, however, founded upon Norman law in many respects.

the sociolinguistic history of the speech community. The most devastating effect was felt on Alderney, where the construction of slave-labour camps meant that, after the German surrender, Alderney was desolate and full of concrete bunkers and, consequently, was unable to be resettled immediately. The community that had existed before the war was lost forever and the dialect was quick to follow (Le Maistre 1982).

Since the war, anglicization has been further strengthened by the fact that low taxation has made the islands a haven for high-income earners and those servicing the finance industry, the latter employing some 20 per cent of the workforce on Jersey and Guernsey. Indeed, the last Census (2001) recorded that, at that time, individuals born in the UK represented around 36 per cent of the population of both of these islands. Clearly, intermarriage between islanders and immigrants has also accelerated the decline of Norman within the family domain. The tourist industry has continued to grow steadily, with daily sea and air services operating between the archipelago and the UK. In 2003, 865,000 passenger movements were made between Guernsey and the UK. Although these are connected with business as well as tourism, they demonstrate how closely linked the Channel Islands are today with mainland Britain.

For all these reasons, the latter half of the twentieth century and the beginning of the twenty-first have witnessed the progressive and widespread decline of Norman as an everyday means of communication, as islanders look increasingly to English. The most recent censuses of Jersey and Guernsey (2001) recorded that, at that time, only 2,874 inhabitants of Jersey (3.2 per cent) and 1,327 inhabitants of Guernsey (2 per cent) were able to speak Norman fluently. A decade ago, it was estimated that fewer than 20 of the 610 permanent inhabitants of Sark spoke Sercquiais (3.5 per cent) (Brasseur 1998: 152). These figures imply that, if the decline continues at the present rate, no speakers of Channel Island French will remain by, at least, the middle of the present century.

It is intriguing to note therefore that, should such a situation come to pass, Norman will persist only in terms of a few place names, patronymics and, as will be explored, the distinctive variety of English spoken in the islands, which may well prove to be the last indicators of their linguistic heritage.

3   Linguistic features

3.1   Phonology

Despite their shared Norman substrate, the varieties of English spoken in the Channel Islands are not phonologically identical. Even when they speak Channel Island French natively, the accents of the now elderly islanders who were evacuated to the UK during the course of the Second World War are often more 'English' than those of their contemporaries who stayed on the islands during the Occupation. The fact that significant numbers of islanders are immigrants means that many UK English accents are prevalent, with intermarriage leading to the presence of non-local features in the English of even island-born children. Moreover, as elsewhere in the British Islands, extralinguistic influence such as the broadcast media may also have a part to play in the increasing presence of TH-fronting and T-glottalization in the speech of younger islanders (cf. Ramisch 2007: 180). The analysis in this section focuses on the English of speakers considered to have a 'broad accent'.

3.1.1 Vowels
Typical vowel realizations in Channel Island English (after Ramisch 2007: 181):

KIT ɪ ~ ï

DRESS ɛ ~ ë

TRAP æ

LOT ɒ ~ ö

STRUT ɔ ~ ʌ

FOOT ʊ

BATH ɑː ~ a̠ː

CLOTH ɒ ~ ö

NURSE ɜː ~ əː

FLEECE iː ~ ɪi

FACE eɪ ~ e̞ɪ

PALM ɑː ~ a̠ː

THOUGHT ɔː ~ oː

GOAT ɔʊ ~ əʊ

GOOSE uː ~ ʉː

PRICE ɒɪ ~ ɑɪ ~ aɪ

CHOICE ɔɪ ~ oɪ

MOUTH aʊ

NEAR ɪə ~ iə[8]

SQUARE ɛə

START ɑː ~ a̠ː

NORTH ɔː ~ oː

FORCE ɔː ~ oː

CURE jʊə

happY i ~ iː

lettER œ ~ ə

horsES ɪ ~ ˙i

commA ə

Popular views about the accent of Jersey in particular include the claim that it 'sounds South African'. This may be due to the tendency towards a close

---

[8] On Guernsey, evidence can be seen of what probably represents input from southern varieties of English in the word *here*, which is pronounced /jœ/, i.e. with a shift of weight from the NEAR diphthong.

realization of DRESS and TRAP and a very back realization of BATH, PALM and START.

3.1.2 Consonants
Particulary noteworthy features include the following:

(a)   All conservative accents of the Channel Islands display H-dropping, leading to hypercorrections such as:

(1)   My mother was very hill and I was the heldest, and I stayed to 'elp my mother.

(b)   Though by no means found in the speech of every speaker, realization of non-prevocalic /r/ is prevalent throughout the archipelago, word-finally (*engineer*, *father* etc.) or medially (*injured*). This may possibly be attributable to transfer from the Norman ending corresponding to French *-eur*, or else to the influence of southern counties English that may have served as input varieties. In unstressed syllables, the pronunciation of *-ing* varies between /ɪn/ and /ɪŋ/ (Ramisch 1989: 175, 1994: 458, 2007: 179). Uvular *r* characterizes the English of Sark and initial prevocalic *r* tends to be trilled throughout the archipelago (Viereck 1988: 473–4).

(c)   Medial yod often appears after an initial voiced consonant such as /gjaːdn/, /bjɪəd/ in all varieties of Channel Island English (Viereck 1988: 473–4).

(d)   [t] and [d] are often dental and unaspirated.

3.1.3 Prosodic features
(a)   In the case of polysyllabic words, the main stress of Channel Island English often falls on a different syllable from that of Standard English: *bed′room*, *Liver′pool*, *daffo′dils*, *rail′way*, *edu′cated*. Moreover, the difference between stressed and unstressed syllables may be less marked than in Standard English, with secondary stress on other syllables: [ˈtɔˈmaˈtəʊz] (Hublart 1979: 47; Tomlinson 1981: 20; Ramisch 1989: 164n.1, 2007: 179). Although Norman influence cannot be demonstrated in each case, it is noteworthy that, where a word of English and Norman share a similar form but a different stress placement – usually due to the fact that the Norman form is an adapted borrowing from English – Norman stress placement is often used in a sentence of Channel Island English. For example: the English word 'gravy' ([ˈgɹejvi]) is borrowed into Jèrriais as *grevîn* in a sentence such as:

(2)   Soulais faithe du grevîn
          'I used to make gravy'.

In Jèrriais, however, the pronunciation is [gɹeˈvi]. When used in a sentence of Jersey English, therefore, the word *gravy* may be given a different stress pattern from that of Standard English, hence:

(3)   I used to make [gɹejˈvi].

(b)   Channel Island English also has a distinctive intonation pattern, with rising intonation in sentence-final position instead of the falling intonation of Standard English.

3.1.4   Conclusions on phonology

Although there has been ample opportunity for the phonological development of Channel Island English to have been influenced by varieties of UK English, the particular prominence of any one English input variety over others cannot be demonstrated conclusively. Certainly, immigrants from the UK have not tended to come from one particular area.[9] However, influence of the Norman substrate may be seen clearly in several of the above features, most notably, the realization of [t], [d], initial prevocalic *r* and the Sark uvular *r*. H-dropping, too, is likely to be due to Norman influence, though clearly this is also a feature of many varieties of English. Ramisch (2007: 180) also suggests that the rounded realization of STRUT, seen in the English of all four main islands, may be attributable to the substrate. The fact that this is such a prominent feature of the English spoken on Alderney, where the Norman dialect died out completely around the time of the Second World War (see above) is testimony to the persistence of such features.

3.2   Morphosyntax

The Norman substrate influence is more clearly demonstrable in the morphosyntax of Channel Island English than in its phonology. This section will be illustrated with examples from Jèrriais (J) and Guernesiais (G). To date, no orthographic conventions have been laid down for Sark French.

3.2.1   Relatively stable features

(i)   'There's' + time reference (Tomlinson 1981: 18; Viereck 1988: 474; Ramisch 1989: 150, 1994: 459–61; Jones 2001: 168; Ramisch 2007: 182)

In Standard English, the present perfect followed by the preposition *for* and a reference to the time involved are required in an expression such as:

(4)   **I've been** a farmer **for** ten years.

In Channel Island English, however, the construction *there's* + time reference + present tense is commonly used:

---

[9] See Ramisch (1989: 164–78) for detailed analysis of this with respect to the English of Guernsey.

(5)   **There's** ten years **I'm** a farmer (cf. y'a dgiex ans qué j'sis fermyi (J)).

As the English construction is a syntactic calque of Norman, its occurrence is clearly due to transfer.

(ii)   The definite article (Brasseur 1977: 101; Ramisch 1989: 113–24, 2007: 179; Jones 2001: 170–1)

Non-standard use is made of the definite article in the following contexts:

    (a) Names of languages:

(6)   Now everyone speaks **the** English

    (b) Before a plural noun with generic reference:

(7)   **The** Jersey people are quite stubborn, you know

    (c) Adverbials of direction:

(8)   Only if you want to, well, do extra shopping then you'd better go into **the** town to do it

    (d) Adverbials of time expressing regular repetition:

(9)   He gives the news out on the wireless in h'm in patois on **the** Friday

Norman would have definite articles in each of these contexts. Compare, for example, the following as translations for (6) and (7): *Auch't'haeure nou pâle tous l'Angllais* (G); *Les Jèrriais sont un mio têtus, dis* (J). Transfer is therefore again the most likely explanation for the English constructions.

(iii)   'Isn't it?' as a tag question (Brasseur 1977: 101; Hublart 1979: 48; Tomlinson 1981: 19; Viereck 1988: 474; Ramisch 1989: 149)

Isn't it is used in Channel Island English as a universal tag question:

(10)   She did well, **isn't it?**

Although this construction also functions as a tag question in other varieties of regional English (Ramisch 1989: 149–50) it is possible that transfer from Norman may account for the presence of this invariable form in Channel Island English, where it could represent a calque of the Norman invariable tag *n'est-che pon?* (J) ('isn't it?'):

(11)   Oulle est hardi belle, not' fil'ye, **n'est-che pon?** (J) (Birt 1985: 237)
           lit. 'She's very pretty, our daughter, isn't it?'

(iv) 'But yes' (Hublart 1979: 48; Tomlinson 1981: 19; Viereck 1988: 474; Ramisch 1989: 154, 1994: 458, 2007: 179; Jones 2001: 171)

The expression *but yes* is used in Channel Island English as an emphatic form of the affirmative with a meaning akin to Standard English 'yes indeed' or 'yes of course'. For example:

(12)   Did your parents speak Jèrriais? – **But yes.**

The presence of this form is clearly due to transfer, representing a calque of the expression *mais oui* ('but yes'), which may be used in the Channel Island dialects as an emphatic form of the affirmative.

(v)   The conditional (Jones 2001: 172)

Conditional clauses of Channel Island English are frequently formed without the word *if*, which would be necessary in standard usage. For example:

(13)   You'd have seen that, you'd never have thought there was any news in it.

This is clearly formed on the basis of a construction such as:

(14)   J'éthais l'temps, j'pouôrrais l'vaie aniet (J)
         lit. 'I had the time, I would be able to see him today', meaning
         'If I'd had the time, I would have been able to see him today',

which is commonly found in Norman – and in spoken Standard French (Price 2008: §423).

(vi)   Object pronouns (Jones 2001: 173)

English and Norman differ in terms of the pronouns used to refer to objects. In English, the gender-neutral *it* is used unless the object has an obvious gender, hence

(15)   **She**'s a girl but **It**'s a dog.

Since all nouns carry a grammatical gender in Norman, the pronoun used to refer to them is also marked for gender. For example, when talking about a chair, which is feminine in Norman, a speaker might say

(16)   Est-**alle** grande? (J)
         'Is it (lit. 'she') big?'

whereas in English *it* would be used in this context.

Under the influence of Norman, a masculine or feminine pronoun may often be used in Channel Island English to refer to inanimate objects, hence:

(17)   **He**'s a Jersey cart
         (the Norman for 'cart', *hèrnais* (J), is masculine)

(18)   Mind that, **she**'s hot, eh! (i.e. the plate)
         (the Norman for 'plate', *assiaette* (G), is feminine).

(vii)   Prepositions

Prepositions used in Channel Island English often differ from those which would be used in the same contexts in Standard English. Again, this is plainly due to transfer. Examples include:

(19)   He wrote a letter **for** thank me (Standard English *to*)
            Il écrit énne laettre **pour** m'r'merciaïr (G)

(20)   That was **on** the 'Evening Post' (Standard English *in*)
            Ch'tait **sus** l' 'Evening Post' (J)

(21)   I bought it **to** the Forest Stores (Standard English *at*)
            J'l'ai acatai **à** la Forest Stores (G)

(22)   The wheel **to** my cart (Standard English 'of')
            La reue **à** mon tchériot (G)

The use of positional *to* (21 above) is widespread in Channel Island English (Viereck 1988: 474; Barbé 1994: 706–17). However, Barbé (1994: 707) also notes evidence of it in certain varieties of English spoken in Hampshire, Somerset and New England.

(viii)   Demonstrative Pronouns (Viereck 1988: 474; Ramisch 1989: 148)

This here and *that there* often replace the demonstratives *here* and *that*:

(23)   When **that there** Jerseyman shows up again (chu Jerriais là (G))
            (Guppy 1975)

3.2.2   *Features typical of bilinguals*

The above transfer features are relatively stable in the English of many older islanders, regardless of their ability to speak Norman. They therefore differ in status to the following which, although they also may be transfer-influenced, are mostly used by bilinguals, hence are likely to be shorter-lived.

(ix)   *Home* is frequently used in the sense of Standard English 'at home' (Tomlinson 1981: 20; Viereck 1988: 474)

(24)   I worked **home**

(x)   The present perfect appears in contexts where the past definite would be more usual in Standard English:

(25)   I've been swimming when **I've been** to get the seaweed in the cart

(xi)   The third person singular form is frequently uninflected (Barbé 1995: 3)

(26)   She **speak**

(xii)   Destinational *at* is frequent after *go* (Barbé 1995: 3)

(27)   They used to go **at** the Catholic school

3.2.3 Features shared with UK non-standard varieties
Channel Island English also contains features of non-standard English with
a non-regional and diffuse distribution throughout the UK. As will be seen
from the examples below, however, it is not always easy to exclude the
possibility of transfer and, in such cases, the features in question may arise
from two reinforcing motivations (Viereck 1988: 475).

(xiii)   Emphatic use of personal pronouns (Brasseur 1977: 101; Hublart
          1979: 48; Tomlinson 1981: 19; Viereck 1988: 474; Ramisch 1989:
          124–9, 1994: 457, 2007: 179; Jones 2001: 169)

Another widespread feature of Channel Island English is the use of the
accusative form of the personal subject pronouns *me, you, him, her, us* and
them as emphatic forms at the beginning or end of an utterance. Thus:

(28)   **Me**, I'm from St. Ouen's / I'm from St. Ouen's, **me**

This is clearly parallel to the emphatic use of such pronouns in Norman:

(29)   Oulle a tréjous 'te d'même, **lyi** (J) (Birt 1985: 238).
           lit. 'She's always been the same, her'

(30)   Jé n'veurs pas y allaïr, **mé** (G)
           'I don't want to go, me'

That this feature is highly salient to speakers of Guernsey English may be
seen by the fact that Le Pelley chose the title *I am Guernsey, me* for his 1975
article. However, Dillard (1985: 107) notes that pronouns may be used in
a similar way in Cajun English and, citing Shorrocks (1981: 542), Ramisch
observes that the emphatic use of personal pronouns may also be observed
in the variety of English spoken in parts of Greater Manchester. While it is
impossible to discount influence from this variety, since there is no intrinsic
demographic connection between Jersey and Greater Manchester, in this
case transfer seems a more likely explanation.

(xiv)   The particle 'eh' (Hublart 1979: 48; Viereck 1988: 474; Ramisch 1989:
         111, 1994: 458–91, 2007: 181; Jones 2001: 168–9)

This is possibly the feature of Channel Island English of which its speakers
are most conscious. In informal speech, the particle *eh* is extremely frequent
and occurs as both a tag at the end of a question, with a meaning akin to
English 'isn't it?'/ 'aren't they?'/ 'don't you think?', for example:

(31)   That's the one, **eh**?

and as a phatic particle used to maintain the connection between speaker and
hearer. In the latter context, it may be used so frequently by some speakers
that it could almost be seen as a marker of the end of a clause:

(32)   You used to get all little shops, **eh**. I mean you get towns in
          England that have changed too, **eh**. No more little shops. Well,
          it's like that in Jersey now too, **eh**. (Ramisch 1989: 111)

Such usage is common in Norman, and also in standard French, where the
particle involved is *hein?*:

(33)   Qu'est-ce que tu fais, **hein?**
          'What are you doing, eh?'

Transfer is, again, a likely explanation. However, as Quirk et al. note (1985:
814) the particle also occurs in varieties of present-day English.

(xv)   'There's' + plural subject (Ramisch 1989: 92–6, 2007: 181; Jones 2001:
       168)

The presentative *there's* may be used in Channel Island English with a plural
subject. This seems to be attributable to the fact that, in Norman, the most
commonly used presentative, *y'a*, contains a singular verb.

(34)   **There's** two castles in Jersey
          (cf. 'Y' a deux chatés en Jèrri (J); standard English 'There are
          two castles in Jersey')

As Ramisch states, this feature may, however, also be observed in many
varieties of non-standard English and is also extremely common in spoken
US English (Miller and Brown 1982: 16; Petyt 1985: 237; Quirk et al. 1985:
8–9).

(xvi)   Pronominal apposition (Ramisch 1989: 156–7)

Linked to (xiii) above is the emphatic use of a personal pronoun immediately
after its antecedent. For example:

(35)   . . . and the teacher, **she** was angry, eh

Although this feature, termed pronominal apposition by Ramisch, who
describes its usage in Guernsey English (1989: 156–7), is also widespread in
colloquial English, in this context, it may reflect transfer of a widely used
device in Norman:

(36)   Et la p'tite fille, **all'** est bouanne (G)
          lit. 'And the little girl, she is good'

(xvii)   FAP (Barbé 1994: 708–12, 1995: 5–20; Viereck 1988: 474)

The term 'FAP' was coined by Barbé in her 1985 study of Guernsey English
to refer to a construction identified by Viereck (1988: 474) more widely in
Channel Island English involving the use of a 'First verb' (usually *go* or *come*)
plus the conjunction *And* plus the **P**lain infinitive, for example:

(37)   We went and live there

(38)   A girl came and see me

A full analysis is given in Barbé (1995: 5–20). Barbé (1994: 710) hypothesized that FAP may have arisen either through contact with Norman, where the use of an infinitive in V2 position is common:

(39)   J'fus veies John (G)
            Cf. Channel Island English 'I went and see John'

or that, alternatively, it may have arisen as an intermediate form (Trudgill 1986) as a conflation of the two standard English alternatives *I went and saw John* and *I went to see John*. Another possibility is that FAP may have arisen by speakers generalizing the pattern V1 + and + uninflected V2, which occurs frequently in standard English when V1 is also uninflected (e.g. *I'll go and see*), or it may even be due to the generalization of a perceived pattern of standard English sentences such as *I went and shut the door*, where the past form (*shut*) is identical to the infinitive.[10] Barbé (1995: 8) has also found casual examples of the construction in American and South African English.[11]

3.2.4   Other non-standard features

Channel Island English also contains features found in several non-standard varieties of English which differ in that these are less likely to be attributable to contact with Norman. The most commonly attested include:

(xviii)   Multiple negation (possibly reinforced by the discontinuous nega-
           tion of Norman) (Viereck 1988: 475; Ramisch 1989: 162; Barbé 1994:
           702–3; Ramisch 2007: 179)

(40)   He **don't** know **nothing**

(xix)   Unmarked plurality with nouns of measurement (Ramisch 1989: 60,
           1994: 458, 2007: 179)

(41)   They pay 200 **pound** a week

(xx)   Adverb formation without -*ly* (Ramisch 1989: 161)

(42)   He runs along quite **slow**

---

[10] For a full analysis and discussion, see Pullum (1990: 231) and Barbé (1995: 5–20).
[11] For other features of Guernsey English, such as assertive 'yet' 3sg. auxiliary usage, prenom-
      inal 'plenty' and the avoidance of inversion, see Barbé (1995). It is possible that these also
      occur more broadly in Channel Island English but no evidence of them has been found in
      the recordings analysed for this chapter.

(xxi)   Non-standard past tense forms (Ramisch 1989: 161; Barbé 1994: 701; Viereck 1988: 474)

(43)   He **seen** him/ I **done** it/ You **hurted** me

(xxii)   The use of *what* as a generalized relative (Barbé 1994: 703):

(44)   He learnt a lot of things **what** was said in the quarry (standard English *which/that*)

(xxiii) *-s* generalized to all persons of the present tense (Barbé 1994: 701; Viereck 1988: 474):

(45)   I goes back home

Some of the above (e.g. vii (21), xi, xiii, xiv) are highly salient to speakers of Channel Island English and feature prominently in items caricaturing everyday speech (such as the Stone de Croze cartoon strip in the Guernsey Press (G), the *Book of Ebenezer le Page* (Edwards 1982) (G) and Jones (1967) (J). Others, however, (such as FAP) are less well documented and are likely to pass unnoticed even by those using them on a daily basis.

3.3   Lexis

Instances of Norman borrowings in Channel Island English are numerous. Nonce borrowings occur spontaneously when a bilingual is unable to recall the exact English term. For example:

(46)   My bike is **foutu** ('broken') (G)

(47)   That's the **faûcheuse** ('mowing machine') (J)

Many established borrowings are from the vocabulary of administration, for example *douzaine* (parish council G, J, S), *connétabl'ye* (J), *connêtable* (G) ('constable', a parish council executive officer in Guernsey and in Jersey and Sark), or the land: *vergée* (J, G) (a unit of measurement in all the Channel Islands).[12] Given its historical role as the official language of the archipelago, borrowings from standard French abound in fields such as administrative, fiscal and legal (especially land administration) matters: *Procureur* (Attorney General), *Jurat* (a member of the Royal Court in Guernsey, Alderney and Jersey), *Greffe* (office of the Clerk to the States and Court), *Billet d'État* (agendas and associated material published prior to meetings of the States in Alderney and Guernsey), *Seneschal* (the island judge and president of Sark's legislative assembly, the Chief Pleas), *contrat* (title deed), *partage* (the

---

[12] As the term *vergée* was once used in standard French, it might be possible to claim that its presence in Channel Island English was due to borrowing from standard French rather than Norman. However, since the term has been obsolete in standard French for many centuries, this seems unlikely. It might even be from the English 'verge' as a linear measurement (Darryl Ogier, personal communication).

official term in the Channel Islands for a division or sharing, most commonly found when an estate is inherited and then divided between heirs). Some of those that have become established in other fields include *bannelais* (organic road sweepings used for compost, J), *branchage* (hedge-trimming and official inspection, J), *chouques* ('logs', J), *temps pâssé* ('time past', J), *côtil* (steep hillside field, J), vraic (seaweed used for fertilizer, J, G), *bachîn* (large metal bowl, J, G), *douit* ('stream', G), *boud'lot* ('Guy Fawkes', G) *gâche mêlaie* (a type of cake, G), *patin* (a device for catching spider crabs, G).

The lexis of older speakers is also peppered with greetings, such as *mon vier* ('old boy', J, G), and exclamations, e.g. *caw chapin* (G) (derived via folk etymology from *gâche à pain* 'bread cake').

4 Concluding remarks

The future of English as the dominant variety of the Channel Islands now seems assured. Its economic relevance and high status outside the archipelago make competition impossible from Norman, a little-spoken dialect with limited relevance beyond the islands. Standard French may continue to be used for ceremonial purposes but, with few native speakers resident on the islands and no-one calling for its retention, it seems destined to become, if it is not already, little more than a widely taught foreign language.

Even though it will probably disappear sometime during the next few decades, the influence of Norman on the English of the Channel Islands has resulted in the production of a distinctive local variety. As discussed above, although not every feature described is necessarily present in the speech of all of the archipelago's inhabitants, it is clear that many of them arose in the speech of bilinguals via the process of transfer. As English has become increasingly dominant, such features may even be found in the speech of monolingual speakers of English whose families are native to the Channel Islands.[13] Moreover, while not officially stigmatized, as in the UK, many non-standard features are consciously corrected at home and school so that the speech of the younger and middle generations also tends to lack many of the features found in the English of more traditional, older islanders who have experienced less contact with outside influences via university education or work in the UK. Where it does remain, it would generally be considered as an L variety in a diglossic relationship with standard English.[14]

For pragmatic reasons, this chapter has focused on a common core of features found in the traditional speech of older islanders. Not all features will necessarily be found in the speech of a single individual. Moreover, as has been discussed, variation is readily apparent across generations, even in

---

[13] The features described in section 3.2 are not generally found in the English of more recent immigrants, since they usually will have little contact with Norman. However, some of the more salient features of the variety (such as xiv) are often adopted.

[14] This comment applies largely to middle-aged and younger people who do not have Norman as their native tongue. Many older speakers are monodialectal in English.

the case of native islanders. Furthermore, although many of these features characterize the English spoken throughout the archipelago, more detailed and systematic studies need to be made of the varieties of Sark and Alderney in order to determine whether any 'superordinate' pan-Channel Islands variety of English that might exist was, in fact, more homo- or heterogeneous than suggested above.

Ramisch's 1989 study of Guernsey English found that the presence of some features differed markedly between the speech of Guernesiais speakers and that of younger monolingual speakers of English who were indigenous to the island and who had lived there all their lives.[15] This suggests that although the Norman colouring of the English spoken in the Channel Islands will almost certainly survive the loss of the local dialect, it may not do so by much. Although it does not automatically follow that Channel Island English will necessarily lose its distinctive character, it does suggest that the Norman substrate might no longer have a major part in its formation. If a regional variety of a language is indeed describable as 'ce qui reste du dialecte quand le dialecte a disparu'[16] (Tuaillon 1974: 576) then, if things continue as at present, the definitive departure of Norman from the Channel Islands will occur, not with the death of the dialect, but rather via the elimination of Norman influence from the variety of English spoken within the archipelago.

References

Anonymous 1847. 'The Channel Islands or a Peep at our neighbours.' In J. Stevens Cox, ed. (1970) *Guernsey in Queen Victoria's Reign*. Guernsey: Toucan Press, 5–23.

Ansted, David T. and Robert G. Latham 1893. *The Channel Islands*. 3rd edn, revised by E. Toulmin Nicolle. London: W.H. Allen.

Barbé, Pauline. 1994. 'Guernsey English: my mother tongue.' *Report and Transactions of La Société Guernesiaise* 23/4: 700–23.

1995. 'Guernsey English: a syntax exile?' *English World-Wide* 16: 1–36.

Berry, William. 1815. *The History of the Island of Guernsey*. London: John Hatchard.

Birt, Paul. 1985. *Lé Jèrriais pour Tous: A Complete Course on the Jersey Language*. Jersey: Don Balleine.

Bougourd, J. M. 1897. 'Our insular dialect.' *Transactions of the Guernsey Society of Natural Science and Local Research* 3: 183–92.

Brasseur, Patrice. 1977. 'Le français dans les îles anglo-normandes.' *Travaux de Linguistique et de Littérature* 16: 97–104.

1998. 'La survie du dialecte normand et du français dans les îles anglo-normandes: remarques sociolinguistiques.' *Plurilinguismes* 15: 133–70.

Bunting, Madeleine. 1996. *The Model Occupation: The Channel Islands under German Rule 1940–1945*. London: Harper Collins.

[15] Cf. for instance the use of the definite article (Ramisch 1989: 123); prepositions *in/to* (Ramisch 1989: 139); present for perfect with time reference (Ramisch 1989: 150–2); deletion of 's in the local genitive (Ramisch 1989: 152–3); *there's* used with time reference (1989: 97–8).

[16] 'What is left of the dialect when the dialect has disappeared'.

de la Croix, M. 1858–60. *Jersey, ses antiquités, ses institutions, son histoire* (2 vols.). Jersey: C. Le Feuvre.

Crossan, Rose-Marie. 2005a. *Guernsey, 1814–1914: Migration in a Modernising Society*. PhD thesis, University of Leicester.

2005b. 'The retreat of French from Guernsey's public primary schools, 1800–1939.' *Report and Transactions of La Société Guernesiaise* 25/5: 851–88.

Dillard, Joey L. 1985. *Towards a Social History of American English*. Berlin: Mouton.

Edwards, Gerald B. 1982. *The Book of Ebenezer Le Page*. Harmondsworth: Penguin.

Ewen, Alfred H. and Allan R. de Carteret. 1969. *The Fief of Sark*. Guernsey: The Guernsey Press Co. Ltd.

de Guérin, Thomas W. M. 1905. 'The English garrison of Guernsey from early times.' *Transactions of the Guernsey Society of Natural Science and Local Research* 5: 66–81.

Guillot, Claude. 1975. *Les Îles anglo-normandes*. Paris: Presses Universitaires de France.

Guppy, Alan W. 1975. *A Selection of 'Stone de Croze' Strip Cartoons as featured in the Guernsey Evening Press and Star*. Guernsey: The Guernsey Press.

Hublart, Claude. 1979. 'Le Français de Jersey.' Unpublished thesis, Université de l'Etat à Mons.

Inglis, Henry. 1834. *The Channel Islands* (4th edn). London: Whittaker and Co.

Jones, D. 1967. 'The 'are and the tortus; Cinderella; Garfawkesnart; Rumple le Stiltskin; Redrardinood.' *Island Topic*, July–December.

Jones, Mari. C. 2001. *Jersey Norman French: A Linguistic Study of an Obsolescent Dialect*. Publications of the Philological Society 34. Oxford: Blackwell.

Le Maistre, Frank. 1982. *The Language of Auregny/La Langue normande d'Auregny* (booklet and cassette recording). Jersey: Don Balleine.

Le Patourel, John. 1937. *The Medieval Administration of the Channel Islands 1199–1399*. London: Oxford University Press.

Le Pelley, Jean. 1975. 'I am Guernsey, me!' *The Review of the Guernsey Society* 21: 17–19.

Marr, L. James. 1982. *The History of Guernsey*. Chichester: Phillimore.

McCammon, A. L. T. 1984. *Currencies of the Anglo-Norman Isles*. London: Spink.

Miller, Jim and Keith Brown. 1982. 'Aspects of Scottish English Syntax.' *English World-Wide* 3: 3–17.

N. N. 1849. 'Les Iles de la Manche, Jersey et Guernsey en 1848 et 1849.' *Revue des Deux Mondes* 4: 937–67.

Petyt, Keith M. 1985. *Dialect and Accent in Industrial West Yorkshire*. Amsterdam: John Benjamins.

Price, Glanville. 2008. *A Comprehensive French Grammar* (6th edn). Oxford: Blackwell.

Pullum, Geoffrey K. 1990. 'Constraints on intransitive quasi-serial verb constructions in modern colloquial English.' *Working Papers in Linguistics* 39: 218–39.

Quirk, Randolph, Sidney Greenbaum, Geoffrey Leech and Jan Svartik. 1985. *A Comprehensive Grammar of the English Language*. London: Longman.

Ramisch, Heinrich. 1989. *The Variation of English in Guernsey, Channel Islands*. Frankfurt am Main: Peter Lang.

1994. 'English in Jersey.' In W. Viereck, ed. *Regional Variation, Colloquial and Standard Languages*. Stuttgart: Franz Steiner, 452–62.

2007. 'English in the Channel Islands.' In D. Britain, ed. *Language in the British Isles*. Cambridge; Cambridge University Press, 176–82.

Sebire, Heather R. 2003. *Frederick Corbin Lukis: A Remarkable Archaeologist and Polymath*. PhD thesis. University of Southampton.

Shorrocks, Graham. 1981. *A Grammar of the Dialect of Farnworth and District (Greater Manchester County, formerly Lancashire)*. PhD thesis. University of Sheffield. (Cited in Ramisch 1989: 126.)

States of Alderney 1974. *Alderney: A Short History and Guide*. Guernsey: Guernsey Press Co. Ltd.

Stead, John. 1809. *A Picture of Jersey*. London: Longman.

Syvret, Marguerite and Joan Stevens. 1998. *Balleine's History of Jersey*. West Sussex: Phillimore and Co.

Tomlinson, Harry. 1981. *Le guernesiais – étude grammaticale et lexicale du parler normand de l'île de Guernesey*. PhD thesis. University of Edinburgh.

Trudgill, Peter. 1986. *Dialects in Contact*. Oxford: Blackwell.

Tuaillon, Gaston. 1974. Review of Marie-Rose Simoni-Aurembou, *Atlas Linguistique et Ethnographique de l'Ile-de-France et de l'Orléanais*, Volume 1. Paris: CNRS 1973. *Revue de Linguistique Romane* 38: 575–6.

Tupper, Ferdinand B. 1854. *The History of Guernsey and its Bailiwick*. Guernsey: S. Barbet.

Venne, Roger and Geoffrey Allez. 1992. *Alderney Annals*. Alderney: The Alderney Society.

Viereck, Wolfgang. 1988. 'The Channel Islands: an anglicist's no man's land.' In J. Klergraf and D. Nehls, eds. *Essays on the English Language and Applied Linguistics on the Occasion of Gerard Nickel's 60th Birthday*. Heidelberg: Julius Gros, 468–78.

Part II

The Americas and the Caribbean

4 Canadian Maritime English

MICHAEL KIEFTE AND
ELIZABETH KAY-RAINING BIRD

1 Introduction

The present chapter gives a brief overview of the dialects of three regions in Nova Scotia: Halifax, Lunenburg and Cape Breton. Although this cannot hope to describe dialectal variation in the Maritimes with any depth, it does serve to give an impression of the major dialectal varieties that exist in the region.

Maritimers are keenly aware of the differences in speech between natives of the region and other Canadians. The English-language dialects spoken across the Maritimes (i.e. New Brunswick, Prince Edward Island, and Nova Scotia) vary considerably in their phonetic characteristics. Indeed, some residents claim they can pinpoint a particular speaker's community of origin based solely on their speech characteristics. The phonetic differences between Maritime dialects can be traced in part to historic settlement patterns over the last three centuries. For example, residents of Cape Breton, Nova Scotia speak dialects very similar to those spoken in Newfoundland given their common Scottish and Irish roots. In contrast, speech along the South Shore of Nova Scotia is largely non-rhotic, similar to the speech of the New Englanders who largely settled in this area. These phonetic patterns are quite distinct from those of more standard Canadian dialects or even from those heard in Halifax, the economic centre of the region. Other equally distinct differences in speech patterns can be heard elsewhere in the Maritimes.

The source of this wide range of dialectal variation can be traced to immigration patterns over the last three centuries resulting in a meeting of several very different cultures. The Maritimes were also sparsely populated with communities separated by large stretches of ocean and wilderness owing to the importance of the fishery and farming. The geographic separation of communities combined with the fact that immigrants tended to settle in relatively small but culturally homogeneous groups encouraged independent development of dialects and sharp contrasts between speech patterns. Although these sharp differences have blurred in more recent times with the advancement of communications and transportation, the characteristic dialects still retain many of their features.

The Maritime population can be subdivided roughly into seven major ethnic groups: English (either directly from the British Isles or via New England), Scottish (both Gaelic- and English-speaking), Irish, French, German, Black, and First Nations or indigenous peoples. Descendants of the English are spread throughout the region as are the French, Black, and First Nations peoples, while the Scottish and Irish immigrated to select areas. The German immigrants settled along the South Shore of Nova Scotia and little remains of the influence they once had on the local dialect. A historic description of the settlement patterns of these groups follows.

2   Sociolinguistic history

The first European settlers, the French, referred to the mainland region as *Acadie* while Cape Breton and Prince Edward Island were known as *Isle Royale* and *Isle Saint Jean*, respectively. With the exception of the two major islands, the entire region was ceded to the British Empire following the Treaty of Utrecht in 1713. At that time and for many years later, there were no British settlements in the area. Halifax was founded in 1749 to counter the French fort of Louisbourg in Cape Breton and a call was subsequently made for settlers to secure the area from French influence. Because Acadians occupied desirable farmland located in the Bay of Fundy region, they were expelled under the pretence that they remained loyal to France and the area was then settled predominantly by American colonists from New England. Cape Breton and Prince Edward Island were captured with the fall of Louisbourg in 1758 and were passed to British hands following the conclusion of the Seven Years' War in 1763. Nevertheless, the French presence was never eliminated in the Maritimes: Acadians returned to the north and eastern shores of New Brunswick and approximately one-third of the New Brunswick population calls French their mother tongue today. French Acadians also returned to Cape Breton and Prince Edward Island where there remains a significant French-speaking presence. Despite official-language status for French both provincially in New Brunswick and federally through the Canada Official Languages Act, there is little influence of the French language on English in the region beyond what already exists elsewhere.

Throughout this early period, a steady stream of *planters* or colonists from New England and Newfoundland arrived in much of New Brunswick and the farming areas of Nova Scotia outside of Halifax, particularly along the South and Fundy Shores and the Canso region. The New England colonists spoke a dialect of English called *Bluenose* which was akin to the Yankee English spoken in colonies to the south. The term *Bluenose* came later to mean any resident of Nova Scotia and has subsequently been used to refer to residents of New Brunswick as well (McConnell 1979). The Revolutionary War in 1775 accelerated the migration of United Empire Loyalists or *Tories* who fled the American colonies. This influx effectively doubled the Maritime population, making the characteristic non-rhotic *Bluenose* speech the dominant dialect in much of the region.

Among the early immigrants, approximately 3,500 free Black Loyalists as well as 2,000 'servants' fled the American Revolution for the Maritimes. Although the majority of these later left for Sierra Leone, the black population was bolstered by approximately 2,000 Jamaican Maroons who were deported to Nova Scotia as well as 2,000 Black refugees from the War of 1812. Many of these black Maritimers preserve many speech patterns that can be traced back to either African American or Caribbean English (Poplack 1993; Poplack and Tagliamonte 1999). Today, approximately 2 per cent of the Nova Scotia population identify as black and most of these live in scattered communities throughout the region, but predominantly in areas in and around Halifax.

In addition, a small group of German soldiers who fought for the British in the American wars disbanded and settled in Lunenburg, Nova Scotia. To counteract the Catholic influence of the remaining French Acadians, a call was made for European Protestants to settle in the Maritimes and this was answered by some thousands of Germans and Swiss, who were naturally drawn to the settlement in Lunenburg. Although the influence of German is evident in many traditional words and expressions (e.g. Poteet 1983), much of the speech of the region bears much stronger similarities to that of the New England planters who occupied the surrounding regions along the South Shore. Surnames such as *Jung*, *Koch*, and *Schmidt* have become *Young*, *Cook*, and *Smith*, making it difficult to trace the origins of many current residents. Outside of terms and phrases often associated with traditional customs and lifestyle, the influence of German on modern-day dialects in the region is largely negligible (Orkin 1970).

Pictou and Antigonish counties in Nova Scotia as well as Cape Breton and Prince Edward Island were settled by Gaelic-speaking Scottish Highlanders as well as English-speaking Lowlanders who arrived after 1773 along with disbanded Highland regiments and Loyalists from the American War of Independence and previously expelled Acadian French. Only in Cape Breton and Pictou did the Scottish immigrants retain much of their language, culture and traditions. However, owing to the decline of the language in their native Scotland, there remained only 3,700 native speakers of Gaelic in Nova Scotia according to a 1961 census and by 2006, not one Cape Bretoner reported Gaelic as their first language. Unlike French, which is still widely spoken throughout the Maritimes, however, Scots Gaelic and Scots English did have a lasting influence on the local dialects in this area and the unique speech of the Cape Breton and Pictou counties is still evident in pronunciation, word usage and sentence structure (Orkin 1970). Although the area is largely dominated by descendants of Scots and Acadians, almost one-quarter of Cape Bretoners trace their ancestry to Ireland (for comparison, approximately half are descended from Scots) owing to the influx of Irish immigrants via

Newfoundland following the Potato Famine in 1846–7. Many Irish also settled in Prince Edward Island during the same period.

As a major British fort, Halifax society was dominated by British garrisons, the clergy and the governing classes, and speech patterns in the region developed somewhat independently from the South Shore and Cape Breton influences. As it is the centre of Nova Scotia government, houses one-third of the Nova Scotia population and is home to the largest universities in the Maritimes, the dialect of Halifax region dominates Nova Scotia society. Likewise, throughout the Maritimes, there is a strong influence from Ontario and Western Canada on the speech patterns in the region owing to public broadcasting, post-secondary education, recent influxes of immigration from outside the Maritimes, as well as the seasonal migration of workers between the Maritimes and the oil-rich regions of Western Canada.

Currently, there are approximately 1.4 million speakers of English in the Maritimes with an additional 280,000 who report French as their first language, the vast majority of whom are in New Brunswick. Almost half of the English speakers in the Maritimes live in Nova Scotia. The total population of Prince Edward Island is approximately 130,000 – only slightly larger than that of Cape Breton. The largest city in the region, Halifax, has a population of about 350,000 and is the centre of government and education for the province of Nova Scotia. New Brunswick has three smaller cities, Saint John Fredericton and Moncton with a population of approximately 100,000 each (roughly one-third of the Moncton population is French-speaking), and is otherwise mostly rural. Despite the close contact between English and French, only a very small proportion claim equal status for both languages and, as mentioned above, there is little influence of the French language on English spoken in the region.

Like many local dialects in North America, Maritime Englishes have been marginalized through the dominance of General American and, more partic- ularly, Canadian English as it is spoken further west. The Atlantic provinces (which includes the Maritimes as well as Newfoundland and Labrador) are frequently referred to as the 'have-not' provinces and, although there is little migration to the Maritimes which would otherwise alter the local dialects, a significant proportion of younger people relocate to the west to seek employ- ment and it is perhaps due in part to this pressure that one sees a general flattening of accents in the region to conform to the prestige dialects spoken further west. In addition, although the Maritimes are still sparsely populated, they are no longer isolated, as the influence of radio and television provides continuous exposure to the speech of Ontario and the Western Provinces (as well as General American). These influences may be most obvious in larger city centres such as Halifax, where one hears accents that are often indistin- guishable from the standard Canadian variety which is described elsewhere (e.g. Wells 1982; Rogers 2000). Nonetheless, when Maritimers do go out west, very often their accent will mark them as 'Easterners'.

In the next sections, several phonetic patterns used by people who live in the Maritimes are described. These descriptions are not intended to be comprehensive. Instead, a few of the more distinctive local dialects are described. Given the homogenizing influences described previously, these dialects tend to be spoken more by older generations, lower social classes, or tradespeople. Younger generations or more upwardly mobile individuals tend to regress to more standard varieties.

There are several patterns in Maritime speech that identify an individual as an 'Easterner' to a Western Canadian: the fronting and raising of the vowels in START, TRAP and KIT, the rounding of the vowel in THOUGHT, the monophthongization of FACE and the more peculiar pronunciations of the diphthongs in MOUTH and PRICE which do not follow the typical Canadian pattern (Labov, Ash and Boberg 2006; and see below).

The following discussion focuses first on the speech heard in the Halifax region followed by a brief discussion of the accents of Cape Breton and of the South Shore of Nova Scotia, samples which illustrate the dialectal diversity of the region. Omitted is any mention of specific differences found in Prince Edward Island or among the English-speaking population of New Brunswick or even the English-speaking population of the Magdeline Islands, of which there are approximately 600. It also does not address the speech of Black Maritimers (which has been addressed elsewhere by Poplack 1993; and Poplack and Tagliamonti 1999) or First Nations peoples. Very little dialect research has been conducted in this region – most of which is cited here – and this chapter represents one of the first broad surveys of selected dialect communities in the Maritimes. The information that has been gathered here comes from several sources which are given in the list of references as well as from recordings that were made by the authors of several speakers from each region.

3 Features of Maritime English

3.1 Halifax

As with many dialects, vowels carry much of the dialect distinctiveness. The stressed vowels of Halifax English can be grossly represented as in Table 4.1.

As the Maritimes shares much of its history with other parts of Canada, there are many similarities between Haligonian English and the description of Canadian English given by Wells (1982). There are very notable differences, however, and these are highlighted below.

As in other Canadian dialects, there is a merger of the low back vowels in PALM, LOT, THOUGHT and CLOTH although the PALM vowel may occasionally be heard as [aː]. However, where the merged vowel is typically /ɑ/ or infrequently the rounded variant /ɒ/ in the rest of Canada, the merged

Table 4.1 *Principal vowels of Halifax English*

KIT	ɪ	FLEECE	i	NEAR	ir
DRESS	ɛ	FACE	eː	SQUARE	er
TRAP	æ	PALM	ɒ ~ aː	START	ar
LOT	ɒ	THOUGHT	ɒ	NORTH	or
STRUT	ʌ	GOAT	oʊ ~ oː	FORCE	or
FOOT	ʊ	GOOSE	u	CURE	ʊr
BATH	æ	PRICE	ɒɪ[a]	happY	i
CLOTH	ɔ	VOICE	oɪ[a]	lettER	ɚ
NURSE	ɝ	MOUTH	ɑʊ[a]	commA	ə

[a] discussed below.

vowel for Halifax and much of the Maritimes is markedly raised and rounded to [ɒ] or [ɔ] in, for example, *body* [bɒ̥di]; *popped* [pɒ̥pt]; and *gone* [gɒn] (or even occasionally [bɔdi], [pɔpt], and [gɔn], respectively). As elsewhere in the country, the merger also results in the homophones *caught–cot* [kɒt] and *stalk–stock* [stɒ̥k]. Although this vowel is frequently lowered to [ɒ], rounding is typically much more pronounced here than in other Canadian varieties. In unstressed syllables, this vowel may be less rounded as [ɑ]. The vowel in BATH is the typical North American /æ/, however. Although we have indicated an occasional merger between PALM and LOT, some authors have reported a front vowel for words such as *father* [faːðɚ], particularly in Nova Scotia (e.g. Wells 1982).

Clarke, Elms and Youssef (1995) have noted that, in other varieties of Canadian English, /ɛ/ and /ɪ/ tend to be lowered in the direction of /æ/ and /ɛ/, respectively, while /æ/ retracts to a low central position. One explanation given for this shift is that the merger of the low back vowels allows the lowering and retraction of front series. Although Halifax English also has the merger of the low back vowels, the shift described by Clark *et al.* is not evident in the traditional dialect. In fact, the front vowels /æ/ and /ɛ/ are frequently raised despite the extra space created by the low back merger in the vowel space. For example, the vowel in *had* is raised to [hæ̝d]; *camera* is raised to [kæ̝mɹʌ]; and *passage* is raised to [pæ̝sədʒ]. Frequently, this vowel can be raised to the quality of /ɛ/ particularly before nasals (e.g. [kɛmɹʌ]). However, no homonyms emerge from this vowel-raising as the vowel /ɛ/ is also frequently raised towards /ɪ/, but just falling short, thereby preserving the phonological distribution of the front vowels, if not the standard North American quality – e.g. *bedroom* [bɛ̝drəm]. McConnell (1979) suggest that some speakers may produce [dif] for *deaf*, but this may no longer be the case for a significant number of speakers. However, there is a tendency to monophthongize the vowel in FACE [feːs]. Although monophthongization has also been reported for the vowel in GOAT (Trudgill 2001), this does not seem to be as prevalent and, in some speakers, this vowel is often merged with the vowel in MOUTH (see below). In unstressed position, the vowel in GOAT is often centralized to [əʊ] or [ɔ̈ʊ] as in *window* [wɪ̈ndəʊ].

Unlike the other low back vowels such as those in LOT, THOUGHT, the vowel in START is not raised in this dialect. Indeed, the treatment of vowels before /r/ also distinguishes Maritime English from other Canadian varieties. Similar to Newfoundland English, these vowels are often fronted in Halifax (in the case of the low back vowel in START – e.g. [a] or [a̠]) or raised (in the case of the front vowels). For example, *parked* is heard as [parkt], while *stairs* is heard as [s̠terz̥] (note also the retraction of /s/ and the devoicing of /z/ – see below). Although Kinloch (1999) suggests that some speakers retain the distinction among /e/, /ɛ/, and /æ/ before /r/ as in *Mary*, *merry*, and *marry*, it is presently difficult to find any Maritimers who still do so. While it is possible that some speakers may still differentiate these, most speakers simply produce the close vowel /e/ before /r/ as in [meri].

One of the most striking characteristics of general Canadian English is the raising of the diphthongs in PRICE and MOUTH before voiceless consonants such that *out and about* can be heard as [ʌʊt n̩ əbʌʊt] (Chambers 1973). Although there is raising of diphthongs in this dialect, the situation is not identical to that of other Canadian varieties in that the pronunciation of these diphthongs in voiced-consonant contexts has partially undergone a diphthong shift. For example, the vowel in PRICE is rounded and retracted as in *I* [ɒɪ]; *died* [dɒɪd]; and *behind* [bihɒɪnd]. Very occasionally one may hear a higher vowel [ɒ̈ɪ] in this context, but not higher. In voiceless contexts, the rounding is often retained as in *like* [lɔɪk] and *frightened* [fɹɔ̈ɪʔnd] suggesting that, although raising is still present, the differences between the two contexts as compared with other Canadian dialects is much smaller. For many speakers, this pronunciation appears to be in free variation with the more general Canadian unrounded variant [ʌɪ] used by younger and more upwardly mobile individuals.

The vowel in MOUTH retains large differences between the two contexts, however. Before voiceless consonants, raising is even more extreme as in *out* [ɔʊt]; *mouth* [mɔʊθ]; and *house* [hɔʊs]. This creates a series of curious homonyms as in [kɔʊtʃ] for both *couch* and *coach*, which causes confusion to outsiders. The phrase *about a boat* is often heard as [ʌbɔʊt ʌ bɔʊt] (see also Emmeneau 1935). The dipthong in MOUTH retains the standard North American quality before voiced consonants or in open syllables as in *mouths* /mauðz/ and *houses* [hauzəz] (although [hɔʊsəz] is also heard).

Consonantal characteristics of the Haligonian dialect are less distinctive than those of the vowels. Although substitution of the flap [ɾ] for /t/ and /d/ in intervocalic position is the norm in much of Canadian English, for a few speakers in Halifax we also occasionally hear the voiceless, alveolar slit fricative [t̞] typical of Irish speech in free variation with [ɾ] in intervocalic position as in *better* [bɛt̞ɚ] ~ [bɛɾɚ]; *water* [wɒt̞ɚ] ~ [wɒɾɚ]. It can also be heard word-finally in words such as *but* /bʌt̞/ and also occasionally in place of /d/ as in *ahead* /əhɛːt̪/. Although this pronunciation is similar to that in Newfoundland English, its incidence is likely much less frequent and restricted to very broad dialects.

Falk and Harry (1999) describe backing of /s/ in a rhotic environment in words such as *strong, street, string, extra* and *grocery*, while /z/ often sounds like /ʒ/ in *misery*. Although the production of /s/ in this context never reaches /ʃ/, there is indeed some retraction of the fricative as in, for example, *started* [s̠tærrəd] and *stairs* [s̠terz̠]. It is difficult to hear the retraction of the fricative /z/ as it is often devoiced both intervocalically and word-finally as in *blizzard* [blɪz̠˳d]; *horizontal* [horəz̠ɒnt̪l̩]; and *neighbours* [nebɚrz̠˳], especially for those same speakers who retract /s/ in these contexts. The devoicing of /z/ has been reported by some authors (e.g. Orkin 1970; McConnell 1979) with reference to the influence of Gaelic on the English dialects of Cape Breton and Pictou counties. However, unless one concludes that the Gaelic language influenced Maritime speech far into the mainland, the incidence of z-devoicing in Halifax calls this connection into question.

Another distinctive characteristic of Maritime speech is the frequent use of ingressives, especially for the word *yes* which is used in very informal speech and can be quite surprising to a visitor to the region (McConnell 1979). Lamb (2003) calls this the 'Gaelic Gasp' even though it has been attested in non-Celtic (Eklund 2008).

3.2   Lunenberg and the south shore of Nova Scotia

The impact of German on the local Lunenberg dialect has been discussed elsewhere and it is perhaps the most closely studied dialect in the region (e.g. Wilson 1958; Orkin 1970; Trudgill 2001). Orkin describes the guttural /ʀ/ of Lunenberg Dutch, while Wilson describes a tendency to devoice word-final stops. However, as Trudgill points out, the Lunenberg dialect today is very much like that of the surrounding region along the South Shore of Nova Scotia and bears far greater resemblance to the Yankee New England speech likely spoken by the early planters. Outside of the treatment of /r/, South Shore speech shares many similarities with other parts of the Maritimes owing to its (indirect) English ancestry. It is for this reason that the description given here can serve as a surrogate for many of the accents heard along the South and Acadian Shores. A broad transcription of the vowels used in this area is given in Table 4.2.

In his 1958 thesis, Wilson attributes much of the distinctiveness of Lunenberg speech to the influences of the German language. For example, he notes a tendency to substitute the labiodental continuant [ʋ] for /w/, the stopping of dental fricatives, the use of velar [ʀ] in place of [ɹ] and the tendency to devoice stops and /dʒ/. With the exception of TH-stopping, none of these features appear to persist, even in the broadest Lunenberg speech, and even TH-stopping is not as frequent as one might expect given its prevalence

Table 4.2 *Principal vowels of Lunenburg English*

KIT	ɪ	FLEECE	i	NEAR	iə
DRESS	ɛ	FACE	ɔɪ	SQUARE	eə
TRAP	æ	PALM	æ ~ a	START	aː
LOT	ɔ ~ a	THOUGHT	ɔ	NORTH	ɔə
STRUT	ʌ ~ ɔ̈	GOAT	əʊ	FORCE	ɔə
FOOT	ʊ	GOOSE	u	CURE	ʊə
BATH	æ	PRICE	ɐɪ[a]	happY	i
CLOTH	ɑ	VOICE	ɔɪ[a]	lettER	ɜ
NURSE	ɜ	MOUTH	əʊ[a]	commA	ə

[a] see discussion below.

throughout Atlantic Canada. Contrary to reports of velar /ʀ/, the most distinctive characteristic of Lunenberg speech is the complete absence of /r/ postvocalically, making it much more similar to neighbouring South Shore dialects, so that it is often confused with the speech of New England by outsiders. Even in prevocalic position, one hears the [ɹ] typical for speakers of English and not a German [ʀ].

The vowel in *lett*ER is given in Table 4.2 as /ɜ/. This vowel can also be heard in a rounded but more open position as /ɐ/ as in *November* [nəʊvɛmbɐ] or *lobster* [lɔpstɐ]. In other contexts, the derhoticization results in a simple lengthening of the previous vowel, as in the vowels in NURSE and START – e.g. *third* [θɜːd]; *markets* [maːkəts] – or substitution with [ə] in NEAR, SQUARE, START, NORTH, FORCE, and CURE (e.g. *or* [ɔə]; *shares* [ʃɛəz], etc.). However, there is a merger of the vowels in NEAR and SQUARE (e.g. *years* [jɛəz]). The vowel in START is significantly advanced relative to RP and conforms more to the pronunciation in New England (Wells 1982). The /r/ is frequently retained for many speakers and is also evident in citation forms or very formal situations. There does not appear to be much evidence for hypercorrection, presumably due to the pervasive exposure to rhotic dialects elsewhere in North America, although Trudgill (2001) reports an intrusive /r/ in, for example, *saw it*.

Although many speakers preserve the distinction between the vowels in LOT and THOUGHT, these vowels are often merged to /ɔ/ even in local dialect speakers. This is a much more closed vowel than the traditional Halifax varieties or elsewhere in Canada – e.g. *on* [ɔn]; *brought* [brɔt]; and even *off the boat* [ɔf ðə bəʊt] (notice also the pronunciation of the vowel in *boat* – see below). For those speakers who do preserve the distinction between the two, the vowel in LOT is typically /a/ (e.g. Wilson 1958; Trudgill 2001). Unfortunately, there are no statistics regarding the prevalence of the LOT– THOUGHT distinction. However, given that it is relatively rare in Canada, one must consider that the distinction is slowly vanishing. The distinction between PALM and TRAP is likewise infrequent, with the vowels produced as /æ/ by most speakers. The vowel in STRUT can have a distinctly retracted and rounded quality best represented by *lucky* [lɔ̈ki], but is often the standard [ʌ].

Unlike Halifax, the vowel in FACE is strongly diphthongized to [əɪ] as in *May* [məɪ]; *bait* [bəɪt]; and *table* [təɪbɫ], while GOAT is diphthongized to [əʊ] as in down [dəʊn]; *home* [həʊm]; and *most* [məʊs] (note also the deletion of the final T in *most*). This latter vowel can range from [öʊ] to [əʊ] to [ʒ̈ʊ], but before voiceless consonants is most typically [əʊ]. The vowel in DRESS, normally [ɛ], can be merged with [ɪ] before nasals and [dʒ] – e.g. *edge* [ɪdʒ]; *men* [mɪn]; *end* [ɪn].

The diphthongs in PRICE, MOUTH and VOICE also show very distinctive patterns. In the casual speech of dialect speakers, one occasionally hears a complete merger of the vowels in PRICE and VOICE (i.e. [ɔɪ]). For example, one hears *ice* [ɔɪs] and *right* [rɔɪt], but also *like* [lɐɪk] and *decline* [dɪklɐɪn], which are very distinct from Halifax speech. For MOUTH, we have *down* [dəʊn] creating a similar situation to the one that exists with Halifax speakers: the vowels in MOUTH and GOAT are very close if not merged.

3.3   Cape Breton

Although it has not been studied extensively, the speech of Cape Breton seems to bear many similarities with the nearby island of Newfoundland and Westerners can perhaps be excused for their inability to differentiate the two accents. These similarities – e.g. the fronting of the low back vowel – owe much to the geographic proximity of the two islands, the fact that approximately one-quarter of the Cape Breton population descends from Irish immigrants – many of whom arrived via Newfoundland – and the Celtic influences in each region (i.e. either Scottish or Irish). There are clear similarities with Halifax speech as well, and the speech of Cape Breton can be seen as part of a continuum between the two extremes. In addition, we see evidence of heavy influence of standard varieties of Canadian English, especially in the diphthongization of the GOAT and GOOSE vowels and the frequent use of Canadian raising. Indeed, because the economic situation in Cape Breton is quite depressed, we see the largest seasonal migration between the island and the Western Provinces and it is entirely possible that this has influenced local dialects in general. Table 4.3 provides a summary of the vowels used in this dialect.

The KIT–DRESS distinction is variably absent in speakers of Cape Breton English and many have difficulty producing words such as *bit* and *bet* as a minimal pair, producing [bɪt] or an intermediate [bɪ̞t] for both. As with Halifax speakers (as well as speakers of Newfoundland English; see Clarke in this volume), the vowel in TRAP and BATH is typically raised relative to the Canadian norm (e.g. *had* [hæ̝d]; *bag* [bæɡ]).

The FACE and GOAT vowels are frequently monophthongized to [eː] and [oː] respectively. For example, *yesterday* is frequently pronounced as [jɛstɚ˞deː], without the final off-glide, while *skate* is pronounced [skeːʔ] (note

Table 4.3 *Principal vowels of Cape Breton English*

KIT	ɪ	FLEECE	i	NEAR	i
DRESS	ɛ	FACE	əɪ	SQUARE	e
TRAP	æ	PALM	a ~ ɑ	START	a
LOT	a ~ ɑ	THOUGHT	ɒ ~ ɔ	NORTH	ɔ
STRUT	ʌ ~ ɝ	GOAT	oː ~ əʊ	FORCE	ɔ
FOOT	ʊ	GOOSE	u	CURE	ʊ
BATH	æ	PRICE	ɐɪ	happY	i
CLOTH	ɑ	VOICE	ɔɪ	lettER	ɚ
NURSE	ɝ	MOUTH	əʊ	commA	ə

the glottal stop as well). For the GOAT vowel, however, we see some adoption of the more centralized and diphthongized [əɔ] in free variation with [oː] and the more standard [oʊ]. For example, the same speaker can produce either [nəɔ] or [noː] for *no*. More commonly, the vowel in GOOSE can show centralizing – e.g. *hoot* [həʊt̠] (note the slit-fricative T); *rooting* [rəʊʔn].

As for the low back vowels, many speakers retain the LOT–THOUGHT distinction. The LOT vowel can be as far forward as [a] or as far back as [ɑ] (e.g. *hockey* [hɑ̜ki]; *on* [ɑ̜n]) while the THOUGHT vowel ranges from [ɒ] to [ɔ]: further back but typically rounded (e.g. *thought* [θɒʔ]; *taught* [tɔt]; *law* [lɔ]; *odd* [ɒd]). It is not known at the present time if this is typical of Cape Breton speech in general or if the sample the authors have collected is somehow biased. More research needs to be done. Nevertheless, this appears to be at odds with reports from other authors who have indicated that these vowels are merged for Cape Bretoners (Labov, Ash and Boberg 2006).

The PRICE vowel shows a typical pattern of Canadian raising, although the quality of the vowel in open syllables and before voiced consonants is further back in quality from the Canadian standard (i.e. [ɑɪ]) as in *time* [tɑɪm]; *find* [fɑɪnd]. Before voiceless consonants, the PRICE vowel is heard as [ʌɪ] as in *quite* [kwʌɪʔ]. For the MOUTH vowel we hear little difference between the two contexts as both are typically pronounced [əʊ]. This parallels the situation elsewhere (i.e. Halifax and Lunenberg), where the MOUTH and GOAT vowels have merged for broad dialect speakers. For example: *out* [əʊt]; *house* [həʊs]; and *now* [nəʊ].

With respect to the consonants, there is some stopping of the dental fricatives, but this is highly variable and not overly common. With the voiceless alveolar stops, there is a tendency to use the slit fricative [t̠] as elsewhere as well as the glottal stop when in word-final position (e.g. *gut* [gʌt̠]; [gʌʔ]).

4 Conclusion

Given the current lack of information regarding Maritime dialects, there is a pressing need for more research in the area. There are several areas that deserve specific attention – not only specific phonetic attributes such as the raising of front vowels, the backing and rounding of many of the dipthongs, etc., but also the dialectal variation that exists across the region. In addition, we have not even touched on syntactic and morphological aspects here. The Maritimes have much to offer to sociolinguists in terms of diversity and the presence of unique dialectal patterns.

References

Chambers, J. K. 1973. 'Canadian raising.' *The Canadian Journal of Linguistics* 18: 113–35.

Clarke, S., F. Elms and A. Youssef. 1995. 'The third dialect of English: Some Canadian evidence.' *Language Variation and Change* 7: 209–28.

Eklund, Robert. 2008. 'Pulmonic ingressive phonation: Diachronic and synchronic characteristics, distribution and function in animal and human sound production and in human speech.' *Journal of the International Phonetic Association* 38/3: 235–324.

Emmeneau, M. B. 1935. 'The dialect of Lunenberg, Nova Scotia.' *Language* 11: 140–7.

Falk, Lilian and Margaret Harry, eds. 1999. *The English Language in Nova Scotia.* Lockeport, Nova Scotia: Roseway Publishing.

Kinloch, A. Murray. 1999. 'The vowel phonemes of Halifax and General Canadian English.' In L. Falk and M. Harry, eds. *The English Language in Nova Scotia.* Lockeport, Nova Scotia: Roseway Publishing, 21–6.

Labov, William, Sharon Ash, and Charles Boberg. 2006. *The Atlas of North American English: Phonetics, Phonology, and Sound Change: A Multimedia Reference Tool.* Berlin: Mouton de Gruyter.

Lamb, William. 2003. *Scottish Gaelic.* Munich: Lincom Europa.

McConnell, R. E. 1979. *Our Own Voice: Canadian English and How it is Studied.* Toronto: Gage Educational Publishing.

Orkin, Michael M. 1970. *Speaking Canadian English.* Toronto: General Publishing.

Poplack, Shana. 1993. 'Variation theory and language contact.' In D. Preston, ed. *American Dialect Research: An Anthology Celebrating the 100th Anniversary of the American Dialect Society.* Amsterdam: Benjamins, 251–86.

Poplack, Shana and Sali Tagliamonte. 1999. 'The grammaticization of *going to* in (African American) English.' *Language Variation and Change* 11: 315–42.

Poteet, Lewis J. 1983. *The South Shore Phrase Book.* Hantsport, Nova Scotia: Lancelot Press.

Reid, John G. 1999. 'Historical introduction.' In L. Falk and M. Harry, eds. *The English Language in Nova Scotia.* Lockeport, Nova Scotia: Roseway Publishing, 1–16.

Rogers, Henry. 2000. *The Sounds of Language.* Harlow, U.K.: Pearson.

Scargill, M. H. 1974. *Modern Canadian English Usage: Linguistic Change and Reconstruction.* Toronto: McLelland and Stewart.

Trudgill, P. 2001. 'Sociohistorical linguistics and dialect survival: a note on another Nova Scotian enclave.' In M. Ljung, ed. *Linguistic Structure and Variation: A*

Festschrift for Gunnel Melchers. Stockholm: Stockholm University Press, 193–211.

Wells, J. C. 1982. *Accents of English*, vol. III: *Beyond the British Isles*. Cambridge: Cambridge University Press.

Wilson, Harry Rex. 1958. *The dialect of Lunenberg County, Nova Scotia: A study of the English of the county, with reference to its sources, preservation of relics, and vestiges of bilingualism*. PhD dissertation, University of Michigan.

5   Newfoundland and Labrador English

SANDRA CLARKE

1   Introduction

This chapter describes the vernacular varieties of English spoken in New-foundland and Labrador, the most easterly province of Canada. Until union with Canada in 1949, the island of Newfoundland, along with its continental portion, Labrador, constituted an independent colony of Britain. Known to European explorers and fishermen from the late fifteenth century, the island represents one of the earliest of Britain's transatlantic colonies, with perma-nent (if sparse) settlement dating back to the first decades of the seventeenth century.

Though perhaps more has been written on Newfoundland and Labrador English (NLE) than on many of the varieties represented in this volume, much of this material is little-known outside the local area.[1] Moreover, this work has dealt largely with the region's rich and unique lexical her-itage, culminating in the 1982 publication of the *Dictionary of Newfoundland English*.

The phonology and morphosyntax of present-day NLE, however, are likewise highly distinct from those of many varieties of English found on the North American mainland. The province also exhibits considerable inter-nal dialect diversity. As late as 1950, much of the island's population was distributed in some 1,300 small fishing villages scattered over 6,000 miles (*c.* 9,660 km) of coastline; many of these communities were linked to the outside world only by sea. This situation, coupled with the region's rela-tively isolated geographical location at the northeastern extremity of North America, is in large measure responsible for the generally conservative nature of local speech, which preserves a number of features no longer current in world Englishes.

---

[1] A bibliography listing over 250 publications on NLE may be accessed at www.mun.ca/
linguistics. NLE materials in digitized format are becoming more readily accessible
via Memorial University's ongoing Digital Archives Initiative (http:/collections.mun.ca/
linguistics/research/language).

2 Sociolinguistic history

Though Newfoundland and Labrador (NL) occupies a landmass larger than that of Japan, its population is small: 2006 Statistics Canada census figures show a total population of only slightly over half a million. The province is the least linguistically diverse within Canada, as almost 98 per cent of its residents have English as their sole mother tongue. Other European languages have not fared well in NL: Irish Gaelic – brought to the island's east coast from the early eighteenth century – had disappeared by the early twentieth, followed half a century later by Scots Gaelic; and (Acadian) French today constitutes the mother tongue of less than 1 per cent of the province's population. The province's aboriginal languages have likewise suffered, and are today spoken only in Labrador, by small native populations.

Despite this, the NL linguistic situation is complex. As noted above, NLE is characterized by its preservation of considerable internal variation. Traditional dialects of NLE differ in many respects from the more standard varieties spoken in much of mainland Canada and the United States – though they share certain linguistic features with other early transatlantic varieties, including Anglo-Caribbean, along with early African American English.

While the earlier settlement of the island of Newfoundland, relative to the North American continent in general, clarifies in part the distinctive nature of NLE, settlement history also played an important role. Unlike the situation in much of mainland North America, NL founder-populations from the British Isles and Ireland originated almost entirely in two highly circumscribed source areas: the West Country of England, and the southeast counties of Ireland. The reasons for this are economic: throughout its early history, most of the region's population was engaged, directly or indirectly, in the pursuit of the cod fishery, which until well into the nineteenth century was largely controlled by West Country merchants operating out of the major ports of Devon and Dorset. Workers in the Newfoundland fishery were typically drawn – initially on a purely seasonal basis – from the immediate hinterlands of these southwest English ports, as well as those of the southeast Irish port of Waterford, which after about 1675 was used as a source of provisions as well as migrant workers (Mannion 1977; Handcock 1989). Despite the late-eighteenth-century influx of post-revolutionary loyalists from the northern American colonies into much of eastern Canada, NL was to receive no such founder component.

British and Irish migrants to coastal NL not only originated in a highly localized geographic area, they also settled in fairly small numbers. It is estimated that no more than 25,000 of these immigrants took up perma-nent settlement, though many thousands more passed through, en route to more attractive economic prospects on the North American mainland. After the mid nineteenth century, in-migration from Britain and Ireland declined dramatically, and the region did not experience the large influxes of twentieth-century immigration that were to characterize much of North America. Even today, less than 2 per cent of the NL population was born outside Canada, as opposed to a comparable figure of almost 20 per cent for Canada as a whole (Statistics Canada, 2006 census of Canada).

On the island of Newfoundland, outside the major towns, population distribution generally followed an ethno-religious pattern. The largely Catholic Irish were to settle in the coastal communities of the southern Avalon peninsula, in the southeastern part of the province. As the province's capital and largest city, St. John's, lies towards the northern extremity of this area, its characteristic speech displays a decidedly Irish flavour. Much of the remainder of the island's coastline was occupied by the (Protestant) southwest English, apart from regional enclaves on the southern west coast, which saw a small amount of nineteenth-century highland Scots and Acadian French in-migration from neighbouring Nova Scotia.

The Labrador or continental portion of the province – under French control until 1763 – presents a more complex settler mix. In the nineteenth century, a small settler base was established in southern coastal Labrador (extending west along the coastline of present-day Quebec). This resulted from West Country English and Channel Island fishing interests, as well as seasonal (later, permanent) migration from the northeast coast of Newfoundland. In the interior and the more northerly regions, there emerged a small mixed (Metis) English-speaking population, descendants of the aboriginal Inuit and Algonquian (Montagnais-Naskapi) inhabitants, and trappers and fur traders from a number of European sources, including the Orkneys, mainland Scotland, and France. Even today, a number of remote coastal Labrador communities are accessible only by sea or air; and though Labrador comprises almost three-quarters of the land area of the province, it possesses only about 6 per cent of the province's total population.

In short, though much linguistic change has occurred since early days of settlement, geographic and socioeconomic factors have contributed to the high degree of linguistic conservatism apparent to this day in NLE. Though obvious 'Southwest English' and 'southern Irish' dialect types can be distinguished within the province, communities within a few miles of one another may display individual community lects, and enclave varieties abound. Thus along the almost exclusively SW-English-settled northeast coast of Newfoundland, the community dialect of Tilting, Fogo Island, retains many of the Irish characteristics of its forebears – some of which differ from those of varieties on the almost exclusively Irish-settled southern Avalon peninsula. Likewise, a cluster of settlements on the Avalon peninsula's Conception Bay north shore displays a confluence of features (regular deletion of postvocalic /r/, retraction of the low vowels /æ/ and /a/) that are not shared by neighbouring communities.

Since the mid twentieth century, however, improvements in transportation, communication and educational opportunities have meant that residents

Table 5.1 *Phonetic realizations of the lax vowels in NLE*

Lexical set (<Wells 1982)	Standard NLE	Conservative Irish-origin NLE (I-NLE): additional variants	Conservative SW English-origin NLE (E-NLE): additional variants
KIT /ɪ/	ɪ, į	iː	iː, ę
DRESS /ɛ/	ɛ, ę	ɪ	ɪ, ęɪ, æ̧
TRAP/BATH /æ/	æ(ː), æ̧(ː)	ę	ę, ęɪ, <aː, ɑː>
LOT/CLOTH/THOUGHT /a/	ɐ(ː), a(ː); ɑ(ː)	ɐ̧(ː), ą(ː)	ɐ̧(ː), ą(ː)
PALM /ɑ/	ɑː, ɒ̧ː, aː	æ(ː)	æ(ː)
FOOT /ʊ/	ʊ	ʊ̧, ʌ, u(ː)	ʌ, u(ː)
STRUT /ʌ/	ʌ, ʌ̧	ɔ̧, ʌ, ɐ	ʌ, ɐ

of NL have come increasingly into contact with supralocal and more standard forms of speech. The loss of the cod fishery in the early 1990s has led to extensive recent out-migration, particularly to Canada's western provinces; once older generations pass away, many small fishing communities are likely to disappear. The future of a number of the traditional features described in the following sections is thus by no means certain.

3   Features of the variety

3.1   *Phonology*

3.1.1   *Vowels*
Though standard NLE possesses the same inventory of vowel phonemes as standard Canadian English (CE), the phonetic realizations of these phonemes often differ, particularly with respect to the lax vowels. The following sections outline the principal vowel features of NLE, using as a general classificatory schema the lexical sets of Wells (1982), each of which is represented by a keyword (e.g. KIT, FOOT).

Lax vowels

The chief phonetic realizations of the NLE lax vowels are grouped in Table 5.1. As in the case of all tables in this chapter, the second column lists standard NLE variants, as may be found in middle-class urban speech. The third and fourth columns present additional pronunciations that characterize the traditional vernacular speech of, respectively, NLE varieties of southeast Irish origin (here labelled I-NLE) and those of southwest English or West Country origin (labelled E-NLE).[2]

---

[2] The descriptors 'traditional' and 'conservative' are used interchangeably in this chapter to designate the speech types identified primarily with rural, working-class, and usually older, speakers. 'Vernacular' designates the least formal speech styles used by speakers of NLE in general.

As outlined below, many of these traditional variants are linguistically conditioned. Highly recessive pronunciations are enclosed in angle brackets (< >) in the various vowel tables.

LOT/CLOTH/THOUGHT; TRAP/BATH

Like speakers of CE, the vast majority of NLE speakers exhibit a merged vowel in the LOT/CLOTH/THOUGHT/FATHER lexical set (though some speakers maintain a length distinction between the LOT and other subsets).[3] Likewise, the vowel of TRAP and BATH is distinguished only by length, and not by quality. Yet the phonetic realizations in both vowel sets constitute perhaps the most salient of the vocalic distinctions between NLE and CE. In all environments, these vowels tend to display more fronted (and in the case of the LOT etc. set, less rounded) articulations in NLE than in CE – trends inherited from both southwest England and southern Ireland, and particularly evident in NLE regional vernaculars. Raising of /æ/ towards [ɛ] is perhaps most obvious in pre-nasal position (e.g. *jam, pants*), as well as in a small set of lexical items (e.g. *catch* pronounced [kʰɛʧ] or even [kʰɪʧ]); before velars, the raised variant may be diphthongized in E-NLE, such that a word like *bag* is pronounced with [ɛɪ].

Among some educated older urban speakers – for whom the British model served as the cultivated norm – the BATH vowel is occasionally heard with a more retracted, [aː/ɑ₊ː]-like quality. The same pronunciation occurs in the earlier-mentioned traditional E-NLE enclave variety in Conception Bay (Seary, Story and Kirwin 1968), in such words as *path, glass* and *dance*; this variety also displays more retracted realizations of the CLOTH/THOUGHT vowels than are usually found in regional varieties of NLE.

KIT/FOOT-tensing; DRESS-raising

As indicated in Table 5.1, the high lax vowels in the KIT and FOOT sets are often somewhat tensed, raised or peripheralized. In standard NLE, this is more frequent in the Irish-influenced variety spoken in the capital, St. John's, than in the urban standards of other areas of the province. All NLE varieties, however, tend to exhibit KIT-tensing in two grammatical morphemes: verbal *-ing* (e.g. *going, leaving*), which may be pronounced as [iːn]; and possessive *his* (the latter possibly through reanalysis as *he's*).

In vernacular I-NLE, KIT- and FOOT-tensing are typical in all environments. This process is however largely phonetically conditioned in E-NLE. There, KIT-tensing occurs most frequently before alveopalatals (as in *fish*), alveolar nasals (*in*), velars (*big*), and to a lesser degree before labiodentals (*skiff*) and laterals (*pill*); FOOT-tensing occurs occasionally before alveolars,

---

[3] The PALM set is anomalous, in that in cultivated and supralocally-oriented speech it may assume a more retracted point of articulation than that of the merged LOT/CLOTH/THOUGHT vowel. In traditional NLE, however, it belongs with the TRAP/BATH set.

as in *wood* pronounced [wu(:)d], as well as velars (as in *brook*). Since the environments for KIT-tensing seem to have been more widespread in the past, this process may also account for such now highly recessive E-NLE past forms as 'loadied' for *loaded* (cf. Noseworthy 1971: 42; Colbourne 1982: 13–14).

Both I-NLE and E-NLE also display variable raising of the DRESS vowel, towards lax [ɪ]. This process is phonetically conditioned, and is favoured by a following stop or affricate, as in *ten, get, peck* and *wedge*. Occasionally, such raised vowels are also subject to KIT-tensing, as in *dead* pronounced [diːd] (Halpert and Widdowson 1996, I: 319). Before voiced velars, the DRESS vowel may be tensed and diphthongized in E-NLE (though not I-NLE), as in *keg* pronounced [kʰe̝ɪg].

KIT/DRESS-lowering

An opposing tendency, lax vowel lowering, occurs only in E-NLE. Again, this is phonetically conditioned: it occurs most frequently in the environment of a following /l/, such that *will* may be homophonous with *well*. In E-NLE a following fricative environment may also promote KIT-lowering towards [e̝], as in *with*. DRESS-lowering is largely restricted to the environments of a following /l/ (as in *yellow*) or a following voiceless velar (e.g. *breakfast, wreck* pronounced with [æ]).

The FOOT/STRUT sets

The /ʌ/ vowel (STRUT) is often realized in NLE as a low-mid back vowel, rather than centralized as in CE; it is frequently rounded to an [ɔ]-like articulation, particularly in Irish-settled areas of the province.

In vernacular NLE, the FOOT and STRUT vowels display a lexical incidence that does not coincide with the standard CE norm. A number of lexical items (*put, took, look*) that belong to the FOOT set in standard varieties are often articulated with the STRUT vowel, particularly in E-NLE. In E-NLE as well (as for many standard NLE speakers), the negative morpheme *un-* is typically realized with the unrounded, central [ɐ] of LOT words, such that *unsure* may be homophonous with *onshore*.

Tense vowels

In standard NLE, the tense vowels of the FLEECE, FACE, GOOSE and GOAT sets are articulated much as they are in standard CE (see Table 5.2). In traditional varieties of NLE, however, all four of these tense vowel phonemes possess more conservative realizations. In E-NLE – and even more so in I-NLE – the high-mid FACE and GOAT vowels occur with non-upglided monophthongal realizations of the type that characterized English in general prior to the nineteenth century. In checked syllables (e.g. *fate, boat*), these high-mid phonemes may exhibit inglided or centring articulations.

Table 5.2 *Phonetic realizations of the tense vowels in NLE*

Lexical set (<Wells 1982)	Standard NLE	Conservative Irish-origin NLE (I-NLE)	Conservative SW English-origin NLE (E-NLE)
FLEECE /iː/	iː, ɪi	<eɪ, eːə>	ɪ <eɪ, eːə, əɪ>
GOOSE /uː/	uː, ʊu, ʊ	ʉː, ʉʊ, ɵʉ, ɛʉ	ʉː, ʉʊ
FACE /eɪ/	eɪ, ɛɪ	ȩː(ə), ȩː(ə)	ȩː(ə), ȩː(ə), ɛ
GOAT /oʊ/	oʊ, ɔʊ	ɔː(ə), ọː(ə)	ɔː(ə), ọː(ə)

Recessive FACE and FLEET pronunciations

Wells' FACE set groups vowels with two distinct Middle English origins: diphthongal (the *maid*-type) vs. non-diphthongal (the *made*-type). Prior to the eighteenth century, these two types had fallen together in standard English (Wells 1982: 193). While the distinction is also no longer made in NLE, it remained however in evidence among at least some traditional speakers of E-NLE born in the early twentieth century (see e.g. Colbourne 1982: 10–11).

The FLEECE set, likewise, encompasses vowels of more than one historical origin. Around 1700, in what is termed by Wells (1982: 194ff.) the FLEECE Merger, *-ea-* words like *meat* fell together with *-ee-* words like *meet*. In both I-NLE and E-NLE, however, *-ea-* words such as *beat* and *heave* may still occasionally be heard with the earlier high-mid vowel of FACE. Somewhat more recessive today is a high-mid [eɪ]/[eː] pronunciation attested in both I-NLE and E-NLE for certain *-ee-* items in the FLEECE set (e.g. *indeed*). Since via the Great Vowel Shift this lexical set would have displayed high [iː]-like articulations since *c.* 1600 (Wells 1982: 195), it is possible that this represents a subsequent lowering in at least some of the source varieties of NLE (cf. Wells 1982: 425 for Irish English). Another possible reflex of a post-Great-Vowel-Shift development is the mid centralized [əɪ]-like realization in such words as *tea* or *see* that is occasionally encountered in enclave varieties of E-NLE (e.g. Harris 2006: 39–40, for an island variety in Bonavista Bay on the northeast coast of the island).

GOOSE fronting

In standard NLE, particularly among older speakers, the GOOSE vowel tends to retain a high back point of articulation – unlike CE, in which more centralized realizations are common (cf. Labov, Ash and Boberg 2006: 143 ff.). That at least some of the area's southwest English and southeast Irish founder-populations used a central-to-front variant of tense /uː/, however, is suggested by the existence of such variants as [ʉː] or [ʉʊ] in regions of Newfoundland settled by both groups. In I-NLE, centralized (often slightly

Table 5.3 *Diphthong variants in NLE*

Lexical set (<Wells 1982)	Standard NLE	Conservative Irish-origin NLE (I-NLE)	Conservative SW English-origin NLE (E-NLE)
PRICE/PRIZE /aɪ/	ɐɪ, aɪ, əɪ, ʌɪ	ʌɪ, ɔɪ	ʌɪ, ɔɪ
MOUTH/LOUD /aʊ/	ɐʊ, aʊ, əʊ, ʌʊ	æʉ, e/ɛʉ, æɪ	æʉ, e/ɛʉ
CHOICE /ɔɪ/	ɔɪ, oɪ	ɐɪ, ʌɪ, ʌ̞ɪ, əɪ, ɑɪ, aɪ	ɐɪ, ʌɪ, ʌ̞ɪ, əɪ, ɑɪ, aɪ

lowered) realizations are particularly evident before /l/, such that *school* may be pronounced [skɵʉəl] or even [skɛʉəl].

Tense vowel laxing

The lexical incidence of several of the tense vowels in NLE is not identical to that found in present-day standard CE. A subset of words in the GOOSE set tends to be articulated in NLE – particularly among older speakers – with lax [ʊ]; these most frequently involve a following nasal (*room, broom, spoon, schooner*) or a voiceless labiodental fricative (*hoof, roof*). In E-NLE, this subset also includes a few lexical items in which the vowel precedes /l/ (e.g. *foolish*) or an alveolar stop (e.g. *food*).

Lax realizations are less common for the FLEECE and FACE vowels, though they are occasionally found in traditional varieties, particularly E-NLE. Thus *keep* may be articulated with [ɪ] rather than [i:], and the past forms *made* and *paid*, with [ɛ].

Diphthongs

For the /aɪ/ diphthong, standard NLE, like CE, displays the feature generally referred to as 'Canadian Raising', whereby the diphthong nucleus is more close (typically, [ə/ʌ]) before a tautosyllabic voiceless obstruent (PRICE words) than in other environments (PRIZE words). For the corresponding /aʊ/ diphthong, however (the MOUTH vs. LOUD sets), this phonetically conditioned vowel-height contrast is considerably less apparent; it is certainly not typical of the Irish-based variety of the capital, St. John's, though it seems to be making some inroads into the speech of younger, upwardly mobile residents of the city (cf. D'Arcy 2005).

A number of traditional speakers of both I-NLE and E-NLE maintain an apparently inherited pattern for both /aɪ/ and /aʊ/, in which in all environments the nucleus is in the mid rather than low vowel range. In addition, /aʊ/ is often fronted to an [æʉ]- or even [ɛʉ]-like realization (see Table 5.3), occasionally accompanied by glide unrounding (as in the [æɪ]-like realization documented by Lanari (1994) for a south-coast I-NLE variety). The nucleus of /aɪ/ is frequently rounded to [ʌ] or [ɔ]. This last process results in considerable overlap with the CHOICE set, which in both I-NLE

Table 5.4 *Phonetic realizations of vowels before /r/ in NLE*

Lexical set (<Wells 1982)	Standard NLE	Conservative Irish-origin NLE (I-NLE)	Conservative SW English-origin NLE (E-NLE)
NEAR /iːr/	iː, ɪ. ɪ	ɪ, ẹ	ɪ, ẹ
SQUARE /ɛr/	ɛ, e	ẹ; (pre-vocalically) ə/ʌ	ẹ; (pre-vocalically) ə/ʌ
START /ar/	ɐ, a̤	ɐ̥, a̤, æ̰	ɐ̥, a̤, æ̰
NORTH/FORCE /ɔr/	ɔ, o	(NORTH words) ɐ̥, a̤, æ̰	(NORTH words) ɐ̥, a̤, æ̰
CURE /uːr/	uː, o, ɔ	–	–
NURSE (also lettER) /ɚ/	ə, ɜ	ə̰, ɵ, ʌ, ɔ̰	ə̰, ɵ, ʌ

and E-NLE tends to display some degree of nucleus-unrounding. Thus in the vernacular styles of some traditional speakers, words like *toy* and *tie* may appear homophonous, both pronounced with [ɐɪ] or [ʌɪ]; for some E-NLE speakers, the *tie*-type may display a greater degree of rounding than the *toy*-type.

Vowels before /r/

While in their formal styles standard speakers of NLE make the same number of vocalic oppositions before /r/ as do their mainland Canadian counterparts, their vernacular styles tend towards near-merger of the lexical sets NEAR and SQUARE, as well as those of CURE and NORTH/FORCE (see Table 5.4). In addition, NLE is characterized by a more fronted articulation of the START vowel than that found in other varieties of CE, outside of Atlantic Canada (cf. Labov, Ash and Boberg 2006: 140). Unlike innovative CE, however, standard NLE continues to distinguish the /æ/ of *marry* from the /ɛ/ of *Mary/merry*.

In traditional regional varieties of both I-NLE and E-NLE, the NORTH and FORCE sets are not merged. Rather, the vowel of the former maintains its inherited unrounded and lowered realizations, similar to those of the START class: thus words like *port* and *part* may appear homophonous. NORTH unrounding is however highly salient, and stigmatized. Also somewhat stigmatized, and today less frequent, is the centralization of the sequence /ɛr/ pre-vocalically, resulting in [ə/ʌ] pronunciations in words like *very* and *bury*. Considerably more common, and largely unnoticed, is the high degree of retroflexion and rounding that accompanies the articulation of the central /ɚ/ vowel of NURSE/lettER, particularly in I-NLE.

3.1.2   Consonants

The consonant system of standard NLE is very similar to that of standard CE. However, several consonant features inherited from Irish and southwest English founder-varieties continue to characterize not only conservative or traditional NLE, but also the vernacular speech of many residents of the province. While some of these features are shared by both I-NLE and E-NLE, others are not. Among the latter are /h/ deletion and insertion, along with the phonetic quality of postvocalic /l/ and postvocalic /t/.

TH-stopping

The interdental fricatives /θ/ and /ð/ are regularly realized in both I-NLE and E-NLE as stops; though alveolar realizations ([t] and [d]) are common, points of articulation range from dental to post-alveolar. Also common are intermediate variants, such as dental fricatives; /θ/ is generally affricated before /r/, as in *thrash*. In unstressed function words such as *the* and *those*, stop pronunciations of /ð/ are frequent even in casual urban styles.

More rarely, in a few regional enclaves settled by the southwest English, labiodental variants are encountered; however, the use of [f] for /θ/ and [v] for /ð/ is restricted to non-word-initial position, as in *with* or *breathe*. More stigmatized, and rarer still, is the use of [s] for non-initial /θ/, as in *path*. To date, this last realization has been documented only in western areas of the south coast of the island; it has no voiced counterpart, so that pronunciations like *breeze* for *breathe* remain unattested (Newhook 2002).

Initial /h/ deletion and insertion

Within the province, perhaps the greatest shibboleth associated with local varieties is found only in E-NLE: the variable loss of /h/ in word-initial (or syllable-initial) position, along with its occasional insertion in vowel-initial words that do not contain historical /h/. In such varieties, pairs such as *ale* and *hale*, or *ooze* and *whose*, may constitute homophones: the articulation of initial [h] in any one of these items is more likely in stressed syllables, as well as in cases where the preceding syllable ends in a vowel rather than a consonant. I-NLE, on the contrary, displays an /h/ patterning identical to that of standard varieties – the only exception being the name of the letter *h*, which is pronounced 'haitch', as in Irish English.

For E-NLE speakers born prior to 1900, /h/ loss was occasionally accompanied by /j/ insertion, such that a word like *here* might be pronounced 'yere'. Since variable deletion of the initial glides /j/ and /w/ also characterized earlier NLE (see Halpert and Widdowson 1996; Clarke 2004a), this may well represent a hypercorrection, though one inherited from southwest England (cf. Wakelin 1986).

Postvocalic /l/

Most standard varieties of NLE share with E-NLE a dark or velar pronunciation of postvocalic /l/ in words such as *heal*, *tall* or *pull*. In I-NLE, however – as in the traditional varieties of the southwestern areas of the island with an Acadian French or Scottish Gaelic heritage – postvocalic /l/ is often realized with a clear or palatal articulation. In certain areas of the province with an exclusively southwest English ancestry, /l/ vocalization has long been typical: there, postvocalic /l/ is frequently realized as dark vocoid [ʊ] or [ɤ]. Though the velar vs. palatal pattern clearly distinguishes southwest-English-settled areas from other areas, phonological conditioning may differ from region to region (see Paddock 1982).

Postvocalic /t/

In I-NLE (including the standard variety of the capital, St. John's), postvocalic word-/syllable-final /t/ may be articulated as a slit fricative, as it is in Irish English (e.g. *pat* pronounced [pʰæt̞]). Slit fricatives also occur in intervocalic position, in words like *better*, *pretty* or *Saturday*, where E-NLE varieties display a voiced stop or flap pronunciation, in all likelihood inherited from southwest England. In addition, though glottalization is infrequent in NLE in intervocalic position, it occurs more frequently in English-settled than in Irish-settled areas (cf. Noseworthy 1971: 40 ff.): for example, in E-NLE, /t/ is glottalized before syllabic /l/, as in *bottle* pronounced [baʔl], an environment in which conservative I-NLE displays a slit fricative.

Rhoticity

Standard NLE, like CE, is firmly rhotic. Yet variable postvocalic /r/ deletion – almost exclusively in unstressed syllables (e.g. *buttER*) – is often encountered among traditional speakers, both on the island and in Labrador. In traditional E-NLE, insertion of non-historical [r] occasionally occurs in unstressed syllables, in words of the type *SusannA*, *tunA* or *tomorroW* [dəmɔɹɚ].

In an earlier-mentioned enclave variety of E-NLE spoken on the north shore of Conception Bay, however, variable deletion of postvocalic /r/ occurs in both stressed and unstressed syllables, and is among the most salient features of this variety (see Seary, Story and Kirwin 1968: 67–9). In addition, in several Irish-settled communities towards the southern extremities of the Avalon peninsula, an original highly marked uvular pronunciation of postvocalic /r/ has disappeared, leading to /r/ loss (cf. Hickey 2002: 296–7).

Other features involving fricatives

Several noteworthy features of conservative NLE are highly recessive today. Initial fricative voicing (e.g. *fat* pronounced as *vat*, *said* as *zaid*) – a well-known characteristic of southwest England – was readily apparent in recordings of many conservative E-NLE speakers born in the late nineteenth and early twentieth centuries, but not in those of their present-day descendants. A second feature appears to be restricted to the conservative speech of southern Labrador, an area of mixed English, Scottish and other input. This is the tendency to pronounce the labiodental fricative /v/ as bilabial [w], or to merge both /v/ and /w/ as a bilabial or labiodental fricative. While most obvious in word-initial position (as in *vine*), this tendency may also occur word-internally (as in *evening*).

Other local fricative features are still common. These include the I-NLE tendency to devoice final fricatives and affricates (as in *rise* or *badge*), along with sibilant assimilation in negative forms of the verb *be* in E-NLE, such that (*it*) *wasn't* and (*it*) *isn't* are pronounced [(t)wʌdn] and [(t)ɪdn]).

Phonotactic and prosodic features

While studies in this area are lacking, it is clear that NLE differs considerably from CE, not the least with respect to speech tempo. Outsiders commonly remark on Newfoundlanders' tendency to 'speak fast'; and to judge from the frequency in vernacular NLE of such sandhi phenomena as elision and assimilation, this observation may well be correct (see Clarke 2004b, 2004c). These prosodic tendencies frequently lead to the deletion of grammatical markers in vernacular NLE, among them *'d* ('would', 'had'), *'ll* ('will'), *'ve* ('have') as well as, in past forms, final postconsonantal /t/ and /d/ (as in *touch(ed)*, *liv(ed)*), as well as the full /əd/ morpheme (yielding such bare past forms as *want* or *start*). The overall effect in conservative vernacular NLE resembles the minimal grammatical-marking patterns often noted of creole varieties.

The influences of substratal languages on regional varieties of NLE have likewise been barely investigated. Yet conservative speech among those of Inuit ancestry along the northern Labrador coast displays substratal effects in stress and intonation patterns; and the English of older residents of the French-settled west coast of the island may exhibit syllable-timing rather than the usual stress-timing. On the Irish-settled Avalon peninsula, Irish-inherited stress patterns involving non-initial stress on certain lexical items (e.g. *inteRESted, appreciATE*) are occasionally encountered. Intonational patterns in I-NLE (as in southern Irish English) remain largely undocumented, though I-NLE and E-NLE clearly differ in this regard.

As in a number of varieties across the North Atlantic (see Clarke and Melchers 2005), both I-NLE and E-NLE may display ingressive pulmonic articulation for the discourse particles *yeah, mm* and *no*. This feature appears to be on the decline. Among younger, more upwardly mobile (and especially female) speakers of NLE, however, two supralocal features that characterize innovative varieties of North American English are making considerable inroads: 'uptalk', or high rising intonation in declaratives; and laryngealization, or creaky voice, particularly in sentence- and phrase-final position.

3.2 Morphosyntax

The grammatical system of conservative NLE differs considerably from that of standard CE. Vernacular NLE shares many features with other English vernaculars, among them absence of nominal plural in measure phrases involving a numerical quantifier (e.g. *three mile, six ton*); unstressed possessive determiner *me* (*me book*); demonstrative *them* rather than *those* (*them people*);

reflexives based on a possessive stem (*hisself, theirselves*); double marking in comparatives (*more cleaner*); negative concord (*I don't have none of them, Nobody didn't go there*); and use of *never* rather than *not* as a generalized negator (*that time she* ('tide') *never come up so far*).

In its pronominal and verbal systems in particular, however, NLE displays a number of features that are considerably less common among present-day world Englishes. The chief of these are outlined below.

3.2.1   Pronouns

Pronoun exchange

Unlike I-NLE, rural E-NLE continues to display a feature inherited from southwest England: the use of subject-like pronoun forms in stressed object position, as in

(1)   He left we in school (Seary, Story and Kirwin 1968: 69)

(2)   He load(ed) she ('boat') full of slabs (Harris 2006: 115)

The opposite – and likewise inherited – tendency occurs much more rarely in E-NLE: the use of an object form in unstressed subject position, particularly in inverted forms:

(3)   Where's 'em to? ('Where are they?') (Halpert and Widdowson 1996, II: 986)

(4)   We lived up on a hill, didn't us? (Harris 2006: 113)

Grammatical gender

Conservative E-NLE displays a pronominal gender system inherited from southwest England (see Paddock 1981; Wagner 2005), involving a three-way contrast for the representation of inanimate objects. The pronoun *it* is reserved for non-count nouns (e.g. *fog, water*), or existential reference, as in

(5)   'Twas ('It was') a nice few down there, wasn't it? ('There was a lot (of people) down there, wasn't there?') (MK, Lanari 1994 Burin corpus)

Count nouns are classified on the basis of mobility; while mobile or self-propelled objects (e.g. *boat, car, tide*) are referred to as *she / her*, other countable inanimates are represented as *he / him* (much more rarely as *she / her*):

(6)   He ('rocking chair') bin down in the store for years (Harris 2006: 117)

(7)   When he ('church') was finished . . . (Seary, Story and Kirwin 1968: 69).

A second system – possibly more recent, and occurring in NLE in general – consists of the use of the feminine pronoun to refer to a general state of affairs or the situation at hand (as in the expression *She's gone, b'y* ('boy'), *she's gone*, which could refer to anything from the economy to the traditional way of life).

Second and third person pronominal morphology

Two pronominal forms inherited from source varieties in the British Isles and Ireland remain fairly current today. These are the object form *un/en* (pronounced [ən], probably derived from Old English *hine*), used in E-NLE instead of *him* or *it* (and, occasionally, *her*) as in (8–9); and the second person plural subject form *ye* [ji:], (along with possessive *yeer's*) found almost exclusively in I-NLE.

(8)   An' he wait(ed) till he got almost to un ('him') an' he fired ('threw') the cake at un (Halpert and Widdowson 1996: 121)

(9)   I tries to keep a bit of paint on un ('house') (Harris 2006: 115)

Also frequent in many English-settled areas of the province is the second person plural form *yous* (pronounced [ju:z] when stressed, [jəz] when unstressed). In addition, such forms as *(y)ee all, y'all* or *all yous* have occasionally been documented (Noseworthy 1971: 78). All of these may be local formations, designed to preserve the distinction between singular and plural – especially in light of the almost total loss of the E-NLE second person singular pronoun *(d)ee* (<*thee*), as in:

(10)   I come in to tell 'ee ('I came in to tell you') (Halpert and Widdowson 1996: 693)

3.2.2 Verbs

Morphological regularization: past forms

Like most vernacular varieties of English, vernacular NLE displays considerable verbal regularization, in the direction of a single binary distinction between non-past/present and past forms. As in many other varieties, levelling of the past tense/past participle distinction occurs in such generalized past forms as *become, begun, come, done, drank, drove, rung, seen, sung, swum, took, tore* and *went*. Conservative NLE also displays full regularization, via the addition of the *-ed* past morpheme, of a host of irregular verbs, among them *blowed, comed, dealed, drinked, falled (down), freezed (up), goed, growed, heared, knowed, leaved, lied (down), maked, rised, runned, seed, teached, throwed*. (As can be seen, some of these – among them *come, go* and *see* – may display more than one regularization pattern.) In a handful of cases, the levelling of the past tense/past participle distinction may lead to a bare past form that is identical with the present, as in the verbs *give* and *eat*. A few verbs may display double past-marking (e.g. *drownded, frozed, cotched* ('caught')), while occasionally historically regular verbs have been made irregular, whether through analogy or hypercorrection (e.g. *sove* rather than *saved*).

Non-past/present marking

A striking feature of vernacular E-NLE, as well as I-NLE, is the extensive use of verbal *-s* as a generalized present-tense marker in lexical verbs; it occurs with all subject types, whether nominal or pronominal. Although *-s*-marked forms express all verbal aspects, they are most favoured for the representation of the habitual, as in

(11)   I always calls him Joseph, see . . . (Clarke 1997: 242)

While habitual aspect may also be represented by unstressed periphrastic *do* forms in both Irish English and southwest British English, such forms have not been attested in NLE, at least for verbs other than *be* (see below; cf. Wagner 2007).

   In traditional varieties, the restriction of the *-s* suffix to lexical verbs results in a morphological opposition – most evident in E-NLE – between lexical and auxiliary uses of the verbs *have* and *do*. The former are (variably) marked with *-s*, and may display generalization of the *have* and *do* stem throughout the paradigm:

(12)   You don't realize what life is until you haves your own youngsters
          (AM, Lanari 1994 Burin corpus)

(13)   . . . an' when they does [duːz] . . . they sees that you got just so
          much enchantment as we got ourself (Halpert and Widdowson
          1996: 93)

Auxiliary uses, on the contrary, are not marked with verbal *-s*; hence the zero-suffix forms in the following third person singular examples:

(14)   'Tis a time to weep to see what 'ave 'appened to Newfoundland
          (CBC Radio (Newfoundland) Morning Show caller, 31 March
          1999)

(15)   (He) comes back right sad, he do (BFK, Lanari 1994 Burin
          corpus)

The verb be

Up to a generation or two ago, rural E-NLE speakers used a number of forms of the verb *be*, inherited from southwest England, that today have all but disappeared. Generalization of *am* (*we'm, you'm, they'm*) was not uncommon in the present paradigm (see e.g. Noseworthy 1971: 64), and, perhaps less frequently, *is* generalization (*I's, you's, they's*). Present *be* forms were often negated, along the northeast coast of the island, via the contracted form *bain't* [beɪnt], from *be + not* (along with *(h)ain't* or its variant *(h)an't*, both of which were also used as contracted forms of *have not*). Affirmative non-inflected *be*, however – the norm in much of southwest England (cf. Upton, Parry and Widdowson 1994: 494) – is barely attested in traditional E-NLE; and the second person singular form *(d)ee bis(t)*, though found among rural speakers born in the late nineteenth century, has since disappeared.

In the past tense, *was* regularization remains frequent with all grammatical subjects in both I-NLE and E-NLE, as it is in most vernacular varieties of English. The opposite tendency – *were* regularization – has been reported much more rarely; the following E-NLE illustrations of first and third person singular *were* come from Harris (2006: 102):

(16)   I were born on Flat Island

(17)   My mother were born . . . on Coward's Island

E-NLE and I-NLE differ from standard English in that both possess special forms of *be* to designate habitual aspect. E-NLE employs the invariable inflected form *bees* for this function (18 below); I-NLE represents the habitual by means of a periphrastic form, *do* [də] *be*, which is found less frequently today (19). In both varieties, the negative habitual is expressed by *don't be/never do be* (along with *never bees* in E-NLE), as in (20):

(18)   I bees home all the time (Noseworthy 1971: 66)

(19)   I do [də] be so hungry I don't know what I'm at (Dillon 1968: 131)

(20)   (He) never do be sick, he don't (BFK, Lanari 1994 Burin corpus)

Verbal aspect: perfect forms

For many speakers of NLE, the standard English perfect form (auxiliary *have* + past participle) is relatively infrequent, at least outside negatives and interrogatives. As in other English varieties (to greater or lesser degrees), recent past events are often represented by simple past forms (e.g. *I just saw him*); and intransitive verbs involving change of state may form their perfect with the auxiliary *be* (e.g. *Times are changed*). However, NLE is additionally characterized by several perfect equivalents inherited from regional source varieties in the British Isles and Ireland. The medial object construction (in which the past participle follows rather than precedes the direct object) occurs frequently in both I-NLE and E-NLE for a full range of dynamic, non-stative transitive verbs. Example (21) below illustrates a past perfect, and (22), a present perfect; the latter usually occurs with *got* rather than *have* in NLE:

(21)   After he had the two of 'em killed . . . ('After he'd killed the two of them') (Halpert and Widdowson 1996: 62)

(22)   I got her outlived by a good many years ('I've outlived her . . .')
          (Harris 2006: 109)

I-NLE also displays two perfect equivalent forms inherited from Irish
English: the simple present, used to represent an ongoing event that began
prior to the point of temporal reference, as in

(23)   I'm here quite a while now (Halpert and Widdowson 1996: 917)

and the *after*-perfect (*be* + *after* + V-*ing*):

(24)   But I mean she was after accepting . . . she accepted one husband
          as dead (AM, Lanari 1994 Burin corpus).

The latter displays a full range of perfect meanings, and not simply the 'hot
news' function that some have suggested as the core meaning of the *after*-
perfect in Irish English. The *after*-perfect is rare among traditional speakers
of E-NLE born prior to the early twentieth century; however, it has since
spread to all areas of the province.

    Two other E-NLE perfect forms are today considerably less frequent.
The first – which retains, in the form of *a-* [ə], the historical prefix on the
past participle – has all but disappeared:

(25)   You can't imagine how much change we have a-seen in our life
          (Harris 2006: 109)

The second is geographically restricted, having been documented only in
parts of the south coast of the island. It involves the auxiliary *been* [bɪn]
rather than *have*, as in the following two examples:

(26)   Have 'ee been eat? ('Have you eaten?') (Noseworthy 1971: 69)

(27)   Dad been a-pulled his weight ('Dad's pulled his weight')
          (Reported by A. Myles for Terrenceville, Burin peninsula, 1998)

According to Noseworthy (1971), this form tends to represent a more remote
past event than that designated by the competing *have*-auxiliary form. As
such, this construction is highly reminiscent of the 'remote *been*' form that to
date has been associated exclusively with early African American varieties.

3.2.3   *Other lexical categories: determiners, adverbial intensifiers, prepositions, nouns*

Space does not permit full treatment of the morphosyntactic features of
NLE; for more information, see Clarke (2004a, 2004c). Noteworthy features
include the use of the determiner *the* both as a proximal demonstrative (e.g.
the fall, meaning 'this past/coming autumn') and in cases where modern
Standard English requires either an indefinite (*when they'd get the cold*) or
zero determiner (*with the fright*). The form *either* (usually pronounced *e'er* or
a'r) has been generalized in NLE as an indefinite determiner for both count

and non-count nouns (e.g. *A'r water in that?*); its negative counterpart is *neither* (*ne'er/na'r*). In vernacular NLE, as in vernacular English in general, adverbial intensifiers often occur in bare form (e.g. *real good*). However, NLE makes regular use of a number of intensifiers which are no longer common in world Englishes (e.g. *right, some, wonderful, terrible*, all of which may modify an adjective like *good*; cf. *a cruel strong day* (Dillon 1968: 135)). Stative uses of the normally dynamic prepositions *to* and *into* are frequent in vernacular NLE (e.g. *stay where you're to*). NLE is also characterized by regular use of the nominal associative plural *and them* (with variants *and they*, *and their*), representing the referent's family, friends or habitual associates.

3.2.4 Sentence embedding
NLE shares with other vernacular Englishes such syntactic patterns as deletion of subject relative pronouns and inversion of subject and object in embedded questions. Subordinating conjunctions in traditional NLE, however, are not identical to those of Standard English; they include *where* [wɔɹ] and *till* ('so that'), *'fraid* ('for fear that') (see Paddock 1981: 16), as well as *without* ('unless'), as in

(28)   You wouldn't touch that without you had to (Harris 2006: 127).

I-NLE displays a construction inherited from Irish English: the use of subordinating *and* + participle (roughly equivalent to 'though') as in

(29)   A present, I thank you, and he payin' me me own money (Dillon 1968: 158).

The use of the complementizer *for to* [fɔɹdə] rather than standard *to* is also common in NLE, and not simply with a purposive ('in order to') meaning:

(30)   Newfoundland is our country. And a darn good country too, you know. For to have to go away and leave it . . . (LK, Lanari 1994 Burin corpus).

4 Conclusion

Traditional NLE displays perhaps more in common with the conservative regional varieties of southwest England or southeast Ireland than it does with standard Canadian English. In the past fifty years, however, the province has experienced considerable socioeconomic change, which has entailed increasing urbanization and out-migration, particularly on the part of younger generations in small rural communities that over the past two or more centuries have depended for their livelihood on the cod fishery.

The overall linguistic result, for both rural and urban varieties of NLE, has been increased contact with supralocal varieties, including standard varieties of North American English. Among younger, and particularly upwardly mobile, speakers, traditional features (such as Irish clear postvocalic /l/) are on the wane, while imported features (including such innovative CE features as the raising of the vowel in *Harry* to sound like *hairy*) are gaining ground. Though the inevitable outcome will be a decrease in the use of traditional NLE linguistic features, and hence a decrease in internal variation, NLE will undoubtedly continue to remain a distinct variety within the North American context for some time to come.

References

Clarke, Sandra. 1997. 'English verbal *-s* revisited: The evidence from Newfoundland.' *American Speech* 72.3: 227–59.

    2004a. 'The legacy of British and Irish English in Newfoundland.' In Raymond Hickey, ed. *Legacies of Colonial English: Transported Dialects*. Cambridge: Cambridge University Press, 242–61.

    2004b. 'Newfoundland English: Phonology.' In Bernd Kortmann, Edgar W. Schneider, Kate Burridge, Rajend Mesthrie, and Clive Upton, eds. *A Handbook of Varieties of English*, vol. I: *Phonology*. Berlin/New York: Mouton de Gruyter, 366–82.

    2004c. 'Newfoundland English: Morphology and syntax.' In Bernd Kortmann, Edgar W. Schneider, Kate Burridge, Rajend Mesthrie, and Clive Upton, eds. *A Handbook of Varieties of English*, vol. II: *Morphology and Syntax*. Berlin/New York: Mouton de Gruyter, 303–18.

Clarke, Sandra and Gunnel Melchers. 2005. 'Ingressive particles across borders: Gender and discourse particles across the North Atlantic.' In Markku Filppula, Juhani Klemola, Marjatta Palander and Esa Penttilä, eds. *Dialects Across Borders: Selected Papers from the 11th International Conference on Methods in Dialectology*. Amsterdam/Philadelphia: John Benjamins, 51–72.

Colbourne, B. Wade. 1982. *A Sociolinguistic Study of Long Island, Notre Dame Bay, Newfoundland*. M.A. thesis. Memorial University of Newfoundland. Available at http://collections.mun.ca/cdm4/document.php?CISOROOT=/theses& CISOPTR=255768&REC=8.

D'Arcy, Alexandra. 2005. 'Situating the locus of change: Phonological innovations in St. John's English.' *Language Variation and Change* 17.3: 327–55.

Dillon, Virginia. 1968. *The Anglo-Irish Element in the Speech of the Southern Shore of Newfoundland*. M.A. thesis. Memorial University of Newfoundland. Available at http://collections.mun.ca/cdm4/document.php?CISOROOT=/theses& CISOPTR=239634&REC=1.

Halpert, Herbert and J. D. A. Widdowson. 1996. *Folktales of Newfoundland* (2 vols.). Publications of the American Folklore Society. St. John's, NL: Breakwater.

Handcock, W. G. 1989. *'Soe Longe As There Comes Noe Women': Origins of English Settlement in Newfoundland*. St John's, NL: Breakwater.

Harris, Linda. 2006. *Two Island Dialects of Bonavista Bay, Newfoundland*. M. A. thesis. Memorial University of Newfoundland.

Hickey, Raymond. 2002. 'The Atlantic edge: The relationship between Irish English and Newfoundland English.' *English World-Wide* 23: 283–316.

Labov, William, Sharon Ash and Charles Boberg. 2006. *The Atlas of North American English*. Berlin/New York: Mouton de Gruyter.

Lanari, Catherine E. Penney. 1994. *A Sociolinguistic Study of the Burin Region of Newfoundland*. M.A. thesis. Memorial University of Newfoundland.

Mannion, John J. 1977. 'Introduction.' In John J. Mannion, ed. *The Peopling of Newfoundland: Essays in Historical Geography*. St John's, NL: Institute of Social and Economic Research, Memorial University of Newfoundland, 1–13.

Newhook, Amanda. 2002. *A Sociolinguistic Study of Burnt Islands, Newfoundland*. M.A. thesis. Memorial University of Newfoundland.

Noseworthy, Ronald G. 1971. *A Dialect Survey of Grand Bank, Newfoundland*. M.A. thesis. Memorial University of Newfoundland. Available at http://collections. mun.ca/cdm4/document.php?CISOROOT=/theses&CISOPTR=187353& REC=3.

Paddock, Harold J. 1981. *A Dialect Survey of Carbonear*. University, Alabama: University of Alabama Press (for the American Dialect Society).

1982. 'Newfoundland dialects of English.' In Harold Paddock, ed. *Languages in Newfoundland and Labrador*, 2nd edn. St. John's, NL: Memorial University of Newfoundland, 71–89.

Seary, E. R., G. M. Story, and W. J. Kirwin. 1968. *The Avalon Peninsula of Newfoundland: An Ethnolinguistic Study*. Bulletin no. 219. Ottawa: National Museum.

Statistics Canada. 2007. 2006 Census of Canada. Available at http:/www12. statcan.ca/english/census06/data/profiles/community.

Upton, Clive, David Parry and J. D. A. Widdowson. 1994. *Survey of English Dialects: The Dictionary and Grammar*. London: Routledge.

Wagner, Susanne. 2005. 'Gender in English pronouns: Southwest England.' In Bernd Kortmann, Tanja Herrmann, Lukas Pietsch and Susanne Wagner, eds. *A Comparative Grammar of British English Dialects: Agreement, Gender, Relative Clauses*. Berlin/New York: Mouton de Gruyter, 211–367.

2007. 'Unstressed periphrastic *do* – from southwest England to Newfoundland?' *English World-Wide* 28.3: 249–78.

Wakelin, Martyn F. 1986. *The Southwest of England*. VEAW text series 5. Amsterdam: John Benjamins.

Wells, J. C. 1982. *Accents of English* (3 vols.). Cambridge: Cambridge University Press.

6   Honduras/Bay Islands English

ROSS GRAHAM

1 Introduction

The Bay Islands ('Islas de la Bahía') is the smallest of the eighteen departments of the Republic of Honduras. The three main islands of the group, Roatan, Guanaja and Utila, lie between 30 and 64 km north of the mainland, and about 170 km southeast of Belize City.

Spanish is the official language of Honduras and the native language of more than 95 per cent of the country's population. Despite constitutional recognition of minority languages since 1995, Spanish is unchallenged as the sole language of the state educational and judicial systems. English does enjoy recognition as the language of an ethnic group – though not as an indigenous language of Honduras. It is listed alongside seven indigenous languages: Garifuna, Miskito and the Amerindian languages Lenca, Chorti, Tolupan, Pech and Tawahka. English is seen as the heritage language of a specific ethnic denomination, the 'negros ingleses': people of Afro-Caribbean descent whose English- or English-creole-speaking ancestors came to Honduras in the nineteenth and twentieth centuries. The last official state census (2001) gives the population of this group as 12,370, making it the fifth largest ethnic group behind Lenca (with an extinct language), Garifuna, Miskito and Chorti.

There are two distinct subgroups of 'negros ingleses'. It is important to distinguish these, as only one has managed to maintain a viable English-speaking community. The first group consisted of emigrants who settled on the Bay Islands in the years following slave-emancipation. The majority emigrated from the Cayman Islands following the ending of slavery there in 1838, though some came from Belize and Jamaica. Their descendants, together with the descendants of white settlers who also in most cases came via the Caymans, form the core group of today's Bay Islands English speech community. The second group included in 'negros ingleses' consists of the descendants of migrant workers who came to work for banana companies on the north coast of Honduras in the first decades of the twentieth century. Most came from Jamaica, but other Caribbean islands, together with Belize, were represented as well. They worked for companies such as the Tela

Railroad and Truxillo Railroad (both later to come under United Fruit) and other North American banana companies which dominated the Honduran economy at that time. Some of their descendants still live in three port cities of the north coast: La Ceiba (where one neighbourhood became known as the 'barrio ingles'), Puerto Cortes and Tela. The rest are scattered across the country. Today, nearly all are Spanish-dominant, and the majority are monolingual Spanish speakers. With elderly speakers numbering only hundreds, the distinctive north coast English variety (referred to in Holm 1989: 482) can be considered moribund. In La Ceiba there is a community of perhaps a thousand speakers of English, but most of these are Bay Islanders who have relocated to the coast (Griffin, p.c. 2006).[1]

The numerous websites devoted to promoting tourism and real estate on the islands unfortunately give the impression that they are mainly English-speaking. This may have been the case until the mid 1980s, but since that time there has been such a large influx of mainlanders that Spanish has become the dominant language. The demographic dominance of Spanish speakers, together with its use in administration and most services, has resulted in displacement of English from its former position. Today, most English-speaking islanders are fully-functioning bilinguals.

1.1   Number of speakers

The 2001 national census gave the population of Honduras as 6,076,885 and the most recent population estimate for July 2008 is over 7.6 million. (CIA country facts website). The Bay Islands is the smallest department, with a population listed as 31,552 in 2001. Roatan accounted for 25,038, Guanaja for 4,535 and Utila, 1,979.

Well-informed residents of the islands consider these figures to considerably underestimate the actual population. In September 2004, the monthly magazine *Bay Islands Voice* published a population estimate of 65,000 for Roatan based on extrapolating from peak domestic electricity demand (with a claimed margin of error of $+/-$ 10 per cent). The calculation was based on current municipal censuses or estimates for the populations of Guanaja and Utila, which were given as 9,300 and 8,500, respectively. The size of the gap between these estimates and official figures is difficult to explain. One point to remember is that the islands have a high floating population, and the population estimates included tourists, non-permanent foreign residents, and mainlanders visiting the island.

---

[1] Holm (1983: 8) gives estimates of 300 English speakers in Honduran Mosquitia and 100 in Trujillo. This seems over-generous. Few Miskitos in Honduras today have functional competence in English. Hardly any English speakers remain in Puerto Castilla (by Trujillo), and there are probably no more than forty to fifty in all of La Mosquitía (Griffin, p.c. March 2005).

What is also certain, however, is that population growth has been rapid since the mid 1980s, very largely due to an influx of poor mainlanders who have come in search of better-paid work. According to Stonich (2000: 99), 'annual rates of population increase on the islands since 1990 are approximately the same as those of mainland urban areas such as San Pedro Sula and Tegucigalpa (4.5%)'. Migration to the islands by ladinos is part of a general drift from rural to urban areas, and in all three islands, mainlanders tend to be concentrated in dense urbanizations, most of which are squatter settlements. If we assume continued growth of 4.5 per cent per annum and the figure of 47,000 given to me in January 1997 by the then Governor is taken as the baseline population of the Bay Islands in 1996, we arrive at an estimated 2008 population of 79,707. The real figure is probably higher, given the need to include a few thousand foreign residents. If we take 90,000 as a current population estimate, the next problem is how to determine the size of the Bay Islands English speech-community. The 2001 census does not give separate information on the number of 'Anglo' Bay Islanders, and the figure of 6,871 given as the number of 'negros ingleses' for the four Bay Islands municipalities combined seems much too small.

In the absence of concrete data, I feel that the estimated English-speaking population of 20,000 given in Graham (2000) can be increased by 2,000–3,000. If this is correct, then indigenous English-speakers do not now account for much more than a quarter of the islands' population.

2 Sociohistorical background and influences on Bay Islands English

The English language has been present in the Western Caribbean since well before 1600, even though Spanish, the language of the conquistadors, preceded it in Honduras. The island of Guanaja was visited by Columbus on his fourth voyage of 1502 and the earliest Spanish settlements on the north coast date from the 1520s. From the 1560s on, English privateers and pirates were the main scourge of the Spanish maritime fleet in this part of the Spanish Main. Due to their convenient location, and the abundance of natural food such as fish, coconuts and wild hogs, the Bay Islands were ideal spots for buccaneers and pirates to hide, careen ships and revictual, before launching raids on the mainland or on Spanish ships.

Although the islands were used by pirates in the late sixteenth and seventeenth centuries, attempts to sustain an organized English settlement were unsuccessful. In 1638, a group of around 400 settlers from Virginia came under the auspices of the Providence Company, and these were later joined by others who had been driven off Old Providence Island (now Providencia). Among these, there were a number of buccaneers. In 1643, William Jackson completely destroyed Trujillo, which was to remain abandoned and undefended for over a hundred years.

This first Bay Islands settlement ended abruptly in 1650, when the Spanish removed the entire population by force, including the original Paya Indian inhabitants. After the 1667 Sandwich Treaty of Madrid, England undertook to suppress buccaneering, and the buccaneers were reclassified as 'pirates'. Still, for at least the next fifty years, the Bay Islands remained a favoured base for pirate activity. Henry Morgan and John Morris had used Roatan as a refuelling point for the sacking of Granada in 1664. Later, pirates such as Jackman, Sharp, Uring, Van Horn, Coxon, Low, Spriggs and Vane used the islands (Harper 2005). Meyer and Meyer (1994: 63) state that 'by 1700 . . . the islands were being repopulated with a motley group of Indians, Africans, Dutch, French, English, Portuguese and Spaniards, among them English pirates expelled from the Bahamas by Woodes Rogers'.

By the early 1700s, the ex-buccaneers had largely settled down to logwood cutting, growing sugar cane and trading in contraband. They lived alongside their slaves in scattered settlements along the coast from Yucatan down through Belize and along the 'Mosquito Coast' of Honduras and Nicaragua. Friendly contacts between the Baymen and the native Miskito date from this time. Together, they were a thorn in the side of the Spanish authorities, but enjoyed somewhat grudging support from Britain. Following the outbreak of the War of Jenkins Ear (1739–1742), Britain decided to actively defend the Baymen by appointing Superintendents on the Miskito Coast and the Bay Islands.

The second attempt at a Bay Islands settlement was no more successful than the first. In 1742, New Port Royal in Roatan was fortified, and some 460 soldiers of the Jamaica regiment and their families, together with some settlers from St. Kitts, Jamaica and Belize, came to Roatan (Davidson 1974: 54, 57). The garrison withdrew after the signing of the treaty of Aix-la-Chapelle (1748), and the islands were emptied. In the following year, the British formally established a protectorate on the Miskito Shore, centred on Black River. This came to an end following a successful Spanish military campaign between 1779 and 1782; the entire Black River population of over 2,000 people, mainly slaves, was forced to evacuate. Most evacuees went to Belize. Roatan became populated again in 1797, with the arrival of a few thousand Black Caribs, transported there from St Vincent following a rebellion. Most of the Black Caribs relocated to the north coast, initially settling around Trujillo, but a few remained on Roatan. The town of Punta Gorda on the north shore is today a mainly Spanish-speaking Black Carib community, where a variety of Bay Islands English is also spoken.

It was, however, the ending of slavery in the British Empire in 1834 that gave rise to what can be regarded as the 'founder settlement' of Bay Islands English. Starting around 1830, formerly slave-owning families from the Cayman Islands began to settle in the Bay Islands. They were followed, after 1838, by a much larger number of ex-slaves and free coloured people. All were attracted by the possibilities for agriculture and fishing. The British administration in Belize backed the settlement and the settlers' demands for incorporation into the Empire.

In the 1840s, some British investors also showed renewed interest in the commercial possibilities of the region, and an attempt was made to re-establish a trading settlement at Black River. The British allied themselves with the Miskito and became involved in confrontations with the Honduran army, as they had with the Spanish before. The state of anarchy on the coast no doubt largely explains why many English-speakers (who probably included some English-creole-speakers) left the north coast and settled on the Bay Islands. The Bay Islands colony, agreed to by the Colonial Office, but never apparently sanctioned by the British Foreign Office, lasted only from 1852 until 1861. The US held that Britain had breached the 1850 Clayton-Bulwer Treaty. This stated that neither country was to seek to fortify, occupy or colonize any part of Central America not already owned. The islands were handed over to Honduras under the terms of the Wyke-Cruz Treaty (1859), which recognized British rights to Belize in exchange for giving up any claims to the Mosquito Coast and the Bay Islands.

The 1858 Bay Islands census, reproduced in Davidson (1974: 81), shows that out of a total population of 1,548 (which included 572 children born on the islands), 144 were born on the Mosquito Coast. This compares with 650 born in the Cayman Islands, 66 in Belize and 28 in Jamaica. A few people had been born in Britain. 'Whites' comprised 22 per cent of the population. Aside from the large number of young people and children who are listed as having been born on the islands, it is clear that the adult population was mainly of Caymanian birth, although other territories must have contributed a definite 'creole' input to the speech mosaic.

Islanders continued for a long time thereafter to believe that they were British subjects and not subject to Honduran laws. Thus, although Spanish was made the official language after the Bay Islands became a department in 1872, this had little or no impact on everyday life. Bay Islanders fished and turtled, and cultivated plantain, banana, yam and pineapples. These products were traded in Belize and also exported to the US. Until the devastating hurricane of 1877, most Honduran bananas exported to the US came from the Bay Islands. Subsequently, agriculture entered a gradual decline from which it never fully recovered.

Still, the trading of agricultural and other products, much of this brought from Belize, was a major activity. The distinctive Caymanian-accented English would have been heard in all the small trading ports along the north coast, including Cauquira, the main port in La Mosquitía, which according to tradition was founded by Bay Islanders (Griffin n.d.: 3). With the banana boom of the first thirty years of the twentieth century, the north coast received its final wave of Caribbean immigrants. The two major employers were United Fruit (which owned the Tela and Trujillo railroads) and Standard Fruit, which operated from la Ceiba. Workers came from Belize, Jamaica and Grand Cayman, and other parts of the English-speaking

Caribbean as far away as Barbados and Trinidad. Many Bay Islanders came to work, and some settled on the coast. Likewise, some of the West Indians married Bay Islanders and went to live on the islands.

Some Bay Islanders of this generation received an American-style education in the company schools on the mainland. Most received only a limited education on the islands, learning Spanish in the state schools and some elements of English in 'home schools'. Public schooling in Spanish was made mandatory in 1917 (Davidson 1974: 95) and many English schools were closed during the Carías era (1932–49). In the mid 1950s, all private English schools were closed by Government order. Sunday schools and 'home schools' were the only means of acquiring English reading and writing skills. The result was that most islanders lacked both proficiency in Spanish and literacy in English.

The US exerted a strong pull for Bay Islanders during most of the twentieth century, not just for work but also in many cases for settlement. During the Second World War, contacts with the outside world widened as many Bay Island men went to work on supply ships for the American navy. Subsequently, many worked for American or Norwegian merchant shipping lines, and on oil tankers and cruise ships. Islanders have always preferred to make a living without going to the mainland, although nowadays some attend high school or university there.

From the late 1950s, money earned offshore enabled development of commercial fishing of shrimp and lobster, which became the islands' major income-generating activity. Despite declining catches due to overfishing, the fish-processing plants operating on Roatan and Guanaja are still a major source of employment, especially for ladinos. Tourism developed gradually, starting with the opening of a few dive resorts at the end of the 1960s, but did not begin to take off in a major way until the airport on Roatan was improved to handle international flights in 1988. In the last decade, the islands have witnessed an unprecedented boom in both tourism and real estate, with the construction of luxury resorts and homes for North Americans. Projects completed or close to completion on Roatan include large cruise-ship docks at Coxen Hole and Dixon Cove, and a luxury golf course resort with a 155-berth marina, another large one due to open in November 2009. It is certain that the establishment of the Bay Islands Free Trade Zone in December 2007 will provide a massive boost to investment. However, development has brought increased crime, social polarization, environmental problems, and a fear of unrest fuelled by resentment among ladinos. Future social stability depends on the ability of the tourist industry to generate employment for the increased population.

2.1 Cultural identity

Two social and cultural factors are significant in terms of defining the identity of English-speaking Bay Islanders. From the beginning of permanent settlement, an awareness of distinctness based on colour has existed. Secondly, islanders have always defined their collective identity in terms of contrast with the Spanish-speaking mainland.

In social terms, a significant feature of Bay Island society remarked on by earlier observers was the separation, amounting to segregation in some places, of white and 'coloured' islanders. Writing in the 1930s, a British visitor described 'rigid strata of society which are unassailable'; coloured people at that time were 'looked upon as an entirely different and quite inferior stratum of society by the rest of the population' (Houlson 1934: 68). This theme is further explored by Evans (1966), who describes a segregated society in French Harbour, Roatan. The segregation was just as marked on Utila, where one account refers to a 'Mississippi-like environment' in which 'white people exhibit horror at physical contact' with 'coloureds' and there were separate dances for blacks and whites (Jones and Glean 1971: 59).

It is only in recent decades that cross-ethnic marriages have become more acceptable, though still frowned upon. On the other hand, islanders of both ethnicities freely take Hispanic partners, so that mixed-race families are common. Today, islanders see themselves as 'Hondureñan'. In spite of this, older islanders still identify themselves as 'English' in opposition to the mainland 'Spaniards'. These terms hark back to colonial times, with all the historical baggage that this entails. It is still possible to hear disparaging terms like 'indios' used to describe mainlanders, while the islanders are sometimes referred to by the latter as 'piratas'.

Contacts between islanders and mainlanders were still minimal until the mid 1960s. Most islanders spoke little Spanish. Writing in 1966, Evans described barriers impeding cultural change, and factors which 'serve to induce and perpetuate ill feelings and mistrust between the people of French Harbour and the mainland ladino population' (1966: v). But immigration by ladinos, which began in earnest in the 1980s, together with greater involvement of administrators and business investors from the mainland, created conditions where 'maintenance of the language barrier' (ibid.: 172) was no longer feasible or desirable. While speaking Spanish was previously frowned upon, using both languages was becoming a normal feature of everyday interaction by the late 1970s. Perhaps the clearest reflection of the extent of hispanicization today is the very high rate of active bilingualism (Decker and Henriksen 2002). Only a few of the oldest islanders are effectively monolingual. This contrasts with a survey of householders in part of western Roatan conducted in the early 1990s (Stonich 2000: 121), which found that only 50 per cent of their parents spoke Spanish. Knowledge and active use of the other language is much greater among the islanders than among the mainland incomers. '84% of islanders who speak English as their primary language also speak Spanish, while only 33% of Spanish-speaking ladinos also speak English' (Stonich 2000: 120).

Even while becoming capable bilinguals, Bay Islanders have resisted cultural assimilation into mainland Honduras. A pragmatic attitude prevails.

Fewer islanders today adopt the stance of cultural superiority and outright rejection of central government which was characteristic of an earlier period. Very gradually, Bay Islanders have come to see themselves as 'Hondureñan' and to understand that bilingualism is an advantage. At the same time, however, the exposure to North American influence has become much greater through the expansion of tourism, the internet and North American television via satellite and cable. These factors have certainly reinforced islanders' sense of belonging to the English-speaking world. It is regrettable that this openness to the outside world has resulted in the loss almost everywhere of traditional manifestations of Bay Islands culture (some aspects of which are described in Graham 2000).

3   Features of the variety

In his introduction to the edited volume *Central American English*, Holm (1983: 15) makes this comment with respect to Bay Islands English: '(it) would seem to be not a Creole but rather a regional variety of English influenced by contact with creolised English, much like the folk speech of the southern United States'. Holm reached this conclusion based on the sketches of Bay Islands English in Ryan (1973) and Warantz (1983); the latter is both more extensive and more reliable, and contains ten pages of transcripts of conversations from Utila. My own investigations, conducted in the early 1990s via interviews and fieldwork observation, show significant differences between the speech of Utila and that of Roatan, with a larger number of creole features among black speakers in Roatan than in either of the other two islands (a summary appears in Graham 2005). For most of Utila's history, whites have outnumbered blacks, and the two ethnicities (with a small number of people of mixed descent) both lived in one main settlement (albeit in separate zones). This suggests that an adequate description of Bay Islands English must account for differences between varieties which show widely varying degrees of restructuring.

Several social dimensions are relevant to such a description: inter-island differences, ethnicity and access to English-medium education and travel are perhaps the most salient. The sketch given here oversimplifies, but an attempt is made at representing some salient differences which separate the most creole-influenced speech of Roatan from 'traditional' white speech. While such speech differences are important, it is essential to point out that Bay Islands English as a whole owes its distinctive character to a history of prolonged co-existence of whites and blacks in close contiguity. Taken as a whole, Bay Islands English (BIE) contains a number of features that result from prolonged close contact between white and black islanders, and there is much evidence of the synchronic effects of linguistic contact between non-creolized and creole or partially creolized varieties.

BIE can be characterized as a spectrum of varieties showing varying degrees of influence from originally separate inputs: a mixed variety from the

Cayman Islands (which has been described as a 'semi-creole' by Schneider, 1990), together with some direct creole input from Jamaica and Belize (and probably the Mosquito Coast).

Williams (1987) characterizes white Caymanian speech as a variety of 'Anglo-Caribbean', the product of koineization of eighteenth century British dialects. The long incubation period during which Caymanian speech was formed would have permitted close approximation of white Anglo-Caribbean by black speakers, in a scenario very similar to that of Barbados. But in contrast to Barbados, the emergence and maintenance of a common shared variety was not disrupted by any large-scale immigration of Africans, so that the linguistic ecology for the subsequent emergence of a creole basilect was absent.

The Cayman Islands was the crucible for Bay Islands English, and it was there that two key processes took place. In a first stage, selection of features from English dialectal inputs took place, resulting in a levelled variety of non-standard English, and second, an approximation of this variety was acquired by black slaves and servants. The unstable and heterogeneous varieties of these acquirers served as input for children of both ethnicities, who would have forged a new, stable and focused variety which became the Caymanian spoken by the first wave of permanent Bay Islands settlers (this speculative account is adapted from the three-stage model of new-dialect formation proposed in Trudgill 2004).

In the nineteeth-century Bay Islands, it would appear that the input of speakers of creole varieties from Jamaica and elsewhere did not significantly alter the dominant speech pattern of Caymanian English, in which black and white speech patterns had mutually influenced each other over a long period. Creole-speakers being a minority, they would have adapted their speech towards the majority variety (with varying results according to local demographics). Native Bay Islanders, including those whose speech shows only small differences from Standard English, have a distinctive accent that is similar to Caymanian.[2] With regard to morphosyntactic features, black Roatan speech bears comparison with mesolectal Caribbean varieties, though it also shows the influence of white Anglo-Caribbean and white BIE (here referred to as AngBIE). Although ethnolinguistic divisions are weaker within BIE today, a system of ethnic labelling of certain linguistic features is still useful. The present account makes use of the labels AngBIE and AfrBIE where this is appropriate. The abbreviation AfrBIE+ denotes those speakers whose speech contains the highest incidence of creole features. Mid-range black varieties that show a more significant degree of convergence with AngBIE are labelled AfrBIE>.

---

[2] I am most grateful to Heather McLaughlin of the Cayman Islands Oral Archive for the loan of audiotapes of four speakers from the oral history collection. My comment on the close similarity of BIE with Caymanian phonology is based on these tapes.

3.1 Phonology

Most of the characteristic features of BIE phonology are shared with Caymanian. The variety of Caribbean English which developed in the Cayman Islands in the late eighteenth and nineteenth centuries was a blend produced by black and white speakers in interaction. Jamaica was the source of slaves in the Caymans, and certain features of Caymanian could therefore have had a dual origin in eighteenth-century English dialects and Jamaican. An example is velar palatalization.

The sketch that follows is an attempt to capture features found in both AngBIE and AfrBIE>, while also mentioning some features restricted to the creole-influenced black speech of Roatan (AfrBIE+).

3.1.1 Consonants

V/W realizations

There are several variants. The variant selected does not always correlate with English spelling, but rather depends on the neighbouring sounds. Syllable-initially, in place of SE [w] or [v], a labial-palatal approximant [ɥ] is used in the environment of a following close or mid front vowel. This may also be used with a following [a] vowel, while [w] with reduced lip rounding is used with back vowels. Thus, *week* may sound like *veek*, and *went* like *vent* (front vowel environment). But we also find *very* sounding like *werry*, and *vexed* like *wex*. To the untutored ear, *vanished* sounds like *wanisht*, and *voice* like *wois* or *wais*.

Syllable-finally, in place of SE [v], we again find the labial-palatal [ɥ]. The impression can be of a lax [y], as there is little or no lip-rounding. This can be noted in a word like *save*, or in *have* which sounds like *how*. The quality of the vowel in *have* is altered by the final consonant; this leads to near-homophony between *show* and *shove*, which are realized as [ʃo] and [ʃɵɥ], respectively.

It may be concluded that merger of the two phonemes in one /w/ phoneme has occurred, with two or more allophones. Some AfrBIE+ speakers may additionally have [b] as an allophone, as in the attested *bek* (vexed).

Unusually for the Caribbean, words spelled with initial 'wh' may be pronounced with aspiration, giving a further variant (or perhaps a marginal phoneme /ʍ/, given the *which/witch* contrast). Examples include the common function words *what*, *when*, *where* and *why*.

TH-stopping

Realization of syllable-initial interdental fricatives /θ/ and /ð/ as the stops [t] and [d] with a dental articulation is variable, even in AfrBIE+, where it is frequent in informal style. But for most BIE speakers, a stop articulation is the norm where the initial *th* is followed by [r] as in *three* [tri]. In Utila, stopped forms are rare in AngBIE. The initial voiced consonant in words like *than*, *that*, *they* and *these*, also *this*, is often omitted.

Rhoticity

Many speakers, including most whites, pronounce /r/ in all positions, and some white speakers have a strong postvocalic /r/ with some retroflexion. Elision of postvocalic /r/ is much more common in AfrBIE, where for many speakers /r/ is unrealized word-finally in an unstressed syllable, e.g. in *mother*, *brother*, *water*, also in *fire*. Exchange of /r/ and /l/ appears in some words. Examples include *unless* [ʌnrɛs] and *fritter* [flɪtɪr].

H-dropping

/h/ is used consistently as in SE, without any tendency to dropping or hypercorrection. This is in marked contrast to Jamaica.

T-voicing

In words like *better* or *little*, the /t/ between vowels tends to be voiced, sounding like [d].

T-glottalling

Many speakers have variable substitution of a glottal stop for /t/ in words like *nothing* or *bottle*, *that* or *it*: [nʌʔn], [bɒʔl], [ðaʔ], [ɪʔ]. Glottalling is not an attested feature of Caribbean English-based creoles (CECs), although found in Barbados (Wells 1982: 584) and Saba (Williams 1985: 40), so this BIE feature may well be a retention of a feature of earlier Anglo-Caribbean.

Velar palatalization

When a word-initial velar stop is followed by [a], the consonant is palatalized, e.g. *cat* [kjat], *garlic* [gjalɪk]. Occasionally this may extend to front mid vowels, e.g. *came* [kjeːm] or to a central vowel, e.g. *girl* [gjʌrl], but not to back vowels, e.g. *cot* [kɒt]. Velar palatalization before /a/ is also a feature of Jamaican Creole, and has its origin in English dialects of the seventeenth–eighteenth centuries (Cassidy and Le Page 1980: lviii).

Reduction of syllable-final consonant clusters

Final consonant cluster simplification is universal, though subject to a good deal of variability. It is not so regular or extensive as in CECs.

a) At the end of a syllable, clusters of any consonant plus /d/ tend to be reduced, with the loss of /d/. For many speakers, this is categorical in the case of [nd] and [ld]: send → [sɛn], told → [tol].

b) Syllable-final fricative plus /t/ is reduced: *left* → [lɛf]; *coast* → [koːs]. But in the case of -*st* final clusters, the final plosive remains present underlyingly, as is shown by the productive strategy employed when

Table 6.1 *Principal vowels of Bay Islands English*

KEY WORDS	realization	KEY WORDS	realization	KEY WORDS	realization
ı KIT	ı ~ i ~ ɛ	iː FLEECE	iː	iː NEAR	iːr ~ iːır ~ ɛːər ~ ɛːr
ɛ DRESS	ɛ ~ e	eː FACE	eː ~ ẹː	eː SQUARE	ɛır ~ ɛːər
a TRAP	a ~ ɑ	a PALM	aː	aː START	ar
ɒ LOT	ɒ	ɒ THOUGHT	ɒː	ɒː NORTH	ɒr
ʌ STRUT	ʌ ~ ɔ	o GOAT	oː	oː FORCE	or
ʊ FOOT	ʊ ~ ɵ	ʊː GOOSE	ʊ	ʊː CURE	ʊr
a BATH	aː	aı PRICE	aı ~ ɐı ~ əı ~ ʌı	ı happY	ı
ɒ CLOTH	ɒː	ɔı CHOICE	ɔı ~ ɐı	ʌ lettER	ı
ʌ NURSE	ʌr	aʊ MOUTH	ɐʊ ~ ʌʊ ~ əʊ	a commA	ʌ

-*s* inflections are added to the base: in order to avoid a difficult consonant cluster, the word is split into two syllables, and the ending realized as [ɛz]: *guests* [gɛstɛz]; *trusts* [trʌstɛz]; *tourists* [tʊrıstɛz]. As in StE, a similar process applies to bases ending in -*ks*, but these include forms produced by metathesis, such as [hʌksɛz] *husks* and [dɛksɛz] *desks*. Interestingly, the [ɛz] variant is sometimes used to avoid an [fs] cluster, for example [lafɛz] *laughs*.

Affrication

In AfrBIE+, there may be affrication in a word-initial *tr*- sequence: *try* [tʃraı]. There is a tendency also among some speakers to substitute [tʃ] for [ʃ]: *sugar* [tʃʊga]. The substitution of [tʃ] for [tr], usual in Jamaican Creole (JC), occurs only in Anancy stories. For some AfrBIE speakers, /ʒ/ is absent, being replaced with [dʒ]: *pleasure* [pledʒa]. But [dʒ] may be hypercorrected, as in *jump* [tʃʌmp]. Note that the voiced affricate is used in words like *dew* [dʒuː]; in this respect BIE resembles British English rather than GenAm.

Devoicing of final stops

In AfrBIE+, final stops may be devoiced: *big* [bık], *stab* [stap].

3.1.2 *Vowels*

Table 6.1 is based on the word-sets in Wells (1982). Where alternative realizations are given, the first is the most common one. Where a variant is associated with a particular group of speakers, phonological environment or lexical subset, this is explained in the notes below. The vowel chart is in Figure 6.1.

Certain distinctions made in the standard accents on the basis of vowel quality are conveyed by vowel length. This applies to the three oppositions

ɪ		iː		ʊ		
ɛ	ʌ	eː		o		
		aɪ	ɔɪ	aʊ	a	ɒ

Figure 6.1 Vowel chart of Bay Islands English

/a, ɑ/, /ʊ, u/, /ɒ, ɔ/. No separate phonemes are introduced for unstressed environments. BIE is basically rhotic and no new phonemes are needed for vowels before /r/. Notes on variation within the vowel system are presented below, in the following order: short vowels, long vowels and diphthongs, vowels before /r/, unstressed vowels.

KIT /ɪ/

Some Roatan and Guanaja speakers have close and lengthened realizations before a nasal consonant: *him* [hiːm], *things* [θiːŋz].On the other hand, lowering may also occur in words with a following nasal: *think* [θɛŋk], *things* [θɛŋz], *since* [sɛns]. In white BIE, lowering is commonly found in the words *it* [ɛt] and *if* [ɛf] and before /k/: *stick* [stɛ̝k], *pick* [pɛ̝k]. Many speakers have homophony between *sit* and *set*.

DRESS /ɛ/

Realizations are varied, and the pronunciation of individual words varies across the islands. In Guanaja, a raised variant [e] has been observed in *red*, *bed*, and *then* [ðen]. Lowered variants often occur in the environment of a following /t/, as in *get* [gɛ̞t] and *set* [sɛ̞t]. The vowel in *whelk*, and the stressed vowels in *pelican*, *engine* and *kettle* place these words in the KIT lexical set.

TRAP /a/

The quality of /a/ is typically an open centralized [a], but both fronted [a̙l] and backed [ɑ] variants are found, the latter occurring more commonly in AfrBIE. There is no relationship between use of these variants and either the BATH or PALM sets, as no phonemic contrast exists within the three sets. The pronunciation of the stressed vowel of 'water' as [aː] is stigmatized and is generally avoided

A distinctive feature, widespread in Utila and Roatan, is the diphthongal variant [ai] found before a velar stop: *back* [baik], *bag* [baig], *sack* [saik]. Cassidy and Le Page (1980: lii) refer to this feature of JC as 'archaic'. Wright (1906: 2) refers to this process, and elsewhere cites a few examples from south-mid Lancashire, but it may have become consolidated in white

Anglo-Caribbean together with the tendency to syllable lengthening and breaking. Many AfrBIE speakers use [ɑ] in these words.

LOT /ɒ/

No tendency to unrounding of LOT and no indication of a merger of the vowels TRAP and LOT, a feature of 'popular speech' in the West Indies (Wells 1982: 131).

STRUT /ʌ/

Often rounded before a nasal, as in *punch* [pɔntʃ], or lungs [lɔːŋz], but in Utila, the vowel tends to be in the region of [ɐ], so that *cup* would sound like *cap*, were it not for velar palatalization in the latter. In the environment of a following sibilant, an off-glide is sometimes inserted: cousin [kʌɪzɪn], does [dʌɪz]. This feature was noted mainly among AfrBIE speakers in Roatan.

FOOT /ʊ/

This vowel is indistinct in quality from the vowel of FOOD, the only clear difference being one of length. Several variants occur, conditioned by the nature of the following segment. A following nasal, as in a word like *spoon*, in the GOOSE class, may result in a vowel intermediate between [ʊ] and [o]. In Utila, some /ʊ/ words with a short vowel may have [ʌ], e.g. *good* [gʌd], look [lʌk].

GOAT /o/

No overall tendency to diphthongization, in contrast with Jamaican Creole (JC). However, in Roatan a diphthong may be heard in *coffee* [kʊɔfɪ], *dory* [dʊɔrɪ] and *coco* (yam) [kʊoko]. A slightly more open pronunciation occurs in some words, e.g. soap [sǫp].

FLEECE /i/

The vowel is generally distinguished by its length and closeness from that of FIT. But the /iː, eː/ opposition is neutralized before a nasal consonant, both being pronounced with a closely articulated [eː]. For many speakers, there is homophony between *keen* and *cane*, *team* and *tame*, *seem* and *same*.

FACE /e/

This vowel has a raised articulation before a following nasal and also, for many speakers, word-finally, as in *way* [węː].

PRICE /aɪ/ and CHOICE /ɔɪ/

The vowels in these two sets are not kept distinct in every word belonging to the two sets. Many speakers use [aɪ] in the words *oil, boil, hoist, join, point* and *poison*. (Also, we find *boy* [bwaɪ] as an interjection.) These pronunciations were widespread in Britain up until the nineteenth century (Cassidy and Le Page 1980: li).

Besides the common [aɪ] realization, a raised version of the /aɪ/ diphthong as [əi/ɐi] is common in words like *night* or *ripe* or *life*, i.e. when the following consonant is a voiceless obstruent. In open syllables, or when followed by a voiced consonant, a lower variant [aɪ] or [ɐɪ] is found. This is similar to 'Canadian Raising'. Trudgill has argued that this results from a process of 'reallocation' in the colonial dialect mixture situation (2004: 88). The picture is made more complex by the variable occurrence of a backed, lengthened and sometimes slightly rounded variant [ʌɪ] or [ɔɪ], when the following segment is voiced. This is illustrated by *tide* [tʌɪd], *flies* [flɔɪz], *child* [tʃʌɪl], *find* [fʌɪn]. It is mainly found among whites, notably in Utila. It is possible that this pronunciation reflects an influence of Southern or Midland English dialects on white Anglo-Caribbean; a similar vowel quality for the PRICE vowel is found in Barbados (Wells 1982: 584).

MOUTH /aʊ/

Many Utilians have a markedly wide diphthong. In contrast, a narrowed diphthong with raised centralized first element, approximately [ɵʊ], is characteristic of CECs, and is sometimes found in AfrBIE+. In AfrBIE+, there is velarization of a following alveolar stop, e.g. *outside* [ɵʊksaɪd].

THOUGHT /ɒː/

This vowel differs from the LOT vowel only in length. This can be seen in the pronunciation of the words *off* and *on* with the same vowel quality [ɒ] with a difference in length only: [ɒːf] versus [ɒn].

NEAR /i/; SQUARE /e/

There is substantial overlap in the range of realizations of these two phonemes. In general, white BIE realizations show a greater tendency to diphthongization. Many speakers have [eə] for both lexical sets, making *hear* and *hair* homophones. *Here* has a variety of realizations ranging from [hiːr]/[hiːər] to [hɛː] to [jɐ].

START /ar/, NORTH /ɒr/, FORCE /or/, CURE /ʊr/

In these lexical sets, BIE has preserved the same phonemes found in TRAP, LOT, GOAT and FOOT/GOOSE, respectively. This in effect was the situation in England before the loss of postvocalic *r* in the eighteenth century (Wells 1982: 212). The Scottish pattern of vowel contrasts before /r/ is maintained, and it is notable that *horse* and *hoarse* are kept distinct.

NURSE (/ʌː/)

The standard accents have merged the vowels in *learn*, *bird* and *burn* in one vowel, referred to by Wells as the NURSE vowel. BIE preserves the main vowel-quality distinctions, although speakers show varying tendencies to production of a front-type vowel or a low central or backed rounded vowel. For example, speakers are divided between those who have [ɪː] or centralized [ɨ] in *bird* and *burn* and those who have [ʌː] or [ɔː], the latter being perhaps an older and today slightly stigmatized form.

For many older speakers, words like *learn*, *stern*, *serve* and *search* are pronounced with a half-open back vowel [ʌː] or [ɔː], This would appear to be an independent development from earlier English dialects' use of a lowered vowel (perhaps [ɑː]) in words of this type; this was common for at least 250 years up until the mid eighteenth century, after which it gradually became a vulgarism (Wyld 1936: 214–15; see also evidence from ships' logs in Matthews 1935: 212).

happY (unstressed vowel)

The most common realization is [ɪ].

lettER, commA (unstressed vowels)

This varies between the most broad vernacular [a] and [ʌ] or [ə]. The word *water* pronounced [waːta] with full vowel in second syllable is regarded on the islands as stereotypical of a broad accent. Although the schwa sound is used variably by some BIE speakers, unstressed vowels tend on the whole to have the same quality as stressed vowels, only shorter.

Vowel lengthening and breaking

Especially in Utila, and mainly in the environment of a following /l/, nasal consonant, or /r/, the long vowels /eː/, /uː/, /oː/ and /ɒː/ are frequently subject to further lengthening: e.g. *field* [fiːːl], *name* [neːːm], *June* [dʒoːːn], *fear* [feːːr]. The lengthened vowel often gives rise to diphthongization, sometimes with syllable-breaking, e.g. fool [fuːːl], *school* [skoːːl], *small* [smɒːːəl], *rain* [reːːɪn], *home* [hoːəm], *years* [jeːːrrz], bread [breːːəd]. Lengthening of stressed vowels is identified by Williams (1985) as a feature of white West Indian English, particularly in Saba.

Vowel nasalization

Vowel nasalization in words with a Vn sequence is common, particularly in AfrBIE. In AfrBIE+, the nasal consonant is variably deleted in *down/town/around*: thus, *down* is rendered as [dəŋ] or [də̃]. Nasalization also affects back vowels and the /a/ vowel, making the latter more backed: e.g. *hunts* [hʌ̃ːs], *want* [wɑ̃ː]. The negator *don't* is sometimes represented by [du]; this rare appearance of close [u] is probably motivated by the need to distinguish the word from main verb *do* [dʊ].

3.1.3   Higher-level phonological features

There is no doubt that the prosody of BIE is deserving of further study, since at this stage only a few impressionistic comments can be offered. Many observers comment on the sing-song intonation. This is most marked in Guanaja, where rising intonation is extremely common.

The stereotypical Utilian drawl is characterized by lengthened vowels, which often become diphthongs or even form two distinct vowel nuclei (breaking). The speech of Roatan and Guanaja, particularly AfrBIE+ in Roatan, is often rapid, with vowels having a clipped quality. There is less variation in vowel length, and elision is extensive.

Certain words ending in [ɪ] may be pronounced with stress on the first syllable as in the standard accents, but with a raised pitch on the second syllable. Examples are *baby* [beːbí], *gully* [gʌlí], *candy* [kandé] and *water* [wɑːté].

There are many words in which stress falls on the syllable following the one which would bear primary stress in RP/GenAm. A few examples are *super^l:market*, *high^l:way* and *mis^l:chievous*.

3.2   Grammar

BIE owes its distinctive character to processes which involve approximation of the speech of earlier white settlers (in the Cayman Islands and subsequently in the Bay Islands) by black speakers, and variable accommodation to Afro-Caribbean speech by white speakers. In general terms, the outcome of linguistic contact was 'convergence'.

For analytical purposes, it is possible to identify 'polar' ethnic varieties together with a wide spread of intermediate varieties. It is convenient to refer to a 'continuum' with upper, mid and lower bands, even though transitions between lects are by no means as discrete and regular as this term suggests. In the description that follows, the term 'acrolect' is used on occasion. This refers here to speech that is closest to StE and at the extreme of the range considered in the study. It should not be taken to imply the existence of a post-creole continuum.

The black dialect of Bay Islanders, particularly in Roatan, conserves certain features that are regarded as typical of CECs. However, the view taken here is that, with the exception of certain features which entered the BIE speech-mix directly from creole-speaking territories, AfrBIE is the product of 'partial restructuring' of white Anglo-Caribbean (Graham 2005), a variety which itself had undergone koineization. For this reason, the term 'basilect' is avoided.

White BIE shows varying degrees of convergence with this partially restructured English. This can be seen in the varying levels of zero morphemes for noun plural, third person non-past, past tense, and the zero

Table 6.2 *Levels of zero morphemes for noun plural, third person non-past, past tense, and zero copula in Bay Islands English*

	6 highest Ø-users overall	6 lowest Ø-users overall
Ø noun plural	45–66	3–15
Ø 3rd. Sing.	67–100	0–46
Ø past tense	55–100	6–22
Ø copula	44–81	4–39

copula (Table 6.2). In my sample of twenty-five speakers, nine can be classi-fied clearly as 'white' (rather than 'mixed'), and thirteen as 'black'. The table below compares the percentage ranges of the six highest-ranked Ø-users overall (all black) and the six lowest-ranked Ø-users overall (all white).

What this demonstrates is the range of variation within BIE. It also suggests a polar opposition between black and white varieties, which indeed reflects the distinctness of their historical development against the background of the social divisions already spoken of. This, however, ignores the large degree of overlap that exists. The mid-range percentage values of all four variables are widely distributed between the ranges indicated above, and black, white and mixed-race speakers are represented in this broad mid range. For reasons of space, the figures demonstrating this are not given here.

In what follows, the following types of feature are presented:

1. Creole features found mainly in AfrBIE, particularly AfrBIE+, unless otherwise indicated.
2. Features which are most readily attributable to British dialect input, where selection, and in some cases simplification, has taken place in the Caribbean.
3. BIE features involving 'partial restructuring' over time as the result of long-term contact between black and white speakers. Although there is much overlap, the results differ somewhat between AfrBIE and tradi-tional AngBIE.

3.2.1 *'Creole' features*
Lists of anglophone 'creole' features have been compiled by linguists, enabling synchronic or diachronic comparisons to be made – see especially Hancock (1987), Schneider (1990) and Baker and Huber (2001). A careful study of the 'creole' features in BIE shows the presence of a great many such features, though some are only marginally present in the speech sample analysed in Graham (1997) (summarized in Graham 2005). Combinations of tense/aspect preverbal markers are absent, and distinctive forms of the creole copula are, if present at all, only very marginal, and are not included here.

Preverbal tense/aspect markers

Past

Bin, was/wuh, had and *did* are found as preverbal past markers in AfrBIE+. However, even in AfrBIE+, *bin* + Ø-verb as in example (1) is less common than main verb *bin* structures, e.g. *I bin there.*

(1)   The man weh [= who] raise me then he tell me this is your father
         . . . so ah've got ah bin meet im and get to know im

(2)   Ah wuh catch one of the turbo [= I caught hold of one of the
         turbos]

The source of *wuh* is any structure involving *was/were* in the superstrate, but a generalization of past-marking function has taken place in AfrBIE+.

(3)   The captain he was down on his belly, he had seasick the whole
         way

Here, *had* is combined with an adjective in AfrBIE. More generally, preverbal *had* indicates that relevance is to a past time period. The functions of preverbal *did* are illustrated in examples (91) and (114)–(118).

Future

Various condensed forms derived from StE *go(ing)* are used to indicate future with intentionality. These consist of the vowels [o] or [ɑ] with or without nasal coalescence, viz. [gon, go, gõ, gwan, ɑn, ɑŋ, ɑ̃]. This is strengthened by the addition of *a*:

(4)   Ah say tell im ah's a go make one bawmie fuh you now [bawmie
         is a type of cassava bread]

For prediction in hypothetical conditional sentences, [*gon*/gõ] is used.

(5)   When you kyaan buy they [gõ] *steal it*

For straightforward prediction from a present time perspective, the future is normally unmarked. Commenting on the future prospects of one young man paralysed as the result of a diving accident, a speaker said:

(6)   When he go then he (Øwill) be happy

This is part of a more general simplification process in AfrBIE+, by which auxiliary verbs do not feature in speakers' grammars.

Habitual

Preverbal *duh* (=[dʌ]), *da* or *a* is used to indicate habitual activity or behaviour. *Do* and *does* are also used.

(7)   He duh say too many things he duh get me vexed

(8)   They just a come in an go back [the planes from la Ceiba]

Completive

Preverbal *done* is used by all BIE speakers to indicate the completion of an activity or sometimes with non-verbal predicates to mark a pre-existing achieved state:

(9)   RG: I talked to him when he was in town
           S: Oh well you done see him

Sequences of three preverbal tense/aspect functors are also possible:

(10)   All of them been done had rot [i.e. the mamey apples had already become rotten]

Other verb phrase constructions

The use of existential structures with *had* or *got* is normal, where StE uses *there* and finite *be*.

(11)   It had a heavy rain this morning

(12)   Got one other man that was smart

Serial verb structures are present in AfrBIE+, though they do not display the range that is found in CEC basilects. They are often found in imperatives directed at children, as in (13):

(13)   Show mek I see [used in an Anancy story]

(14)   Go so full the bucket come back hurry [said rapidly]

The *say* complementizer (transcribed as *seh*) is found with the verbs *tell*, *hear* and *know*.

(15)   The tourists-them don't know seh Roatan is part of Honduras

Infinitive complements of verbs do not require a marker:

(16)   They tell we present weself

To emphasize that a dependent clause expresses purpose or directed activity, *for* or its variants *fuh* and *fi* are found in AfrBIE.

(17)   Ah neva use sweet soap fi bathe with yet you know

(18)   They gotta fuh know why

Example (18) parallels the Guyanese creole example cited by Winford (1993: 315): 'Ram gat fu mek plenty moni'.

Interestingly, there are also examples in AfrBIE of the *for to* infinitive.

(19)   They did that for to get disturb the people

(20)   tryin to push for to them to go to school

For to operates as a single morpheme, its use being associated with the expression of purposive behaviour. It is unclear which came first chronologically, the *fuh/fi* or the *for to* infinitive, and if the latter is found also in AngBIE.

Pronouns

With the exception of 1sg. and 3sg.f., the same forms are commonly used for subject and possessive: *you*, *he*, *we*, *they* [ðe/de]. The use of *fi-* prefixing is attested, though rare (21). *We-all* is also found (22). Sometimes, *him* or *them* may be employed as possessives. First person has subj. *ah* [aː] or occasionally *ahm* [aːm] and poss. [mi/mɪ]; 3sg.m. subj./poss. is generally *he* or gender-neutral [i], although notably, *her* is the norm for 3sg.f. poss.

(21)   da fi-mi pen [= that's my pen – example heard in a primary
             classroom]

(22)   Ahm savin we-all life

Subject and object personal pronouns are normally distinct as in StE. [a]/[mi], [i]/[ɪm], [ʃi]/ [ʌr], [ðe/dɛm]. However, *we* is used as subj./obj. in AfrBIE. In the Flowers Bay area of Roatan, *her* and *them* may be found as Subjects:

(23)   [hʌ] don't get up that early

(24)   Them plan to go away, them plan to sell out

In AfrBIE in Roatan and Guanaja, the form *annuh* [ɐnʌ] is frequent. Used as a subj./obj./poss. form, it corresponds to JC *unu*, but differs in that it can be used to address just one person as well as more than one.

(25)   If annuh don hush ah gon beat annuh [mother to her small child]

(26)   Ah'll beat the two of ye annuh

In (26), the use of *ye* [ji], a British dialectal form, with *annuh* as reinforcement, is striking.

There are other forms of the 2pl. pronoun. At least for some speakers, the morpheme *all* can be added to create the plural forms *all-they* (27) or *all-um* (29).

(27)   All-they live off lobster

The morphological process of adding *all* to a plural pronoun is probably the result of calquing from West African languages (Allsopp 1996: 26). In AfrBIE, it is unclear if this extends to the forms *all-you* and *all-we*, cited in the Dictionary of Caribbean English. Across BIE, *we-all* (see (28)) and *you-all* (subject) are fairly common.

On Utila, and particularly the Utila Cays, the 2pl. pronoun *among-you* is used for subject, object and oblique case:

(28)   We-all call among-you from the island gringos

This form (or *amongst-you*) is listed by Allsopp (1996: 29) as Grenadian or Guyanese, and Hancock (1987: 296) cites an example from St. Vincent. It may have been an innovation in one or in several contact varieties. Its presence in the white community of Utila Cays, which was among the earliest settlements exclusively of whites, is suggestive of an origin in earlier Anglo-Caribbean.

When referring to animates, and even sometimes inanimate objects, *he* or *she* is preferred to *it*. A third person singular neuter pronoun *um* [ʌm] is attested for both Roatan and Guanaja and for both ethnicities:

(29)   All-um pull um in together see

In (29), *um* refers to a seine net. The origin of this pronoun is disputed (Williams 2001), but variants are attested in many Atlantic anglophone creoles, and also in Caymanian. It is most likely that the latter is the immediate source of this feature, which evidence suggests may be an early product of language contact.

The use of a resumptive pronoun in subject position is related to topic-fronting, which is extremely common.

(30)   Is many young men roun here they pick this habit up

Noun phrases

One feature which tends to be restricted to AfrBIE is postnominal *-dem* as pluralizer. This generally occurs with a noun denoting a human group.

(31)   Me an my breda-dem wuh there too a lot [breda = 'brothers']

In contrast, all varieties of BIE make use of associative *an them*.

(32)   Oh they Bowman an them they was good plaiters in them days

Possession is indicated by two nouns in sequence without *'s*. In BIE generally, this is a linguistic variable comparable to plural *-s*/Ø.

Although *fi*-prefixing is rare overall (see (21)), the use of the construction Possessed + *for* + Possessor is found throughout BIE.

(33)   a cay out there for a white man

Another creole feature, general in AfrBIE and sporadic in AngBIE, is the use of 'indefinite specific' *one*. This determinative is used to individuate an entity, often to foreground it, but does not pick out a previously mentioned referent.

(34)   Somebody take it away from here on one plate – for stealin and rape [*it* refers here to a man's severed head]

For truly non-specific reference with a count noun, *a* is used, although zero article is more usual in AfrBIE, and is common across BIE. This is symptomatic of the loss of the StE count/mass noun distinction. The indefinite quantifiers *much/how much/so much* are used with both mass and count nouns.

(35)   900 yards, ah dunno how much acres that would be

Someone and *something* are treated as fully nominal, admitting the indefinite article.

(36)   Cassava's a heavy something

Negation

In AfrBIE+, the most characteristic forms are preverbal *no*, *na* or *not* (usually [nɒ]) and [dʊ], an adaptation of *don't*. In BIE generally, the extension of *na* and *not* to most structural contexts of negation is striking.

(37)   You [nɒ] *see im?* [= in this context 'you hadn't seen him?']

(38)   It [dʊ] be too thin, it be soft [referring to the texture of bawmie, a cassava bread]

Bimorphemic question forms

Interrogative words consisting of a questioning and a questioned element are typical of pidgins and creoles and are present in early Atlantic creole texts (Bruyn 1999). In (39), the question word serves as introducer of a subordinate clause.

(39)   Nobody didn know what part ah was

Adjectives

Hot, full, ripe and *dead* may occur with preverbal *had* (see also (3)). The construction *pass* + adjective is sometimes used for intensification, e.g. *it pass expensive*.

3.2.2 British dialect input

There are a number of features besides the *for to* infinitive ((19), (20)) which seem likely to have their origin in British dialects, although other sources may contribute (as with emphatic particle *na* below). Some have undergone minor adaptation. Most features are widespread, though some (see *thee* and *mines*, Scottish words, adjective structures, and *take and V* below) are more limited in their distribution.

Relativiser *weh*

In addition to the commonly occurring zero relativizer and the relative pronoun *that* (often in reduced form), BIE employs reduced forms of *what* [we/ʍe/wɑ/ʍɑ], regardless of animacy of the antecedent. The full form [wɑt] also occurs, though is less common.

(40)   Ah have some pumpkin under there [we] we bring on the farm

(41)   Then ah speak a little Spanish [wɑt] ah know

As in BIE, reduced forms are found in JC, Belize creole and across the Anglophone Caribbean. The *what* relativizer is 'ubiquitous' in English rural dialects (Wakelin 1984: 79).

Demonstrative determinative *them*

This feature, which is general in BIE, is noted by Wright (1906: 76) as present in all British and Irish dialects. There is a single instance of [ðe] in the BIE data, which may correspond to Scots *thae*. *Them* is not rigidly tied to plural count nouns, and likewise *that* is sometimes found with plural nouns.

(42)   Them big shot people in Coxen Hole they didn want give the poor people nothin

(43)   I don't fool with that highland cows

There is a single instance of demonstrative [ðə] in the BIE data, which may correspond to Scots *thae*.

Negation using *neva*

As in British dialects, *neva* can be used to negate in a non-emphatic way a past action or event; this is quite distinct from the StE use meaning 'not even once'. Its range of use is widened in BIE.

(44)   I never been down there for two days now (= 'I haven't been down there . . .')

In some varieties of BIE, *neva* may function as a general negator.

(45)   You neva need no cake for the people comin behind? (= 'you don't/won't need . .)

Negative concord

As in earlier English, patterns involving negative concord are the norm. This is true of AngBIE as well as AfrBIE, and the pattern extends to negative concord outside the clause. For some speakers, sequences of two negative preverbal markers are possible.

(46)   Nobody not interested in nothing like that now

(47)   It ain [dõ] have big ears [referring to the island rabbit]

(48)   They [nɒ] ain goin back [referring to mainlanders who come to
          the islands]

The personal dative construction

In StE, the benefactive meaning 'for X' may be expressed within the verb
phrase either by reflexives or indirect object constructions. The reflexive
can be regarded as a special case where X is co-referential with the subject.
In BIE, reflexive pronouns are present in the grammar, but for expressing
benefactive meaning in relation to the subject, they are replaced by object
pronouns.

(49)   I dug me five nest of egg that mornin

    This structure is found in some dialects of English found in the American
south, such as Appalachian English (Christian 1991); it is not considered to
be a form which originated in black speech.

Use of *it* as dummy subject in existentials

Besides the creole-like existential structures with *got / had*, there are two types
of structure with *be*, one using *there* as in standard dialects, the other using
dummy *it*.

(50)   It's a lotta money circulatin

    While *there* and *it* expletive forms are found in both AfrBIE and AngBIE,
the high frequency of dummy *it* in AngBIE suggests that this form originated
in the Anglo-Caribbean koiné. All that would have been necessary is a small
extension of the range of application of 'empty' *it* in structures such as 'it's a
nice day'.
    The same structure is also used for focusing purposes in discourse.

(51)   Time ran on that the war started or was on directly *it wuh* men
          started to go an ship out

    An alternative realization is clause-initial *iz* or [ɪs]:

(52)   [ɪs] many young men roun here they pick this habit up

Double modals

Sequences of two modal verbs with *might* as first element and *can* or *could* as
the second element are found.

(53)   He might could sell them down there

(54)   He thought she might couldn't born it

Double modals are a well-known feature of Scots, and *might could* is perhaps the most typical combination, though other modals are available for both slots (Millar 1993: 119–20).

The modal adverbs *might-be* and *oughta-be* participate in a parallel construction.

(55)   I might-be can put back enough to look after my children

(56)   If you can talk it you oughta-be can translate it

a-prefixing

The construction in which the prefix *a*- is followed by a present participle derives from OE *on* preceding a verbal noun, and was still present in various Midlands and some southern English dialects in the mid twentieth century (Wakelin 1977: 121); Upton, Parry and Widdowson (1994) list numerous examples mostly from northern and midland counties. In BIE, it is found with *be* and with verbs of starting and continuing:

(57)   Ah was still young an probably ah was still a-growin

(58)   They start a chasin and makin noise

(59)   He burst out a-laughin

(60)   They just keep a-jumpin

The pronouns *thee* and *mines*

A form with a long lineage in English, but not otherwise attested in the Caribbean, is second person singular *thee*.

(61)   I'll send him stay with thee (Roatan speaker to me, referring to
            her misbehaving son)

(62)   Get out or ah gwine lick thee

Wright (1906: 74) writes that *thee* 'is in use in almost all the dialects of England to express familiarity or contempt'; this is exactly the way it is employed in BIE, often to children.

The rarity of *thee* in Scotland, as reported in Wright's *English Dialect Dictionary* (1905), suggests a stronger English component in BIE. On the other hand, the possessive pronoun *mines* found in AngBIE suggests Scottish input.

Some Scottish words

In Scotland and Northern Ireland, the conjunction *whenever* is often used when referring to a specific time, whether this is punctual or extended. This usage has been noted as well in Appalachia and some parts of the American

South (Montgomery and Kirk 2001). It appears in AngBIE, though perhaps not in AfrBIE.

(63)   I will see my aunt whenever I get to La Ceiba.

Clause-final adversative *but* is a feature that is considered characteristic of Scots.

(64)   [Ø 1st sing. pronoun] thought a only roun to Honduras that happen but [*a* = it's]

While not confined to any particular dialect of the British Isles, a strong tendency to use *though* clause-finally may also be associated with Scots. This same tendency exists in BIE (see (109)).
     Propositional *to*, pronounced [te] and written as *tae*, is common in BIE, and can be used in the sense of 'until', as in Scots. Also found are *wouldnae*, *couldnae*, *doesnae*, and *usetae* (see (111)). The next example illustrates [te] and [wʌdne], as well as the AfrBIE [dʊ] (='don't').

(65)   [Our children] if you put them to college they not interested in stayin [te] the end . . . (The Spaniard) he know if you [dʊ] stay till the end to come out to college he wouldnae own the job

Adjective structures

The use of 'double comparatives' like *more easier*, *more scarcer*, double inflection as in *betterer/worserer* and generalization to yield *gooder/goodest* or *badder/baddest* are all recorded British dialectal forms (Wright 1906: 73–4).
     Reduplication or pairing of attributive adjectives is a common feature. Examples are *a wee wee tree*, *a lil young girl*, *a happy sweet life*. The first of these is distinctively Scots.

(66)   The spirit have more power nor a livin

Wakelin (1977: 119) lists *nor* as a variant of than, 'used throughout the north and (in scattered examples) the east and west midlands'.

The inceptive *take* and V construction

This structure, which lends a certain emphasis to the second verb, occurs in older English dialects, and also in Barbados (Niles 1980: 132)

(67)   Old Tom McFeal took and told that in court

Niles gives examples of this structure from southern and southwestern English dialects.

Utterance-final emphatic particle *na(h)* or *nuh*

(68)   He didn feel too good from the fever na

(69)   They's human like us nuh

Allsopp (1996: 407) describes *nuh* as a terminal tag found in the anglophone Caribbean, with the meaning 'adding friendly persuasion to a statement or request'. This fits BIE usage. Niles (1980: 130) gives examples from Barbadian English. There is some evidence of the use of a terminal interjection *nan* marking queries in earlier English dialects (the OED records its use in Sussex and Shropshire dialect: 'archaic by 19th century'), but Allsopp (1996) argues for West African substrate influence, citing Twi particles *no* and *ana*. Convergence of superstrate and substrate, with a degree of functional shift, could account for the feature, which functions both to add emphasis to statements and also as a question tag inviting listener assent.

3.2.3   BIE features involving 'partial restructuring'

Although direct linguistic evidence is lacking, it can be assumed that contact between white and black speakers in the Cayman Islands in the eighteenth and nineteenth centuries gave rise to forms of restructured English. This 'restructuring with convergence' has involved three main types of result. These are (1) omission of grammatical functors, (2) absence of grammatical forms or categories and creation of substitute structures, and (3) resetting of form–function relationships. These dynamic processes of adaptation can be seen throughout the BIE continuum, resulting in a wide variety of structures. While complex to describe, partial restructuring (by contrast with the radical restructuring that characterizes creole basilects) is the central defining feature of BIE.

Removal of grammatical functors

Considered from the point of view of British dialect input, processes of simplification in the interethnic contact variety resulted in variable loss of grammatical affixes and functors, including the copula. Ellipsis of many types of grammatical element is variable in BIE as a whole, though in certain constructions and for many speakers ellipsis is (near-) categorical.

Copula

In both AfrBIE and AngBIE, the copula is almost always present before a following NP, with much higher rates of omission before adjective, locative and V-ing forms (in increasing order). This matches the pattern found in studies of the 'creole copula' (Winford 1992). The fact that AngBIE patterns in a similar way to AfrBIE is strong evidence for convergence.

Verbal auxiliaries

Omission of auxiliary *Have* is general and omission of *will*/*would* is frequent.

(70)   The fishin business in this island (Ø-has) been pretty poor

(71)   When he go then he (Ø-will) be happy

(72)   What (Ø-do) you say master?

Across BIE, little use is made of auxiliary *do* in questions. Where an auxiliary is present (as in the case of modals) there is no subject–aux inversion. Rising intonation, generally placed on the last stressed word, distinguishes a polar interrogative from a statement.

(73)   You could come and live here?

   In the absence of intonational cues, a yes-no question may be signalled by the question tags *nuh* or *not true*.

(74)   You hear about Crawfish Rock nuh?

(75)   You didn know im not true?

Object pronouns (in addition to omitted subject pronouns)

(76)   Ah had done know the road so he couldn keep (Ø-me) there again
           no more

Relative pronoun with subject antecedent

(77)   Everybody in [is] town (Ø-relativizer) makes a dollar makes it off
           the sea

Subordinating conjunction *if* in conditionals

(78)   (Ø-if) ah ain got nothing (Ø-subj.) just go an look somebody goin
           fishin

Indefinite article

(79)   When I'm fishin here in (Ø-art.) dory I use (Ø-art.?) hand-line,
           when I'm fishin on (Ø-art.) boat I use reels

Infinitive marker *to*

(80)   Ah like (Ø-to) go in the bush

Preposition to

(81)   Ah wen (Ø-to) Oakridge.

Loss of grammatical forms/categories and their substitution

How and *Be*

The use of forms of *Have* and *Be* is central to StE passive and perfect constructions. The general loss of auxiliary *have/has* in BIE (it is infrequent even in the acrolect) has led to a number of substitute structures for StE perfect: present and past structures (82–84), *got/had* (85–6), and occasionally also substitution of *Have* by forms of auxiliary *Be* (=*am/are*) (87).

(82)   She don't come out yet [=hasn't come]

(83)   Ah didn bin in Tela to visit [=haven't visited]

(84)   Today the Spaniard took it over [=has taken]

(85)   I got about 26 years goin to the high seas

(86)   She only had two years since she left home [=it's only been]

(87)   This lady up here weh [=who] am open up this other hotel

Passive constructions are also substantially restructured. Only the *get* passive, with past participle or more commonly a verb base form, is found at all levels of the continuum.

(88)   We got more or less populated from Caymans

   In most varieties of BIE, the passive with past time reference is formed using either *was/wuh* or *been* followed by a past inflected or base form. The present tense passive with *Be* is less common. A frequent substitute is the 'basic passive' formed by a verb with a subject that cannot be given an agent role.

(89)   All the churches build close to the beach

(90)   They eats ripe ['they' = small chata bananas]

Structures using *V-ing* are sometimes used with the function of passive:

(91)   You did see them makin not true? [i.e. coconut breads]

In the StE passive, the nominal complement is raised to subject, but in BIE the resulting 'trace' may sometimes be filled by an explicit element after the verb, so that the construction may superficially resemble the active voice. The speaker in the next example is referring to the effects of a prolonged drought on his Seville orange trees ('they' in the following example).

(92)   They gonna just burnt it man no rain

Here, *it* is a placeholder element. Alternatively, a pronoun subject is copied after the verb and case-marked as object.

(93)   Now he's gone he is miss im

It is noteworthy that forms of the passive with *being* + verb are absent even in the acrolect, and the same applies to *to be* + verb. This is linked to the general weakness of the finite/non-finite distinction.

Finite/non-finite distinction

The finite/non-finite distinction is tenuous in BIE. Many speakers treat *Do* + lexical verb combinations as finite verb complexes where tense is marked on both elements:

(94)   I didn seen him when he come [both *seen* and *come* are non-standard past tense forms in BIE]

(95)   It's something that dozn goes into the wood

Instead of non-finite verb complements, BIE generally uses finite forms, often without *to*. The verb agrees in tense with the matrix clause verb, if the latter has tense explicitly marked.

(96)   The guy didn want gave none

(97)   What made me didn worry about them . . .

A special form of this is the 'manipulative predicate' with *must*, a creole structure (Winford 1993: 324).

(98)   They aks im mus walk with im

Even where *to* is present, as in the following examples, a kind of tense concord is followed (*had been* in (101) may be considered as the past form of *Be* specialized for non-finite use).

(99)   My sister hadda went and get her papers

(100)   Before he died he told her mother to don't told her that he had plenty property in Roatan

(101)   He told me that he want me to had been here, he want me spend the Christmas in Diamond Rock

Negation

Don't and *didn't* (pronounced [don] and [dɪdn]) are present in the grammars of all BIE speakers. This is in addition to *never*/*neva* used in both punctual and non-punctual contexts (see (44–45)). Indeed, the entire range of forms is quite consistent across BIE, apart from *doesn't* being absent in AfrBIE+. In most varieties, there is widening of the range of application of *don't* and *didn't* and also of *na/not*, and this occurs even in the case of speakers who show control of the StE forms.[3]

Present tense *don't* + ØV and past tense *didn't* + ØV are in all speakers' grammars, though *didn't* may be combined with a past marked verb:

(102)   They didn went no further

Not/na+ØV is commonly used in present, past, or present perfect contexts. *Ain* is employed by some speakers.

(103)   You na get no more of 'at [= 'you don't get any more of that']

(104)   This was her maybe just her first year here teachin here, she not understand anything in English [= 'she didn't understand . . .']

(105)   Ah not [dɛsaidɛ] yet [= 'I haven't decided yet']

(106)   He ain dive any more [= 'he doesn't dive any more']

The main use of *not* is in constructions with *Be* (or *ØBe* in the case of copula deletion). Only *not* may co-occur with *is* or *was*: the contracted form *wasn* is found, but not *isn't*. The absence of *isn't* may point to Scottish influence.

In general, *not* and *na* and *ain* occur in the same range of environments, including the future *go* + V structure. With *got*, constructions with *don't*, *not* and *ain* are all found, the latter two being more common. The detailed factors conditioning each variant remain to be investigated.

Resetting of form–function relationships

The cross-community language for interethnic communication which developed over time showed not just reduction of forms and substitution of patterns, but also new form–function mappings with an impact on the grammar. Some of the ways in which English was remoulded can be seen in the meanings and functions of *bin*, *did* and *had* in present-day BIE. A further example is the development of habitual marking with the *-s* suffix.

Relative tense-marking; *bin* and *had*

Within AfrBIE, we can observe patterns of synchronic variation that reveal something of how a 'creole' system of relative tense-marking co-exists with, and influences, the StE system based on a fixed deictic point of reference in Speaker Time (ST).

In AfrBIE+, *bin* is used to express the relevance of the event or state to a Reference Time before the present. It is not used to express temporal anteriority to the Reference Time, neither is it used to advance a narrative sequence once this has begun. This can be seen in example (1), repeated here.

---

[3] A preference for non-standard structures among such speakers may reflect a feeling that these are more 'authentic' forms: their use does not in all cases imply 'loss' (i.e. unavailability) of the StE forms.

(107)   The man weh [= who] raise me then he tell me this is your
           father . . . so ah've got ah bin meet im and get to know im

Pollard (1989) provides evidence of the use of *(b)en* in JC to mark information that has a supportive or backgrounding function, and this analysis
fits preverbal *bin* in AfrBIE+. Sometimes *bin* appears in this backgrounding
function with a verb that encodes how information was transmitted to the
speaker:

(108)   Many time ah bin hearin them say . . .

The principal carrier of relative past marking with a backgrounding function in BIE is *had* + ØV. This is used across the islands by speakers of both
ethnic groups.
    One context in which preverbal *had* often appears is in the presentation of
evidentiary sources using *hear*, *tell* or *say*.

(109)   You had hear about the hurricane though?

The use of *had* to mark primary relevance to a time before the present is
illustrated by the next example.

(110)   Beforetime now, the young girl-them they had know about raisin
           a chicken an helpin their Mama an Papa raise a hog

Had + ØV is not associated with temporal anteriority to some specified
time in the past:

(111)   When ah first moved down here ah usetae go tae dance an had
           plenty a funs but ah'm thankful to know that the Lord had touch
           my heart and ah had change that so now ah livin on a better life

Although *had* + ØV very often represents a 'remote past' context, this is
not invariably the case. Provision of less salient information is the key to its
use.

(112)   A coupla weeks ago ah went round there an she had one she had
           give me a piece man that wuh real real nice

The same white speaker provides the next example, where preverbal *had*
has a narrative staging function at the start of a hunting story. Here, *had* is
combined with a past verb form:

(113)   A coupla days ago me an one lil boy had went with some dog
           from up the road

Approximation of the form of StE past perfect, as here, is often associated
with a relative tense-marking system rather than with marking chronological
anteriority to a past Reference Time (RT). The co-existence of both systems
in a speaker's grammar means that a structure identical or very similar to
StE may be used with a different meaning.

In contrast, use of the non-standard *had* + *done* + ØV does involve the encoding of temporal anteriority to a past RT. This structure occurs with both unmarked and past-marked verb forms, and is available even in AfrBIE+, so that it can be regarded as a 'bridge' between the two systems involving *had*. It allows the meaning of StE past perfect to be conveyed unambiguously even when an unmarked verb is used:

(114)   The man had done talk Sam about it

Functions of *did*

Winford (1993: 65) claims that in CEC mesolects, a similar supportive function to *(b)en* is realized by *did*, which is also a relative tense-marker. This is debatable for preverbal *did* in BIE. Largely absent as question-forming auxiliary, and replaced by *done* as a past tense form of the lexical verb, *did* has a range of other functions in BIE, which are illustrated in (115)–(118).

(115)   Ah forget that she did ava go down one hill [describing a bicycle running out of control]

(116)   They ever did give him but he would shove it in his pocket

(117)   We never did get ah'd have to say get to any school

(118)   He born the thirteenth an ah did born the fourteenth

Did may mark a degree of highlighting of a salient fact (115), or it may be used in habitual/iterative contexts (116). It occurs frequently with *never* in a highlighting function (117). *Did* may mark tense with certain stative predicates like *born* and *worth* (118).

Stripped-down perfect *bin* and stressed *BIN*

The present perfect with a past-inflected verb or participle is found in the mid to upper range of BIE; when present, it is generally used in accordance with StE, i.e. with Speaker Time (ST) as the deictic reference point. In the lower range, *had* may be substituted for *has/have*:

(119)   I never had been that distant yet [with RT=ST]

Non-realization of auxiliary *have* has the consequence that lexical verb *bin* develops a general experiential meaning with past reference:

(120)   Codumel, Isla Mujer, boy ah bin all about roun them place . . . ah went plenty places

The absence of an auxiliary linking the predication to a present or past RT allows the stripped-down 'bare *bin*' structure to be used unrestrictedly with reference to any past time period. In the next example, the speaker is referring to the notorious nineteenth-century pirate Lafitte:

(121)   Lafitte he even bin all up to Cape Gracias.

When *bin* is used with *V-ing*, the structure enters into contrast with *was+V-ing*. *Bin* retains its function of marking primary relevance to a past timeframe. There is no implication of continuation of the state or activity into the present, as with StE present perfect progressive.

(122)   My mother bin livin then in Helene [the mother no longer lives in Helene]

(123)   Ah [bɪ] [=bin] signin check with that name Blinky, signin check an neva come back neitha [the check-signing may have been at any time in the past]

(124)   An she say she bin seein those Spaniard get the machete an walk to one nother an chop that head off [a middle-aged speaker is recounting her mother's experience of living on the mainland during the banana boom era]

The difference between this structure and *was/wuh+V-ing* is that *bin+V-ing* sets the state or activity within a non-specific past timeframe, while *was/wuh* provides a local frame for a narrative event in the same way as in StE.

With *bin+V-ing*, there is no indication whether the time frame involved was long or short, nor (in the case of non-statives) whether the event was reiterated or not. BIE does, however, have a specific means of encoding 'for a long time'. This is by means of stressed 'Remote Phase' BIN (described in Rickford 1974).

(125)   RG:Do you spend any time at all on the mainland or most of the time you spend
         C: Yeah I BIN livin there for some years
         [C is not actually living on the mainland at present]

Note that as with comparable uses of unstressed *bin* (121), it is not necessary that the situation is continuing up to the present. This marks a difference from African American English (AAE) Remote Phase Continuative BIN, described in Green (1998). Another difference is that BIE does not allow the use of *BIN having* or *BIN knowing*, as found in AAE (Green 1998). Other uses of Remote Phase BIN in BIE conform to the pattern documented for AAE: a state which has been in existence for a considerable time (including being in a given place), or an event which took place a relatively long time ago. BIN 'situates the initiation of a state in the remote past, and the state continues until the moment of utterance' (Green 1998: 133).

(126)   I BIN had it ready. I waitin on you

(127)   It's not too long that this bin in vogue but these house that BIN there they wouldn move them

With non-statives, BIN indicates that the event took place a long time ago:

(128)   It BIN gone up the road [referring to a truck that functioned as the community taxi]

Modal *shoulda* + *BIN* can be used to comment on the inordinate length of time elapsed since an event was expected to occur:

(129)   He shoulda BIN bring them up here

Verbal *-s* and habitual marking

Habitual aspect is marked in the verb group in at least six ways in BIE: by the use of a preverbal marker *doz*, *duh*, *da* or *a* (the last two being found only in AfrBIE+), *would* + V, zero-marked verb in past contexts, *useta*, the verb ending *-s*, and invariant Be(s).

The preverbal markers *duh* and *a* were illustrated in (7) and (8). At least in the form *does*, a habitual structure can also be negated. The speaker has been asked if people fish at night:

(130)   In the night they [do] does do that ([do] = 'don't')

Would(a) + V is used to express past habitual meaning (mainly in AngBIE):

(131)   Who did the most shoutin in the air and the most beerin woulda
           win

In a past narrative, *would* (or other past marker) is often omitted when habitual meaning is inferable:

(132)   What ah could feed hogs on today is what ah have to eat, because
           he always had good potatoes, cocoes, yams

Useta is mainly used in past time contexts, although it also occurs with non-past reference, indicating a present pattern of behaviour:

(133)   He just now useta go to the States

In verbs with non-past and non-future time reference, the *-s* ending (*V-s*) occurs variably in all persons. Overall, it is most frequent in third person singular, where it serves to mark number concord as in StE, followed by third person plural. It is rare in second person.

(134)   When the tree fall they inspects it to see if it have branches and
           they inspect the branches to see if there's any hollow

This example illustrates the typical pattern of zero inflection on the verb in a time clause (also the pattern in 'real' conditional clauses), and variability in the marking of habitual aspect. There is, however, a much stronger tendency for habitual meaning to be associated with *V-s* than with *V-Ø*.[4]

The extent to which *-s* is grammaticized as a habitual marker is brought out in the next example, where it unusually attaches to a *V-ing* form:

---

[4] In Graham (1997: 201) tokens of non-concord *V-s* (non-3sg. tokens) and the same number of non-3sg *V-Ø* tokens were coded as either 'habitual' or 'neutral': the respective percentages for habitual meaning were 71 per cent and 32 per cent.

(135)   They didn useta be drinkin like how they doins these days

V-s habitual marking extends to *Have* and *Be*. The latter is interesting because invariant *be* is also used aspectually, so that strictly *-s* is redundant.

(136)   It mostly bes by the dock where we stays

(137)   When you not use to them boy it be hard to pelt off you know so much hundred of them you gotta pelt off [speaking of lobster traps]

One source of aspectual *be* is reduction of *do / does be*:

(138)   That why I do be askin him to heal me . an I be askin him oh yeh

One problem is that although *do / does be* also co-occurs with locatives, it would seem to have a more limited range than *be(s)*, which also collocates with adjectives and nominals:

(139)   It [a he-crab] bes bigger than the she-one

(140)   They have a clown inside the pole but he don have to plait . . . C always be that for us

For some black speakers, invariant *be* can be used to signify any non-varying state:

(141)   He tell us why he be Christian

All uses of *be* except this one (but not *bes*) can be negated using *don't* or *doesn't*.

Speakers with low levels of concord *V-s* (i.e. 3sg.) tend also to have low levels of non-concord *V-s* and to use invariant *be* rather than *bes*. On the other hand, some of the highest frequencies of non-concord *V-s* are found in AngBIE. This suggests that habitual *V-s* has developed out of a pattern of *V-s* marking in all persons in the early British dialectal input to what became Anglo-Caribbean (habitual *V-s* is a shared feature of the white varieties described in Williams 1987).

The pattern of *V-s* marking in all persons was widespread in British dialects by the end of the eighteenth century, although a particular pattern, whereby *V-s* was found with plural nouns though not with pronouns, was particularly associated with Scotland and the north of England. In Graham (1997), I investigated whether the Northern Subject Rule applies in BIE, but identified only a weak tendency. On the other hand, a VARBRUL study of variation between forms of finite *Be* and Ø-copula found a very strong statistical association between the use of *is / 's* and noun plural subjects. In white BIE at all levels, a pronoun subject favoured *'re*.[5] This pattern is typical of Scots.

---

[5] The Northern Subject Rule was also found to apply in AfrBIE>, though slightly less strongly. The main difference between this group and AngBIE was a tendency to favour *'s* rather than *'re* with pronominal subjects. Overall, the results suggest convergence of AfrBIE toward a traditional AngBIE pattern of use of finite *be*.

A periphrastic *do* structure (once much more widely found than now), invariant *be* and *V-s* in all persons were most likely present in the eighteenth-century British/Irish dialectal input which came to be reformed into Anglo-Caribbean. The seventeenth- and early eighteenth-century ships' logs examined by Bailey and Ross (1988) contain all these features. It is likely that there was already some association between periphrastic *do/does* and the expression of habitual meaning, given that habitual markers in CECs appear to have been modelled on these forms in the superstrate. A source for habitual *be* is the phonological reduction of *does be* to [z bi], followed by the loss of [z] (Rickford 1974: 105). Invariant *be* in the superstrate would then have become invested with habitual meaning in the intercommunal speech variety. Alternatively, the [z] could have reattached enclitically to *be*, giving *bes*. In the same manner, a gradual grammaticization of habitual *V-s* would be assisted by reattachment of reduced form [z] to lexical verbs. That this is a real possibility is suggested by the co-occurrence of both types in the final example.

(142)   They stays with the heft of the money and then theys keep a building theirself up [theys < 'they does']

Such processes could only take place in conditions where there was a strong disposition to mark habitual aspect. Central American English creoles (see Escure 2004) employ *de* as a marker of both categories of imperfective – progressive and habitual – but the precursor to BIE would already have had *V-ing* for progressive, so that only habitual remained to be marked. As in creole-forming contact situations, this was achieved by matching a selection of resources from the superstrate together with reallocation of functions to accommodate the semantics of substrate languages. Forms deriving from *do-does* and *V-s* marking of habitual were the result. Over time, *V-s* appears to have become the preferred form among traditional AngBIE speakers and for converging AfrBIE speakers, while a preverbal marker has remained in use among some traditional speakers, particularly in AfrBIE.

3.3   *Lexis*

The vocabulary of BIE reflects the various sources which have shaped its development. In most cases, we cannot say how the words arrived in the Bay Islands, whether from Britain, the Cayman Islands, Jamaica, the Mosquito Coast of Honduras, or Belize. In any case, BIE has preserved many words and usages which were current in British/Irish vernaculars of the nineteenth century and earlier. A large number of these are shared with the Mosquito Coast Creole (MCC) of Nicaragua; Holm (1980) found that the highest percentage of traceable British dialect vocabulary in MCC (as listed in Wright 1905, henceforth EDD) was Scots or North Country in origin. A caveat is that pre-nineteenth-century, some of the words and usages may have had a wider distribution.

The most probable regional origin of the following selection of BIE words, based on EDD, is indicated by the abbreviations Sc (Scotland), NC (North Country), Ir (Ireland), S/M (Southern/Midlands), WC (West Country), HC (Home Counties around London). Words with a wider, though still restricted, distribution in British dialects are indicated as 'Dial'. Most of the items marked as 'archaic' have latest attestations in OED no later than the nineteenth century.

Sc: *a blow* (= a rest); [gi] (= give); *mines* (= mine); *thonder* (= yonder); *wee*

Sc/NC: *dodge* (= hide); *fass* (= meddle); *punish* (= suffer); *reach* (= arrive); *soon* (= early)

Sc/Ir: *learn* (= teach); *dotin*/*doted* (= senile)

Ir: *bog* (= become stuck)

Ir/NC: *carry* (= take)

NC/HC: *mannish* (= impudent)

S/M: *heft* (= weight)

WC: *pitch* (= land)

Dial: *gedderin* (= a boil); *limber* (= pliant); *onliest* (= only); *whicker* (= neigh); *yonder* (= over there).

Archaic: *beforetime* (= in the past); *beg* (= ask for); *bide* (= stay in a place); *do*, in phrase *what do* ──── ? (= what is wrong with ──── healthwise?); *engage* (= to place an order); *favour* (= resemble); *form* (= pretend); *gig* (= spinning-top); *glass* (= mirror); *punish* (= suffer); *tinnen* (= tin metal) *wish* (= want).

An interesting archaism is the use of *without* meaning 'unless':

(143)   She not gonna marry again without she find a husband like him

Likewise the two conjunctions used in place of 'except' have a slightly archaic ring:

(144)   The liberals don't have but very few seats.

(145)   You pick the bone-them out, outside that you can't eat him

Conjunctions with an intrusive -*n* at the end include *becausin*, *besiden*, *whichin*, *iffen*; the first three have a loose clausal linking function. Such forms are found in CECs (see Cassidy and Le Page 1980 and Allsopp 1996): *Whichin* may have been spread via Irish/English bond-servants in Barbados (Edwards 1990), and the same may apply to the other cases (*becausin* has also been noted in Black AmE; Allsopp 1996: 88). This -*n* is not to be confused with the reanalysis which produces the forms *fishenin* and *huntenin*.

Some archaisms in BIE are shared with Barbadian (see Allsopp 1996): e.g. *blackguard* (to abuse with strong language); *ever* in the sense of 'always'. *Either* in the sense of 'any' and *neither* in the sense of 'no/not any' are also found in Barbadian – and interestingly are also listed in the *Dictionary of Newfoundland English* (Story et al. 1999).

(146)   We didn punish either day for nothing to eat.

(147)   It's not neither year I don't have breadkind

Nautical English is responsible for many typical BIE usages. These include: *hoise* (pron. [hais] = raise); *haul up* (= move in a certain direction); *heave* (pron. [hɪq] = to throw down something forcefully); *spyglass* (telescope); *tack* (pron. [taɪk] = change direction (also figurative)); *tackle* (pron. [teːkɪl] = pulley).

African substrate influence is responsible for the use of *hand* for 'arm and hand'; likewise for *foot* = leg and foot. *Joog* (= to prick, cf. JC *jook*) derives from a Fulani word. The word for Indian artefacts, *yabbadingding*, is partly derived from the Twi word for an earthen pot. Many common words are shared with most Caribbean varieties, e.g. *breadkind* (starchy vegetables); *mauger* (= thin); *duppy* (ghost); *pop* (= break); *renk* (= foul-smelling); *tief* (= steal). The infinitive forms *to broke, to left, to married* are characteristic of CECs. The use of *make* for *let* as in *make me explain* is also characteristic, as is the use of *one* as an adverbial complement of personal pronouns: e.g. *me one* = me alone.

Similarly, certain adaptations of StE meaning are shared with CECs: *directly* (= exactly/specifically as well as later/soon); *fit* (= nearly ripe); *next* (= other); *scorn* (= find repulsive). A few words may be shared only with West Caribbean varieties (e.g. *buck* = strike against, *buck up* = meet), Caymanian (e.g. *back* = carry) or Belize (e.g. *lone* + noun = *only*). Some may possibly be unique to the Bay Islands (e.g. *bunkie* = buttocks; *pucky* = muddy; *fud/furt* = far; *hant* = ghost). Like other Caribbean Englishes, BIE shows a tendency to augment lexemes with a particle: *brag off, change up, steal out, drunk-up.* Neologisms using English affixes include *sailorise* (= go to work at sea), *conversate, murderation.* From the Miskito language, BIE has borrowed a few words such as *cohone* (= a type of palm), *duori* (= simple boat), *weewee* (= leaf-ant) and *wishy-willy* (a kind of iguana). Spanish influence on traditional BIE was limited, although some words were thoroughly integrated into everyday speech, and given English inflections as appropriate. Some examples noted in 1990–92 are *aguantar* (to put up with), *aprovechar* (make use of), *castigar* (to punish), *cobrarin* (getting paid), *pasearin* (strolling), *vagarin* (loafing around), *jalón* (lift), *mandado* (errand), *pasaje* (fare), *prensa* (gossip), *tía* (aunt). Transfer of meaning from Spanish is occasionally observable, e.g. in *gain* (= earn < Sp. *ganar*) and the common use of *molest* (= bother < Sp. *molestar*), also in a few fixed expressions like *what time you have?* or *when I had three month* (= when I was 3 months old).

4   Conclusion

Bay Islands English presents many examples of retention, mutual convergence and innovative restructuring and displays a fascinating range of varieties in contact. The metaphor of convergence is apt, given the continuous history of cross-influence between varieties which has formed its complex character. Clear traces remain of the role played by British dialectal input, for example in the provision of verbal *-s* in all persons and in the lexis. The British input was subjected to processes of levelling, simplification and a degree of reanalysis in the ancestor variety, white Anglo-Caribbean, as this was formed over a considerable period via contact with black approximative varieties. Black varieties have been influenced more directly by contact with creoles via speakers of Jamaican and Belize Creole (or the undocumented earlier Miskito Coast Creole of Honduras).

The broad spectrum of varieties in contemporary BIE reflects ethnic and inter-island differences, so that only a general picture has been presented. The many changes of the last decade will have brought certain changes to speech which unfortunately could not be documented here. The influx of tourists, particularly from North America, and the presence of many foreign residents, will have provided new models of speech which younger islanders may have partially adopted. These new influences serve only to deepen the already considerable complexity of BIE.

Economic development has proceeded apace while the ethnic composition of the islands has continued to change, with mainlanders accounting for an ever-increasing proportion of the population. While accepting their membership of two language communities, islanders remain proud of their English-speaking identity, and resentful of the cheap labour influx. One of the greatest challenges for the islands' leaders is to develop English literacy, amongst many other skills, so that all native Bay Islanders can benefit from widened employment horizons. The recent creation of the Bay Islands Free Trade zone opens up many possibilities for reinvestment of money now freed of the burden of taxation. It is to be hoped that the challenges of the present and future will be met in ways that enhance the vitality of English, ensuring its continuing presence in this cultural border-zone.

References

Allsopp, Richard. 1996. *Dictionary of Caribbean English Usage*. Oxford: Oxford University Press.

Bailey, Guy and Garry Ross. 1988. 'The shape of the superstrate: Morphosyntactic features of Ship English.' *English World-Wide* 9/2: 193–212.

Baker, Philip and Magnus Huber. 2001. 'Atlantic, Pacific, and world-wide features in English-lexicon contact languages.' *English World-Wide* 22/(2): 157–208.

Bruyn, Adrienne. 1999. 'Early forms of question words and relativizers in Atlantic English Creoles.' In Philip Baker and Adrienne Bruyn, eds. *St Kitts and the Atlantic Creoles.* London: University of Westminster Press, 289–314.

Cassidy, Frederick and Robert Le Page. 1980. *Dictionary of Jamaican English.* Cambridge: Cambridge University Press.

Christian, Donna. 1991. 'The personal dative in Appalachian speech.' In Peter Trudgill and Jack Chambers, eds. *Dialects of English: Studies in Grammatical Variation.* London and New York: Longman, 11–19.

CIA Country Facts website. www.cia.gov/cia/publications/factbook/geos/ho.html (accessed 19 March 2008).

Davidson, William. 1974. *A Historical Geography of the Bay Islands of Honduras.* Birmingham, Ala.: Southern University Press.

Decker, Ken and Lee Henriksen. 2002. 'A Report on the English of the Bay Islands of Honduras.' Summer Institute of Linguistics.

Edwards, Walter. 1990. '*Whichin* in Guyanese Creole.' *International Journal of Lexicography* 3/2: 103–10.

Escure, Genevieve. 2004. 'Belize and other Central American varieties: Morphology and syntax.' In Bernd Jortmann, Edgar W. Schneider, Kate Burridge, Rajend Mesthrie, and Clive Upton, eds. *A Handbook of Varieties of English*, vol. II: *Morphology and Syntax.* Berlin: Mouton de Gruyter, 517–44.

Evans, David. 1966. *The People of French Harbour.* Unpub. PhD dissertation. University of California, Berkeley.

Graham, Ross. 1997. *Bay Islands English: Linguistic Contact and Convergence in the Western Caribbean.* Unpub. PhD dissertation. University of Florida.

2000. 'The Bay Islands English: Stages in the evolution of cultural identity.' In Oliver Marshall, ed. *English-speaking Communities in Latin America.* London and New York: Macmillan and St. Martin's Press, 287–313.

2005. 'Partial creolization, restructuring and convergence in Bay Islands English.' *English World-Wide* 26/1: 43–76.

Green, Lisa. 1998. 'Remote past and states in African-American English.' *American Speech* 73: 115–38.

Griffin, Wendy. n.d. *The Past, Present and Future of English Speakers on Honduras' North Coast.* Unpublished monograph.

Hancock, Ian. 1987. 'A preliminary classification of the Anglophone Caribbean creoles, with syntactic data from thirty-three representative dialects.' In Glenn Gilbert, ed. *Pidgin and Creole languages: Essays in Memory of John E. Reinecke.* Honolulu: University Press of Hawaii, 264–334.

Harper, Matthew. 2005. 'When pirates ruled . . .' www.bayislandsvoice.com/issue-v3-3.htm (accessed 23 July 2009).

Holm, John. 1981. 'Sociolinguistic history and the creolist.' In Albert Highfield and Arnold Valdman, eds. *Historicity and Variation in Creole Studies.* Ann Arbor: Koroma, 40–51.

ed. 1983. *Central American English.* Heidelberg: Julius Groos Verlag.

1989. *Pidgins and Creoles.* Cambridge: Cambridge University Press.

Houlson, Sarah. 1934. *Blue Blaze: Danger and Delight in Strange Islands of Honduras*. Indianapolis: Bobbs Merrill.

Jones, David and Carlyle Glean. 1971. 'The English-speaking communities of Honduras and Nicaragua.' *Caribbean Quarterly* 17: 50–61.

Matthews, W. 1935. 'Sailors' pronunciation in the second half of the seventeenth century. *Anglia* 39: 193–251.

Meyer, Harvey and Jeanette Meyer. 1994. *A Historical Dictionary of Honduras*. Metuchen, N.J.; London: Scarecrow Press.

Miller, Jim. 1993. 'The grammar of Scottish English.' In James Milroy and Lesley Milroy, eds. *Real English: The Grammar of English Dialects in the British Isles*. London and New York: Longman, 99–138.

Montgomery, Michael and John Kirk. 2001. '"My Mother, Whenever She Passed Away, She Had Pneumonia": The history and functions of *whenever*.' *Journal of English Linguistics* 29: 234–49.

Niles, Norma. 1980. *Provincial English Dialects and Barbadian English*. Unpub. PhD dissertation. University of Michigan, Ann Arbor.

Pollard, Velma. 1989. 'The particle *en* in Jamaican creole: A discourse-related account.' *English World-Wide* 10/1: 55–68.

Rickford, John. 1974. 'The insights of the mesolect.' In David De Camp and Ian Hancock, eds. *Pidgins and Creoles: Current Trends and Prospects*. Washington, D.C.: Georgetown University Press, 92–117.

Ryan, James. 1973. 'Blayk is white on the Bay Islands.' *University of Michigan Working Papers in Linguistics* 1/2: 128–39.

Schneider, Edgar. 1990. 'The cline of creoleness in the English-oriented creoles and semi-creoles of the Caribbean.' *English World-Wide* 11/1: 71–113.

Stonich, Susan. (2000). *The Other Side of Paradise: Tourism, Conservation and Development in the Bay Islands*. Elmsford, N.Y.: Cognizant Communication Corp.

Story, George Morley, W. J. Kirwin, and John David Allison Widdowson 1999. *Dictionary of Newfoundland English* (2nd edn). Toronto: University of Toronto Press.

Trudgill, P. 2004. *New-Dialect Formation: The Inevitability of Colonial Englishes*. Edinburgh: Edinburgh University Press.

Upton, Clive, David Parry and John Widdowson. 1994. *Survey of English Dialects: The Dictionary and Grammar*. London: Routledge.

Wakelin, Martin. 1977. *English Dialects: An introduction*. 2nd edn. London and Atlantic Highlands, N.J.: Athlone Press.

1984. 'Rural dialects in England.' In Peter Trudgill, ed. *Language in the British Isles*. Cambridge: Cambridge University Press, 70–93.

Warantz, Elissa. 1983. *The Bay Islands of Honduras*. In John Holm, ed. *Central American English*. Heidelberg: Julius Groos, 71–94.

Wells, John. 1982. *Accents of English*. Cambridge: Cambridge University Press.

Williams, Jeffrey. 1985. 'Preliminaries to the study of the dialects of white West Indian English.' *Nieuwe West Indische Gids* 59: 27–44.

1987. *Anglo-Caribbean English: A Study of its Sociolinguistic History and the Development of its Aspectual Markers*. PhD dissertation. University of Texas, Austin.

2001. 'Arguments against a British dialect source for *um* in Bajan English Creole.' *Journal of Pidgin and Creole Linguistics* 16/2: 355–63.

Winford, Donald. 1992. 'Another look at the copula in Black English and Caribbean creoles.' *American Speech* 67.1: 21–60.

1993. *Predication in Caribbean English Creoles.* Amsterdam: Benjamins.

Wright, James. 1905. *English Dialect Dictionary.* Oxford: Oxford University Press.

1906. *English Dialect Grammar.* Oxford: Oxford University Press.

Wyld, Henry C. 1936. *A History of Modern Colloquial English.* 3rd edn. Oxford: Basil Blackwell.

7   Euro-Caribbean English varieties

JEFFREY P. WILLIAMS

1   Introduction

This chapter describes a continuum of lesser-known varieties of English spoken in small, relatively isolated enclave white communities in the West Indies that I refer to here as Euro-Caribbean English.[1] The white minority that is in focus in this chapter is not the white elite that are so often thought of in any use of the cultural descriptor 'white.' Instead, this is a group that has not made any historical claims to social privilege. They have been traditionally referred to as 'poor whites' or more derogatorily as 'Redlegs', although most white West Indians refer to themselves as being 'clear-skinned people'.

The geography of whiteness and of the Euro-Caribbean English (ECE) varieties spans the circum-Caribbean region even including areas that are typically considered to be outside the region, such as the Bahamas (see Reaser, this volume) and Bermuda. The region where varieties of Euro-Caribbean English are spoken covers more than 2,754,000 square kilometres; however, the communities that speak these dialects are scattered widely and thinly throughout. In most cases, the communities where ECE is spoken are very small, typically numbering less than one hundred individuals.

What makes the dialects of Euro-Caribbean English lesser-known varieties of English and why? Trudgill (2002: 30) first uses the term 'lesser-known varieties of English' to refer to a set of relatively ignored, native varieties of English in more obscure parts of the anglophone world. The sociolinguistic features that further define the lesser-known varieties of English are:

  i.   that they are identified as distinct, salient varieties within the sociolinguistic environment;
  ii. that they are the mother-tongue varieties spoken within established communities whose external boundaries are relatively impermeable;
  iii. that they are frequently taken to be identity carriers by their respective communities;

---

[1] Elsewhere I have referred to these varieties as Anglo-Caribbean English (e.g. Williams 1988).

iv.   that they were typically originally transmitted by settler communities, or adopted by newly formed social communities that emerged early in the colonial era;

v.   that they have been shaped by the processes of dialect/language contact;

vi.   that they are often endangered.

This list of six features clearly defines the origin, status and structure of the dialects of Euro-Caribbean English. Point (v) above addresses Mufwene's (2008) concerns regarding a lack of focus on the role of contact in the evolution of the varieties of English spoken by European Americans. Instead of viewing the lesser-known varieties of English as following a different structural path in their geneses, I view them as evolutionarily parallel.

Why have researchers ignored these varieties of English? Many of the communities where varieties of ECE are spoken have been characterized as being closed to outsiders. For example, in his ethnographic study of kinship and family life on the island of Carriacou, the cultural anthropologist M. G. Smith writes of the village of Windward and Carriacou's dependency at that time, Petit Martinique:

Like Petit Martinique, Windward is a closed community, and together they contain about one-sixth of the Carriacou population. In view of their social and cultural peculiarities and numerical insignificance, I did not attempt to study either community in detail; and except for the survey of domestic groupings, which included fifty households at Orange Vale and Windward, my account does not refer to those villages except where they are specifically mentioned. (Smith 1962: 29)

In spite of the fact that this was written over forty years ago, the belief that these enclave communities are closed still persists.[2] Communities of Euro-Caribbean English speakers have been socially secluded from the remainder of the population on the islands where they are found. This social isolation has lead to the conservative and emblematic nature of these varieties of English. However, social isolation has not necessarily entailed geographical isolation. In the case of the Mount Moritz enclave community on Grenada, the village is in very close proximity to St. George's – the capital of the island. The same geographical situation holds for the Dorsetshire Hill community on St. Vincent, which is within walking distance of the town centre of Kingstown – the capital and most populous town on the island. Notwithstanding the proximity of these communities to the major population centres of Grenada and St. Vincent, these enclave

---

[2] In the relatively recent popular non-fiction account of several enclave white communities, Orizio (2001) presents these groups as living in deliberate isolation, clinging to false notions of racial superiority. Orizio's book is an unfortunate account of how the colonial attitudes to whiteness continue into the present day.

populations, like most others in the region, have been 'invisible' to most of the outside world.

Table 7.1 provides an inclusive listing of both the documented extant communities in which a variety of Euro-Caribbean English is spoken as well as those communities which are attested in historical sources but are known to no longer exist.

Many of these varieties remain completely undocumented and undescribed, with some of the most important varieties being only minimally described, such as Euro-Barbadian English (EBE). With approximately forty communities where Euro-Caribbean English is spoken, it would prove impossible to provide information on each and every variety in a chapter such as this; so instead I will focus on Euro-Anguillian English (EAE) and incorporate comparative data from other islands where relevant.

2   Sociolinguistic history and current status of Euro-Caribbean English

The vast majority of speakers of Euro-Caribbean English dialects are the descendants of indentured servants, *engagés*, sojourners and small-scale planters who were part of the European colonization of the West Indies which began in earnest in the seventeenth century. The earliest permanent English settlement in the West Indies took place on St. Kitts in 1624, with Barbados following closely behind in 1627. These two locations became the dispersal points for servants, settlers, merchants and other founder-populations in the anglophone Caribbean.

Barbados quickly became a major destination point for the transportation of the landless poor, religious dissenters, political enemies and other groups that were marked as 'undesirables' within mainstream seventeenth-century English society. A large portion of those who were transported became the backbone of the labour force in seventeenth-century Barbados and other parts of the colonial Caribbean.[3]

There is considerable historical documentation regarding the escape of white servants throughout the West Indies during the seventeenth century (cf. Beckles 1990). In some cases, these individuals may have formed their own separate communities, possibly based on ethnic identity. Karras (1993), in writing about the eighteenth-century sojourners of Jamaica, discusses the clustering of settlers and sojourners of the same ethnicity (ibid.: 127). According to Karras, Scottish residents of Jamaica chose to live in particular parishes and within these parishes in concentrated pockets (ibid.: 129). Karras goes so far as to state that sojourners in the Caribbean formed ethnically based social webs (in current sociolinguistic parlance 'communities of practice') to

---

[3]   Chinea (2007) discusses the place of Irish indentured servants in Puerto Rico and other parts of the Hispanic Caribbean.

Table 7.1 *Euro-Caribbean English-speaking communities*

Island	Community Name	Ethnicities	Languages
Abaco, Bahamas	Cherokee Sound	E, A	LD ~ LC (E)
	Great Guana Cay	E, A	LD ~ LC (E)
	Hope Town	E, A	LD ~ LC (E)
	Man-O-War Cay	E, A	LD ~ LC (E)
Anguilla	Canafist†	I	n.s.
	Island Harbour	I, S	LD ~ LC (E)
	Stoney Ground	I, S	LD ~ LC (E)
Barbados	Blades	I, S, E	LD (E)
	Church View	I, S, E	LD (E)
	Clifton Hall	I, S, E	LD (E)
	Glebe Land	I, S, E	LD (E)
	Martin's Bay	I, S, E	LD (E)
	Newcastle	I, S, E	LD (E)
	Superlative	I, S, E	LD (E)
Bequia	Mt. Pleasant	I, S, E	LD (E)
	Sugar Hill†	I, S, E	n.s.
Bermuda	n.s.	n.s.	LD (E)
Carriacou, Grenada	Windward	S	LD (E)
Cayman Brac	West End	I, S, E	LD (E)
Eleuthera, Bahamas	Spanish Wells	E, A	LD ~ LC (E)
Grand Cayman	East End	I, S, E, A	LD (E)
	West Bay	I, S, E, A	LD (E)
Grenada	Mt. Moritz	I, S, E	LD (E)
Guanaja, Bay Islands	n.s.	I, S, E	LD (E)
Inagua, Bahamas	Northwest Point	E, A	LD ~ LC (E)
Jamaica	Cave Valley	G	LD ~ LC (E)
	Seaford Town	G	LD ~ LC (E)
Long Island, Bahamas	Grays	E, A	LD ~ LC (E)
	Mangrove Bush	E, A	LD ~ LC (E)
	Salt Pond	E, A	LD ~ LC (E)
Montserrat	Carr's Bay†	S, E	n.s.
New Providence, Bahamas	n.s.	E, A	LD ~ LC (E)

(*cont.*)

Table 7.1 (*cont.*)

Island	Community Name	Ethnicities	Languages
Petit Martinique, Grenada	Madame Pierre	S, F	LD (E)[a]
Roatan, Bay Islands	French Cay	I, S, E	LD (E)
	French Harbour	I, S, E	LD (E)
Saba	Hell's Gate	I, S, E, D	LD (E)
	St. Johns	I, S, E, D	LD (E)
	Windwardside	I, S, E, D	LD (E)
St. Kitts	Dieppe Bay†	I, S, E	LD ~ LC (E)
St. Lucia	Roseau Valley†	I, S, E	LD (E)
Sint Maarten	Simson Baai	I, S, E, F	LD ~ LC (E)

[a] A local French creole language was also spoken in Madame Pierre village up until recently.

Key
A = American loyalists   LD = local dialect/non-creolized
D = Dutch   LC = local creole
E = English   n.s. = not specified/unknown
F = French   (E) = English language
G = German   (F) = French language
I = Irish   † = community no longer exists
S = Scottish   ~ = variation in use of the two languages

assist them in their goals of accruing financial wealth (ibid.: 170). On Saba and Anguilla, we find ethnohistory, folk linguistic accounts, and the clustering of surnames that indicate that different European ethnic groups settled in different areas of the islands, formed their own villages, with each developing its own distinctive accent. As one Euro-Saban put it

Like I said, in each village 'tis different. Also, less than 1,000 people... St. John's, those people they talkin' more like Irishmen. In the Bottom, well they have different. They have the old white ones, those who are English, they spoke London English, or tried to.

Given the diverse origins of the founder populations and the relative isolation of the developing dialects throughout time, it is very difficult to generalize across the linguistic and sociolinguistic boundaries. In the subsection that follows, I will outline the sociolinguistic history of one variety of Euro-Caribbean English: that spoken on the island of Anguilla in the northern Leeward Antilles. The sociolinguistic history of Euro-Anguillian English is both typical and atypical of other varieties of English spoken in enclave Euro-Caribbean communities.

2.1   Anguilla

Anguilla is the northernmost of the Leeward Antilles, being situated approximately eight kilometres north of the island of St. Martin. It has an area of
ninety square kilometres, being twenty-six kilometres long and five kilometres in width. Anguilla is a low-lying limestone island with a maximum
elevation of only sixty-six metres above sea level. There are very few sources
of fresh water on the island: no rivers or streams and very little annual rainfall. The lack of rainfall and scarcity of freshwater made Anguilla a difficult
environment in which to establish the sort of extensive plantations based
on the production of sugar that were to become typical of the European
colonization of the West Indies.

The population of Anguilla is dispersed primarily along the extensive
coastline in a number of villages. The most recent census of 2001 gives
a population for Anguilla of 11,300. The Valley, which functions as the
administrative centre of the island, is the only major settlement located
inland. A good system of hardtop roads links all of the villages together. The
island is connected to the larger world through air service to Puerto Rico,
Antigua and St. Martin as well as frequent ferry service to St. Martin.

2.1.1   Early European settlement history

All of the existing colonial records indicate that the English established the
first permanent European settlement on the island in 1650. Anguilla was
somewhat unusual in the history of its settlement in that the island was
settled without any commission from the King or the Governor-in-Chief of
one of the other islands, and this left Anguilla out of the purview of most
colonial administrators. Anguilla did not receive protection from the English
Crown until 1660. The Crown's action to bring the island under its direct
rule and protection was due in large part to a massive raid that took place in
1656. According to correspondence housed in the Anguillian archives, the
raid dispersed much of the original English settler population. The groups
that were to repopulate the island who came after the 1656 raid were mostly
freed and runaway indentured servants from nearby St. Kitts, Nevis and
Antigua. The archival records on Anguilla also indicate that a percentage of
the settlers were made up of smallholders, debtors and criminals. Anguilla
underwent another large-scale raid in 1666 at the hands of the French, and
once again, a large portion of the settler population was forced to leave the
island. William Willoughby sailed with a group of settlers – mostly 'time out',
a colonial term that refers to settlers who had only recently been released
from servitude – from Barbados in 1667 to resettle the northern Leeward
Islands of Montserrat, Saba, Antigua and Anguilla. Archival sources indicate
that another shipment of settlers from Barbados reached Anguilla in 1668.

Late in the seventeenth century – somewhere around 1688–9 – there are
references in the archival correspondence to a group called the 'Wild Irish'

coming to Anguilla from the French portion of St. Kitts. The 'Wild Irish' ravaged the settlements of Anguilla after their arrival, forcing the existing settlers to take refuge in the scrubby, harsh interior of the island.[4] Some Anguillians were also removed from the island and resettled on Antigua in 1689 (Jones 1936: 16).

2.1.2   Slavery on Anguilla

The sugar industry on Anguilla had suffered throughout the seventeenth and eighteenth centuries due to a lack of dependable rainfall and a lack of investment capital on the part of local planters. The Anguillian cash-crop enterprise was not able to entice large-scale planters with capital to invest in large tracts of land, or in amassing a large labour pool comprised primarily of slaves. Instead, Anguillian settlers owned small plots of land, and typically only a few slaves who worked with them and their family members in the fields and pastures.

Slavery did not become fully established on Anguilla until late in the eighteenth century; even then the ratio of slaves to whites and free coloureds never matched the proportions that we find typical in most of the Eastern Caribbean during the height of slavery. Slave mortality on Anguilla was reportedly lower than that in many of the other English islands in the region (Knight 1997: 92). The 1750 population information for Anguilla, albeit incomplete, shows 350 whites, 38 free coloureds, and 1,962 blacks (Knight 1997: 48).

By 1830, the white population had diminished by over 40 per cent. The census of that year breaks down the overall population into groups of 200 whites, 399 free coloureds, and 2,600 blacks (Knight 1997: 51). A partial reason for the decline in the white population is the growing discontent among the Anguillian population with living conditions on the island.

The 1830s on Anguilla saw a period of prolonged droughts that destroyed food crops and animals, and caused human famine. Slaves who had become idle as a result of the adverse conditions were permitted to leave the island by their masters and earn a living on other islands. Some of these slaves were able to acquire enough money to buy their own or their family members' freedom. A remittance-type economy developed during this time that became the model for economic life on the island for decades to come.

Slavery on Anguilla came to an end in 1838 when the St. Kitts Legislature abolished the apprenticeship system that had been provided for by the Emancipation Act of 1833 (Carty and Petty 1997: 61). By this time, the already fragile sugar industry had all but disappeared from the landscape.

---

[4] The present-day Harrigans of the village of Island Harbour claim to be, in part, descended from the 'Wild Irish' of seventeenth-century Anguilla.

2.1.3   Post-emancipation Anguilla

After emancipation, a number of white colonists left the island to settle in North America and other parts of the Caribbean. Their estates were sold piecemeal to the descendants of the slaves who had worked them, or acquired through the practice of quiet possession (Jones 1936: 22). Other ex-slaves were able to rent land through a system of in-kind payments, since cash in the poverty-stricken economy was scarce. Anguilla developed into a society of independent peasants who settled on any cultivatable piece of land that they could find.

The general distressed conditions of Anguillian life prompted some Anguillians to work as indentured labourers on the sugar plantations in St. Croix during the 1870s (Jones 1936: 24). The 1880 census of the island shows 202 whites and 3,017 free coloureds and blacks (Knight 1997: 53). There was relative stability of the overall population of the island during the eighteenth and nineteenth centuries, with a gradual decline in the white population. Although the status of blacks and coloureds changed after emancipation, their numbers did not fluctuate dramatically at any point during this time. Overall, the population of the island has been stable, which has promoted a degree of linguistic stability that many other Eastern Caribbean islands have not experienced due to drastic influxes of new slaves and the large-scale exodus of whites.

2.1.4   Present-day settlement patterns on Anguilla

Many settlements on Anguilla have their origins in the early colonization of the island. A few villages are situated in areas very near to pre-Columbian settlement sites on the island – most near sources of fresh water. There is a social and linguistic divide between East- and West-enders. The polar extremes along this continuum are the villages of Island Harbour and West End respectively.

Development has come to Anguilla slowly, but its growth has been rapid. Phone service was not available on the island until the mid 1960s. Communication between communities before this was minimal. Individuals might only rarely leave their natal village. Electricity was not brought to the far eastern end of the island, to the villages of Island Harbour, East End and Mount Fortune, until the 1980s. Concrete-block houses did not become the common sights that they are nowadays until after Hurricane Luis devastated the island in 1995. Before that, many poorer Anguillians lived in wattle-and-daub houses.

2.2   Setting of Euro-Anguillian English

Presently, Euro-Anguillian English is spoken primarily in the village of Island Harbour, which is located along a natural harbor with a protective cay on the northeastern coast of the island. In spite of the fact that Island

Harbour has grown considerably over the past several decades, attracting residents from other West Indian territories including Guyana, St. Martin and St. Kitts, the village still retains a parochial, isolationist attitude and the opinions of Anguillians from other parts of the island are that the residents of Island Harbour are haughty, aloof and 'in-bred'. Euro-Anguillian English is also spoken in the village of Stoney Ground[5] and used to be spoken in the village of Canafist, which is now abandoned.

The origins of the village of Island Harbour are not specified in any of the archival records of the island; however, the community's ethnohistory provides some details on the settlement history of the community. Utilizing genealogical reckoning, ethnohistory, and the record of shipwrecks on the island (cf. Berglund 1995), it is apparent that a group of Scottish-born settlers bound from Grenada to England were shipwrecked on Scrub Island – a relatively small island just off the northern tip of Anguilla and visible from Island Harbour.[6] The ship was the English brigantine *Antelope*, which had left Grenada for England in 1771 (Berglund 1995: 5). Ethnohistorical accounts state that there were only three survivors of the shipwreck – all brothers, sharing the surname Webster. They are thought to have made their way to the main island of Anguilla shortly after the wreck, in search of a source of fresh water. Two of the brothers settled somewhere near the centre of the present-day village near a site of fresh water called 'The Fountain', which had also been a pilgrimage site for pre-Columbian peoples in the region. The local accounts go on to provide information that these two brothers found wives from the local white population that lived in the area south of Island Harbour, most likely in the historical village of Canafist. The third brother is thought to have settled at a location called Sandy Point; however, no further information is known about him or any of his descendants. The ethnohistorical account of the late arrival of the Webster brothers on Anguilla is reinforced by the archival records of settler lists, wills and other legal documents, where the surname Webster does not appear in any transactions or records until 1832.

According to Anguillians, each village had its own distinctive dialect in the past. Again, the social isolation that prevailed between villages was the likely cause of this pattern. However, these distinctions have been eroding steadily as communication between villages has become quick and simple with an extensive telephone service provided through Cable and Wireless, and a system of hard-surfaced roads that connects all of the major settlements on the island.

---

[5] The Stoney Ground community has a different history and their dialect differs slightly from that of the residents of Island Harbour.

[6] The Harrigans of Island Harbour recount that the ship was coming from Barbados. I can find no record of a ship from Barbados to St. Kitts at that time, but it might be that the *Antelope* had originated in Barbados.

In section 3, I will focus on describing the salient features of Euro-Caribbean English, with an emphasis on Euro-Anguillian English.[7] I will include comparative data on other varieties where relevant.

3   Features of Euro-Caribbean English

3.1   Segmental phonology

There is considerable variation in the segmental and suprasegmental aspects of Euro-Caribbean English phonology. Each variety has a different sociolinguistic history and ecology and the linguistic inputs to the developing phonological system were different. These differing inputs and component strengths provided for similar yet distinctive outcomes. As Milroy (1981) has shown, the phonologies of non-standard varieties are more complex than those of standard varieties, and additionally mergers are more common in koinés as well. ECE varieties are both non-standard and koinéized, making them complex in a variety of ways. What follows only touches upon the more interesting and salient aspects of Euro-Caribbean English phonology.[8]

3.1.1   Short vowels

KIT /I/

EAE follows RP and General American Englishes in the realization of the KIT vowel. However, following suit with Newfoundland English, ECE exhibits KIT-tensing in two grammatical morphemes: gerundive -ing and possessive his (cf. Clarke, this volume).

DRESS /ɛ/

DRESS vowels are typically more open in ECE dialects than they are in either General American or RP. This corresponds with the general tendency of Barbadian English as discussed by Wells (1982c: 585).

TRAP/BATH /a ~ a:/

As in many other LKVEs, TRAP and BATH are distinguished by length and not vowel quality.

---

[7] The data for the description that follows were collected by the author during approximately six months of field research in the village of Island Harbour spread over four different trips to the island. The corpus of recorded data consists of spontaneous discourse, conversation about the history of the village, formal elicitation, and life history narrative. All of the consultants for this study had been born in the village. Many of the men had spent considerable time working abroad, while the women had remained on the island for the majority of their lives. My consultants ranged in age from 44 to 83 years in 2000. The oldest clear-skinned female Webster died in late 2000, at the age of 83.

[8] A complete and accurate phonological account of the anglophone Caribbean has yet to be developed.

STRUT /ʌ/

As opposed to the creole-related varieties of the West Indies, the dialects of Euro-Caribbean English have mid-central vowels. Therefore, the realization of the STRUT vowel is as in most varieties of English found in the British Isles.

FOOT /ʊ/

As with /ɛ/, the FOOT vowel is relatively open in the dialects of ECE. This feature may be due to the Barbadian origins of many of the Euro-Caribbean dialects of English. The presence of /ʊ/ in ECE systems demonstrates that these dialects are not simply transported varieties of Scottish English, where the phoneme /ʊ/ is absent (cf. Wells 1982b: 401–2).

3.1.2   Diphthongs

FACE /ei ~ eː/

Not unlike Barbadian English, ECE dialects sometimes exhibit a monoph-thongal realization of FACE words. A diagnostic feature of Euro-Carriacouan English of Windward village on Carriacou is the inclusion of FLEECE words in the FACE set, realized with diphthongization; accordingly, a lexical item such as *tea* is realized as [tei].

PRICE/CHOICE /ɔi ~ oɪ/

There is a wide range of phonetic realizations of the first vowel in this diphthong in the dialects of ECE. The most widespread is [ɛ] with the pronunciation of *nice* as [nɛis]. Lexical items such as *boy* which are typically part of the CHOICE set are found in the PRICE set in many ECE varieties.

GOAT /oː ~ ou/

In most varieties of ECE, this vowel is long as in Barbadian English (cf. Wells 1982c: 584), although some speakers also produce this as the diphthong [ou]. This might be due to influence from the co-existing anglophone creoles of the region.

MOUTH /uː ~ ɛʊ/

Lexical items in the MOUTH set are highly variable in terms of realization. Typically, though, MOUTH items are realized with either the Scots pronunci-ation /uː/, which as Wells (1982: 406) states, 'is well-known as a Scottishism outside of Scotland', or with the diphthong that is associated with Scotland, again according to Wells (1982a: 152).

FLEECE /i ~ iː/

This vowel is typically a long monophthong in many varieties of Euro-Caribbean English; however it is also realized as a short vowel in some contexts.

3.1.3 Consonants

/h/

The realization of /h/ varies among the dialects of ECE. The ECE dialects of Cherokee Sound in the Bahamas and of Windward village on Carriacou evidence initial *h*-dropping, while Euro-Anguillian English does not.[9] Examples (1) and (2) are from the village of Windward on the island of Carriacou.

(1)   [ʔatʃ]   *hatch*

(2)   [ʔɔt]   *hot*

/r/

Euro-Caribbean English dialects are primarily non-rhotic, although *r* is pronounced in some contexts by speakers who have had more formal education. Examples (3) through (5) are from Euro-Anguillian English.

(3)   [gjɑnʔfaðə]   *grandfather*

(4)   [wɑːmz]   *worms*

(5)   [yɑːd]   *yard*

/w, v, ꞵ̞/

Euro-Anguillian English exhibits the pre-stressed-syllable merger of /v/ and /w/ that is characteristic of a number of other colonial varieties of English as well as that of nineteenth-century southeastern English (Trudgill et al. 2004). In several dialects of ECE, the realization is with the intermediate value of [ꞵ]; a voiced bilabial approximant.[10] Examples (6) and (7) are from Euro-Anguillian English and example (8) is from the Euro-Grenadian English (EGE) spoken in Mount Moritz, Grenada.

---

[9] According to Reaser (this volume), Euro-Bahamian English also evidences *h*-insertion in some contexts.

[10] A detailed set of arguments is presented in Trudgill et al. (2004) for this phonetic realization. The use of the subscript diacritic [¢] with the bilabial fricative symbol indicates a more open stricture, with no audible friction, no lip rounding (except before round vowels), and without approximation of the tongue towards the velum as in [w].

(6)   [ʙ̝ɪlɪdʒ]   *village*

(7)   [ʙ̝ɛbstɛ]   *Webster*

(8)   [oʙ̝ɝ]   *over*

Both of these dialects differ from the Euro-Bahamian dialect of Cherokee Sound where only the use of *v* in place of *w* was recorded by Childs, Reaser, and Wolfram (2003).

In Euro-Anguillian English, the postvocalic realization of this phoneme is the voiced labial plosive [b] as shown in examples from Euro-Anguillian English.

(9)   [drɛib]   *drive*

(10)   [lʊbd]   *loved*

TH-stopping

This feature, whereby the interdental fricatives /θ/ and /ð/ merge with /t/ and /d/ respectively, is common in the dialects of Euro-Caribbean English. Examples (11)–(13) from Euro-Anguillian English show the pronunciation in casual, relaxed speech.

(11)   [dɑt ẽnʔ fo mi naʊ]   *That ain't for me now.*

(12)   [diːz]   *these*

(13)   [doz]   *those*

There is a degree of variation in the replacement of the fricatives with the corresponding stops, especially in careful speech. Context and the effect of vernacular language loyalty are the factors that affect which pronunciation of /θ/ and /ð/ will occur.

Palatalization of velar plosives

Euro-Caribbean English dialects evidence the feature of palatalization of velar plosives before the vowels /a/ and /i/.

The dialect of Anguilla provides examples in (14)–(16) below.

(14)   [gjɑnʔfɑðə]   *grandfather*[11]

(15)   [gjɝlz]   *girls*

(16)   [kjɑrɪdʒ]   *carriage*

---

[11] Example (14) is noteworthy since it shows the palatalization of the initial velar plosive in a lexical item where it is not typically reported for any dialect of English, due to the fact that the /r/ is normally present and blocks the secondary palatalization process.

The dialect of Mount Moritz, Grenada provides examples in (17)–(19) below.

(17)   [gjɑdŋ]   *garden*

(18)   [skjɜ˞t]   *skirt*

(19)   [gjIrlz]   *girls*

This feature is likely attributable to input from northern Irish English, although the context of palatalization has expanded from only low front vowels to include high front vowels as well.

Other features of consonants

Other features of the dialect include the voicing of intervocalic /f/ as in [nɛvu:z], and velar realization of /n/ in word final position after MOUTH vowels, as in (20) and (21) from the Euro-Grenadian English dialect of Mount Moritz.

(20)   [daʊŋ]   *down*

(21)   [taʊŋ]   *town*

Consonant clusters are typically reduced in Euro-Caribbean English. Examples (22) and (23) are from Euro-Grenadian English.

(22)   [mos]   *most*

(23)   [frɛn]   *friend*

3.2   Morphosyntax

3.2.1   Pluralization
Pluralization is variably realized in Euro-Caribbean English. In nouns that undergo suppletive changes for plurality, double marking often occurs as in forms such as *womens*. Zero-marked forms such as *fish* are often rendered as *fishes*. Unlike other LKVEs such as those spoken on Tristan da Cunha and in the Bahamas, Euro-Caribbean English does not evidence any use of the postposed plural marker [dɛm], except in those cases where influence from the local creole is being realized.

3.2.2   Pronouns
The pronominal systems of Euro-Caribbean English dialects vary regionally and socially. It is almost impossible to generalize across the entire region. Case-marking in pronouns differs from what is typical in Standard English. For example, in Euro-Anguillian English, utterances with *take* as

the predicate most often have the object pronoun realized in the nominative case as in examples (24) and (25) below:

(24)   I takes she to her patient.

(25)   I go take he Scrub tomorrow.

In Euro-Anguillian English, *all we* is used as the first person plural pronoun.

Some varieties of ECE use of *mi* as first person possessive pronoun, but typically *mi* is not found in subject position. Examples (26) and (27) are from Euro-Grenadian English.

(26)   . . . to gi *mi* mother.

(27)   So when I pack *mi* basket with *mi* pan of water ontop *mi* head . . .

3.2.3   *Possession*
In vernacular ECE, possession is marked solely by the juxtaposition of nouns in the order possessor–possessed, as examples (28)–(31) show.

(28)   My mother father . . . my daddy father were brothers.   EAE

(29)   . . . the big Webster yard.   EAE

(30)   My mother race from St. Martin.   EAE

(31)   . . . and *mi* mother father . . . he was a Barbadian   EGE

The Standard English possessive *-s* is also used in Euro-Caribbean English, but typically in more formal contexts or with individuals of European descent from outside the community.

3.2.4   *Tense and aspect*
Verbs in the dialects of ECE are typically marked for both tense and aspect. Many of these categories are marked by preverbal articles, or auxiliaries, as is typically found in the anglophone Atlantic creoles and other contact varieties of English.

Present and past tense

As in most dialects and varieties of English in the Eastern Caribbean, the present tense in Euro-Anguillian English is often indistinguishable from the past tense. In vernacular usage, neither is marked in any significant manner. As will be discussed below, the third person present *-s* is often used with all persons; however, the usage does not reflect an extension of the number and person system in the present tense but instead is used to mark the habitual aspect.

Past perfect

In Euro-Anguillian English the past perfect is commonly used in a variety of contexts. This use of the past perfect has been widely associated with the structure of AAVE (African American Vernacular English) narrative style. In Anguillian Englishes, the form is common both in black and white varieties on the island, and is associated, to some degree, with formality and level of education. Its use is not restricted to the narrative style as has been reported in AAVE. Little work has been done regarding the provenance of this feature, and when it is reported in West Indian varieties, it is sometimes attributed to influence from AAVE. However, its presence in Euro-Anguillian English provides preliminary evidence that the form does not likely derive from a North American source, and instead probably has a source, or sources, in English dialects.

(32)   My friend, Eddie, he had call yesterday.

(33)   I had buy it.

(34)   I never did had it.

Future tense

The future is marked with the preverbal particle [gɔn] in the Euro-Caribbean English dialect of Anguilla and also in many other regional dialects of Euro-Caribbean English.

(35)   Someday I [gɔn] call you too, you know.

Habitual/continuative

The habitual/continuative aspect in all varieties of Euro-Caribbean English is a very salient feature. There is a continuum of marking for this category in the present tense that ranges from [də] to [də bi] to [dʌz]. The use of [də] and [də bi] is a marker of Euro-Caribbean identity. Dəz is the typically mesolectal creole variant that co-exists within Euro-Caribbean English social networks and also can be heard in conversations among elderly Euro-Caribbeans.

(36)   It [də] leak   EAE

(37)   Those rooms [də] come hot   EAE

(38)   See why we [də] check um   EAE

(39)   Everymornin' I [də] get a snack.   EGE

(40)   I [də] wake up early [fə] di mornin' an cook   EGE

(41)   From noon 'til three o'clock, it [də bi] hot   EAE

(42)   When the lady comes, she usually [dʌz] call me.   EPME[12]

(43)   Every night she [dʌz] come for you   EAE

(44)   When you goin down, the wind [dʌz] come up.   EAE

(45)   We [dʌz] like the small ones   EAE

(46)   I [dʌz] send it always   EAE

(47)   Shallow water [dʌz] feather the sea funny   EAE

Verbal -s

The extension of third person -s to all persons in the paradigm is a feature of Euro-Caribbean English. Examples (48)–(53) provide only a few examples of the usage from a few dialects.

(48)   I goes there every Sunday.   EAE

(49)   I works here every night.   EAE

(50)   The Chinese drinks plenty tea.   ESE

(51)   They puts on shoes.   ESE

(52)   They sells it at Decker Shop.   EBE

(53)   Yes, we makes coconut bread sometimes.   EBE

This feature is also common in many of the English dialects of the British Isles, including Scotland. In the southwestern counties of England, Elworthy (1879) provides information that the present habitual can be formed either with preverbal *do* [du] or with the use of the third person singular present tense form (verbal -s).

Past habitual

The past habitual in ECE is typically marked with the preverbal 'used to', with the verb in the unmarked or infinitive form, as in example (55) below.

(54)   I . . . I [dʌz] . . . I used to . . . now I takes too long.   EAE

(55)   It used be only white-skinned up here.   EGE

Progressive aspect

Euro-Caribbean English evidences significant variation in the forms and constructions that are used to mark the progressive aspect. This formal variation is a product of the koinéization that gave rise to the ancestral dialects (cf. Williams 1988).

---

[12] Euro-Petite Martinique English.

Prefixed gerundive

(56)   . . . and the new ones did now start [ə-] comin' in.   EAE

Copula + gerundive

(57)   She is goin' college in Maryland.   EAE

(58)   I's deliver' mi milk.   EGE

Bare gerundive

(59)   She workin' hard.   EGE

do be + gerundive

(60)   February, March corn *do be* comin'.   EAE

Completive aspect

The use of *done* to signal completive aspect is a feature of most of the varieties of Euro-Caribbean English. Its use, however, is highly variable, dependent upon context, interlocutors and other social features. *Done* is also used both pre- and postverbally as a completive marker, as examples (61)–(63) show.

(61)   He die *done*.   EAE

(62)   I *done* fire already.   EAE

(63)   I *done* gone.   EAE

Copula

The presence/absence of the copula has been a focus of discussion and debate for many contact varieties of English, including those lesser-known varieties spoken in the Eastern Caribbean (cf. Walker and Meyerhoff 2006). In Euro-Caribbean English, the copula is variably realized. I have not engaged in an exhaustive study of the variables that may affect its usage, and the examples that follow simply provide raw data.

(64)   That Ø how the Island Harbour folk get so close   EAE
            one to another.

(65)   The telephone *is* another something.   EAE

(66)   That Ø why my mother and father are in that way.   EAE

(67)   She Ø workin' hard.   EGE

3.2.5 Questions

Euro-Caribbean English questions are signalled through intonational cues and not by syntactic inversion of subjects and predicates as in Standard Englishes.

(68)   You did go?   EAE

3.2.6 Negation

Negation in Euro-Caribbean English is typically marked with preverbal *ain't* or *t'aint* or *tisn't*.

3.3 Lexicon

The lexicons of the dialects of Euro-Caribbean English have some archaic forms and regionalisms that set them apart from other varieties in the region.

(69)	gi	'to give'	EAE, EBE, EGE
(70)	lass	'girl or unmarried woman'	EAE, EBE, EGE
(71)	sempriss	'seamstress'	EAE
(72)	corn on the hub	'corn on the cob'	EAE
(73)	latitude	[used as a directional indicator on land]	EAE
(74)	strangled up	'tangled up'	EAE
(75)	stone sack	'scrotum'	EAE
(76)	jig	'to dance vigorously'	EAE, EBE, EGE, EPME
(77)	fegary[13]	'an annoyance often accompanied by excessive noise and lewd behavior'	EAE
(78)	macadam	'a paved road'	EGE

[13] This form is possibly from the Scots form *feegarie* ~ *fleegarie* that has the following meanings: (i) a vagary, whim, (ii) finery, (iii) a 'jaw harp', (iv) a fastidious person, one fond of trifles (Warrack 2002: 187). While the form in Euro-Anguillian English is very similar phonetically to the Scots form, the semantic relationship between the two forms is obscure at best.

(79)	bier	'a portable frame on which a corpse is placed or carried to the burial site'	EGE
(80)	ligaroo	'men who can change themselves into animals or objects at night and then suck blood from their victims'	EGE, EPME
(81)	ladiabless	'beautiful women who have one human foot and one cow foot. These women, concealing the abnormal foot, lure men off into the woods for sex, and then break their necks.'	EGE

4   Conclusion

Euro-Caribbean English is highly endangered. The variety is no longer being transmitted to children and in most communities the youngest speakers are in their late forties. The linguistic endangerment of the varieties of ECE is a consequence of identity shift on the part of younger Euro-Caribbeans as well as the discontinuation of the practice of colour endogamy.

The use of these varieties provided the sociolinguistic delineation of clear-skinned individuals in a broad colour spectrum of West Indian societies. On the island of Anguilla, the ECE dialect spoken in the village of Island Harbour by members of the Webster *deme* has functioned as a marker of social identity (cf. Williams 2003). In the past, when colour integration was not a social practice on Anguilla, EAE would have been the social variety spoken within the territorial confines of the village of Island Harbour. However, with the growing permeability of the village and colour boundaries, ECE has been diminishing in its role as a boundary maintenance mechanism. And now, ECE has become a marker of the past, when peoples of different colours did not get along on the island. One of my consultants from Island Harbour told me in response to my question about why things were changing – both linguistically and socially in the village – 'Anguillians don't like racism'. Locally, the dialects of ECE have become identified with racism in the modern Caribbean sociolinguistic ideology.

The speech of younger Euro-Caribbeans is shifting towards the local creole varieties. The passing of each of the elderly Euro-Caribbeans takes with it important linguistic and cultural information about these misunderstood peoples. I am certain that within the next twenty-five years, the varieties of Euro-Caribbean, which arose out of koinéization and within the social contexts of isolationism and endogamy, will disappear from the West Indian sociolinguistic landscape.

References

Beckles, Hilary McD. 1990. 'A "riotous and unruly lot": Irish indentured servants and freemen in the English West Indies, 1644–1713.' *The William and Mary Quarterly* 47: 505–22.

Berglund, David C. 1995. *Shipwrecks of Anguilla 1628–1995*. Basseterre, St. Kitts: The Creole Publishing Company.

Carty, Brenda and Colville Petty. 1997. *Anguilla*. London: Macmillan Education Ltd.

Childs, Becky, Jeffrey Reaser, and Walt Wolfram. 2003. 'Defining ethnic varieties in the Bahamas: Phonological accommodation in black and white enclave communities.' In Michael Aceto and Jeffrey P. Williams, eds. *Contact Englishes of the Eastern Caribbean*. Amsterdam, Philadelphia: Benjamins, 1–28.

Chinea, Jorge L. 2007. 'Irish indentured servants, papists and colonists in Spanish colonial Puerto Rico, ca. 1650–1800.' *Irish Migration Studies in Latin America* 5: 171–82.

Elworthy, Frederic. 1879. 'The grammar of the dialect of West Somerset.' *Transactions of the Philological Society* 1877-8-9: 143–256.

Jones, S. B. 1936. *Annals of Anguilla*. Belfast: Christian Journals Ltd.

Karras, Alan. 1993. *Sojourners in the Sun: Scottish Migrants in Jamaica and the Chesapeake, 1740–1800*. Ithaca, N.Y.: Cornell University Press.

Knight, Franklin, ed. 1997. *General History of the Caribbean* (6 vols.). London: UNESCO Publishing.

Milroy, James. 1981. *Regional Accents of English: Belfast*. Belfast: Blackstaff.

Mufwene, Salikoko. 2008. *Language Evolution: Contact, Competition and Change*. London: Continuum Publishing.

Orizio, Riccardo. 2001. *Lost White Tribes*. New York: The Free Press.

Smith, M. G. 1962. *Kinship and Community in Carriacou*. New Haven: Yale University Press.

Trudgill, Peter. 2002. 'The history of lesser-known varieties of English.' In Richard Watts and Peter Trudgill, eds. *Alternative Histories of English*. London: Routledge, 29–44.

Trudgill, Peter, Daniel Schreier, Daniel Long and Jeffrey Williams. 2004. 'On the reversibility of mergers: /w/, /v/ and evidence from lesser-known Englishes.' *Folia linguistica historica* 24.1–2: 23–45.

Walker, James and Miriam Meyerhoff. 2006. 'Zero copula in the eastern Caribbean: Evidence from Bequia.' *American Speech* 81: 146–63.

Warrack, Alexander. 2002. *Scots Dialect Dictionary*. New Lanark: Waverley Books.

Wells, J. C. 1982a. *Accents of English*, vol. I: *An Introduction*. Cambridge: Cambridge University Press.

1982b. *Accents of English*, vol. II: *The British Isles*. Cambridge: Cambridge University Press.

1982c. *Accents of English*, vol. III: *Beyond the British Isles*. Cambridge: Cambridge University Press.

Williams, Jeffrey P. 1988. 'The development of aspectual markers in Anglo-Caribbean English.' *Journal of Pidgin and Creole languages* 3: 245–63.

2003. 'The establishment and perpetuation of anglophone white enclave communities in the eastern Caribbean: The case of Island Harbour.' In Michael Aceto and Jeffrey P. Williams, eds. *Contact Englishes of the Eastern Caribbean*. Amsterdam, Philadelphia: Benjamins, 95–119.

8   Bahamian English

JEFFREY REASER

1   Introduction

Situated in the southern Atlantic Ocean, the Commonwealth of The Bahamas (henceforth 'the Bahamas') is an archipelago of more than seven hundred islands – of which twenty-nine are inhabited – extending over 750 miles from near southeastern Florida to northern Hispaniola. The landmass of approximately 5,400 square miles supports around 300,000 people (CIA, 2006). The islands tend to be relatively flat, exposed coral formations, with few rising more than fifty or sixty feet above sea-level. They also tend to have relatively thin soils that are poorly suited for most agriculture, which has tied Bahamians closely to ship-building and farming the abundant marine life in the shallow seas (the name *Bahamas* come from the Spanish *baja mar*, meaning 'shallow sea'). Despite technically not being a part of the Caribbean, the Bahamas joined the Caribbean Community in 1983 (without joining the Common Market). Recently, commercial fishing has given way to tourism, which now makes up over 60 per cent of the Bahamian economy. Banking has become the second largest sector of the Bahamian economy.

Just as the Bahamas has traditionally been overshadowed by other Caribbean destinations, the speech of Bahamians has not garnered the linguistic attention of some Caribbean creoles, despite being relevant to a number of interesting questions. For example, has Bahamian English retained traces of early Spanish exploration beyond its name? Has the geographical and cultural closeness to the Caribbean resulted in any linguistic accommodation to Caribbean creoles? Has the islands' relative isolation resulted in linguistic basilectalization? Has the nearby Spanish-speaking population from Cuba or the French Creole population from Haiti influenced the linguistic variety of the islands? Given the often great distances between population centres, is there a relatively homogeneous Bahamian English? The relative dearth of linguistic study of the Bahamas leaves these and other questions ripe for exploration. This chapter does not attempt to answer these questions in any definitive way; however, it does bring together information on the history and status of this Bahamian English that may provide the starting point for scholars investigating these or other questions in the future.

2   Sociohistorical status of the variety

Prior to Columbus' arrival in San Salvador in 1492, what is now the Bahamas was inhabited by seafaring Lucayan or Arawak Indians. The Spanish enslaved the indigenous population for labour in the gold mines of Hispaniola. Despite this early exploration and exploitation, the Spanish made little attempt to settle The Bahamas since the islands lacked riches, and the soils were unsuitable for farming (Craton and Saunders 1992). Over 150 years later, in 1648, a group of British settlers seeking religious freedom left Bermuda and founded the first permanent colony on Eleuthera, in the northern Bahamas. Another group of British colonists from Bermuda settled Nassau – the present-day capital – in 1666, which became the entry point of slaves and other 'social undesirable[s]' from Bermuda (ibid.: 78). It is unknown whether slaves arriving in the Bahamas were born in Bermuda or Africa; nevertheless, some speculate that the initial Afro-Bahamian dialect was likely to be a pidgin or creole variety (see e.g. Holm 1980).

A second important group of British settlers came to the Bahamas from the Carolinas and Bermuda through much of the seventeenth century. During this early period, whites substantially outnumbered blacks; however, as colonists realized the poor soils would not support traditional plantation agriculture, many abandoned their slaves and deserted the islands. Former slaves often found employment in maritime activities including the importation of other slaves to America or the Caribbean and pirating.

The Afro-Bahamian population grew steadily in the eighteenth century as a result of importation and birth-rate, overtaking the white population by about 1760 (Craton and Saunders 1992: 119–20). Even then, however, the population was not homogeneous as the urban areas such as Nassau had higher percentages of Afro-Bahamians than did more remote locations, often termed 'out islands'.

An additional linguistic input was the nearly 8,000 British loyalists leaving the newly formed United States for the Bahamas following the American War of Independence. This group nearly tripled the total population of the colony. Many of these loyalists settled previously uninhabited out-islands, such as Abaco, further separating the social and linguistic histories of these locals from those of places like Nassau (Dodge 1995). Today, Abaco is home to the third largest Bahamian city, Marsh Harbour, and remains vastly different from the rest of the Bahamas. In addition to substantially different demographics (50 per cent of Abaco is white compared to 15 per cent of the Bahamas as a whole) (CIA 2006), Abaco is culturally different as well: in 1971, 75 per cent of the island's population signed a petition to remain a part of the British Commonwealth if the Bahamas sought 'premature independence'

(independence was granted on 10 July 1973). As Abaco historian Steve Dodge notes, places like Abaco have had little impact on modern Bahamian culture and existence (1995: vi–vii); however, it is this independent settlement and subsequent isolation of places like Abaco that make any singular description of Bahamian English difficult.

3   Sociolinguistic status of the variety

Much of the early linguistic examination of Bahamian English occurred in the context of cataloguing the pidgin and creole varieties of the world, despite the fact that there was no consensus on Bahamian's status as a creole (cf. e.g. Hancock 1971 and 1977). Subsequent works attempting to profile the world's English language varieties, be they creole or non-creole, included overviews of the lexical, phonological and morphosyntactic systems of Bahamian with little attention paid to inter- or intra-variety variation (Wells 1982; Holm 1988, 1989). The first substantial examination of variation in Bahamian English was Shilling's (1978) dissertation, *Some non-standard features of Bahamian Dialect syntax*, which primarily focuses on the verb phrase. Shilling attempts to situate Afro-Bahamian English as a transitional variety, existing between African American English and creoles such as Gullah, Jamaican and Guyanese Creoles. Shilling posits a similar creole genesis to such varieties but dissimilar subsequent decreolization. While Shilling's informants are from a number of settlements throughout the archipelago, she condenses variation in a way that assumes two Bahamian Englishes split along ethnic lines. The assumption that Afro-Bahamian English is monolithic is, in fact, false, but continues to this day (see e.g. McPhee 2003) despite the fact that Albury (1981), in a Master's thesis, found variation of simple past marking within Afro-Bahamian, differentiating four distinct groups of speakers: basilectal, mid-mesolectal, upper-mesolectal, and acrolectal. The assumption that Afro-Bahamian is monolithic is further complicated by the fact that there are few clear ethnic boundaries in the Bahamas, as residents claim ties to diverse groups including British, American, African, American Indian, Haitian and mixed heritages of all combinations. Bahamian English may have received its most prolonged examination in a series of articles by John Holm (1980, 1983, 1984, etc.). These works, as well as a few others (e.g. Shilling 1980), sought not to document variation in the islands but to establish connections to Gullah or African languages.

One early study of Bahamian that is notable for its attention to the variation within the speech of islanders is Holm and Shilling's *Dictionary of Bahamian English* (1982), which catalogues regional and ethnic differences in the lexicon. Recent studies of Bahamian English have continued to probe regional and ethnic variation by examining specific segments of the population, such as urban speech (Hackert 2004), southern Bahamian speech (Holm and Hackert 1997), or the speech of insular communities on out islands (e.g. Sellers 1999; Childs, Reaser, and Wolfram 2003; Reaser 2004). Even recent overviews of Bahamian have been more inclusive of variation in Bahamian both in terms of phonology (Childs and Wolfram 2005) and morphosyntax (Reaser and Torbert 2005); however, even these treatments lament the need to condense linguistic variation in the Bahamas into three oversimplified groupings: white, basilectal Afro-Bahamian, and mesolectal Afro-Bahamian. The present overview, likewise, condenses language variation in the Bahamas into imperfect groupings for two reasons: space constraints would not permit a complete description and the scholarship on Bahamian English is still relatively sparse. One further complication for such a description is that many Bahamians are skilled register-shifters and may have access to both creole and non-creole varieties. Thus, even defining speech norms for a single speaker is a complicated task: as Reaser and Torbert (2005: 393) note, 'what is true Bahamian English [is] a difficult or impossible question to answer'.

Despite these difficulties impeding concise description, some generalities can be made about Bahamian English. For one, no study of Anglo-Bahamians has found evidence of past creolization (e.g. Shilling 1978; Reaser 2004). No consensus exists, however, on the creole status (past or current) of Afro-Bahamians. Shilling (1978) concludes a creole history and subsequent decreolization whereas, at least in one community on Abaco Island, Reaser (2004) finds no compelling evidence for a creole past. Hackert (2004) convincingly demonstrates that the language variety spoken in the urban centre of Nassau is best thought of as a creole, though it is not conclusive whether creolization is an older or current process. Generally speaking, islands that were settled earlier and historically have had higher percentages of Afro-Bahamians are more likely to have residents whose speech exhibits creole-like features. Islands that were settled later seem to follow one of two paths: islands in the northern Bahamas that were settled primarily by loyalists leaving from New York (the settlers themselves may have been from as far south as the Carolinas) tend to exhibit little or no evidence of a past creole history. Islands in the southeast, settled by loyalists departing from Florida who attempted to establish Southern-style plantations, seem to have some echoes of what was either an earlier form of Gullah or a variety influenced by Gullah (Holm and Hackert 1997). The sundry settlement histories combined with the style-shifting abilities of residents make it difficult to estimate the numbers of speakers who speak any Bahamian dialect; however, drawing solely from demographic data, about five in six Bahamian residents (or, roughly 250,000 people) live on either New Providence Island (where Nassau is located) or Grand Bahama (where Freeport is) (CIA 2006). These more urban areas are where much of the creole Bahamian basilect can be heard (Hackert 2004). The remaining approximately 50,000 residents are spread throughout the rest of the islands and vary considerably in their speech patterns. The Bahamas is also home to emigrants from French Creole-speaking Haiti and

Spanish-speaking Cuba, though these populations make up only an estimated 2 per cent of the total population.

4   Features of the variety

4.1   Lexicon

The lexicon may be the best-documented part of Bahamian English. Holm and Shilling's *Dictionary of Bahamian English* documents over 5,500 'words and expressions used in the Bahamas which are not generally found in the current standard English of Britain or North America' in hopes of establishing 'a link between the Caribbean creoles, such as Jamaican English, and the English spoken today by many black people in the United States' (1982: iii). For support, the dictionary documents connections between lexical items in the Bahamas and varieties such as Gullah (e.g. *gutlin* 'greedy' and *Hoppin' John* 'beans and rice') and African languages (*obeah* 'witchcraft' and *gumbay* 'social gathering'). Unfortunately, however, the authors also extend African genealogy to the grammatical system of Bahamian, asserting controversial notions as fact: '[Bahamian word order] follows African patterns' (ibid.: x). The pronunciation information in the volume is also occasionally problematic in that it has a tendency to underestimate variation. For example, it claims falsely that all Bahamians participate in the *pin/pen* merger (cf. Childs, Reaser, and Wolfram 2003). Despite these shortcomings, it remains an outstanding resource for regional and social lexical variation.

One important set of words are the many terms used to identify and taxonomize Bahamians. Many of these terms are used to denote people from particular towns or islands; for example, *Crabs* live in Hope Town and *Cigillians* are from Spanish Wells. Other terms index skin colour. The term *white* is used broadly to describe Bahamians with Anglo ancestry as well as those light-skinned Afro-Bahamians of mixed ancestry (Holm 1984: 254). The Afro-Bahamian community sometimes uses the term *Conchy Joe* or *Conky Joe* to describe people of Anglo descent. Generally, however, Bahamians self-identify simply as *white* or *black* along lines similar to the distinction made in the US.

4.2   Consonants

Folk accounts of the dialect, such as Glinton-Meicholas' *More Talkin' Bahamian* (1995), primarily document lexical variation in the Bahamas; however, in an attempt to highlight the differentness of Bahamian English, the book depicts some pronunciation patterns as lexical variation, which allows for many examples of a single feature. For example, there are many lemmas reflecting *h*-dropping or *h*-insertion patterns (e.g. *'am* for 'ham' and *heggs* for 'eggs'). This pronunciation pattern is summarized succinctly by Holm as 'in the Bahamas *ear* is what you do with your *hear* (or vice versa)' (1988: 76). The same is true of *w/v* alternation, in which both consonants in initial positions are realized as the intermediate [v]. Both of these features are more commonly associated with Anglo-Bahamian varieties though they are found in the acrolectal speech of some Afro-Bahamians (Childs, Reaser, and Wolfram 2003: 15–18). Phonological variation in Bahamian typically is a matter of frequency rather than absolute difference.

A quantitative difference exists between Afro and Anglo varieties with respect to syllable-coda consonant cluster reduction (CCR). While acrolectal Afro-Bahamian has rates of prevocalic CCR similar to American vernaculars, Anglo-Bahamian speech has elevated rates when compared to white working-class US varieties. Childs, Reaser, and Wolfram (2003) speculate that this may reflect accommodation to or at least influence from the majority Afro-Bahamian population on the speech of whites. In both varieties, phonological and morphemic-status conditioning factors are identical to those found in American varieties.

As is common in varieties of English throughout the Caribbean, Afro-Bahamians tend to have TH-stopping as the primary allophone of the inter-dental fricatives in pre-, post-, and intervocalic environments (*dese* for 'these' and *wit* for 'with'). Bahamians have occasional labialization (*smoov* or *wif*) and deletion in postvocalic environments, a characteristic that is rare in creoles but common in African American English. While Anglo-Bahamians do have TH-stopping as the most common variant of the TH-sound, they are far more likely than their Afro-Bahamian cohorts to delete or assimilate the initial TH-sounds.

Postvocalic *r*-vocalization is not common in Bahamian English, even in stressed syllabic vocoids such as NURSE. Unstressed postvocalic *r* (as in *lettER*) is nearly categorically absent in the casual speech of both Afro- and Anglo-Bahamians. Hackert (2004) notes that many Bahamians perceive *r*-full productions to be more standard than *r*-less productions, reflecting, perhaps, a recognition of American norms. Some speakers will occasionally hypercorrect and insert *r* in words that do not typically contain one.

4.3 Vowels

The vowels of Bahamian English vary by region, ethnicity and class (and basilectal/acrolectal status). Therefore, the summary of the vowel systems of Anglo-Bahamians and acrolectal Afro-Bahamians found in Table 8.1 ought not be generalized beyond the local context of the Abaco Island communities from which this description stems (for more on these systems, see Childs, Reaser, and Wolfram 2003, and Childs and Wolfram 2005). Table 8.1 summarizes the vowels of Bahamian English excluding

Table 8.1 *Principal vowels of Anglo- and Afro-Bahamian English*

Key Word	Anglo-Bahamian	Afro-Bahamian	Key Word	Anglo-Bahamian	Afro-Bahamian
KIT	ɪ	ɪ	FLEECE	i ~ ii	ɪ
DRESS	ɛ	ɛ	FACE	ei	ɛi
BATH/TRAP	a ~ æ	a ~ æ	LOT/PALM	ɑ	ɑ
THOUGHT/CLOTH	ɔ	ɔ	GOAT	ɘu	ou
FOOT	ʊ	ʊ	GOOSE	ʉ˙	u˙
PRIZE	ɑi ~ ai	aˑ	PRICE	ɑi	ai ~ ɑi
MOUTH	aɵ ~ aɛ	aɔ	CHOICE	oi	ɔi
STRUT	ʌ	ʌ	commA	ə	ə

pre-*r* and pre-*l* environments and is organized according to the standard lexical set of Wells (1982).

A number of interesting observations can be made based on Table 8.1. Perhaps most important is that the vowel systems are quite dissimilar from prototypical Caribbean vowel systems such as Jamaican, which have vowels with diphthongal qualities; instead, the vowel systems are more similar to those of US varieties despite the fact that neither of the described systems aligns isomorphically with Gullah, African American English or Southern White English.

One particularity of the vowel production in the younger male speakers in the Afro-Bahamian community on Abaco involves the BATH/TRAP vowel, which is usually pronounced in the front to mid portion of the mouth; however, when the term 'man' is used as an address term, the vowel is realized further back, akin to Jamaican 'mon'. Thus, a speaker may say, 'hey mon, check out that man on the roof'. Such a pronunciation may stem from the linguistic capital associated with a Caribbean identity in an emerging tourist economy. The young men who do this are typically employed in the tourist fishing business and rely on customers' tips for most of their livelihood. Whether this production generalizes in the future remains to be seen. In the TRAP/BATH class, older Anglo-Bahamians occasionally raise the vowel to near [ɪ] before a word-final *d*-sound (e.g. *sad*), a pattern not found in the younger Anglo- or the Afro-Bahamian speakers. The other front vowels of these varieties, including the FACE and lax vowel classes are relatively similar to productions common in African American English.

The back vowels reveal a stronger ethnic divide than do the front vowels. Anglo-Bahamians have more fronted GOOSE and COAT vowels than do Afro-Bahamians: a production found commonly in Southern White but not African American English (see e.g. Thomas 2001). It is not known whether this fronting in the Anglo-Bahamian community is a recent innovation (or accommodation to US norms) or a preservation of an older form. This fronting is not quite as radical as is found in the Southern US, nor do the vowels lower in their onsets; however, in Bahamian English, the ethnolinguistic divide with respect to fronting of back vowels mirrors that in the US. The vowels in THOUGHT and LOT remain unmerged despite the fact that the vowel in LOT has backed somewhat in both speech communities. This aligns these varieties more with Southern US varieties than other Caribbean creoles.

The central vowels of Bahamian are the only group that aligns more with Caribbean norms than US norms. The STRUT vowel is slightly backed and rounded in both Anglo- and Afro-Bahamian varieties. This variant has been documented in Jamaican Creole as well as Gullah. However, this single vowel variant does not provide sufficient evidence for concluding a connection to creole varieties.

The diphthongs of Bahamian are among its most distinctive and potentially most diagnostic vowels. Older Anglo-Bahamians share a number of vowel productions with the Pamlico Sound dialect in North Carolina and the Virginia Chesapeake, especially the backed and raised onset of the PRICE and PRIZE vowels. The diphthong in MOUTH, with its forward glide, is occasionally misdiagnosed as Canadian Raising; however, this production is quite different and, again, aligns with the distinctive vowels of the Pamlico Sound dialect. The diphthongs of the Afro-Bahamians are less exotic and are more similar to the productions found in African American English. For example, the pre-voiced PRIZE vowel tends to be monophthongal whereas the pre-voiceless PRICE has a full off-glide. The MOUTH diphthong's off-glide backs and rises in a manner similar to African American English and quite dissimilar from the variant found in Anglo-Bahamians.

4.4 Morphology and syntax

Among the most studied morphosyntactic structures of English is the copula. Shilling (1980) finds no alternate copular forms such as Jamaican Creole's *da* in the Bahamian basilect. Instead, the copula is either omitted or levelled to *is*. In the more acrolectal varieties, including Anglo-Bahamian, the standard copula forms *am, is, are, was* and *were* do occur, though not without occasional levelling to *is* in the present tense and *was* in the past tense. Past-tense levelling to *was* seems to be undergoing intensification in the Anglo-Bahamian communities on Abaco.

Zero-copula occurs in all varieties of Bahamian, with substantially more in the basilectal than the acrolectal Afro-Bahamian varieties and the least in the Anglo- varieties. Both Afro- and Anglo-Bahamian varieties have *are* absent more often than *is*, mirroring the hierarchy found in American varieties; however, Afro-Bahamian also features rates of *am*-absence that are even higher than *is*-absence, a pattern not found in any US variety. All varieties have elevated rates of absence when the copula is an auxiliary (i.e. preceding verb + *ing* or *gonna* constructions), though the Anglo-Bahamian speakers also have substantial absence before predicate adjectives (*she_ nice*): a pattern also found in Gullah and Jamaican Creole. Mesolectal Afro-Bahamian has some occurrence of zero-copula with past tense forms (Reaser 2004).

As with pronunciation features, there are qualitative and quantitative differences in the ethnic Bahamian varieties. Further, though these varieties have more copula absence than is found in the speech of ethnic cohorts in the US, they have none of the alternate particles found in creole varieties. The elevated rates of absence in the Anglo- variety may have been preserved from settlement or may demonstrate some historical accommodation to the majority Afro-Bahamian population but current divergence with respect to levelling: a potentially diagnostic ethnolinguistic marker.

Finite *be* demonstrates similar ethnolinguistic patterning. Anglo-Bahamians occasionally use finite *bes* with third person singular subjects and *be* with other subjects in habitual, durative or occasionally punctual contexts, such as 'Where the boats's be now?' (elderly Anglo-Bahamian speaker). Afro-Bahamians do not use *bes* at all; however, they use uninflected *be* more commonly than Anglo speakers and more consistently in habitual contexts. In the Basilect, *be* occurs most commonly in *does* + *be* + V-*ing* constructions, as in 'We does be reading play every time' (Shilling 1980: 138). Such constructions may be similar to earlier forms of the habitual *be* found in African American English (see Rickford 1974). As with the copular forms discussed above, this construction does not align Bahamian with other creoles.

Perfective aspectual patterns also differ ethnolinguistically in the Bahamas. Anglo-Bahamians often use a conjugated form of *be* in place of the standard English *have*, especially with first person singular subjects, as in 'I'm been there before', or less commonly with other subjects: 'you're been there before.' This construction, occasionally called 'perfective *I'm*', was widespread in the seventeenth century and can still be found in some communities in the American Southeast. This form seems to be absent from the speech of Afro-Bahamians, with acrolectal speakers alternating between full and contracted forms of *have* much like in Standard English. Basilectal speakers often delete *have* altogether, especially when followed by verbs such as *been* and *got*.

Another verbal auxiliary in Bahamian English is *done*, which denotes completed actions and is found in both Southern White English and African American English. In acrolectal speech, like US varieties, the verb following *done* is most often in the past tense, as in 'I done sent the pictures'. Hackert (2004) found that urban basilectal Bahamians have extensive *done* + bare root, as in 'I done send the pictures', a pattern common to other creole varieties.

Similar subtle differences among populations exist in other facets of the tense and aspect systems of varieties in the Bahamas, demonstrating that linguistic patterning continues to reflect the sundry settlement histories of islands. In general, areas of the Bahamas that are urban tend to have more

Table 8.2 *Summary of verbs in Bahamian dialects and comparison varieties*

Grammatical Structure	Anglo-Bahamian	Mesolectal Afro-Bahamian	Basilectal Afro-Bahamian	Jamaican Creole	Gullah	AAVE
Ambiguous forms, e.g. *he come home*	✔	✔	✔	✔	✔	✔
Preterite for past participle, e.g. *she had went*	✔	✔	(✔)		(✔)	✔
Past participle for preterite, e.g. *I seen her*	✔	✔	(✔)		(✔)	✔
Bare root, e.g. *he run yesterday*	✔	✔	✔	✔	✔	✔
Regularization, e.g. *he growed up tall*	✔	✔	(✔)		(✔)	✔
Different strong form, e.g. *It riz up out of the water*	✔	✔	✔	(✔)	✔	✔

structures that reveal a potential creole past than do areas settled more recently, especially those settled by expatriates following the American War of Independence. Table 8.2 summarizes some of the variation in the verb system across different dialects of Bahamian, as well as Gullah, Jamaican Creole, and African American Vernacular English. In this table, a check indicates the feature is common in the variety while a check in parentheses indicates it is present but uncommon.

Table 8.2 makes it clear that Anglo–Bahamian and mesolectal Afro–Bahamian on rural islands differ more quantitatively than qualitatively. The structures in these varieties overlap substantially with US varieties, reflecting a possible historical tie between locales. Basilectal Bahamian, on the other hand, aligns more with Gullah than with the more heavily creolized Jamaican Creole. It is worth noting that the basilect has near-categorical bimorphemic consonant cluster reduction and zero past-tense marking: tense, when crucial to understanding, tends to be marked through adverbs (*yesterday*, *last year*, etc.) (Albury 1981). In the mesolect, marking is more variable, especially among strong verbs.

Other non-standard subject–verb concord patterns are also found in Bahamian. As is common in African American English, Afro-Bahamian has absence of the inflectional -*s* on verbs following third person singular subjects (*he walk_*). While many dialects attach -*s* to third person plural subjects (*they walks there*), mesolectal Afro-Bahamian also attaches -*s* frequently to verbs following the pronoun *I* (e.g. *I works hard*). Both absence and attachment co-occur in the speech of individuals and whether the subject is a pronoun or noun phrase seems not to correlate with any usage; indeed, in mesolectal Afro-Bahamian, -s marking on verbs appears to be an optional process. Not surprisingly, the verbal -s is categorically absent in basilectal varieties.

Inflectional morphology on nouns is likewise variable in Afro-Bahamian varieties. Plural -s is commonly absent especially when the noun follows a quantifier (*I have two pig_*) and the creole plural marker *dem* occurs in many Bahamian varieties (*the boy-dem fishing* 'the boys are fishing'). However, double marking also occurs, with the noun taking both a standard -s and *dem* suffixes (*the boys-dem fishing*). Unlike other creoles, however, no Afro-Bahamian variety has categorically unmarked plurals. Anglo-Bahamian has essentially standard plural marking.

All lects of Afro-Bahamian have near categorical absence of the possessive *'s*, marking possession through adjacency instead (*my son_truck*). Anglo-Bahamians tend to use the possessive marker in such cases, but seem not to distinguish between possessive and objective pronouns such as *my* and *me* (*them me grandchildren*). Similar usage of *they* and *theys* for *their* and *theirs* exists in the Afro-Bahamian varieties as well.

Other hallmark vernacular features are present in Bahamian varieties, including alternate second person plural pronouns (*oonah* on San Salvador, *yonner* on Andros, *y'all* on Abaco, *yinna(h)* in other locations), negative concord patterns, lack of subject–verb inversion in questions, variation of comparative and superlative forms, alternate or archaic intensifiers, and variation in prepositional use. The preposition *to*, for example, has generalized in usage, allowing for constructions such as *she's to the store*; *put [the shoes] to your feet*; *he works to Marsh Harbour*; *he's been here to* [since/during] *Christmas*; and *they hunt more to* [from] *Marsh Harbor*.

5 Conclusion

Despite not being as extensively studied as other Caribbean and US varieties, Bahamian English seems to be continuing much as it always has: somewhere between yet fundamentally different from American and Caribbean norms. This is not to suggest that Bahamian English is a static variety. There is some evidence of possible basilectalization in urban areas, continued decreolization and accommodation in others, and, of course, linguistic innovation throughout the islands. In emerging tourist areas, there may be superficial alignment with Caribbean norms among those involved directly in the industry; however, it is unknown whether this will eventually result in linguistic realignment or continue to exist as a performance style. The Bahamas also continues to receive Haitian and Cuban immigrants, which further clouds predictions of the future of the variety.

While a good bit of work has gone into positioning Bahamian in relation to American and Caribbean varieties, it is important to note that the English of all classes, ethnicities and regions of the Bahamas is uniquely Bahamian.

Much remains to be learned about these varieties by scholars who approach them as interesting and important independently of questions of creolization, decreolization and alignment with other varieties. Perhaps as the Bahamas continues to increase its profile in the world through tourism and banking, even more attention will be paid to the language varieties of the islands' inhabitants.

References

Aceto, Michael, and Jeffrey P. Williams, eds. 2003. *Contact Englishes of the Eastern Caribbean*. Amsterdam and Philadelphia: Benjamins.

Albury, Anne. 1981. *The Status of the -ed Suffix in Black Bahamian English*. MA thesis. University College London.

Childs, Becky, Jeffrey Reaser and Walt Wolfram. 2003. 'Defining ethnic varieties in The Bahamas: Phonological accommodation in black and white enclaves.' In Aceto and Williams, eds. 1–28.

Childs, Becky, and Walt Wolfram. 2005. 'Bahamian English phonology'. In Schneider et al., eds., vol. I: 435–49.

CIA. 2006. *The World Fact Book*. www.cia.gov/library/publications/the-world-factbook/index.html.

Craton, Michael, and Gail Saunders. 1992. *Islanders in the Stream: A History of the Bahamian People* (2 vols.). Athens, Ga.: University of Georgia Press.

Dodge, Steve. 1995. *Abaco: The History of an Out Island and its Cays*. Decatur, Ill.: White Sound Press.

Glinton-Meicholas, Patricia. 1995. *More Talkin' Bahamian*. Nassau: Guanima Press.

Hackert, Stephanie. 2004. *Urban Bahamian Creole: System and Variation*. Amsterdam and Philadelphia: Benjamins.

Hancock, Ian F. 1971. 'A survey of the pidgin and creole languages.' In Dell Hymes, ed. *Pidginization and Creolization of Languages*. Cambridge: Cambridge University Press, 509–25.

1977. 'Appendix: Repertory of pidgin and creole languages.' In Albert Valdman, ed. *Pidgin and Creole Linguistics*. Bloomington, Ind.: Indiana University Press, 277–94.

Holm, John. 1980. 'African features in white Bahamian Speech.' *English World-Wide* 1: 45–65.

1983. 'On the relationship of Gullah and Bahamian.' *American Speech* 58: 303–18.

1984. 'Variability of the copula in Black English and its creole kin.' *American Speech* 59: 291–309.

1988. *Pidgins and Creoles*, vol. I: *Theory and Structure*. Cambridge: Cambridge University Press.

1989. *Pidgins and Creoles*, vol. II: *References Survey*. Cambridge: Cambridge University Press.

Holm, John and Stephanie Hackert. 1997. 'Southern Bahamian: Transported AAVE or transported Gullah?' Paper presented at the Annual Meeting of the Society for Pidgin and Creole Linguistics, London: University of Westminster.

Holm, John and Alison Shilling. 1982. *Dictionary of Bahamian English*. Cold Spring, N.Y.: Lexik House.

Kortmann, Bernd, Edgar W. Schneider, Kate Burridge, Rajend Mesthrie and Clive Upton, eds. 2004. *A Handbook of Varieties of English: A Multi-Media Resource* (2 vols.). Berlin: Mouton de Gruyter.

McPhee, Helean. 2003. 'The grammatical features of TMA auxiliaries in Bahamian Creole.' In Aceto and Williams, eds., 29–50.

Reaser, Jeffrey. 2004. 'A quantitative analysis of Bahamian copula absence: Morphosyntactic evidence from Abaco Island, The Bahamas.' *Journal of Pidgin and Creole Languages* 19: 1–40.

Reaser, Jeffrey and Benjamin Torbert. 2005. 'Bahamian English: Morphology and syntax.' In Schneider et al., eds., vol. II: 391–406.

Rickford, John R. 1974. 'The insights of the mesolect.' In David De Camp and Ian F. Hancock, eds., *Pidgins and Creoles: Current Trends and Prospects*. Washington, D.C.: Georgetown University Press, 92–117.

Sellers, Jason. 1999. *A Sociolinguistic Profile of Cherokee Sound, Bahamas: Analysis of an Out Island Community*. MA thesis. North Carolina State University.

Shilling, Alison. 1978. *Some Non-Standard Features of Bahamian Dialect Syntax*. PhD dissertation. University of Hawaii.

  1980. 'Bahamian English – a non-continuum?' In Richard R. Day, ed *Issues in English Creoles: Papers from the 1975 Hawaii Conference*. Heidelberg: Groos, 133–45.

Thomas, Erik R. 2001. *An Acoustic Analysis of Vowel Variation in New World English*. Durham: Duke University Press.

Wells, J. C. 1982. *Accents of English*, vol. III. *Beyond the British Isles*. Cambridge: Cambridge University Press.

9   Dominican Kokoy

MICHAEL ACETO

1 Introduction

This article examines the grammatical features of Kokoy, a creole or restructured variety of English spoken on the island of Dominica in the eastern
Caribbean. It is part of an ongoing project to document neglected or undocumented English-derived languages of the Caribbean via fieldwork (see Aceto
and Williams 2003; see Aceto 2002a for a complete list of undescribed and
underdescribed languages of the anglophone Americas). There is no published research focusing on Kokoy and references to the existence of this
language variety are sparse. In fact, I only encountered my first reference to
this language when editing Aceto and Williams (2003). Bryan and Burnette
(2003) focused on language usage on the island of Dominica, and one of the
languages mentioned was Kokoy. As a fieldworker interested in undescribed
languages, this reference caught my eye and, on the basis of a generous fac-
ulty grant from my institution and help offered by Rosalind Burnette, I was
able to carry out fieldwork in Kokoy-speaking locations for a few weeks in the
summer of 2002. Subsequently, I have encountered two further references
in the published literature by Christie (1990, 1994) referring to Kokoy or
Cocoy (as it is sometimes spelled).

Dominica, an island in the eastern Caribbean situated between Guadeloupe and Martinique and sharing a partial francophone history, reveals
at least three European-language-derived varieties. The oldest variety is
a French-based creole; the more recent development is an English-based
variety that has emerged in the last fifty years largely, it seems, due to
varieties of Caribbean English spoken within governmental and educational
institutions. According to the prevalent (yet flawed; see Aceto 2003) terminology of creole studies this latter variety would be designated a so-called
mesolectal or intermediate variety. The subject of this chapter, however,

I would like to thank Rosalind Burnette for her help in vouching for my research with customs
officials in Dominica and for arranging housing for me in Marigot during my stay on the
island of Dominica in 2002. I would also like to thank Margaret James, Vincent James,
Arnold Tellemach as well as the people of Marigot in general for sharing their time and
language with me. The research in question and this subsequent paper could not have been
realized without their gracious help. As always, any errors or shortcomings are mine alone.

is an English variety called Kokoy, which was brought to the island in the post-emancipation period. Its contributing populations are believed to have emigrated from Antigua and Montserrat (Honychurch, p.c., as well as my many informants) in response to requests from plantation owners looking for workers in the large-scale fruit business in the nineteenth century. Thus, the ancestors of Kokoy-speakers were from strictly anglophone locations; speakers of the creole French variety are historically related to the emergence of colonial French varieties. The intermediate English variety is spoken, in some form or another, by nearly all residents of the island, including those of African and Carib descent (Carib as a distinct language has unfortunately disappeared), and is similar to other such varieties spoken throughout the anglophone Caribbean. This paper focuses on the heretofore undocumented English-derived variety called Kokoy spoken by those in two general areas of Dominica, Marigot and Wesley, though it is heard in at least two other areas of the island as well (mainly around Portsmouth).

2   Historical background to the island

The island of Dominica is twenty-nine miles long and sixteen miles wide at its widest point. It contains a land area of approximately 300 square miles or 751 square kilometres. Dominica is mountainous and has abundant natural water resources. The average height of mountains in the central range is 3,000 feet, with three mountains even higher. This central range of mountains receives over 300 inches of rain per year, with coastal areas receiving approximately 50 inches.[1]

The first humans on Dominica were an Arawakan-speaking people called the Igneri who settled the island around 400 CE. This group was later in contact with and subsequently displaced by another Arawakan-speaking group in the fifteenth century, before contact with Europeans: the Caribs or Kalinagos.[2] Kalinagos arrived in Dominica approximately 100 years before Europeans and managed to control Dominica for 300 years, until about 1700. In that century, under pressure from both French and English settlers, the Kalinago retreated to more inaccessible parts of Dominica. The British granted them 3,700 acres on the island in 1903. Unfortunately, their traditional language has not survived and the Kalinago today speak a mostly English-derived and/or French-derived variety. The last fluent speaker of the language died early in the twentieth century (Honychurch 1995: 26).

---

[1]   All the information in this section is from Honychurch (1995), the most authoritative source on the history of this Caribbean island. I also spoke with Honychurch during my fieldwork on the island.

[2]   The name 'Carib' appears to be an exonym, a name given by outsiders. It seems Columbus picked up the name Carib for these people from Tainos of the Great Antilles. In the seventeenth century, a French priest recorded the name the group gave themselves: 'Kalinago', which also appears to be the source of the word 'Garifuna' used in Belize (Honychurch 1995: 20).

The island was named Dominica by Columbus in 1493 because he sighted it on a Sunday. Europeans made no great impact on the island or the Kalinago (who vigorously defended themselves from slave raiders and sailors) for almost 200 years. In fact, the Kalinago took European and African captives from visiting ships; but it also seems that some Kalinago traded with visiting European ships as well (37). By 1625, the Kalinago were offering military resistance to French and English attempts to colonize the island. Honychurch (47) writes that in early 1700, 'the Kalinagos were still in total control of the island'. However, by 1730, due to ongoing battles with the British and the French, as well as ravaging illnesses, the Kalinago numbers were reduced to approximately 400, whereas in 1647 they had numbered 5,000 persons. By the eighteenth century, the Kalinago had heard themselves called Caribs so long by Europeans that they adopted this exonym for themselves as well.[3]

French settlers established a small settlement in 1635, but it was soon abandoned by all but missionaries. In 1642, Father Raymond Breton arrived in Dominica to Christianize the locals. It was here that he compiled his 'Dictionaire Caribe–Français'. During the next century, both French-speaking and English-speaking colonists began to settle the island. Honychurch writes (49), 'by 1727 there were fifty to sixty French families in Dominica along with a few Spaniard, Portuguese and English Catholics'. The French settlers and colonists were largely raising crops to feed slaves in nearby Martinique and Guadeloupe. There was also a big trade in lumber for building ships and houses. The French-speakers were more significant during this phase and they introduced the varieties out of which would emerge the island's first creole, a French-derived variety that would become a lingua franca for much of the island until the twentieth century.

Dominica was occupied by the British in 1761 and officially became part of the British colonial empire under the Treaty of Paris in 1763.[4] Honychurch writes (6), 'despite British political power, the French language, customs, religion and place-names would remain forever strong in the island's history'. Since French plantations were well established, the British allowed them to continue operating as a source of revenue for their empire. Sugar production came to Dominica relatively late and not on a large scale until the British took control of the island.

During the American Revolution, the French reoccupied the island for five years beginning in 1778. The British retook the island in 1782. After the

---

[3] Other often self-applied exonyms are the term 'Indian' or 'Indio' given by Columbus and his crew to the natives of the Americas because the Europeans mistakenly thought they were in the East Indies. Another exonym is the name 'Gypsy', which is due to the fact that Roma were mistakenly thought to be from Egypt.

[4] It was at the signing of this treaty between the British and French that Tobago, St. Vincent, Grenada and the Grenadines, as well as Dominica, were transferred from French to British colonial control.

French Revolution in 1789, French Republicans attempted to take back the island in 1795; they were defeated by the local British-run militias. These militias confronted Maroon communities in the mountains as well during this period. The last French attack on the island occurred in 1805.

Emancipation for slaves in the British West Indies occurred in 1834; in the French West Indies emancipation came fourteen years later. In the intervening years, several hundred French slave refugees from nearby Martinique and Guadeloupe made their way across the seas in open boats. The French-creole-speaking communities of Dominica presumably absorbed many of these refugees (127).

After 1763, and especially after the abolition of slavery in the British Caribbean in 1834, when the ancestors of Kokoy-speakers began to arrive, English-speaking colonists and people of African descent began arriving in significant numbers that would begin a tilt towards significant English language emergence in the former French colonial island. A French-derived creole is still the first language of many in both rural and urban communities on the island, except for the historic Kokoy-speaking communities of Marigot and Wesley (the subject of this article and the residences of all informants documented in this article). The third 'creole' language heard on Dominica is an intermediate English-derived variety that has emerged largely through educational institutions (and by educators from Barbados) in traditional French-derived creole-speaking areas as well as Kokoy-speaking areas, often displacing the latter varieties in the linguistic repertoires of many young people. That is, Kokoy is better known among folks in their forties and older than among younger people, though younger males typically are more familiar with the language than females, who often reflect common social prejudices that associate vernacular dialects with lack of education and 'bad' English. That is not to say that there isn't pride in Kokoy because there is, but only that the same negative stereotypes about so-called 'improper' vernacular English forms are at play here as they are in many areas of the English-speaking world, especially in the Caribbean.

3   Linguistic features of Kokoy

3.1   Introduction

The data for this chapter was gathered from approximately fifteen hours of recorded data. Data was recorded from approximately twelve informants, ranging from teenagers to elders of the community. At all ages, there were both males and females who were willing to share their language with me. Recordings were made of naturally occurring discourse (recorded in my presence) and corroborated by a set of interviews with key informants. All informants were recorded with their consent. The data is presented with an IPA transcription.

The recordings were made in two towns: mostly in Marigot but I also made one long recording in Wesley with a respected elder of the community. There are several people in these two areas who are associated with a radio programme called *A Fu Awi* ('It's ours' or 'It's for us'), which focused on Kokoy language and culture for the local populations. I was informed that the programme, while it lasted, was a source of great pride in the community, but it unfortunately was defunct by the time I arrived on the island in 2002. Locals still spoke about the programme with fondness, but it was not without its own politics and critics. Kokoy is a minority language, and one that seems to be receding, in Dominica.

One participant in the radio programme and a respected elder of Wesley provided me with the following quote: 'Those people who don't know Kokoy . . . there are people whose Kokoy is poor. This is how one's English can be poor. They speak poor English just as one speaks poor Kokoy.' The sense of pride in the local language is transparent, and among many of the elders there was a kind of lamentation that Kokoy seems to be receding in the face of intermediate and institutional varieties of Caribbean English.

3.2 Distinctive features of Kokoy

Articles such as Aceto (2002a) and the contributions to Aceto and Williams (2003) made the case that many of the English-derived varieties of the Caribbean, such as Jamaican, Guyanese and the creoles of Suriname, have received the bulk of attention from linguists (for a list of undescribed and underdescribed varieties consult those works). To correct this balance, in this chapter, I will highlight features or a constellation of features that are unique to this dialect/creole. It will also be unavoidable to discuss features commonly associated with other, better-documented varieties.

In this paper I will use the terms 'dialect' and 'creole' interchangeably. I am convinced that so-called creole languages are normal languages that exhibit the same emergent characteristics and processes found in so-called non-creole languages. In the last several years, it has been asserted that so-called creole languages manifest structural characteristics different from non-creole languages (McWhorter 1998, 2000; Parkvall 2001), but many researchers have remained unconvinced that these assertions or alleged diagnostic structural features are exclusive to the group of languages researchers call creoles (Plag 2001).[5] Rizzi (1999: 466) concludes that 'creoles do not look different from other natural languages in any qualitative sense'. Many creolists would probably agree with Mufwene (2000, 2001) that

---

[5] Many of the ideas displayed in the Plag (2001) publication were anticipated by the detailed written comments of Michel DeGraff, which appeared on Creolist, a now defunct subscriber service for those interested in pidgin and creole languages.

'creolization' is a social process designating that these languages were born within the crucible of colonialism and imperialism, and not (yet) a structurally defined one.

The name of the language itself is a subject of some debate and no one answer is entirely satisfactory. Kokoy may be an example of an exonym. It seems the historically prior population named these immigrants largely from Montserrat and Antigua (and, some present-day locals say, St. Kitts as well) and their subsequent variety of English after a banana fruit called *kokoy* harvested on these plantations in the post-emancipation period. Or perhaps it was a kind of insult referring to the people and/or their language because the fruit, though edible, is considered a bit tough and difficult to digest. Allsopp (1996: 333) reveals that this banana fruit is called *bluggo* in Belize and also referred to as *kokoy* in Guadeloupe. Perhaps the name reflects their uncomfortable immigrant/outsider status vis-à-vis the earlier populations of African descent, who were descended from local slaves. Or perhaps the name *kokoy* for the language is a pejorative related to the assumed 'crude' quality of the language; there is no shortage of pejoratives used by local folks in the Caribbean to refer to their local English varieties.

There is another meaning for *kokoy* that seems related to shame. For example, one consultant shared the following expression with me: [mi mi gi yu a kokoi] 'I shamed you' or 'I gave you a shame.' Another consultant suggested that Kokoy may be related to the term Cockney, but that explanation seems unnecessarily complicated given the fact that the local banana and the previous expression already share the same form.[6]

One of the implications of this language variety's well-known and robustly used name is that it eclipses other well-known labels in the Caribbean such as 'Bad English' or 'Raw English' that are common in many areas. That is, locals sometimes still describe Kokoy with some pejorative adjective but the adjective plus the word 'English' is *not* the name of the language. Some may not like it, know it or speak it, but the name of the language for all is Kokoy. My fieldwork in Barbuda revealed that many people referred to the local language as either 'Dialect' or 'Broken English' (among other pejorative labels) and sometimes even just as 'English'; my fieldwork in Bastimentos, Panama revealed a similar pattern, except a minority of speakers referred to the language as Guari-Guari. In neither location was the same pride in the local language anywhere near the level I encountered among Kokoy speakers.

[6] Allsop (1996: 162, 333) uses two spellings for these homonyms. He uses 'cocoy(e)' for the language and people and 'kokoy' for the fruit, though in neither entry in his dictionary does he explain why. I prefer 'kokoy' for the language (and people, I suppose, though I never heard anyone referred to as Kokoy, only as the name for the local language) since it represents a more phonetic spelling.

3.3   Local use of the word nega

One of several unique features of this dialect is the common use of the word [nega], which is clearly derived etymologically from 'nigger'. The history of 'nega' and its racist associations outside of Kokoy-speaking areas is not lost on the locals. All my consultants were aware that this word is often objectionable among other English-speaking communities. However, within the Kokoy-speaking context it simply means 'people' and is only used in the plural, not the singular; and Kokoy-speakers use it to refer to themselves and any group of people outside of their community. It doesn't even have to be used in reference to so-called black folks. I recorded 'white nega', 'black nega' and 'French nega', for that matter, and the latter form didn't mean only Francophone Afro-Caribbeans, just any French-speaking people or people of French ancestry. This example is a remarkable illustration of how the relationship between sound and meaning is arbitrary or how meaning is locally constructed by the speech community in question.

(1)   di frɛnč nega an dɛm 'The French people'

(2)   di nega dem e taak gud kokoi 'The people talk good Kokoy'

(3)   aalawi a blak nega 'We are all black people'

(4)   an di nega dɛm aa rispansibl fu di program
         'the people are responsible for the programme'

(5)   hau di nega de lɪv? 'how do the people live?'

(6)   mi no ʌndrstan hau dɛm nega de lɪv
         'I don't understand how those people there live'

(7)   hau di nega dɛm tap so 'How do these people live?'

(8)   wamek dɛm nega tap laika dat 'Why are those people like that?'

(9)   dɛm nega ya 'These people here'

(10)   dɛm nega de lʌv ič/wan ada 'Those people love each other.'

3.4   Archaic (and receding) usages in Kokoy

In this section, I present archaic usages that seem to be fading from Kokoy in general due to prolonged contact with the metropolitan variety of English that has emerged within institutional settings in Dominica. Many features of general Caribbean English are permeating enclave communities like those in Marigot and Wesley. I am not in any way suggesting that purported 'decreolization' is at play here, but only that many younger speakers are speaking a different variety of English from their parents or their grandparents or any earlier generation.

There is a tendency, particularly among younger speakers, to ignore the traditional pronoun *om* for 'him/her/it' (in object position) in favour of the more metropolitan pronoun *(h)im* or *(h)er*. Traditional words like *pa* 'road, path, space' are used less than the more contemporary form *ruod* 'road' (all examples were provided by consultants; the following example illustrates both examples); my consultants also informed me that [bɪg pa] is Kokoy for 'main road/street'. The traditional form [gi] is being replaced by [gɪv] 'give':

(11) a.   wɛn mi go doŋ a pa doŋ de, mi miit wan man . . . mi tɛl om gi mi pa.

     b.   wɛn mi go doŋ a ruod, mi miit wan man . . . mi tɛl hɪm fu giv mi rum.
            'When I went down the road, I met a man . . . I told him give me space.'

In Kokoy, the traditional Atlantic creole form [nyam] is being replaced by [iit] 'eat', and [vɪkl] (< vittles) is being replaced by the word [fud] 'food':

(12) a.   me go nyam mi vɪkl

     b.   me go iit mi fud
            'I'm going to eat my food.'

What was called [dakta šap] 'doctor's shop' in the past is what is called a 'pharmacy' or 'drugstore' today.

3.5   Kokoy lexicon and expressions

The following list represents words and phrases I encountered in Kokoy that may be of some interest to creolists and dialectologists. Whenever possible I have noted correspondences in other Caribbean Englishes (JC = Jamaican; S = Sranan; DCEU = *Dictionary of Caribbean English Usage* = Allsopp 1996; DJE = Dictionary of Jamaican English = Cassidy and Le Page 1967). This list in no way pretends to be exhaustive.

[frak] 'dress'; JC
[kum] 'come', come a fashion 'come in style'; JC
[ye] 'eye'
[nyam] 'to eat'; *common in many areas:* [nyan] S
[ninyam] 'food'; JC; [nyanyan] S
[akka, lɛka] 'like'; [laka] J; [leki (fa)] S
[nez] 'noise'; *often* [nais] *in W. Caribbean*
[fufu] 'hummingbird'; *in* DCEU *as* 'fou-fou'
[krebɪn] 'greedy, ravenous' < *craving*; [kriebɪn] J

[fars] 'noisy'; 'interfering' in DCEU; 'meddlesome' in Barbados < 'fast';
  [fasi] S 'to get into a problem, conflict, or quarrel'
[vantəpul] 'something/person that is no good, leave it alone'
[ven] 'vine'
[haudi] 'hello'; JC
[sʌnu] 'something'
[wanwan] 'little by little'; JC
[uše, we, wiše, če, wiče, iče, wičpaat, upat] 'where'
[beheŋ] 'behind, bottom'
[daab, darb] 'to rush something'
[bwel] 'boil'; [bwail] JC
[spwel] 'spoil'; [spail] in W. Caribbean
[lambesɪŋ] 'to talk nonsense'; [langabere] S 'longwinded'
[ol mor an yu, oldə an yu] 'older than you'
[wa, waar] 'want'
[ha] 'have'
[zɪnk] 'drink' (archaic)
[tumari, tumaro, tumara] 'tomorrow'; [tamara] S
[ton] 'stone, testicle'
[lundi wal] 'mannish, sexual experience'; most likely from some French
  variety
[aayu oi] 'you' (pl.) + urgency
[beč] < bitch, [yu mis a faal] 'you almost fell'; [(yur) beč] 'acknowledgment
  of a mishap'; sort of like 'what a bitch!'
[higas] 'a fight'
[bari, baro] 'to borrow'
[bara] 'barren'; [bara] means 'bother' in DJE
[kʌtlɪs, čaplɪs] 'machete'; back-formation 'cutlass' to 'choplass', based on 'to
  chop'
[ʌndənid, pandənid] 'underneath'
[pan om] 'on it'
[tan op pan om] 'stand up on it'
[fut an dɛm] 'feet'
[kum aaf pan om] 'come away from it'
[nansi tori, kokoi tori] 'folk tales'
[pupu] 'shit'; JC
[pɪdl, pɪgl] 'to urinate'; see [lega]/[leda] 'ladder' for [d]/[g] alternation for
  DJE
[tidi, tide] 'today'
[monki se aal čɪn tiit nat smail] 'Just because someone's face is full of teeth
  doesn't mean they are smiling at you.'
[i mi ha wa eda haas] 'he had another horse'
[mi e yer yu] 'I'm hearing you'; [yere] 'hear' S
[wif] 'with'; [bafrum] 'bathroom'; [ɛvrifɪŋ] 'everything'

[lɪv] 'live' *in Dominica, not* [lɪb] *as in Antigua;* [lʌv] 'love' *in Dominica, not* [lʌb] *as in Antigua; however,* [nebl] 'navel' *in Kokoy; no* [ie] *but* [e] *in Kokoy*

[vɛks] 'angry' *in Dominica, not* [bɛks] *as in Antigua*

[pe le le] *an exclamation for* 'there's going to be trouble' (*often sung*)

3.6   Pronouns

The first features that one notices when listening to Kokoy is how the pronominal system is different from other English varieties, especially in the Western Caribbean. One interesting observation is the complete absence of 'unu' and any of its reflexes. I never recorded the pronoun and I asked every interviewed informant about its occurrence and each consultant insisted it was not a Kokoy form and that to the best of their knowledge it never was (and I interviewed elders of the community who rejected it as well). The presence of *aayu* as a second person plural pronoun (as well as *awi* as the first person plural pronoun) and *om* as an object pronoun are a unique constellation of grammatical features heard in Eastern Caribbean Englishes (Table 9.1).

Table 9.1   *Pronouns in Kokoy*

	Sing.	Pl.
1st	mi/ami	awi
2nd	yu	aa(l)yu
3rd	i/om (obj).	dem/de

These features seem to suggest that the location and/or history of Eastern varieties is different from those for the Western varieties that display *unu*, *wi* and *im* for these same features.[7]

(13)   mos awi 'Most of us'

(14)   mi muma e kaal mi 'My mother is calling me'

(15)   ayu pupa e kaal ayu 'Your (pl.) father is calling you'

(16)   ayu muma 'Your (pl.) mother'

(17)   ayu onkl; ayu anti 'Your (pl.) uncle/aunt'

(18)   mi mi fait wɪt om 'I fought with him/her/it'

---

[7] In the Eastern Caribbean, some varieties of Barbadian English in fact display a reflex of *unu*, but this occurrence is somewhat of an anomaly for the region. Of course, there is no reason to expect only a single pronoun for a specific grammatical function to have emerged even from the earliest century of English language emergence in the Caribbean. That is, the baseline assumption for so-called creole languages should be that variation was a natural part of these languages, especially during language emergence, as it is for all human languages (see Satyanath 2006).

(19)   ami hav a kwarɪl 'I have a quarrel'

(20)   mi sisa; mi brada; awi brada 'my sister; my brother; our brother'

(21)   mi bʌs i as 'I busted his ass'

(22)   mi patrɪša 'I am Patricia'

(23)   awi e taak Kokoy 'We're talking Kokoy'

(24)   tumaro mi e go antiga 'Tomorrow I am going to Antigua'

(25)   ami hav a paati yɛstide 'I had a party yesterday'

(26)   ami de de 'I am there/I'm OK'

(27)   awi de de 'We're there/we're OK'

(28)   awi du ok 'we're alright'

(29)   mi gɛt vɛx kwɪk 'I get mad quickly'

(30)   aalayu/ayu hafu du om 'You (pl.) have to do it'

(31)   mi ne [no + e] go du om 'I'm not going to do it'

(32)   mi ha wa saŋ fu aalayu sɪŋ 'I have a song for all of you to sing'

(33)   mi hav a gyɪrl pɪkni 'I have a girl child'

(34)   ami pɪkni dɛm 'My children'

(35)   so wat me [mi + e] taak 'So what am I saying?'

(36)   mi mi kwarɪl wid am 'I quarrelled/I had quarrelled with her/him'

(37)   mi mi kwarɪl wid i 'I quarrelled with her/him'

The first person singular pronoun *ami* kept popping up in my data. It seems to be marginal to the general pronominal paradigm, but it may be emerging based on four-part analogy with the plural pronouns *awi* and *aayu*, which are unique to the Eastern Caribbean anglophone region, i.e. mi: wi :: awi : x, x = ami. (The first person plural pronoun [wi] can be heard throughout the Caribbean in Jamaican, regional standard Caribbean English, and the intermediate variety of English that has emerged on the island in the last fifty years or so.) It could also be a collapsing of [a] 'I' with [mi] into one pronoun due to contact with metropolitan varieties where [a] is commonly heard. It's difficult to be certain which dynamic is at play.

The vowel in the pronoun [mi] also elides when it is before the progressive aspectual marker [e] (see next section). It is common in Kokoy to hear [mi] become [me] as in (35) above, i.e. [mi] + [e] → [me]. Note the similar contraction process is governing the replacement of the vowel [o] in the preverbal negative marker [no] when it occurs before the aspectual marker [e] as in (31) above, i.e. [no] + [e] → [ne].

My key consultant in Wesley informed me that one difference between Marigot and Wesley Kokoy varieties is that in Marigot they use [i] when the referent is living yet in Wesley they use [om] for all referents in object position (see (36) and (37) above). In Wesley you can also in rare instances get [a] in this same position as in: [tɛl om mi se] or [tɛl aa mi se] 'Tell him I said . . . ' and [tek om gi mi]/[tek aa gi mi] 'Take it for me'. Both dialects use [i] in third person singular subject position.

3.7   Progressive aspectual markers

The progressive preverbal aspectual marker in Kokoy is [e], which appears historically derived from [de], though [de] never appeared even as a single token in my data. The connection between [e] and [de] was made clear to me by my more grammatically aware and sophisticated consultants (of which I had no fewer than three as key consultants). Often in the Eastern Caribbean, [a] is heard robustly for this same function. I had heard it and recorded it frequently in Barbuda as the most common progressive aspectual form, yet it is absent from Kokoy. It was also rejected by all informants as not part of Kokoy, though sometimes it seems the [e] can become unstressed and sometimes sound quite close to [ə]. Furthermore, the full preverbal aspectual form [de] was also rejected as not being part of Kokoy, even if some consultants recognize it as the form from which [e] derives diachronically; however, [de] is heard in Kokoy as the locative copula. Note that the first person singular pronominal subject [mi] often contracts with [e] to form [me] as in (40) and (41) below.

(38)   wa yu e du 'what are you doing'

(39)   Awi e waak pan di ruod 'we're walking along the road'

(40)   me [< mi + e] go fiks di bʌlb tumaro
        'I'm going to fix the bulb tomorrow'

(41)   me [< mi + e] want yu fiks dat bʌlb tumaro
        'I want you to fix that bulb tomorrow'

(42)   patrıša dɛm e kʌm 'Patricia and her friends are coming'

(43)   mi hir mi muma e taak 'I hear my mother talking'

3.8   Pluralization

Strategies for indicating plurality in Kokoy are similar to those found in the anglophone Eastern Caribbean in general: postnominal [dɛm] or [an dɛm]. There seem to be no differences in meaning between those two strategies that I could tease apart. The more common dialectal form heard across the English-speaking world of a pre-nominal [dɛm] as in (46) below is also heard on the Kokoy-speaking areas. In instances of the latter case, a redundant postnominal plural marker is rarely if ever heard.

(44)   di pɪkni dɛm 'the children'

(45)   mi pɪkni an dɛm 'my children'

(46)   dɛm pɪkni de 'those children there'

(47)   mi pɪkni an dɛm 'my children'

(48)   bikaz yu lɛf di pɪkni dɛm de 'because you left the children there'

(49)   patrɪša dɛm no de 'Patricia and her friends are not there'

(50)   patrɪša dɛm gaan aut 'Patricia and her friends have gone out'

3.9   Copula

3.9.1   Equative
The equative copula [a] in Kokoy functions in a similar manner as it does anywhere in the anglophone Caribbean, except that in Kokoy the form appears to be strictly [a] and not forms like [ɪz] or [bi] as can be heard in other regions. Sometimes Ø forms can be heard as well (e.g. (54), (57)).

(51)   dat a mi hous 'That's my house'

(52)   a mi pupa hous 'it's/that's my father's house'

(53)   dat man de a mi frɛn/mi paadna 'The man there is my friend'

(54)   da wa de tɛl awi 'That's what they tell us'

(55)   i a plɛnti 'there is plenty'

(56)   dat a no awi marigat pipl saun
         'that is not how we Marigot people sound'

(57)   dat a lai 'that's a lie'

(58)   dɛm pɪkni a me pɪkni dɛm 'those children are my children'

(59)   dɛm de a mi pɪkni an dɛm 'Those there are my children'

(60)   dɛm pikni de a fu mi 'those children there are mine'

(61)   dat a mi pɪkni 'that's my child'

(62)   dat a mi muma vais 'that's my mother's voice'

(63)   da daag ya a fu dat man ova de
         'this dog here belongs to that man over there'

(64)   da daag de no fu mi a da man de
          'That dog is not mine; it's that man's'

(65)   mi a mi oon baas; mi kan du ɛnitıŋ mi want
          'I am my own boss; I can do anything I want'

3.9.2   Attributive copula

The most common attributive strategy is Ø between the pronoun and
the adjective as in (68). One interesting equivalent of the attributive
copula is [tap] in which etymological *stop* seems to have provided a
model for this particular function of the *to be* verb; see (66) and (67)
below.

(66)   wa mek yu tap laika dat? 'why are you like that?'

(67)   wamek yu tap so? 'why are you like that?'

(68)   mi sirias 'I'm serious'

3.9.3   Locative copula

The locative form is [de] with rare instances of [bi] serving this function as
well.

(69)   luk mi sısa de de 'look, my sister is there'

(70)   we i bi? 'where is she?'

(71)   an no bika de de pan di redio e se čupıdnıs dat de kan taak kokoi,
          ya no
          'and not because they are on the radio talking stupidness that
          they can talk Kokoy'

3.10   Past tense marking

As with almost any variety of Caribbean English, non-stative or dynamic
unmarked verbs can be interpreted as marked for the past by default; see (72)
and (82) below. However, the overt past tense marker (sometimes marking
past before past, especially with non-stative verbs) in Kokoy is [mi] in all
instances. This sole past tense form without apparent variation is unusual
even in the Eastern Caribbean, where some reflex of [mın] (e.g. [mi], [miŋ])
is quite common. I recorded all three of the previous forms, for example, in
Barbuda (see Aceto 2002b). The form [mın] appears transparently related
to [bın] with the bilabial onset nasalized. However, the codeless form [mi]
is a bit problematic to resolve in an easy manner, since there are no correspondences in any anglophone Caribbean variety that I am aware of in which
the common past tense form [bın] also displays the reflexes [bıŋ] or [bi], as

one would expect if [mɪn] is straightforwardly accounted for by the nasal-ization of the onset.[8] Regarding the case of [mi] in Kokoy: why did none of the assumed historical variants documented in other nearby areas arise as part of the grammatical system? One would expect them to be a normal part of variation, and yet when my consultants were explicitly questioned about forms like [mɪn], they were always rejected as not part of the local language.

(72)   mi waak pan di ruod yɛstide 'I walked along the road'

(73)   mi mi ha čri a mi frɛn de wɪd mi
         'I had three of my friends there with me'

(74)   čri a mi frɛn mi de wɪd mi 'three of my friends were with me'

(75)   mi mi waak 'I walked/I had walked upon the road'

(76)   mi mi rait 'I was right'

(77)   mi mi kwarɪl wid am 'I quarrelled/I had quarrelled with her/him'

(78)   i sɪŋ an fɪnɪš 'she finished singing'

(79)   wamek yu no mi tɛl i sari 'Why didn't you say "sorry" to him?'

(80)   yu mi aks mi ɪf mi wan go wɪd yu
         'Did you ask me if I wanted to go with you?'

(81)   mi mi so hongri mi almos dɛd 'I was so hungry I almost died'

(82)   i paŋ di kaan wɪd di maata pɛsl
         'she pounded the corn with the mortar and pestle'

(83)   mi mi jʌs e taak gi om 'I was just talking to her'

3.11   Future tense markers

The primary future tense marker in Kokoy is [go] with some apparent instances of [e go] which are most likely progressive aspectual forms with the verb *go* as in (95) below. There appear to be even rare instances of [e go] as a future tense as in (92) below. Winford (1993) presents a discussion of future tense markers, focusing only on *go* and *a go* in what he terms Caribbean English Creole (note the use of the singular here); there is no mention of *e go*. Hancock (1987: 290) reveals only one possible analogue to this construction for Afro-Seminole, a related form of Gullah spoken in south Texas and northern Mexico: [mi ɛ̃ go suun] 'I will go soon'.

---

[8] However, Saramaccan and Matawai exhibit preverbal [bi]; Kwinti, Boni, Paramaccan and Ndyuka display [bɛ] (see Hancock 1987: 282).

(84)   Wa mi go se? 'What am I going to say?'

(85)   yu go se dat wan taim laika dat
          'you're going to say that one time like that'

(86)   Yu go fain wan o tu nega i se dat
          'you're going to find one or two people who say that'

(87)   Yu no go fain aalbadi i taak so
          'you're not going to find everyone who speaks like that'

(88)   Mi hafu go wok jʌs nau 'I have to go to work now'

(89)   mi go go jʌs nau 'I will go'

(90)   sʌmbadi we go gi yu di kokoi gud
          'somebody who is going to give you good Kokoy...'

(91)   i go sɪŋ gi awi 'she will sing for us'

(92)   i e go sɪŋ 'she is going to sing'

(93)   i go sɪŋ tumara 'she will sing tomorrow'

(94)   mi gon go wok 'I'm going to go to work'

(95)   yu e go a rozo 'you are going to Roseau'

(96)   yu go a rozo 'you will go to Roseau'

3.12   Interrogative constructions

There is robust variation in the interrogative form for 'where' in Kokoy; there are no fewer than six different forms: [upaat, wepaat, wɪčpaat, wɪče, iče, we]. According to Hancock (1987: 285), [učpaat], a form similar to [upaat], is heard in Providencia; [wɪčpaat] is found in St. Vincent and Trinidad; [wepaat] is heard in Jamaica. The common form [we] is heard throughout the anglophone Caribbean. Hancock (1987: 285) does not report [wɪče, iče] for any area of the Atlantic region; of course, this does not mean it is not heard beyond Dominica, but only that Hancock's consultants did not report it as a form.

Hancock (1987: 311) reports [wamek] 'why' for the following islands and areas: Guyana, Providencia, Jamaica and St. Vincent. It is also commonly heard among Kokoy-speakers in Dominica. It is surprising that this form is not even more robustly documented, since any English-speaker in any dialect can utters sentences similar to 'What makes you say so?' in which *what + makes* is a substitute for the interrogative form *why*. The construction [hu fu] equals 'whose'; see (101) below.

(97)   wɪče i de? we i de? 'where is she/he/it'?

(98)   wɪče i pʊt ʌm 'where did he put it?'

(99)   wɪče yu pʊt ʌm 'where did you put it?'

(100)   wɪčepaat i de 'where is he/she/it?'

(101)   hu fa (fu + a) da 'whose is that?'

(102)   wamek yu no tɛl yu pɪkni fu tɛl di man i sari
            'why didn't you tell your child to tell the man he's sorry?'

(103)   wamek yu kyaan du dat laika dat 'why can't you do that like that?'

(104)   wamek yu kyaan du om 'why can't you do it?'

3.13   Negation

The common, solitary strategy for negating verb phrases is the preverbal
form *no*. Furthermore, this form is changed via contraction when it occurs
before the progressive aspectual marker [e] and it thus becomes [ne]:

(105)   nʌθɪn ne hapɪn 'nothing's happening'

(106)   i ne sɪŋ fu awi 'she isn't singing for us'

(107)   i ne sɪŋ 'she/he isn't singing'

(108)   i no mi sɪŋ 'she didn't sing'

(109)   i ne go sɪŋ 'she is not singing'

(110)   i no sɪŋ yɛt 'she hasn't sung yet'

3.14   Habitual constructions

In the anglophone Caribbean, some reflex of [dʌz] is the most common preverbal habitual marker; unmarked verbal forms can often indicate habituality
as well (see Hancock 1987: 288). In Kokoy, preverbal [e] is the only habitual
marker I encountered. Preverbal [dʌz] forms were rejected by all consultants
as not part of the local variety of Kokoy. According to Hancock (1987: 288)
only the Surinamese English-derived languages Kwinti, Boni, Paramaccan,
Ndjuka and Sranan also use preverbal [e] as a habitual marker. Nigerian,
Krio and Antiguan reveal preverbal [de] to indicate habituality; preverbal
habitual [de] is also heard in Bastimentos Creole English spoken in Panama.
In Kokoy, preverbal [e] contracts with preceding negator [no] to create the
new form [ne] (see (119) and (120) below).

(111)   mi e go a rozo ɛvri satəde 'I go to Roseau every Saturday'

(112)   mi e go a rozo go si mi brada
         'I go to Roseau to see my brother (frequently)'

(113)   mi e si mi sɪsa ɛvri satəde 'I see my sister every Saturday'

(114)   maagrɪt e taak kokoi gud 'Margaret talks good Kokoy'

(115)   i aalwez e du dat an dat e bada mi
         'he/she always is doing that and it always bother me'

(116)   i e du dat aal taim an i e bada mi
         'he does that all the time and it always bothers me'

(117)   i aalwez e du om 'he's always doing it/he does that all the time'

(118)   i e du om aal taim an i e bada mi
         'he does that all the time and it always bothers me'

(119)   i ne go kʌm agɛn 'he isn't going to come again'

(120)   i ne kʌm agɛn 'he isn't coming again'

3.15   Possession

In Kokoy, possession is indicated by juxtaposing a possessor noun with a possessed noun without any inflectional morphology, in the manner common among so-called creole languages, e.g. *mi muma haus* 'my mother's house'. Additionally, prenominal [fu] can also indicate possession, as is indicated below.

(121)   dat a fu mi kaa 'that's my car'

(122)   dat a fu mi haus 'that's my house'

(123)   dɛm pɪkni de aar fu mi 'those children are mine'

3.16   Benefactive constructions

Benefective [gi] meaning 'for' and even 'to' in some instances is robust in Kokoy. This type of construction is heard in the Surinamese creoles as well as in the Englishes of Antigua and Carriacou (Hancock 1987: 298–9).

(124)   go tek dat gi mi 'go take that for me'

(125)   pɪkni tek dæt gi me 'child, take that for me'

(126)   no taak kokoi gi mi pɪkni 'don't talk Kokoy to my child'

(127)   if yu no taak kokoi gi yu pɪkni, di pɪkni ne go larn di kokoi
'If you don't talk Kokoy to the child, then the child will not learn
the Kokoy'

(128)   keri dat doŋ de gi mi 'carry that down there for me'

(129)   tes dat vɪkl de gi mi 'taste that food there for me'

(130)   i no wan sɪŋ gi awi 'she doesn't want to sing for us'

(131)   i no go sɪŋ gi awi 'she will not sing for us'

(132)   mi ne go sɪŋ gi ayu 'I am not singing for you (pl.)'

(133)   mi ne go sɪŋ gi dɛm 'I am not singing for them'

(134)   luk pan dɛm pɪkni de gi mi
'take care of those children there for me'

(135)   luk pan di haus de gi mi, ren e go faal
'take care of the house there for me, rain is going to fall'

(136)   wamek kaan nobadi brɪŋ da sʌŋ gi mi
'why can't anybody bring that thing for me?'

3.17 Verbal fronting

The nominal copula is fronted in order to indicate emphasis or contrast as is
common in the Atlantic anglophone creoles.

(137)   a rait mi rait 'I'm right'

(138)   a dat mi jʌs ə tɛl yu, di nega dɛm we lɪv a sauθis, awi kaal dɛm
patwa nega
'That's what I'm telling you. The people who live in the southeast, we call them patois people'

3.18 Infinitivals

The infinitival marker in Kokoy is always [fu], and not [fi] or some other
reflex of *for*, as is the case in many of the Atlantic Englishes:

(139)   wɛn i kʌm fu taak di ɪŋlɪš, i kaan taak di ɪŋlɪš gud, so i taak kokoi
'when he tries to talk Enlgish, he can't talk it so well, so he talks
Kokoy'

(140)   so de ha di aportunɪti fu de pan di redio fu taak di kokoi
'so they have the opportunity to be on the radio to talk Kokoy'

(141)   mi laik fu dans 'I like to dance'

(142)   awi laik fu dans 'we like to dance'

(143)   dem de laik fu dans 'those there like to dance'

(144)   mi wan fu aks yu wan kwɛsčan 'I want to ask you a question'

(145)   a kʌm fu aks yu wan kwɛsčan 'I came to ask you a question'

(146)   mi nɪrli dɛd fu hongri 'I was nearly dead I was so hungry'

(147)   mi fiil fu nyam 'I feel like eating'

3.19   Comparatives

As with many varieties of Caribbean English, Kokoy exhibits some inflectional morphology with comparative forms like [smaala] 'smaller' and [bɪga] 'bigger'; see Hanock (1987: 294) for other varieties that display this same morphology. Note also that possessive pronouns are often constructed with [fu] plus subject pronouns like [yu] and [mi].

(148)   fu yu oon pɪkni bɪga dan fu mi 'your child is bigger than mine'

(149)   dɪs pɪkni bɪga dan fu mi 'this child is bigger than mine'

(150)   wɪč pɪkni smala dan fu mi 'which child is smaller than mine?'

(151)   fu yu oon pɪkni smaala da(n) fu mi
           'your child is smaller than mine'

3.20   Completives

As with many of the Atlantic Englishes completive aspect is indicated by preverbal [dʌn] 'done'. Note that the form [i sɪŋ dʌn] with the completive marker in the postverbal position was rejected by all consultants as not a Kokoy construction (see Hancock 1987: 296–7, 302–3). In some rare instances, Kokoy-speakers use preverbal *finish* with the same meaning as *done*; see (155) below.

(152)   mi dʌn tes di vɪkl aarɛdi 'I already tasted the food already'

(153)   i dʌn sɪŋ/i sɪŋ arɛdi 'she's already sung'

(154)   i dʌn sɪŋ arɛdi 'she's already sung'

(155)   ši fɪnɪš sɪŋ 'she's already sung'

(156)   i dʌn let; i ne kʌm agɛn 'he's already late; he isn't coming again'

(157)   a dʌn gaan 'I already left'

3.21   Conditionals

In Kokoy, conditional constructions like 'should have' are represented by reflexes like [šuda] and not by combinations of past + future markers (see Hancock 1987: 306–7).

(158)   mi šuda rimɛmba fu du dat
           'I should have remembered to do that'

(159)   mi šuda rimɛmba fu du om 'I should have remembered to do it'

(160)   mi šuda rimɛmba fu brɪŋ om
           'I should have remembered to bring it'

3.22   Relativizer

The relativized clause marker in Kokoy is [we], which is homophonous with [we] 'where'. Note also that [a] represents existential 'it's' in Kokoy.

(161)   a mi pupa we taak de 'It's my father who's talking there'

4   Some phonological features of Kokoy

One of the most striking phonological features of Kokoy in Dominica is that many speakers exhibit voiceless labiodental fricatives, i.e. [f], in syllable onsets that correspond to voiceless interdental fricatives in metropolitan varieties, i.e. [θ], and [t] in other Caribbean Englishes. For example, the words *three* and *thing* are often realized as [fri] and [fɪŋ] respectively. Another common feature of Kokoy is a general lack of postvocalic [r], which is common enough among Caribbean Englishes, but nearby varieties in Barbados often exhibit postvocalic [r]. Additionally, unlike Englishes heard in the Western Caribbean, Kokoy does not exibit off-glides after velar stops; thus *car* is [kaa], not [kyaa] as is often the case in other varieties. Lastly, many vowels that are represented by diphthongs in Western Caribbean varieties are monophthongs with an off-glide, e.g. [spwel] *spoil* in Kokoy is often [spail] in, for example, Jamaican.

5   Discussion and conclusions

The cluster of grammatical forms presented and discussed above appears to represent a unique variety of Caribbean English among many other similar varieties in the region. What I designate as 'unique' is the bundle of features associated with Kokoy, not in the uniqueness of any one individual feature, though there does appear to be one such feature: progressive aspectual preverbal [e], which, to my knowledge, is not heard in any English-derived area outside of Suriname.

In Aceto (2002b) I presented data on Barbudan Creole English, also spoken in the Eastern Caribbean. There I suggested that the past tense marker [mɪn] and its various reflexes were rather common in the Eastern Caribbean (which is unusual, since the same construction is uncommon elsewhere, e.g. in Jamaica). Some reflex of [mɪn] is also heard in Barbuda, Antigua, St. Kitts and Nevis. What is different about Kokoy is that the overt past tense marker is always [mi]; I never encountered a single token of the form with the bilabial nasal coda. The onset [m-] may be transparently considered as a nasalization of the onset [b-] in [bɪn].[9] Is this [m-] onset a regional Eastern Caribbean innovation? If so, from where did it emerge and spread? My feeling after having documented this form and its reflexes in Barbuda and now in Dominica is that it most likely emerged in the Eastern Caribbean, perhaps in St. Kitts, whose historical varieties have been the subject of some detailed investigations (see Baker and Bruyn 1998).

The forms documented by this research as well as those documented in Barbuda (Aceto 2002b) suggest strongly that the historical nexus of the anglophone Eastern Caribbean was different from that of the Western Caribbean, which has many similar but also substantially different forms. Some of the forms that are more or less 'unique' to the Eastern Caribbean are the second person plural pronominal form [aayu] and the multifunctional third person singular pronominal form [om]. When the verbal markers [mi] and [e] are also considered, what emerges is a grammatically idiosyncratic English variety heard in Dominica.

Even if St. Kitts is convincingly demonstrated to be one location from which Africans and their descendants were distributed across the Eastern Caribbean with their emerging English varieties, from a more recent historical perspective of the last 150 years it must be remembered that nearly all Kokoy-speakers insist that their ancestors came from Antigua and Montserrat. It may never be determined to what extent earlier speakers of Montserrat English contributed to the emergence of Kokoy since the recent volcanic activity of the mid 1990s dispersed speech communities across the Americas and they are only now being reconstituted as speakers return to the island, presumably with some changes to their grammars due to their time in other locations. Gauging the effects on Antiguan English is a little easier since there is better documentation for earlier varieties and more recent published fieldwork. Antiguan reveals some similar features like various reflexes of [mɪn] (though Kokoy has the sole form [mi]) and though it reveals progressive aspectual [de], it does not display, to my knowledge, the form [e].

What research on Kokoy also suggests is that different speakers made different 'choices' (albeit probably mostly unconscious) about their emerging grammars. Just because Kokoy-speakers are knowledgeable about from

---

[9] From a diachronic perspective, it may be considered as a weakening of the onset as it assumes the nasal feature.

where their ancestors immigrated to Dominica does not necessarily mean that the historical immigrants all displayed homogeneous grammars upon landing in Dominica. Some choices were likely made *in situ* while this new community coalesced into a new ethnic and linguistic community vis-à-vis the earlier and more dominant French-creole-speaking community.

Many of the older residents who mostly spoke Kokoy in their youth were insistent that Kokoy is still spoken, but its numbers of speakers are declining. Many of these same key consultants reported that a process of shift occurred fairly rapidly within one generation in the 1950s to 1970s, in which young people started identifying the intermediate institutional English variety used in schools as the most prestigious target. Kokoy-speakers exhibit almost no mixing of Kokoy and intermediate English features. When motivated, one switches between these varieties as if one were switching from one grammatically unrelated variety to another, such as from the local French Creole to English. That is, Kokoy-speakers do not exhibit the purported continuum of varieties associated with so-called decreolization. For some speakers, Kokoy is simply not part of their repertoires; for some it is, and these folks can switch from Kokoy to another language variety in the same manner as traditional code-switching. The concept of decreolization has been undergoing a process of re-examination and deconstruction in the last ten years (see Aceto 1999, Satyanath 2006) and certainly data from Kokoy does not validate this abstraction as having any linguistic reality in Dominica.

References

Aceto, Michael. 1999. 'Looking beyond decreolization as an explanatory model of language change in Creole-speaking communities.' *Journal of Pidgin and Creole Languages* 14: 93–119.

    2002a. 'Going back to the beginning: Describing the (nearly) undocumented Anglophone Creoles of the Caribbean.' In G. G. Gilbert, ed. *Pidgin and Creole Linguistics in the 21st Century*. New York: Peter Lang, 93–120.

    2002b. 'Barbudan Creole English: Its history and some grammatical features.' *English World-Wide* 23: 223–50.

    2003. 'What are creole languages? An alternative approach to the Anglophone Atlantic World with special emphasis on Barbudan Creole English.' In M. Aceto and J. P. Williams, eds., 121–40.

Aceto, Michael and Jeffrey P. Williams, eds. 2003. *Contact Englishes of the Eastern Caribbean*. As part of the series *Varieties of English around the World*. Amsterdam/Philadelphia: John Benjamins.

Allsopp, Richard. 1996. *Dictionary of Caribbean English Usage*. Oxford: Oxford University Press.

Baker, Philip and Adrienne Bruyn. 1998. *St. Kitts and the Atlantic Creoles*. Westminster: University of Westminster Press.

Bryan, Beverley and Rosalind Burnette. 2003. 'Language variation and language use among teachers in Dominica.' In Aceto and Williams, eds., 141–53.

Cassidy, F. G. and R. B. Le Page. 1967. *Dictionary of Jamaican English*. Cambridge: Cambridge University Press.

Christie, Pauline. 1990. 'Language as expression of identity in Dominica.' *International Journal of the Sociology of Language* 85: 61–9.

1994. 'Language preference in two communities in Dominica, West Indies.' *La Linguistique* 30: 7–16.

Hancock, Ian. 1987. 'A preliminary classification of the Anglophone Atlantic creoles, with syntactic data from thirty-three representative dialects.' In Glenn G. Gilbert, ed. *Pidgin and Creole Languages: Essays in Memory of John E. Reinecke*. Honolulu: University Press of Hawaii, 264–334.

Honychurch, Lennox. 1995. *The Dominica Story: A History of the Island*. London: Macmillan.

McWhorter, John. 1998. 'Identifying the creole prototype: Vindicating a typological class.' *Language* 74: 788–818.

2000. 'Defining "creole" as a synchronic term.' In Ingrid Neumann-Holzschuh and Edgar W. Schneider, eds. *Degrees of Restructuring in Creole Languages*. Amsterdam: John Benjamins, 85–123.

Mufwene, Salikoko S. 2000. 'Creolization is a social, not a structural, process.' In Ingrid Neumann-Holzschuh and Edgar W. Schneider, eds. *Degrees of Restructuring in Creole Languages*. Amsterdam: John Benjamins, 65–84.

2001. *The Ecology of Language Evolution*. Cambridge: Cambridge University Press.

Parkvall, Mikael. 2001. 'Creolistics and the quest for creoleness: A reply to Claire Lefebvre.' *Journal of Pidgin and Creole languages* 16: 147–51.

Plag, Ingo. 2001. 'The nature of derivational morphology in creoles and non-creoles.' *Journal of Pidgin and Creole Languages* 16: 153–60.

Rizzi, Luigi. 1999. 'Broadening the empirical basis of universal grammar models: A commentary.' In Michel DeGraff, ed. *Language Creation and Language Change: Creolization, Diachrony, and Development*. Cambridge, Mass.: The MIT Press, 453–72.

Satyanath, Shobha. 2006. 'English in the New World: Continuity and change, the case of personal pronouns in Guyanese English.' In Parth Bhatt and Ingo Plag, eds. *The Structure of Creole Words: Segmental, Syllabic and Morphological Aspects*. Tubingen: Max Niemeyer Verlag, 179–99.

Winford, Donald. 1993. *Predication in Caribbean English Creoles*. Amsterdam/Philadelphia: John Benjamins Publishing Company.

10   Anglo-Argentine English

JULIAN JEFFERIES

1 Introduction

More than a hundred years of mutually beneficial commerce relations between Britain and Argentina, from the middle of the nineteenth century to the end of the Second World War, established an enclave of English-speaking people in Argentina that reached a peak of 28,300 (Cortes Conde 2000) in 1914. While there is little data that differentiates the regional origins of the flow of immigrants, except for a well-known Welsh enclave in Patagonia, the main bulk of the flow were middle-class merchants of mostly English origin who worked in the meat-packing and railroad industries and settled in the northern suburbs of Buenos Aires. Creating their own newspaper, hospitals, schools, churches and clubs, the enclave remained relatively isolated from the host country language and culture until 1950. Due to Britain's economic decline and economic relations between the two countries coming to a near stop, many of the immigrants returned to Britain, with the Anglo–Argentine community halving in size to 17,500 by 1976 (Graham-Yooll 1981). This number has remained relatively stable in the last thirty years, a time marked by a greater amount of cultural and linguistic contact with the Argentinian population. From this tracing of the English-speaking people in Argentina, this chapter describes the sociolinguistic history and some phonetic characteristics of this little-known variety of Southern Hemisphere English.

2 The rise of the community

The immigration of English-speaking peoples to Latin America started in the early seventeenth century, but a more stabilized establishment came when these colonized countries obtained independence from either Spain or Portugal, and 'the region opened up to overseas trade and investment' (Marshall 2000: xvii). Immigration from the United Kingdom to Argentina started as early as 1744, when it was a Spanish colony and where a local census reported seven English people out of a total of 16,091 (Table 10.1 gives the census returns from 1869 onwards). Before Argentina's independence from Spain in 1810, Britain 'regarded Argentina as a possible place to invade in

Table 10.1 *Argentine population compared with foreign-born and British-born nationals (Cortes Conde 2000)*

	Total population	Other foreign-born	British-born
1869	1,737,080	210,299	10,637
1895	3,954,911	1,004,527	21,788
1914	7,885,237	2,357,952	28,300

order to gain access to a trading post' (Graham-Yooll 1981: 25) that would allow them to control new markets and extend their naval supremacy to the South Atlantic. After two failed attempts to invade the city of Buenos Aires in 1806 and 1807, British settlers became very friendly and generous with the new independence movement and provided intellectual support to recognize the revolution. At the same time, they were eager to establish good trading relations with the new independent country. The 'Treaty of Friendship, Navigation and Commerce' between Britain and the United Provinces of the Rio de la Plata in 1825 followed, and 'was to govern relations for almost a century' (Graham-Yooll 1981: 188).

This treaty would be responsible for a considerable flow of capital and most of the immigration of British people to Argentina. The next two hundred years witnessed a flow of immigrants from Ireland, Scotland, Wales and England. Although this immigration is numerically less significant than the Spanish and Italian immigration during the nineteenth century, British immigration was to play an important role in the economic development and the building of the infrastructure of Argentina. It is believed that although this flow of English-speaking people started as early as 1840, the bulk of immigration came during the second part of the nineteenth century.

Although there is no concrete data in terms of the regional origin and destination of each population, it is well known that Welsh immigrants settled in an isolated community in Patagonia and still have a vigorous, identifiable culture. The literature on the subject generalizes the English-speaking population as belonging to a British community, while little detail is available in terms of distinguishing original regional differences among them. Frequently, older members of the Anglo-Argentine community acknowledge a distinction between English immigrants and those of Scottish and Irish background in terms of social class and geographical location. English immigrants were typically from an educated middle class, either with capital to invest, or administrators of this capital or employees in British companies. A large number of the latter worked in the railway and meat-packing companies and settled in the northern suburbs of Buenos Aires. Due to their social and economic capital, their language and culture was maintained. Irish and Scottish immigrants, however, were of working-class origins, and settled in the southern suburbs of the city. These populations seemed to assimilate into

Argentine culture more readily and have therefore not survived as a linguistic and cultural enclave. Although there exists a number of communities of British origin spread throughout Argentina, historical accounts have mostly followed the most numerous and homogenous population: that of English middle-class immigrants concentrated in the northern suburbs of Buenos Aires.

During the earlier portion of the migration from England, several patterns of interaction demonstrate an intentional resistance to assimilating into the new country and an attitude towards it as a temporary residence to conduct business. Notably, they replicated most of the institutions of their country of origin, building churches, clubs, hospitals and schools in the English way, even bringing English teachers to fill the schools. Furthermore, it was a common occurrence to send the women back to Britain in order for the children to be born there in order to retain their citizenship. During the First and Second World Wars, many of the second- and third-generation English men living in Argentina enlisted on the side of the allies, even though they were not born in England, and had no obligation to enlist.

Deborah Jakubs (2000) describes this attitude against assimilation into a new country as different from most other immigrant groups. She stresses that 'the special position they occupied as members of the "progressive race"' made it possible for them to 'maintain their English ways and [use] selective hybridization' (155). Most interestingly, she comments on how most English immigrants had in the back of their minds what she calls a 'psychological escape hatch: the belief that they could always go home' (155). As opposed to other immigrant populations, the British had more chances of going back to the home country if they were not pleased with their situation.

Having little use for it, the first English settlers did not learn Spanish very well; in fact, 'to keep their shocking accent in the native Spanish tongue was a symbol of status, of power' (Graham-Yooll 1981: 228). Most of these immigrants established themselves above the middle classes of Argentine society, they were well received by the host country and their language enjoyed a high status among Argentines. Parents sent their children to schools where instruction was in English only, or directly sent them to school in England. Most of the social life in clubs and churches together with the intermarrying practices of this community preserved the cultural parameters of this professional middle-class enclave. In terms of language use, the particular characteristics of this immigrant group set the stage for a high degree of language maintenance.

2.1   *The world wars and their effect on the community*

In the Argentine 1914 census, there were approximately 28,000 people of British descent in Argentina. The next fifteen years would be the most fruitful economically in terms of trade between these two countries, and even though the Anglo–Argentine community lost many of its members to the First World War, some British interests continued to expand. The railways built by the British were already run by well-established corporations, and the meat-packing industry, also dominated by the British, became one of the most profitable industries in the 1930s.

However, the end of the 1930s marked the end of an era. The influence of the United States began to grow in South America and in Argentina as North Americans competed with British interests in commerce, banking and capital goods investments (Graham-Yooll 1981: 242), but it was the Second World War that dealt the major blow to British interests in Argentina. Towards the end of the war, Britain's economic decline began, and the community in Argentina felt it. The war effort made it difficult for the British to manage its overseas investments, especially in Argentina where there was no colonial authority. It was a relief to British shareholders, then, when the Argentine government bought the British-built-and-run railroads. At this time, most British capital left the country, and trading relations came to a near stop. The general in charge of Argentina, Juan Domingo Perón, was also not very sympathetic to the British, and there were isolated instances of harassment (Graham-Yooll 1981: 244).

All these factors contributed to the exodus of British subjects from Argentina. After the railways, many other employees of British-owned companies followed in the exodus. However, not all the members of the community left: those who had lost close economic or family contact with Britain remained, comprising the core of what would become the Anglo–Argentine community. Graham-Yooll reports that the number of recorded British subjects reached 17,500 in 1976 (1981: 245), a little more than half the former population after sixty years of decline.

3   A sociolinguistic study of the community: A look at the present

Twenty years later, in 1996, the number of Anglo–Argentines living in Buenos Aires and the suburbs was estimated at 15,000 (Cortes-Conde 1996: 114). Many of the institutions created by the long years of economic exchange remain, as in the case of *The Buenos Aires Herald*, an English newspaper with a circulation of approximately 17,000, a British Hospital and approximately twenty-five English/Spanish bilingual schools (ibid.: 115). These institutions are no longer restricted to British descendants; in schools, the majority of the children attending are upper- and upper-middle-class Argentines, aware of the importance of English for social mobility. Churches and hospitals, furthermore, have to cater to the Argentine public in order to subsist.

A sociolinguistic survey of the Anglo–Argentine community conducted in 1996 found that it was more common for the younger members of the community to speak Spanish than English, exhibiting a higher proficiency in the former. Most of the younger respondents used English with older relatives, but switched to Spanish when talking to siblings or peers. Older respondents, on the other hand, were more proficient in English overall. Regarding language use patterns, older respondents claimed they used English more than Spanish in all domains except at work. Age as a variable was significant, where the author saw a language shift occurring from a more proficient English-speaking older generation to a younger generation that relies more heavily on Spanish as their language of choice (Cortes Conde 1996: 115).

These findings show that the process of language shift in this community does not imply that there is a complete loss of the mother tongue, but 'rather the loss of that language as the community's mother tongue, that is, the symbolic power of that language as a marker of group membership' (Cortes Conde 1996: 113). Anglo-Argentines do not all speak English among themselves, as English is ceasing to be their native language, but it has not been lost: it is shifting towards being a second language for the younger generation. One of the main reasons that English is not lost is because younger community members are retaining it for its instrumental value: it is an asset when looking for a job in a country with a high unemployment rate.

The Anglo-Argentine community, even though it has a prestigious language (English) and is living in a country where a less prestigious language is spoken (Spanish), still struggles to maintain stable bilingualism. Among the most important reasons for this phenomenon, Cortes Conde argues, is that peers strongly discourage each other from speaking in English. Even in bilingual English schools, speaking in English causes the child to be ridiculed and seen as a 'snob', and thus to feel isolated. For young children growing up it is important not to seem different. The prestige of the English language seems to be working against itself in this case, as young locals perceive it as snobbish. However, young Anglo-Argentines keep their English and use it selectively and to suit their own purposes. Another important reason for the loss of stable bilingualism is related to changes to the practice of marrying within the community, a common occurrence before the 1950s. In the last fifty years the community has halved in size and marriage outside of the community has become the norm. This means that there is now often only one parent in the household who speaks English, making it more difficult for the children to speak English at home and thus be more proficient in it.

As we can see, the Anglo-Argentine community has a very particular history. More than a hundred years of mutually beneficial commercial relations built a community of approximately 30,000 people at its peak, a number that was drastically reduced at the end of the Second World War. Sixty years later, and after an armed conflict between these countries, the community exhibits some interesting sociolinguistic characteristics, including a maintenance but also a concurrent displacement of English as a mother tongue in the younger generations. As such, the contemporary uses of English within this community are worthy of further investigation, including analysis of

Table 10.2 *Range of age groups and*
average age per group

	Age Range	Average Age
Younger	18 to 35	25
Middle	31 to 60	50.25
Older	Above 60	78.5

specific features. This provides an opportunity to describe some of the phonetic characteristics of a variety of Southern Hemisphere English practically
unknown to the rest of the world.

4   Two phonetic variables in Anglo-Argentine English

In order to evaluate some of the phonetic features of the variety on a preliminary basis, twelve informants were interviewed in Argentina during
December 2003. The first part of the interview focused on their language
practices and attitudes about language and the community. Additionally,
phonetic data was gathered when informants read a story out loud with various instances of postvocalic /r/ and intervocalic /t/, two features of English
that exhibit variability across dialects. Although the sample is limited in
terms of the analysis of two phonetic features, a small number of informants
and a prompted read-aloud technique, it will enable us to start describing
some of the patterns of this variety.

4.1   The informants

All the informants were born in Argentina, except one, who was born in
England but moved to Argentina at a young age. The twelve informants
were chosen according to gender and age, so that I had two female and two
male informants for each age group. The informants were classified into
three groups according to their age: Older (60 and more), Middle (31 to 60)
and Younger (18 to 30; Tables 10.2 and 10.3).

The older generation, born between 1919 and 1930, experienced the transition of the community after the Second World War. All of them attended
school in English in Argentina. The men in this generation worked for
English companies in either the textile industry or for a construction company, where English was spoken, while the women in this generation did not
work. All of them have travelled to England in their lifetime, though some
more often than others: two of them travelled every year or every other year
most of their life, while the other two have been there only five times. All of
them, additionally, speak English at home.

Table 10.3 *Age of informants*

Informant	Age	Country of birth
Martin J.	22	Argentina
Terence R.	23	Argentina
Cecilia J.	26	Argentina
Cynthia T.	29	Argentina
Kevin S.	41	Argentina
Cathy O.	41	Argentina
Susan J.	59	United Kingdom
Harry J.	60	Argentina
Edith M.	81	Argentina
William G.	77	Argentina
Peggy L.	83	Argentina
Ronnie J.	73	Argentina

The middle generation, born between 1942 and 1962, were all born in Argentina, except one who was born in England and moved to Argentina when she was two years old. All of them attended bilingual schools in English and Spanish. Two of the informants are teachers of English, one a retired employee in a farm management business owned by Anglo-Argentines, and the other works for the United Nations, where her command of English is needed. Three of them reported that they speak both English and Spanish at home, while one said that he speaks only Spanish. Three of them actively engage in community, religious and social activities that are linked to the community. Although these activities are linked to the Anglo-Argentine community, they are not always conducted in English.

The younger generation, born between 1973 and 1980, also attended school in English and Spanish. Two of them are pursuing tertiary education, one in a bilingual university and the other in an all-Spanish one. Their use of English in their work environments differs from other generations. Two of the informants use English at work: one of them in a management company where both Spanish and English are used, and most of the English spoken is with General American speakers; the other is under direct management of a person from the United States. The rest of the informants in this generation use only Spanish at work, and all of them speak Spanish at home. Regarding their participation in events of the Anglo-Argentine community, only one of the informants participates actively in religious and social activities. For the rest, the only contact with the community is through family or old friends from school.

All of the informants spoke English at home, in some degree, before they attended school, and they all have the same level of education: a high school degree. Geographically, they live in the same region of the city of Buenos Aires: the northern suburbs. The Anglo-Argentine community, in this part of the city, belongs to a middle class employed in white-collar jobs.

Table 10.4 *Omission of postvocalic /r/ by social and linguistic factors*

	%	Factor Weight	Significance	Number of tokens
Age Group				
Younger	82	.32	p < 0.005	217
Middle	90	.53	p < 0.005	223
Older	93	.65	p < 0.005	224
Gender				
Male	92	.61	p < 0.005	331
Female	85	.39	p < 0.005	333
Stress				
Stressed	91	.62	p < 0.005	296
Unstressed	85	.41	p < 0.005	368
Following sound				
Vowel	61	.11	p < 0.005	84
Consonant	93	.60	p < 0.005	496
Pause	88	.40	p < 0.005	60
Approximant	83	.40	p < 0.005	24

4.2 *Postvocalic /r/*

Varieties of English exhibit a high degree of variability in terms of rhoticity of postvocalic /r/ in final or preconsonantal position. Historically, Bailey (1996) argues that the English of England shifted from consonantal to vocalic /r/ roughly at the end of the eighteenth century, while Strang (1970) and Lass (1992) place this transition between the late seventeenth and early eighteenth centuries. However, new sets of data analysed by Trudgill (1999) suggest that rhoticity was still present in most dialects of English spoken in the mid nineteenth century, suggesting that 'the loss of rhoticity is something that has occurred subsequently in both New Zealand and England' (233).

The reading aloud of the passage for the Anglo-Argentine informants yielded 664 tokens for postvocalic /r/, with approximately 55 tokens for each informant. Each informant produced the same number of environments, since they were reading from the same passage, and there were thirty-six different words with a postvocalic /r/ in the reading passage. Tokens were coded for social factors (age and gender), along with stress (stressed or unstressed syllable), following segment (vowel, consonant, pause or approximant) and preceding segment (/ə/, /ae/ or /o/); see Table 10.4.

The first considerable finding is that, even though this feature shows variability, postvocalic /r/ was not pronounced in the informant's reading 88 per cent of the time. The input value, the average frequency of occurrence of the application value of the dependent variable, is 0.93, showing the lack of rhoticity for speakers of Anglo-Argentine English. The age of the informant was found to have a very strong influence on the dropping of /r/ (see Figures 10.1–3). It is clear that the older generation favours this application (factor weight = 0.65), while the middle generation does so in a smaller

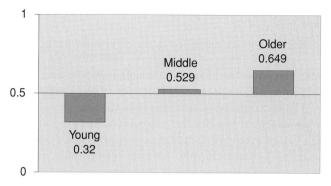

Figure 10.1 Factor weights by age group

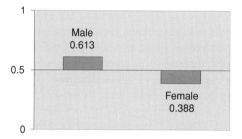

Figure 10.2 Factor weights according to gender

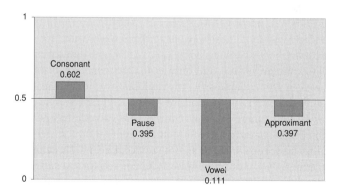

Figure 10.3 Factor weights by following sound

degree (0.53), and the younger generation is more prone to pronounce /r/ (0.32).

The lack of rhoticity exhibited in the older informants corresponds with other varieties of Southern Hemisphere English, although there is not enough phonetic data about the history of the community to determine if this shift occurred in Argentina or was brought over by the English-speaking immigrants. The rhoticization of this feature in the younger generation could be due to phonological transfer from Argentine Spanish, stemming from the unstable nature of bilingualism in the community and the shift from English to Spanish as a mother tongue. Another reason could be the contact that younger members are experiencing with American English, although a bigger sample would be needed in order to determine if this type of interaction is a notable trend in the Anglo-Argentine community.

4.3   Intervocalic /t/

The realization of intervocalic /t/ word-internally and across word boundaries in English dialects is rich in variants. Bailey (1996) suggests that glottalling of this feature started as early as 1860 in London and Scotland, spreading to other English dialects in England, although only very recently (Trudgill 1999). As we look at other varieties of English, Wells (1982: 250) affirms that the voicing of /t/ 'is sometimes to be observed in southern hemisphere English, and also in certain casual styles in British accents ranging from RP to Cockney'. He then speculates that this influence is 'the first distinctively American phonetic innovation likely to spread in time to all accents of English' (ibid.). Furthermore, in Canada, Woods (1991) and De Wolf (1990) say that it is well established in Canadian English.

For the Anglo-Argentine community sample, the social factors considered were age and gender. There were twelve words where the tokens were produced: *latest, better, native, Peter, city, party, forty, thirty, computer, invited, reported* and *cheating*. Nearly twenty tokens were coded for each informant, making a total of 215 tokens. Of these, 192 (89 per cent) were marked with a voiceless alveolar plosive, and only 23 (11 per cent) were not.

As we can see in Table 10.5, the high distribution of the voiceless plosive /t/ is reflected in the generations of Anglo-Argentines. The older generation has a high percentage of production of the variable (98 per cent), but this number drops severely for the younger generation (76 per cent), which is replacing this feature with the voicing of /t/. The middle generation produces the variable 93 per cent of the time. The chi-square test shows this data to be significant: the probability of a younger informant producing the variable is very low (factor weight 0.18), while the older generation is much more likely to use it (factor weight 0.83).

Although glottal stops could have been brought by British immigrants to Argentina, there is no evidence of this feature in the speech of the Anglo-Argentine community. This could be an example of 'the post-colonial

Table 10.5 *Intervocalic voiceless plosive /t/ according to social and linguistic factors (factor weights in brackets are not significant)*

	%	Factor Weight	Significance	Number of tokens
Age Group				
Younger	76	.18	p = 0.000	72
Middle	93	.48	p = 0.000	72
Older	98	.83	p = 0.000	71
Gender				
Male	92	[.60]	p = 0.012	108
Female	85	[.40]	p = 0.012	107

survival of earlier phases of mother country culture' (Marckwart 1958; in Trudgill 1999) or 'colonial lag', due to the isolated nature of the enclave up to the 1950s. The data further demonstrates the highly unstable nature of the variety, with the younger generation moving from a voiceless plosive stop towards the voicing of /t/, probably due to the influence of American English in the community.

5   Conclusions

A sociolinguistic and phonetic evaluation of the community points to a high degree of instability across generations in the variety of Anglo–Argentine English. While older generations of Anglo–Argentines use English more often and in more contexts while retaining phonetic features reminiscent of the 'mother country', younger generations are losing English as the mother tongue, with cases of phonological influences from American English and/or Argentine Spanish. The older generations' speech patterns further exemplify cases of 'colonial lag' in Southern Hemisphere Englishes, attesting to the isolated nature of social life for the community before the Second World War. A more comprehensive study of the community's language patterns, including morphology, syntax and lexicon, can shed light regarding the nature of the phonological transfer. In terms of its future, the relatively high status of English in Argentina due to its economic advantages will secure its survival, although a high degree of phonological transfer seems likely. Further study of the community's phonetic characteristics with a more representative sample in different regions of the country are needed to shed light on this highly fascinating and previously unacknowledged variety of Southern Hemisphere English.

References

Bailey, Richard W. 1996. *Nineteenth Century English*. Ann Arbor: University of Michigan Press.

Cortes Conde, Florencia. 1996. 'Is stable bilingualism possible in an immigrational setting? The Anglo-Argentine case.' In Ana Roca and John B. Jensen, eds. *Spanish in Contact*. Somerville, Mass.: Cascadilla Press, 113–22.

2000. 'New nations and old identities: Anglo-Argentines and the South Atlantic conflict.' In O. Marshall, ed. *English-Speaking Communities in Latin-America*. New York: St. Martin's Press, 159–77.

De Wolf, Gaelan D. 1990. 'Patterns of usage in urban Canadian English.' *English World Wide* 11: 1–31.

Graham-Yooll, Andrew. 1981. *The Forgotten Colony: A History of the English Speaking Colonies in Argentina*. London: Hutchinson.

Jakubs, Deborah. 2000. 'The Anglo-Argentines: Work, family and identity, 1860–1914.' In O. Marshall, ed. *English-Speaking Communities in Latin-America*. New York: St. Martin's Press, 135–57.

Lass, Roger. 1992. 'Phonology and morphology.' In N. Blake, ed. *The Cambridge History of the English Language*, vol. II: *1066–1476*. Cambridge: Cambridge University Press, 23–155.

Marckwardt, Albert H. 1958. *American English*. New York: Oxford University Press.

Marshall, Oliver. 2000. *English Speaking Communities in Latin-America*. New York: St. Martin's Press.

Strang, Barbara M. H. 1970. *A History of English*. London: Methuen.

Trudgill, Peter. 1999. 'A window to the past: "Colonial Lag" and New Zealand Evidence for the Phonology of Nineteenth Century English.' *American Speech* 74: 227–39.

Wells, John. 1982. *Accents of English* (3 vols.). Cambridge: Cambridge University Press.

Woods, Howard. 1991. 'Social differentiation in Ottawa English.' In Jenny Cheshire, ed. *English Around the World: Sociolinguistic Perspectives*. Cambridge: Cambridge University Press, 134–49.

Part III

The South Atlantic Ocean

11   Falkland Islands English

DAVID BRITAIN AND ANDREA SUDBURY

1 Introduction

The Falkland Islands comprise a group of 780 islands in the South Atlantic Ocean, 480 km off the east coast of Argentina. Together, the islands cover 12,173 km² (slightly larger than Jamaica and Kosovo, slightly smaller than Connecticut, about half the size of Wales and a third the size of Baden-Württemberg), with a resident population of 2,955, according to the 2006 census. There are two main islands, East and West Falkland, and the capital is Stanley, on East Falkland, where 85 per cent of the resident population live. In addition to the resident population, around 2,000 British military personnel are based at RAF Mount Pleasant, 50 km west of Stanley. Politically, the Falklands are an Overseas Territory of the United Kingdom.

Closely associated with the Falklands, but now technically independent of them, are South Georgia and the South Sandwich Islands (SGSSI) (capital Grytviken), another UK Overseas Territory situated 1,390 km east-southeast of the Falklands. South Georgia, at 3,528 km² the same size roughly as Luxembourg, Saarland or the county of Dorset in England, was once an important whaling station. The 1909 census found a population of 720, of which over 90 per cent were Scandinavian, predominantly Norwegian. The whaling stations began to decline in the mid twentieth century, with the last closing in 1966, and today there is no settled civilian population, although there are two permanently staffed British Antarctic Research Stations, as well as Government Officers and curators staffing the museum and shop that are visited by passing cruise ships. The South Sandwich Islands (310 km² – the same size as Malta), a further 640 km southeast of South Georgia, are uninhabited. Today South Georgia and the South Sandwich Islands constitute a UK Overseas Territory distinct from the Falklands, but are administered by a Commissioner who also holds the post of Governor of the Falkland Islands.

Further south is the British Antarctic Territory, a UK Overseas Territory comprising part of Antarctica, the South Shetland Islands and South Orkney, which covers an area of 1,709,400 km² (slightly larger than Iran). Like SGSSI, the British Antarctic Territory has no settled population, but is home to a number of research stations, with around 500 scientists and support staff in winter, rising to well over 2,500 in summer, from a number of countries, including Poland, Russia, South Korea, Spain, as well as Argentina, Chile and the UK. The Territory is administered by a Commissioner, who also holds the post of Head of the Overseas Territories Department at the British Foreign and Commonwealth Office. Because of the lack of a settled civilian population, no more will be said here about SGSSI and the British Antarctic Territory.

The Falklands have been continuously settled by anglophones for only just over 175 years, making the variety of English spoken there one of the most recently developed 'Inner Circle' (Kachru 1985) Englishes in the world. Unlike many of the other Inner Circle Englishes that formed at roughly the same time, such as those of New Zealand and Australia, the anglophone community that developed there was not in contact with an indigenous non-anglophone population, providing (almost – see below) the sort of *tabula rasa* contact situation for the English dialects brought by settlers and migrants that has been the subject of recent theoretical speculation (Gordon et al. 2004; Trudgill 2004) in English dialectology. Furthermore, although formed only slightly later than Australian (AE) and New Zealand Englishes (NZE), Falkland Islands English (FIE), as we will see, was formed from the dialects of settlers from rather different parts of the British Isles than those who went to the South Pacific. This settler mix, the *tabula rasa* situation, as well as an extremely sparsely distributed population and low absolute numbers of migrants have all contributed to making Falkland Islands English a distinctive variety, sharing some but not all features with the other Southern Hemisphere Inner Circle anglophone countries.

2 Falkland Islands: History and anglophone settlement

Although the British first set foot on the islands in 1690, uninterrupted anglophone settlement of the Falklands dates back to the mid 1830s, when, on 2 January 1833, Captain Onslow on the HMS *Clio* landed at Port Louis in the northeast of East Falkland and raised the Union Flag (Gough 1990: 270). According to Pascoe and Pepper (2008: 18–19), there were thirty-three residents already there, along with an Argentinian garrison of twenty-six soldiers and their families that had been on the islands since 6 October 1832. The garrison was forced to leave, and the other residents given the option of staying or leaving. Eleven residents left, leaving twelve Argentinians, four Charrúa Indians from Uruguay, two British, two Germans, one French and one Jamaican. Seven more civilians arrived in March 1833 (four gauchos, of unspecified nationality, one Argentinian and two British) (Pascoe and Pepper (2008: 20), though by this time Onslow had left, leaving no official presence on the islands to enforce sovereignty besides 'the storekeeper William Dickson [who] was instructed to hoist a British flag on

Sundays and when a ship approached' (Pascoe and Pepper 2008: 20). The murder of five settlers by eight of the resident gauchos in mid-1833 led to the return of the Navy in early 1834, who arrested and expelled the gauchos and established a permanent garrison on the islands (Royle 1985: 205). The presence of the garrison did not straightforwardly lead to the development of a viable colony, however. Throughout the remainder of the 1830s the population of the islands struggled to reach sustainable levels. In 1836 seventeen people – mostly British – arrived (Royle 1985: 205). The 1838 census counted forty-three people, of whom fourteen were sailors working from docked ships and seven were temporary gauchos. The population saw high turnover and of the forty-nine non-military residents at the time of the 1842 census only ten of the 1838 population were still present (Royle 1985: 206). Of those forty-nine, none were independent settlers: there were missionaries en route to Patagonia, temporary gauchos and sealers, a private group of horticulturalists and fish-curers and some other temporary government workers (Royle 1985: 206). Throughout the 1840s there were numerous references to a population that was described by the first governor, R. Moody, as 'men of reckless character, irregular passions unchecked by moral impulses, far less discipline' (in Royle 1985: 209). Royle reports that, in 1842, for the total population of sixty-two souls, 541 gallons (over 2,400 litres) of spirits and 200 gallons (over 900 litres) of wine were imported, suggesting, rather amusingly, that 'perhaps some of it was destined for the supply of passing ships' (1985: 209).

It was clear that the islands required a more formally organized strategy to bring migrants to the islands, and it was soon recognized that, given the climate and the agricultural conditions, 'there seemed to be general agreement that the best colonists would be Scottish islanders' (Royle 1985: 207). From the 1850s onwards, the population began to increase. The 1851 census found a population of 384, of whom 140 were children under 15 (Pascoe and Pepper 2008: 24), reaching 540 in 1860 and 662 in 1867 (Royle 1985: 211). By 1901, following a committed recruitment drive in the UK, the population had reached over 2,000, according to the Falkland Islands Government Census Report. There were few migrants from South America in the nineteenth century – Spruce (1996: 1) suggests no more than 100, and most had returned by the end of the century. We do know, however, that the nineteenth century population was constantly in a state of flux, partly caused by a large proportion of the workforce being contract employees, who came, served their time and then left, partly by unexpected arrivals – e.g. a good number of Scandinavians who had been shipwrecked or jumped ship on their way around Cape Horn – and partly by the return of migrants who had intended to stay but couldn't acclimatize to life in the Falklands (see Sudbury 2000, 2001). Unlike, then, in New Zealand and Australia where an indigenous non-anglophone presence was large in number and remained, this cannot be said to be true of the Falklands, where, in the early years, people from places other than the British Isles were few, temporary and often accidental.

The total population remained at just over 2,000 throughout the twentieth century, but again there was considerable demographic instability – in 1952 alone, for example, over 12 per cent of the population emigrated from the islands and another 9 per cent arrived to settle there (see, for example, Sudbury 2000: 26). There was a general decline in the population between the Second World War and 1982 – a fall of over 19 per cent between the censuses of 1946 and 1980, caused by economic decline and the gradual fall of the price of wool on international markets, a key Falkland export at the time.

In April 1982, the Falklands were invaded by Argentina, and were recaptured by British armed forces seventy-four days later. The consequences of this conflict for the Falklands and their people have been considerable. The establishment of a fisheries licensing zone in 1986 has generated considerable wealth for the islands, and their general prosperity has triggered an upsurge in migration, with the population rising by more than 36 per cent since 1980. The population is becoming more and more urban, however. Today 85 per cent of the population live in Stanley – with the rest living in 'Camp', the local term used to describe settlements elsewhere on East and West Falkland, or on one of the other islands of the archipelago – up from just 58 per cent in 1980. Sudbury (2000: 29–30) shows that the population surge occurred mostly in the 1980s, in the years immediately after the conflict, and that since then there has been less immigration but also less emigration – the population is becoming more stable.

The 2006 census shows that the largest groups in the population not born in the Falklands are from Great Britain (838 people or 28.4 per cent of the population), St Helena (394, 13.3 per cent), Chile (161, 5.4 per cent) and Australia (36, 1.2 per cent). In all, 55 per cent of the population were born outside the islands, a level of immigration as a proportion of the total population only exceeded in Europe by Andorra and Monaco. The islands may be distant from the more metropolitan parts of the northern hemisphere, they may have a small population, but they should in no way be seen as demographically homogeneous or monocultural. People born in sixty-two different countries were resident on the islands at the time of the 2006 census (Pascoe and Pepper 2008: 38).

Accurate details of the places of birth of the earlier settlers who remained in the Falklands are harder to come by. As Sudbury (2000: 119–21) outlines, many of the records have been lost or destroyed and those that remain are often vague and inconclusive. Although dominated by the English, the origins of the very early residents of the Falklands in the mid nineteenth century were quite diverse, with small numbers of Spaniards, Irish and Scandinavians. By the late 1860s, the British government's efforts at encouraging migration were beginning to show signs of success, leading to a steady increase in migration, especially from Somerset, Devon and other parts of the southwest of England, from Hampshire in the south of England, and from (especially Gaelic-speaking areas of) Scotland (Strange 1983; Trehearne 1978). As Trehearne notes, 'a great proportion . . . were of Scottish origin, often emigrants from the Western Highlands and Islands, especially Lewis . . . Applicants from the Western Isles would have obtained favourable consideration for these free passages, coming as they did from a part of Britain not unlike the Falklands in climate and way of life' (1978: 124). Indeed, William Blain, a shepherd from Dumfries, noted on his arrival in the Falklands in 1878 that 'Scotland has equally as good a claim to the Falklands as England. At the time I am speaking of, the majority of the inhabitants was Scotch or of Scotch descendants. Besides, the Scotch language was fairly well represented' (quoted in Cameron 1997). Whilst it is probable that Gaelic did not survive long in the Falklands, the question of what sort of English these migrants spoke and thus contributed to the feature pool remains open, and there has been disagreement in the literature over whether the English of the late nineteenth century Highlands and Islands was standard-like (see Bailey 1996: 301) or strongly influenced by Scots (Clement 1980: 14; see also Ó Baoill 1997: 566). Of course the migrants to the Falklands from the Highlands and Islands of Scotland may well also have been Gaelic monolinguals or a mixture of monolinguals and bilinguals and may have acquired all or most of their English en route to and on arrival in the South Atlantic. Overall, though, it is clear that the predominant accents and dialects of English shaping the emergent Falkland Islands English are those of the south and southwest of England, and the northwest of Scotland.

3   A description of Falkland Islands English (FIE)

Below is an outline of some of the main structural and lexical characteristics of Falkland Islands English. It is based on analyses of the first large-scale social dialectological corpus of FIE, collected by Andrea Sudbury (see Sudbury 2000: 133–63 for more details of data collection and corpus structure). The corpus contains over 100 hours of informal conversational data from eighty-seven Falkland Islanders.

3.1   Vowels

In order to briefly describe the vocalic system of Falkland Islands English, we will adopt Wells' (1982) lexical set classification system.

KIT, DRESS, TRAP
Unlike Australian and New Zealand Englishes, FIE has but slight, sporadic and isolated raising of the front short vowels. Raising appears to be lexically determined to some extent, with 'get' particularly vulnerable (as it is in a

number of varieties in England), and is generally more common in DRESS than KIT or, especially, TRAP. In general, then, we can say that these vowels are realized as [ɪ], [ẹ] and [æ] in FIE (see Sudbury 2000: 285–314 for more detail). It has been suggested, in studies of New Zealand English, for example (Trudgill, Gordon and Lewis 1998), that slightly raised variants of these vowels were imported from England, and raised further in New Zealand (and Australia). The FIE evidence suggests this variety is conservative with respect to short front vowels, therefore. The lack of raising of TRAP is, according to Trudgill (2004: 43), due to the fact that the FIE speech community developed later than that in New Zealand and Australia, and consequently adopted a later, less close variant of TRAP than settlers to the South Pacific. Also notable is the fact that in FIE some of these vowels are slightly long, particularly in the TRAP and DRESS classes. Both Wells (1982) and Piercy (forthcoming) have noted that this is typical of varieties of English in the southwest of England.

LOT/CLOTH

For the most part, LOT/CLOTH are realized as [ɒ]. Some speakers, of all ages, retain pre-fricative lengthening to [ɔː], especially in the words 'off', 'often' and 'across', as is still heard among (esp. rural) older working-class speakers in England. Perhaps more noteworthy, however, is the fact that some Falklanders have unrounded short [ɑ] variants of LOT. Both Kurath and Lowman (1970: 22) and Wells (1982: 347) suggest such unrounded vowels were common in the southwest of England (and elsewhere) in traditional varieties, and so their continued presence in FIE and their absence in NZE and AE suggest, once again, that FIE is conservative in this respect (see Sudbury 2000: 171–2 for more detail).

STRUT

FIE has undergone FOOT–STRUT split, like the south of England and the other major southern-hemisphere varieties. STRUT, although fronted somewhat, is not nearly as fronted as in NZE and AE, however: [ɐ].

FOOT

Like many Southern British and NZ varieties, FIE is beginning to succumb to FOOT fronting, with fronted unrounded variants [ɨ ˑ ɯ] found among some speakers, especially in the words 'good' and 'could', alongside a more back rounded [ʊ]. FOOT fronting, though, is noted by Wakelin (1986: 25) as a traditional feature of parts of southwest England, where many of the FI settlers came from.

BATH/START/PALM

These vowels are variable in FIE, with a good deal of intra- and inter-speaker variation. For START and PALM, a mid or front fully open long realization was dominant: [aː], or even [æ̞ː]. More variation is present for BATH, with mid long variants most frequent, but more back ones also found. Some speakers, sporadically, had short vowels in BATH words, but such forms were extremely variable and not consistent across individual words or individual speakers. Furthermore, the short vowels were mid and fully open, unlike the fronted short vowels found in some BATH words in AE, for instance, and, again unlike AE, they were not restricted to certain phonological environments. It is clear, however, in examining the British dialect origins of FIE, that this variability is not entirely unexpected. English dialects of both the southwest of England and of Scotland showed considerable variability for these vowels, according to Ellis (1889) and, for the southwest only, Kurath and Lowman (1970: 20–1). The southwest retains considerable variability to this day (Piercy forthcoming), with especially older speakers showing TRAP–BATH split only variably and inconsistently (see Sudbury 2000: 173–7 for more detail on BATH/START/PALM).

NURSE
This vowel shows variability between an unrounded mid-central vowel [ɜː] and a raised, fronted and lip-rounded one [ö: ˎ œː], like that also found in AE, NZE and SAE. This appears to be a southern-hemisphere innovation and not straightforwardly ascribable to British importation.

THOUGHT
This vowel is generally a back half-close vowel [oː]. Only a few speakers diphthongize it to [ɔə ~ oɐ].

FLEECE, GOOSE, FACE, GOAT, MOUTH, PRICE
These vowels are usually grouped together in discussions of southern-hemisphere Englishes, since it is often claimed that they have undergone 'diphthong shift', a term coined by Wells (1982) to describe a set of coordinated changes to some diphthongs and long vowels. As a result of diphthong shift:

- /iː/ in FLEECE words diphthongizes, with the nucleus falling to become [əi];
- /eɪ/ in FACE words undergoes a lowering and often backing of its nucleus to become [æɪ – ɐi];
- /aɪ/ in PRICE words backs and sometimes raises its nucleus to [ɑi – ɒi – ɔi];
- /uː/ in GOOSE words diphthongizes, with a lowering of the nucleus to [əu];
- /ʌʊ/ in GOAT words fronts and lowers the nucleus (and sometimes fronts the off-glide too) to [ɐʊ – ɐʏ – ɐi]; and finally
- /aʊ/ in MOUTH words fronts and raises the nucleus to [æʊ – ɛʊ].

Whilst there is solid evidence that the *outcomes* of diphthong shift are present in NZE, AE and traditional varieties of southeast England, the routes by which some of these changes got to these positions have been questioned (Britain 2005, 2008a, 2008b; Britain and Sudbury 2008). The Falkland Islands have not undergone diphthong shift anywhere near as vigorously as these aforementioned varieties, to such an extent that the realizations of these vowels constitute another major difference between FIE and NZE/AE. Sudbury (2000) and Britain and Sudbury (2008) outline FIE developments in PRICE and MOUTH in some detail, but to summarize here we can say that:

- FLEECE is generally realized as [iː] with relatively little significant diphthongization.
- GOOSE is commonly fronted to [ʉː], as in many other varieties of English, but is not diphthongized.
- FACE is generally realized with very little opening or backing of the nucleus: [eɪ ~ ɛɪ].
- GOAT, like FACE, has variants that are relatively standard-like, and have not undergone the extensive fronting of both nucleus and off-glide found in some other southern-hemisphere varieties: FIE has [ɤʊ ~ ʌʊ ~ əʊ].
- PRICE, far from being realized with back and raised nuclei, is mostly central and mid: [əɪ ~ ʌɪ]. Firstly, this realization suggests a good degree of conservatism – it is a stage on the route from ME [iː] to the proposed [ai] that is but the *starting point* of 'diphthong shift'. Secondly, it represents a retention of the dialectological forms brought over by settlers from southwest England and Scotland, and finally, it is a mark of significant divergence from AE and NZE. PRICE is subject to the allophonic conditioning known as 'Canadian Raising' (Chambers 1973) whereby variants before voiceless consonants are less open than in other contexts. Unlike in Canadian English, however, the difference between the pre-voiceless and other contexts is relatively slight, although consistent.
- MOUTH shows considerable diversity in the Falkland Islands. The dominant variant, especially before voiceless consonants, is [ɛʊ], similar to NZE and AE in terms of the quality of the nucleus, but with much less glide reduction (cf Britain 2008a). A significant minority variant is [ɐʊ], with a central, mid-open nucleus. Standard variants [aʊ] are relatively uncommon, with higher levels before voiced consonants, but a minority variant nevertheless. Britain and Sudbury (2008) argued that, on the balance of historical dialectological and apparent-time evidence, present-day FIE front mid-open realizations of MOUTH probably result from a fronting from [ɐʊ], rather than from a raising from [aʊ] (see also Sudbury 2000).

CHOICE
This diphthong is realized with a back, mid-open nucleus in FIE: [ɔɪ].

NEAR and SQUARE
For the most part NEAR and SQUARE are distinct in FIE, though the nucleus of SQUARE is relatively close and has considerable glide weakening. For some speakers, there is evidence of the beginnings of a merger of the two diphthongs, though this is not in any way as established as it is in NZE. We could transcribe NEAR and SQUARE, then, as [ɪə] and [eə].

WantED
[ə] largely dominates as the vowel of checked unstressed syllables such as those in past tense -ed and plural -es morphemes. However, [ɪ] and an intermediate vowel can also be found, suggesting that the Falklands are not as focused as NZE and AE with respect to this particular feature.

HappY
FIE has HappY-tensing – the final vowel in 'lovely' and 'busy' is [iː].

-OWN
As in NZE and AE, -own and -ewn past participles can be realized disyllabi-cally, following the epenthesis of schwa. Consequently, 'grown' and 'groan' are variably distinct in FIE.

3.2   Consonants

Rhoticity
FIE is, for the most part, non-rhotic, despite the fact that an overwhelming majority of migrants came from areas of the British Isles which were not only rhotic in the mid nineteenth century, but are also, at least variably, rhotic today – Scotland and the southwest of England. Many Falklanders use intrusive and linking /r/. Just a few, especially older, speakers were variably rhotic, however.

H-dropping
H-dropping is not usual in FIE, though a few older speakers do drop variably. This neatly parallels the situation in NZ, for example, where H-Dropping has been found to be obsolescent (Bell and Holmes 1992).

ING
As in most anglophone societies, /ɪŋ/ is realized variably [ɪŋ ∼ ɪn ∼ ən]. In words ending -thing, [ɪŋk] is also possible, as in some other parts of the anglophone southern hemisphere.

L

Although /l/ has clear and dark allophones in FIE, there is a tendency for it to be quite 'dark' in 'clear' /l/ positions, e.g. prevocalically. Some vocalization is found among the young.

YOD

On the whole, yod-dropping is not a widespread feature of FIE. It occasionally occurs after coronals, but not after labials or velars as in East Anglian English.

TH

Generally, TH-fronting is extremely rare in FIE, though Sudbury's (2000) data did pinpoint two young female speakers with high levels of fronting. Two older residents of the Camp, on the other hand, occasionally replaced voiced TH with [d], especially in the context /t#_/ – 'but there's' [bʌʔdeᵊz]. In the word 'with', as in Scottish English, and some other southern-hemisphere speech communities, the final consonant is often voiceless.

T

Unlike NZE and AE, FIE demonstrates very high levels of T-glottaling in word-final preconsonantal contexts, and apparent time analyses (Sudbury 2000: 315–54) show that these glottaling levels are on the increase. In prevocalic contexts, however, glottaling, although on the rise across apparent time, is used less frequently than flapping. Alveolar stop variants are on the decline as glottaling and flapping become more common.

WH

For the vast majority of FIE speakers, /ʍ/ and /w/ are totally merged as [w], so *which* and *witch* are homophones.

Prosody

High Rising Terminals are quite common in FIE, and although they appear to be more prevalent among the young and among women (corresponding to the broad social patterning in Australia and New Zealand; Guy et al. 1986, Britain 1992), they are found right across the speech community.

3.3   Morphosyntax

Along with AE and NZE, FIE has relatively little morphosyntax that characterizes it as particularly distinct from other varieties, and any differences are likely to be quantitative (requiring a detailed variationist analysis) rather than qualitative. A large number of the non-standard grammatical forms found in FIE are common to a number of non-standard varieties of English. These include:

- The use of *them* as a determiner, e.g. *some of them shearers*;
- The regularization of reflexive pronouns, e.g. *he had to buy them all hisself*;
- Non-standard past tense verb forms: *She give that to Paul*; *he come to our door*; *they might have went*;
- Non-standard subject–verb concord: *they was covered in concrete*; *five geese eats as much as one sheep can*; *there's tapestries and there's penguins* (see Britain and Sudbury 2002);
- Absence of plural marking: *about two year ago*.

The Scottish origins of Falkland settlers may be responsible for the albeit sporadic use of AUX contraction in the negative of *will*. Some Falklanders, therefore, say *we'll not go* rather than *we won't go*.

Generally, *that* is favoured over WH- as the relative pronoun of choice, though a few examples of *what* relative pronouns can also be found.

Unlike Standard English, FIE (variably) has distinct second person singular and plural pronouns. *Youse* is used by some Falklanders as the plural pronoun, as is also found in Australia and New Zealand and a number of places in the British Isles, especially those with Irish influence.

Adverbial *but*: several examples were found of this feature which is also found in AE: *not that I ever used it much but*.

Some FIE speakers variably lack allomorphy in the article system, using, for example, the preconsonantal *a* and *the* [ðə] forms in prevocalic position. This has also been noted in NZE, SAE and some (especially contact) varieties of British English (see Britain and Fox 2009, for a review). One relatively distinctive feature of FIE is the non-use of the definite article preceding some country acronyms: *unless you go to UK*.

3.4   Lexicon

There is not the space here to devote too much attention to the distinctive lexicon of the Falklands. A few distinctive words (especially in connection with horse-riding) and place names have Spanish origins, probably from contact with South American gauchos. These include the word 'Camp' (from Sp. 'campo') to refer to Falkland settlements other than Stanley, as well as the land itself, and 'passar libre' (cattlegrid). Sudbury (2000: 191) noted that a number of these words are losing currency because of contact with non-Islanders, especially with the British military based on the islands. Generally, those words borrowed from Spanish have undergone heavy integration into the local phonological system.

4   Discussion

Structurally, perhaps what is most remarkable about FIE is just how unremarkable the variety is, despite its settler origins in the southwest of England

and Scotland which the traditional dialectological literature portrays as divergent varieties in the British context. So, for example, present in traditional southwestern varieties, but absent in FIE are:

- Onset fricative voicing: the voicing of /f s θ ʃ/ to [v z ð ʒ];
- Loss of /w/ before /ʊ/, so *woman* becomes [ʊmən];
- The distinctive uses of pronoun exchange, gendered pronouns and the use of *ich* and *utch* as first person pronouns;
- The use of periphrastic do;
- /θr/ realised as [dr].

And common to Scottish English, but again absent in FIE are, for example:

- Velar fricative /x/
- Distinct /ʍ/ and /w/
- Scottish Vowel Length (Sudbury 2000: 208–47)
- Double modals

And, of course, common to both is rhoticity, which has now largely disappeared. The levelling of these forms over the past 150 years is symptomatic of a great deal of dialect contact (Trudgill 1986) throughout the anglophone history of the Falklands, and provides solid linguistic evidence of the relative turbulence of the speech community. Generally, though, FIE is a relatively unfocused variety and sustains rather considerable levels of inherent heterogeneity – this can perhaps best be seen in the considerable variability found in the BATH and MOUTH lexical sets, but Sudbury's variationist analyses of a number of linguistic variables demonstrate significant inter- and intra-speaker variability more generally. This variability may partly be put down to the sparseness of the Falklands population (in the world, only Greenland has a sparser population density than the Falklands), especially in Camp, producing conditions that are not conducive to focusing. Sudbury (2000: 371, 381) discusses how a number of older Islanders remembered people in their Camp communities once having distinctive Irish, or Scottish or southwestern accents, and it was once the case that the dispersed Camp settlements often tended to consist of different clusterings of people all or mostly from one particular part of the British Isles. Since the Falklands conflict of 1982, however, mobility within the islands has increased and the islands have been becoming more and more urban, with an ever greater proportion of the islands' population living in Stanley, and coming into contact not only with the large British military presence on the islands, but also with rising numbers of non-Falklanders and an ever increasing number of foreign tourists.

5   The future

It is likely that, for the foreseeable future, the presence of a sustainable anglophone presence on the Falkland Islands is assured. UK governments of all political colours have robustly defended the Falklanders' rights to self-determination, and, importantly, the economy has developed significantly in the quarter-century since the conflict. The establishment of a fisheries licensing zone around the Islands, as well as the issuing of licences for oil exploration and a booming tourist industry (55,000 visitors in 2006–7; Taylor and Miller 2007: 56) have meant that the Islands are largely economically self-sufficient, except in the area of defence. What is less clear is how increased contact with non-Falklanders will affect the local variety of English, whether the presence of significant populations of St Helenians on the Islands will have any lasting linguistic consequences, and the extent to which Falkland Islands English will converge with or diverge from the Englishes to which it is presently typologically similar.

References

Bailey, Richard. 1996. *Nineteenth Century English.* Ann Arbor, Mich.: University of Michigan Press.

Bell, Allan and Janet Holmes. 1992. 'H-Droppin': Two sociolinguistic variables in New Zealand English.' *Australian Journal of Linguistics* 12: 223–48.

Britain, David. 1992. 'Linguistic change in intonation: The use of high rising terminals in New Zealand English.' *Language Variation and Change* 4: 77–104.

　　2005. 'Where did New Zealand English come from?' In Allan Bell, Ray Harlow and Donna Starks, eds. *The Languages of New Zealand.* Wellington: Victoria University Press, 156–93.

　　2008a. 'When is a change not a change? A case study on the dialect origins of New Zealand English.' *Language Variation and Change* 20: 187–223.

　　2008b. 'On the wrong track? a Non-standard history of non-standard /au/ in English.' *Essex Research Reports in Linguistics* 57 (1): 33–77.

Britain, David and Susan Fox. 2009. 'The regularisation of the hiatus resolution system in British English: A contact-induced "vernacular universal".' In Markku Filppula, Juhani Klemola and Heli Paulasto, eds. *Vernacular Universals and Language Contacts: Evidence from Varieties of English and Beyond.* London: Routledge, 177–205.

Britain, David and Andrea Sudbury. 2002. 'There's sheep and there's penguins: "Drift", "slant" and singular verb forms following existentials in New Zealand and Falkland Island English.' In Mari Jones and Edith Esch, eds. *Language Change: The Interplay of Internal, External and Extra-linguistic Factors.* Berlin: Mouton de Gruyter, 209–42.

　　2008. 'What can the Falkland Islands tell us about Diphthong Shift?' *Essex Research Reports in Linguistics* 57 (1): 1–32.

Cameron, Jane. 1997. 'Catalysts of change: The impact of war and prosperity on a small island community.' Paper presented at the International Conference on the Cultural Heritage of Islands and Small States, Malta, May 1997.

Chambers, J. K. 1973. 'Canadian Raising.' *Canadian Journal of Linguistics* 18: 113–35.

Clement, R. D. 1980. 'Highlands English.' *Scottish Literary Journal: Supplement* 12: 13–18.

Ellis, Alexander. 1889. *On Early English Pronunciation: Part V.* London: Truebner and Co.

Gordon, Elizabeth, Lyle Campbell, Jennifer Hay, Margaret Maclagan, Andrea Sudbury and Peter Trudgill. 2004. *New Zealand English: Its Origins and Evolution.* Cambridge: Cambridge University Press.

Gough, Barry. 1990. 'The British reoccupation and colonization of the Falkland Islands, or Malvinas, 1832–1843.' *Albion: A Quarterly Journal Concerned with British Studies* 22: 261–87.

Guy, Gregory, Barbara Horvath, Julia Vonwiller, Elaine Daisley and Inge Rogers. 1986. 'An intonational change in progress in Australian English.' *Language in Society* 15: 23–51.

Kachru, Braj B. 1985. 'Standards, codification and sociolinguistic realism: The English language in the Outer Circle.' In R. Quirk and H. G. Widdowson, eds. *English in the World: Teaching and Learning the Language and Literatures.* Cambridge: Cambridge University Press, 11–30.

Kurath, Hans and Guy Lowman. 1970. *The Dialectal Structure of Southern England.* Tuscaloosa: University of Alabama Press.

Ó Baoill, Colm. 1997. 'The Scots-Gaelic interface.' In Charles Jones, ed. *The Edinburgh History of the Scots Language.* Edinburgh: Edinburgh University Press, 551–68.

Pascoe, Graham and Peter Pepper. 2008. 'Getting it right: The real history of the Falklands/Malvinas: A reply to the Argentine seminar of 3 December 2007.' Unpublished manuscript. Available at www.wildisland.gs/atlantis/gettingitright.pdf (last accessed 30 September 2009).

Piercy, Caroline (forthcoming). *One /a/ or two? The phonetics, phonology and sociolinguistics of change in the TRAP and BATH vowels in the South-west of England.* PhD dissertation. Colchester: University of Essex.

Richards, Eric. 2001. 'Highland and Gaelic Immigrants.' In James Jupp, ed. *The Australian People.* Cambridge: Cambridge University Press, 649–55.

Royle, Stephen. 1985. 'The Falkland Islands, 1833–1876: The establishment of a colony.' *The Geographical Journal* 151: 204–14.

Spruce, Joan. 1996. 'Falkland words.' Unpublished manuscript.

Strange, Ian. 1983. *The Falkland Islands.* (3rd edn). Newton Abbott: David and Charles.

Sudbury, Andrea. 2000. 'Dialect contact and koineization in the Falkland Islands: Development of a Southern Hemisphere Variety?' Unpublished PhD dissertation. Colchester: University of Essex.

  2001. 'Is Falkland Islands English a southern hemisphere variety?' *English World-Wide* 22: 55–80.

Taylor, Claire and Vaughne Miller. 2007. *The Falkland Islands – Twenty Five Years On.* London: International Affairs and Defence Section, House of Commons Library.

Trehearne, Mary (1978). *Falkland heritage: A record of a pioneer settlement*. Ilfra-
combe: A H Stockwell.

Trudgill, Peter. 1986. *Dialects in Contact*. Oxford: Basil Blackwell.

2004. *New Dialect Formation: The Inevitability of Colonial Englishes*. Edinburgh:
Edinburgh University Press.

Trudgill, Peter, Elizabeth Gordon and Gillian Lewis. 1998. 'New dialect formation
and Southern Hemisphere English: The New Zealand short front vowels.'
Journal of Sociolinguistics 2: 35–51.

Wakelin, Martyn. 1986. *The South West of England*. Amsterdam: John Benjamins.

Wells, John. 1982. *Accents of English*. Cambridge: Cambridge University Press.

12   St Helenian English

DANIEL SCHREIER

1   Introduction

The volcanic island of St Helena lies in the mid-central South Atlantic Ocean, 1,930 kilometres west of Angola, south of the equator. Its nearest neighbour (geographically speaking) is Ascension Island, more than 1,000 kilometres to the northwest. St Helena covers an area of 122 square kilometres and its topography mostly consists of steep, relatively barren and rocky territory, mostly unsuitable for cultivation. Despite the island's locality within the tropics, the micro-climates of the main valley of the island, Jamestown Valley, and the central highlands as well as the island's southwest are mild, favoured by the southeast trade winds. The island's capital and only town is Jamestown, although there are other smaller settlements such as Half Tree Hollow, Blue Hill, Sandy Bay and Longwood (the latter serving as the residence of Napoleon Bonaparte, who was exiled on the island from 1815 to his death in 1821).

The origins of St Helenian English (StHE) can be dated to the mid seventeenth century (the East India Company (EIC) established the colony in 1658). It is thus the oldest variety of Southern Hemisphere English (SHemE), more than a century older than the major varieties of South African, Australian and New Zealand English and pre-dating other lesser-known SHemEs (TdCE, FIE; this volume) by more than 150 years. There has been a continuous native-speaker tradition on the island ever since a short Dutch interregnum in the early 1670s, when the Dutch fleet under Jacob de Gens took control of the island for a few months. The population has undergone extensive ethnic mixing (and also language contact, see below), since the founders of the community came from England, France, West Africa and the Caboverde Islands as well as the Indian subcontinent and Madagascar. The evolution and development of StHE involved a complex interplay of dialect and language contact, which makes it difficult to assess the typological status as a variety of postcolonial English (Schreier 2008).

Today, the island is still comparatively isolated and a difficult travel destination. St Helena does not have an airport and the single government-subsidized ship that connected the island with the United Kingdom has changed its route to become more cost-efficient, now only serving Ascension, St Helena and Cape Town (the annual run to Tristan da Cunha was cut as well). Today, many Saint Helenians (or 'Saints', as they call themselves) take on contract work on the military bases on Ascension and the Falkland Islands; since 1999, when the British Government conceded full citizenship rights to the islanders, they have full access to United Kingdom workplaces. This affected the community heavily, as perhaps up to 30 per cent of the population, mostly younger Saints, left the island in search of better job opportunities. St Helena's population is now (2010) approximately 4,000.

2 Sociolinguistic history and current status of the variety

Originally uninhabited, St Helena was discovered in 1502 by the Portuguese, who, just like the other European seafaring nations who followed in their wake, used the island as a refreshment station and sick bay on their journeys to and from the East. Until claimed by the EIC in 1658, the island was never permanently or formally settled (Gosse 1938). From this date, a concerted settlement policy was implemented, and soldiers, servants and planters (employed and contracted by the EIC, who held direct control over the island until the 1830s) were recruited to St Helena, along with slaves supplied on request by the Company's ships. The exact origins of the British settlers are not known, but many – if not most – of them came from southern, perhaps southeastern, England. Moreover, the majority of the planters had working-class origins and the EIC recruited many of its soldiers (and settlers as well, for that matter) from among the unemployed in England (Gosse 1938: 72). There are occasional reports that quite a lot of them were illiterate, as evidenced by an entry in the *St Helena Consultations* (quoted in Brooke 1808) on 2 February 1774: 'On 31st Jan. six soldiers deserted in the night taking two Boats . . . The deserters were illiterate men of bad character and only a few days provisions and must inevitably perish at sea.'

The origins of the non-white population are better documented: slaves were imported from the Guinea Coast, the Indian subcontinent and Madagascar, and to a lesser extent from the Cape and Larger Table Bay area, the West Indies, Indonesia and the Maldives. In 1789, the importation of slaves officially ended, but the lack of cheap labour was compensated by the arrival of Chinese indentured workers in the early nineteenth century. However, very few, if any, stayed on permanently and slavery was finally abolished in 1832 (Melliss 1875). In 1815, the total population was 3,342, comprising 694 whites, 1,715 non-whites, and 933 non-permanent army personnel (see Table 12.1, adapted from Schreier 2008: 110).

The situation was to change dramatically, when in 1834, St Helena's administration was transferred from the EIC to the British government and St Helena officially became a crown colony. Poverty led to out-migration and

Table 12.1 *The sociodemographic situation on St Helena in 1815*

	Men	Women	Children	Total
White	109	202	383	694
Non-white	342	245	610	1,197
Army personnel (white)		933 (combined)		933
Company slaves (black)		98 (combined)		98
Free blacks		420 (combined)		420
Total				3,342

the remainder of the nineteenth century was characterized by extreme hardship. Crucially, this period saw an increase in mobility and also ethnic mixing. Governor Charles Elliot remarked in 1868 that 'there can be no position on the face of the earth where it would be more difficult to discriminate between the various strains of blood of which the body of the population is composed than here in St Helena' (quoted in Gosse 1938). The population loss due to out-migration was compensated for by the arrival of immigrant groups: the indentured labourers from China; liberated African slaves, brought to the island after 1840, when St Helena was used as a temporary residence for rescued slaves from captured ships (some of them chose to stay while the majority were sent on to the West Indies or repatriated back to the African mainland); and hundreds of Afrikaans-speaking Boer War prisoners in 1902, only very few of whom stayed behind upon their release.

The increasing use of steam-driven ships and the opening of the Suez Canal voided the island's strategic purpose as a refreshment station. With the exception of a short-lived flax industry (that ended in 1965 when the British postal service switched to cheaper synthetic fibre), no industry has provided a viable means of sustaining the island.

The sociolinguistic status and the origins of StHE are by no means clear-cut. We need to address a number of questions in order to reconstruct the history of StHE and, by doing so, to understand how StHE came to be the way it is. To begin with historical, social and sociodemographic issues, there is no doubt that the founding populations were socially and ethnically diverse. Settlers, planters, administrative staff, soldiers and slaves, i.e. all those *could have had* an impact on the emerging variety, came to the island from three continents and had the following origins:

- England (mainly south(eastern) England)
- France
- St Iago, Guinea, Nigeria, southern Africa, Madagascar, Maldives, India, Indonesia
- China (indentured labourers in the 1820s and 1830s)
- South Africa (POWs from the Boer War, 1898–1902)
- West Africa (liberated slaves from 1850s)

The strong early presence of English settlers and planters is evidenced by the first account of life on St Helena. Henry Gargen's (1665) diary describes the little community in detail and leaves no doubt that there were Company personnel (administration and soldiers), planters and their families as well as slaves, mostly in the possession of the Company. Their origins are unknown, but order was given that 'In case at St. Iago you can procure five or six blacks or Negroes, able men and women, we desire you to buy them, provided they may be had at or under 40 dollars per poll' (*Company Instructions*, quoted in Gosse 1938: 46–7), which is supported by later reports that Portuguese was spoken on the island. A later entry in the *St Helena Consultations* (collected by Janisch 1885) points to Guinea as a place of origin: 'There are but twelve out of 42 Guinea Blacks now living yet more dyed from want of care or victuals.' From the 1700s on, the preferred place of origin of slaves was Madagascar, and requests were made to provide slaves from that island exclusively. According to other sources (Brooke 1808; Janisch 1885; Gosse 1938), some of the inhabitants came from France as well (Huguenots who fled from persecution in France). Consequently, then, the historical account of the local community allows us to pinpoint the founders and to speculate on their sociolinguistic input, which is particularly important for the question of whether there was a potential for 'founder effects' (Mufwene 1996). Historically speaking, these were predominantly the English planters and their offspring (other groups were too small in size and keen to integrate and accommodate, e.g. the French Huguenots, or they left the island before they could make an impact on the evolution of the local variety, e.g. the South African POWs), as well as the slaves, the majority of whom came from Madagascar.

Sociodemographically, the question is how the populace developed generally and how stable and transient it was. In the years following the 1672 Dutch Interregnum, there were countless conflicts in the island community, affecting soldiers and planters alike. Promises of land grants were broken and the late seventeenth century was characterized by quasi-feudal relationships between the Company directors in London, the local administration and the settlers and their families, who were in fact nothing else than indentured labourers. Most of the planters were dissatisfied with these conditions and left the island at the first opportunity. There were heavy fluctuations among army and administrative staff as well. The fort saw revolts and rebellions, which led to casualties, death penalties and forced emigration. In 1693, for instance, during the infamous 'Jackson Conspiracy', twenty-seven soldiers seized the fort (killing the Governor), and escaped from the island on a Company ship. As for the slaves, the St Helena Records (Janisch 1885) mention dozens of escapes, mostly by young male slaves. Several slave uprisings were reported in the 1680s and 1690s, and slaves were tried and brutally punished, often without proof or following a forced confession. As a result, slaves seized every opportunity to flee the island and the loss of manpower was compensated by the importation of new labour, preferably from Madagascar (more than one hundred slaves arrived from that island in 1716 alone).

In addition, illness and disease ravaged the community in the first half of the eighteenth century; diseases like chickenpox spread on the island like wildfire. Thirty planters died in the first half of 1718 alone and there were large numbers of victims in the black population as well. Mortality rates in this period were exceptionally high indeed. An entry in the *Consultations* (Janisch 1885) from 26 May 1719 reads: 'We usually decrease here among the white people five in a hundred per annum – but in each of the two last years not lesser than 10 per 100!!' Census and shipping lists show that there was a massive population turnover on St Helena, and the population only stabilized from the 1740s onwards. Consequently, then, we can exclude 'founder effects', simply because many of the founders did not stay on the island long enough to leave an impact. Rather, StHE must have emerged when the social conditions were favourable, and that is around the middle of the eighteenth century. It evolved in a setting of ethnic mixing and sociodemographic homogenization and was accompanied by language shift (mostly from Malagasy to English), dialect levelling and bilingualism (Portuguese-English and Malagasy-English are historically attested).

3   Features of the variety

3.1   Segmental phonology

3.1.1   Short vowels

StHE has six short vowels (i.e., KIT, DRESS, TRAP, CLOTH, STRUT and FOOT), with the following realizations:

KIT /ɪ/

StHE KIT displays considerable variation. While a stable KIT is found (in words such as *livin'*, *fish*, *little* or *itchy*), which resembles modern mainstream EngE (but not the other SHemEs), both KIT-raising (in words such as *big* and *tin*) and KIT centralization (*trip*, *pick*, *mill*) feature as well, the latter one being quite prominent (resembling advanced modern NZE). As in many South of England and American accents, some DRESS words have KIT rather than DRESS, particularly when an alveolar consonant follows the vowel: /t/ in *get* or *kettle*, /d/ in *head*, or /n/ in *engine*.

DRESS /ɛ/

DRESS displays a considerable amount of variation also. Most speakers have a mid-close realization ([ɛ]) and slightly raised realizations (most usually [ɛ̝ ~ e̞]). Raised variants ([e̞]) are common and particularly noticeable in voiced pre-velar environments (*leg*). Some speakers have [iə] for the word *dead*, which, quite interestingly, is also found in KIT (at least for one speaker). Lowering does not occur.

TRAP /æ/

A similar pattern is found in the most open of the short front vowels, TRAP. [æ] is the most common realization. The pattern is complicated, however, since raising and (slight) lengthening accompanied by off-gliding are found as well ([ɛ� ~ æˑˀ ~ æ̝ˀ ~ ɛ̞ˀ ~ ɛˀ]). Glides are most common in pre-alveolar and pre-velar environments and before nasals. [ɛ̞] is unusual, though. Generally speaking, TRAP raising is not as prominent as it is in most other accents of SHemE.

FOOT /ʊ/

This vowel is unremarkable. FOOT is commonly close-mid/close and fully back, though, as in many parts of the English-speaking world, unrounded, though slightly centralized variants occur as well. Words such as *room*, *roof*, or *hoof* take the FOOT vowel.

STRUT /ʌ/

The most common realization of STRUT is fully-mid back. Most speakers have fronting to [ɐ̟], however, and one speaker has [ʊ] (only on one occasion, in the word *rub*). One could make a case in point that this is a remnant feature of an older five-vowel system, but [ʌ ~ ɐ] are quasi-normative, so this is exceptional.

CLOTH /ɒ/

Unrounded [ɑ] variants are more common than rounded ones, but most speakers have both. The realization of CLOTH is complex since there are two more realizations. Raising to [ɔ̞] before labiodental fricatives (*off*) occurs (a feature widely attested in nineteenth-century BrE; Wells 1982) and there is lengthening and slight off-gliding (as in [oˑᵘ], *long*) as well, which resembles varieties of English in the Caribbean. Perhaps the most diagnostic realization is found in speakers from the Sandy Bay area, which I would somewhat hesitantly identify as [ɜː], i.e. as an open-mid central vowel that has both unrounding and lengthening. My field notes indicate that this is found in other speakers as well (and it certainly is highly salient; visitors from Tristan da Cunha, for instance, consider it so prominent that they stereotype it, and the Saints themselves list this as a prime candidate for regional variation).

Also of interest is the fact that some words may have /ɔə/: *gone*, *daughter*, *cost*, etc., which could be indicative of a partial overlap with the THOUGHT/FORCE/NORTH/POOR sets, which are merged (see below).

3.1.2 Rising/closing diphthongs

FACE /eɪ/

StHE FACE has what Wells (1982: 210–11) refers to as 'long mid diphthonging', so the most common realization is a diphthong. However, the nucleus may be lengthed and slightly raised, which means that the off-glide ([ɛˑⁱ]) is less prominent. Alternative realizations exist: some have a monophthong (most commonly [ɛ̝ˑ]), which differs from accents elsewhere (North of England, Scotland or Ireland) in that it is not as tense and may have a slight offglide [ɛˑᶦ]. It is certainly noteworthy that 'diphthong shift' (Wells 1982: 256) to [aɪ] does not occur.

PRICE /aɪ/

The most common realization of StHE PRICE is [ɔ̝ɨ], with a back open-mid onset, though a more open [ɑ] is found as well. At least one speaker has [ɐ̝ɪ]. Consequently, in contrast with FACE, PRICE demonstrates diphthong shift since its nucleus has backed its place of articulation (Wells 1982: 256). It displays some mild *glide weakening* as well ([ɨ]). Moreover, the nucleus is raised to a mid-central [ə ~ æ̝] when it precedes voiceless environments, the well-known 'Canadian raising' pattern.

CHOICE /oi/

This vowel has a rather close first element, around [o̝ɨ]. The nucleus of CHOICE is thus raised and the diphthong has shifted too. Moreover, at least one speaker has the archaic dialectal feature where PRICE occurs instead of CHOICE. This is attested in earlier forms of British English (Strang 1970: 112).

GOAT /ou/

Though monophthongal [o̝ː] variants are found occasionally, GOAT is typically diphthongized ([ɔ̝ụ ~ ɔ̞ụ ~ ɔ̝u]). The onset is an open-mid and fully rounded [ɔ], and there are no traces of onset shift to /ʌ ~ œ ~ a/ or glide weakening. Even though StHE GOAT has to some extent partaken in long-mid diphthonging, the realization of this vowel remains conservative.

MOUTH /aʊ/

The most usual pronunciation is [aʊ ~ ɑ̞ʊ̣ ~ ɔʊ]. A back /ɔ/ onset is found in function words (*out*, *about*), whereas the onset of lexical words tends to be somewhat more front (without shifting to TRAP or DRESS, however). Glide weakening is uncommon. There is an apparent asymmetry between front and back vowel pairs in that, in contrast to PRICE, there is no Canadian raising pattern in MOUTH (reported in TdCE – see Schreier and Trudgill 2006: 126; Schreier, this volume – which attests to the impact of StHE in the formation phase of TdCE).

3.1.3 Long Monophthongs and Centring Diphthongs

FLEECE /iː/

This vowel is most commonly a long monophthongal [iː]; some speakers occasionally have an off-glide [iᶦ] and slight diphthongization. Centralization, backing and breaking do not occur.

GOOSE /uː/

GOOSE is genuinely monophthongal: a fully back and close [uː]. There is practically no fronting (this has been documented in many varieties of English around the world, though it is changing quickly, e.g. in AusE or SAfrE, where fronting is prominent in younger speakers).

NURSE /ɜː/

NURSE is characterized by little lip-rounding in StHE. The vowel is open-mid central; fronted or back variants are not found.

START /ɑː/

START has a number of realizations in StHE. First of all, some speakers have both /ɑː/ and /æ/, the latter in pre-nasal environments (*dance*, *sample*, *demand*, *plant*, etc., which resembles Irish and American English). This is not common, however, since a fully back [ɑː] prevails.

   Words such as *heart*, *car*, *smart*, or *mark* may have [ɔə] rather than /ɑː/. The overall incidence of START provides further evidence of a possible overlap with the THOUGHT/FORCE/NORTH/POOR set, which also shows up in the case of CLOTH.

THOUGHT/FORCE/NORTH/POOR /ɔə/

One of the most striking features of the StHE vowel system is that the four vowel sets THOUGHT, FORCE, NORTH and POOR are closing diphthongs. They are generally merged, being pronounced [ɔə], with a rounded close-mid nucleus and with an off-glide /ə/, sometimes even /ɐ/. It occurs in all five lexical sets, so both the *First* and the *Second Force mergers* (Wells 1982) are completed. It is unusual, perhaps diagnostic, that /ɔə/ is also extended to include lexical items from the CLOTH and START sets (see above).

NEAR /iə/ ~ SQUARE /ɛə/

Most StHE speakers have merged NEAR and SQUARE (pivot [iə]), even though a few exceptions remain (the word *there* is very often /dɛə/). Only one speaker keeps the two vowels separate on a regular basis.

3.1.4 Other vowel features

Other features common in English accents around the world are the weak StHE vowel merger, H-dropping, happʏ-tensing and Yod-dropping. StHE, in line with SHemE, has /ə/ in unstressed syllables in all or nearly all cases where southeast England has /ɪ/ (*David, market, wanted*). 'happy tensing' (Wells 1982: 595, 616) is common as well, so that words like *happy, money* have word-final /iː/ rather than /ɪ/. As for Yod-dropping, all four speakers have a strong tendency to drop /j/ before stressed syllables (*Tuesday, few, tune, leukaemia*), but it may occasionally be retained in *music*. Another interesting feature is the so-called PIN/PEN merger: KIT and DRESS are merged (pivot /ɪ/) when followed by a nasal: one speaker has /də mɪn/ (*the men*). LettER is occasionally /ɐ/, as in *bigger* [bigɐ].

3.1.5   Consonants

As for the consonants, StHE is genuinely non-rhotic. None of the speakers analysed pronounced /r/ in preconsonantal (*farm, sort*) or pre-pausal environments. Some speakers have linking and intrusive /r/ ('he went to South Africa /r/ eh', 'after he saw /r/ it'), which is reminiscent of SAfrE. The pronunciation of /r/ is an [ɹ] approximant, although it is occasionally post-alveolar and somewhat more retroflexed than elsewhere. By the same token, none of the four speakers has H-dropping in stressed content words (in unstressed function words, however, /h/ is commonly dropped, just as elsewhere, so this is not at all unusual). There is no trace of H-insertion (or 'hypercorrect /h/').

Another prominent (and much remarked on) feature of StHE is the /v∼w/ interchange. StHE has a pre-stressed-syllable merger of /w/ and /v/, just like many other postcolonial English and nineteenth century southeastern England varieties (Trudgill et al. 2004). Phonetically, the single consonant is realized as an approximant [β̞], a bilabial fricative, or, less often, [β] (which, as argued in Trudgill et al. 2004, may explain why this merger is historically reported with both pivots /v/ and /w/, the approximant being perceived and reported as either). In any case, StHE does not have /ʍ/, the labio-velar approximant in *where, wheel*, etc. (which features prominently in Scottish, Irish and (Otago) New Zealand English). However, at least one speaker has bilabial stops for /v/, a prototypical creole feature.

Intervocalic /p/ and /k/ are often pre-glottalized. Intervocalic /t/, on the other hand, (as in *better, letter, butter*) is nearly always a voiced flap. StHE has pre-glottalization (Wells 1982: 260), i.e. a glottal stop before /p, t, k, tʃ/. Syllable-final /k/ is often uvular, particularly in pre-pausal environments and when following back vowels: *clock* [klɑq], *work* [β̞ɘq], *back* [bæʳᵊq]. This is found in TdCE as well (Schreier, this volume).

Dental fricatives are uncommon in StHE. The most common realization is TH-stopping to /t/ and /d/, not only in function words, which is also found in IrE and other varieties of English, but also in stressed lexical items (*think, through, cathedral*). Some speakers have a palatalized stop. TH-fronting to /f/ and /v/ is uncommon by contrast (occasionally found in words such as *both*). Clear /l/ is usual in prevocalic position and after front vowels, but dark /l/ occurs after back vowels, displaying the usual type of allophony. L-vocalization is not found.

A final characteristic of the consonantal system of StHE is the deletion of consonants from word-final clusters (so-called consonant cluster reduction, or CCR), which occurs frequently and affects both monomorphemic words (*post, cask, left*, etc.) and bimorphemic ones, where the final plosive represents an *-ed* tense suffix and thus carries morphological meaning (in *passed, laughed*, etc.). This process is extremely frequent (cf. Schreier 2005).

3.1.6 The segmental phonology of StHE: First conclusions
A close look at the segmental phonology of StHE features reveals complex genetic affiliations with varieties of English around the world (in the British Isles, particularly in the southeast, throughout the southern hemisphere, the Caribbean, etc.). There are striking similarities (e.g. Canadian raising) with a number of structurally and geographically distinct varieties. The short front vowels, first of all, are qualitatively similar to the major SHemE varieties. KIT, DRESS and TRAP all display variation and their places of articulation tend to be closer rather than more open. StHE KIT in particular mirrors variants found in other SHemEs, where raising (AusE) and centralization (SAfrE, NZE) are well-documented. The common trend in StHE is one of raising, though impressionistically, DRESS and TRAP seem to be more open than in varieties such as FIE (Britain and Sudbury, this volume), SAfrE or AusE. Also, DRESS and TRAP vary less than the highest of the short front vowels: KIT displays stable, raised and centralized variants, which is both unstable and complex.

As for the back vowels, CLOTH displays a similar amount of variation: raising is common (in words such as *off, froth*, etc.) and /ɔə/ occurs as well. Several speakers have an overlap with the THOUGHT/FORCE/NORTH/POOR set (also found in some of the START words), which seems a highly characteristic local development. FOOT and STRUT, finally, are distinct so that StHE has six short vowels and is in line with the vast majority of English varieties around the world.

The long monophthongs, in contrast, are conservative. FLEECE and GOOSE are close and mostly monophthongal (though a few speakers have sporadic – but slight – off-glides in FLEECE). Tendencies toward fronting or breaking are practically absent. NURSE-unrounding is common; lip-rounding, very frequent in SAfrE, is not found. One of the most striking features is that THOUGHT, FORCE, NORTH and POOR are not distinct (pivot /ɔə/), and START is [ɑː], even though words like *car, smart, mark* have /ɔə/, which is indicative of an overlap of the START, CLOTH and THOUGHT/FORCE/NORTH/POOR sets, an unusual pattern that – to the best of my knowledge – has not been reported elsewhere. It is also noteworthy that the so-called 'START backing innovation' (dated to the early

1800s by Wells 1982: 234) is the norm, and a fully back [ɑː] is most common in all the lexical sets where it would occur in southeastern EnglE, e.g. *start*, *last*, *path*, resembling SAfrE. As for the diphthongs, both FACE and GOAT display 'long-mid diphthonging' (Wells 1982: 210); conservative monophthongs, though rare, are reported as well. PRICE and CHOICE have backed and raised onsets (/ə̞ ~ ɑ/ for PRICE, /o̞/ for CHOICE), which means that they have the 'diphthong shift' which is common in 'Cockney, also the local accents of much of the south of England and the midlands, together with those of Australia and New Zealand' (Wells 1982: 256). The backed and raised onset in PRICE resembles Cockney and working-class AusE. PRICE, on the other hand, has 'Canadian raising' while MOUTH has not (which is unusual). Glide-weakening is not prominent either. Quite remarkably, FACE, MOUTH and GOAT remain stable and have not shifted in line with the other two diphthongs, being quite conservative in that they have fully back (MOUTH, GOAT) or open-mid front onsets (FACE). As for minor vowel features, StHE has the NEAR ~ SQUARE merger (attested in NZE), happY-tensing (common in accents of English around the world), as well as Yod-dropping and the weak vowel merger (normative in SHemE).

3.2   Morphosyntax

The most prominent morphosyntactic properties of StHE are the following.

3.2.1   Plural formation

As for pluralization, nouns often take -*s* suffixation (with the exception of nouns of measurement). -*s* is context-sensitive in that it is bisegmental after sibilants and dental fricatives.

(1)   you pick the *blackberries* off the blackberry *bushes*

With agent nouns and animate subjects, the so-called associative plural *dem/n' dem* (suffixed to plural NPs) is also found:

(2)   they stay over there my daddy *n' dem* you know

Nouns of measurement, on the other hand, are rarely marked. Plural is not overtly marked and has to be interpreted using context.

(3)   Her weddin' never cost no more than sixty seventy poundØ

(4)   I stay there for over twelve monthØ

However, the absence of plural markers is widespread in StHE and plural NPs (other than mass or count nouns) may take zero marking as well.

(5)   there wasn't many houseØ. you never had you own house. one
          or two houseØ was there

Interestingly, even the place name *Falkland Islands* or the generic term *Chinese* may lack plural -*s*:

(6)   Down the Falkland IslandØ (DF, Sandy Bay)

Some speakers refer to the Chinese indentured labourers as /tʃaɪni/ ('I come off the /tʃaɪni/ breed'), so this is quite possibly a reanalysis and misinterpretation of -*s* suffixation, which is indicative of weakened pluralization in StHE as well.

3.2.2 Pronouns
Subject personal pronouns are occasionally absent in StHE:

(7)   Ø met with two girls on the train. trying to sleep had to keep
             wake

(8)   Ø don't get nothin' much only 14 pound a week

A personal pronoun that is non-specified and generic, such as *one* or *you*, may be absent as well:

(9)   Oh yes, Ø gotta pay for you water now. Ø get nothing for free
             now

When personal pronouns are present, then the singular forms match the general patterns found in most varieties of English around the world (*I* for first person singular, *you* for second and *he/she/it* for third). The first person plural pronoun is categorically *us*:

(10)   *us* come up Peak Hill way see

(11)   *us* had a very saucy school master

The second person plural pronoun is typically *you all/y'all*:

(12)   But one thing I will tell *y'all*, thing was cheap them days

(13)   So *y'all* be goin' back soon?

Object personal pronouns resemble the paradigms found in most other varieties of English (*me* for first person singular, *you* for second and *him/her/it* for third). *Y'all* is the most common pronoun for second person plural objects.

(14)   I say you can't blame *her* and you can't blame *him*

(15)   I always tell '*em* I will see *y'all* before you see *me*

The possessive pronouns are unremarkable for first and third person singular (*my*, *his*, *her*, *our*) and first person plural (*our*), the second persons are *you* and *y'all*:

(16)   us used to put a bit of egg shell on top of the cake to mark it. to
          say that is *my* cake and that is *you* cake

(17)   when you put *you* head down it scratch *you* head

(18)   *y'all* been seein' anything like that in *y'all's* countries?

(19)   so you follow *y'all's* own way roun' yesterday?

Third person plural is often *they*:

(20)   that's *they* occupation

(21)   those people on *they* way out now

The second persons and third person plural have (at least in part) merged
with the subject pronouns: *you* functions at the same time as a subject and
object pronoun as well as a possessive pronoun, and *they* is both subject
and possessive pronoun. It is also interesting that the second possessive
plural is *y'all's*, i.e. a pluralized form of the subjective and objective *y'all*
that takes genitive *-s*. What is equally remarkable is that third person plural
possessive *they* can be complemented by *own* (*they own*), for which I have no
evidence in the other persons. The reflexive pronouns are merged as well.
The second person singular is *youself* (perhaps for both numbers, though
this cannot be verified in all cases) and the third singular masculine is *hisself*.
The latter is widespread in varieties of English around the world (Kortmann
and Szmrecsanyi 2004).

(22)   he was all to *hisself* that's the sort of person he was

Reflexives, finally, may be reinforced by *own self* (*my own self, they own self*,
etc.), possibly a marker of personal involvement and a narrative intensifier,
which has also been reported in Caribbean English, e.g. on the Bahamas,
in Earlier AAE and is very common on Tristan da Cunha as well (Schreier
2003):

(23)   I don't know if she think I was only hittin' *on my own self* or what

3.2.3   *Verb forms (principal parts, endings)*
-ed past tense affixation of regular verbs is frequently absent:

(24)   I never walkØ around much them days

(25)   She passØ it over and I grabØ it as fast as I could

Mussy co-occurs with infinitives and even with modal verbs (such as *can*
or *could*), resembling modal verbs (cf. Wilson and Mesthrie 2004):

(26)   Mr Solomon had the mills see. you *mussy* hear about it hey

(27)   They *mussy* take that down and buil' the house

(28)   You *mussy* hear some histories about people on St Helena eh

Another striking feature of the StHE verb phrase is invariant *be* with habitual meaning, as in:

(29)   the Jack o' Lanterns generally *be* round there too, up top the mountain

(30)   it don't *be* nothing much for them. get 14 pound a week for it, you see

(31)   see that hill that *be* on the side. it all up top yonder

However, there are also contexts where the meaning is non-habitual or where there is future reference:

(32)   He don't *be* well now

(33)   He *be* home this September

Futurity may alternatively be expressed by *will* (and, with negative polarity, *won't*), or even *go*:

(34)   one thing I'*ll* tell y'all the pay was very small

(35)   if you pick up sweet potatoes, if it's one kilo, two kilos, it *go* be expensive

(36)   yeah, the weather nice up here, but you don't know what it *go* be Sandy Bay

(37)   in two weeks time I *go* be 82 (GY, Half Tree Hollow)

The copula, finally, is very often absent, no matter whether followed by personal subject pronouns, NPs, adjectives, locatives (LOC), Verb + *-ing* or *gonna*.

3.2.4 *Adjective comparison*

StHE has two techniques of expressing comparatives and superlatives, an analytic one (*more/most ADJ*) and synthetic one (with *-er* and *-est* affixation). Analytic techniques are more common so that *more/most* is used with monosyllabic ADJ as well.

(38)   people were *more genuine* than what they are today

(39)   They *humaner* now, they shoot 'em

On the other hand, the two techniques are also mixed, resulting in *more* co-occurring with an adjective that is affixed:

(40)   It was a bit *more better* . . . it wasn't as bad as this but it got *worser*

(41)   Those days was *more rough* but *more kind* you know. *more rough* but *more kinder*

3.2.5   Negation

The StHE negation system is rich and complex. On the one hand, there is a standard negation type that takes *do*-support, as in:

(42)   we *didn't* have imported eggs. imported chickens like we get now

(43)   so nevertheless he got this job down Solomon's office so he *didn't* go back to secondary school

However, there are alternative techniques; for one, like many varieties of English around the world, StHE has merged *am not*, *is not* and *are not* to *ain't*. *Ain't* may also occur in combination with preverbal markers such as *done* (see below):

(44)   No way, I *ain't* goin' in for that

(45)   They *ain't* plannin' that

(46)   He *ain't done* examine you

Negative markers include *never*, *no* and, quite unusually, *not* (all of which occur in preverbal positions):

(47)   But after members *never* join so the societies went down. there was no more money

(48)   Jessie, they say to me, Jessie, you *no eat no* food

(49)   I got more pictures but I *not* got them close by

Multiple negation is frequent:

(50)   I a young girl only then, *don't* know *nothin'* and *nowhere none* to help me *nothin'*

3.2.6   Interrogatives

WH-question words are often monomorphemic, though compounds occur also. The former contain the classical WH-words (*who*, *what*, *where*, etc.), with no notable difference from their equivalents in BrE or SHemE generally, whereas the latter include *what-thing*, *what-time*, but no combinations with *which* (*which-place*, etc.). The most likely explanation is that *which* as an interrogative or relative pronoun is generally rare in StHE.

It is striking that StHE does not have word-order inversion in WH-questions. As a result, syntactic complexity is reduced and the order of S and V remains as in declaratives (which reinforces the use of high-rise patterns in intonation). Moreover, *do*-support is rare:

(51)   Where she is?

(52)   Where you lef' you car?

(53)   You was on the island then?

3.2.7   Tense, aspect and modality

In present tense, *do* (mostly in the form of unstressed /də/) is often used as a marker of emphasis or habituality:

(54)   When I *do* kill I send half a pound to Cape Town

(55)   that's what all of us *do* query

Done very often functions as a preterit of do:

(56)   I never *done* no lace that day

(57)   the last two tests they *done*. they *done* on the 26th of March

As pointed out above, weak verbs very rarely take *-ed* suffixation and rely on context:

(58)   My husband liveØ in Jamestown all his life and I liveØ in Jamestown all my life

This also applies to passive sentences, as in:

(59)   I got two grandsons in Germany. one nameØ Gary and the other nameØ Steve

It is open to debate whether this is a phonological process (namely the reduction – or simplification – of a cluster of consonants through the deletion of a final stop) or, alternatively, a grammatical one (namely that past tense is not expressed via suffixation, mirroring the process of bare root extension). Generally speaking, one can say that overt past tense marking is rare in StHE (Schreier 2005, 2008). Irregular verbs typically undergo bare root extension, so that infinitives come to be used with past tense reference as well:

(60)   I *make* so many trips to get the wood in

(61)   I *leave* school when I was fourteen

Completive *done* is very frequent in StHE:

(62)   I *done* beat him now, I seventy-five see

(63)   I *done* scotch up there myself see . . . I *done* scotch down the mill too

Preverbal *been* occurs with regular frequency also, very often carrying a meaning of remoteness and anteriority:

(64)   I scotch, I sort, but I not *been* bale (talking about work in the flax industry)

(65)   I *been* ride up on a donkey up this road here, up Peak Hill, when the [school] treats was on the plain (GC, Jamestown)

Unstressed preverbal *did* is in use as well:

(66)   he *did* really like. he *did* love it

(67)   I know some weeks they *did* give out the numbers what used to come here

Note also *do be*, which is possibly used for special emphasis or as an expression of emotional involvement:

(68)   that place *do be* terrible now

(69)   that place *do be* cram. about a hundred

Aspect markers can also co-occur in the same VP. Most common are the combinations *done + been*:

(70)   if you *done been* down there Collie Williams I don't know if you know him

On the other hand, *a*-prefixing, is extremely uncommon, and I found only one example in my corpus:

(71)   you see that house up there? He's *a*-livin' there

Functions of modality (irrealis, etc.) are often expressed by *would*:

(72)   I *would* take you a fine [?] day and explain to y'all

(73)   those who had big families, they *would* give more bread than I *would* give with only two of us

On the other hand, *may*, *might*, *could* and *couldn't* take this (or at least a similar) function as well:

(74)   then us all put it in a basket and then we raffle it. what she bring, somebody else *may* draw out

(75)   there *might* be a possibility to cut down the electricity see

(76)   we didn't have imported eggs. imported chickens like we get now. people had it on the island. were their own and they *could* sell or give you one

Double modals occur occasionally:

(77)   what I bring you *may can* draw out

Go may also occur instead of *would*. In the following example, a man from Sandy Bay recalls the hard work in the flax plantations in the 1940s and 1950s and describes how flax was collected and produced in the factory buildings:

(78)   then you gotta you got it uh and then uh the people gotta roll it
          up like hanks like you know. and then the dray *go* take it in for
          the scotcher. scotcher in the same place

The same usage is found in the following example, where a woman
recounts where her husband used to hide his money:

(79)   and never worry over money. as soon as he come he *go* say to me
          you find my money down the side of my drawer

Deontic and epistemic modality are often expressed with *must* (for present
tense) and *had to* (past tense), or even, though this is very unusual, *must have
(to)*:

(80)   whatever they want you to do you *must* do it maybe pipelines
          fittin' in compressors trucks all like that

(81)   when you boil that you put salt or anything you boil of a pig –
          you *must have to* add a bit of salt in you food

Present tense progressives are typically expressed by *-ing*. On occasion,
however, this suffix may be zero:

(82)   you legs was painØ?

(83)   they got some Ascension and they tell me they's workØ very
          successful

3.2.8 StHE morphosyntax: First conclusions

The morphosyntactic profile of twentieth-century StHE shows that grammatical complexity is reduced quite drastically. For example, there is no
word-order inversion in question-type sentences ('Where she is?'), analytic
techniques are more commonly used than synthetic ones for comparatives
and superlatives, there is a strong trend to merge pronouns (so that *you* is
used as a possessive pronoun as well), there is no environment-conditioned
constraint on allomorphy (so that the indefinite article *a* is invariant and used
in prevocalic contexts as well), etc.

As in the case of segmental phonology above, one can establish parallels
between features found in StHE and varieties elsewhere. Though the following observations are based on a short overview only (see Schreier 2008 for a
more detailed description), some features can be traced to the British Isles
(and better still: to different parts of the British Isles). Here I would include
what and *that* as relative pronouns, extensive levelling of past *be* with pivot
form *was*, no pluralization of nouns of measurement, *them* as a demonstrative,
mergers of reflexive pronouns (e.g. *hisself*), invariant *be*, *ain't* as merger for
am not, *is not* and *are not*, *never* as a negator ('she *never* talk to him las' week'),
double modals ('it *may can* draw you out'), or present tense *be* regularization
with pivot form *is* ('*I's* quite happy here'), all of which are documented in

regional varieties of EngE. StHE also has a number of features that are now archaic or obsolete in the British Isles, such as: *yonder* as a locative, perfective *be*, or *for to* 'in order to' (the last two are found in TdCE as well).

By the same token, a good number of the morphosyntactic features are predominant in English-based creoles: absence of definite and indefinite articles before NPs ('that was Ø long time ago', 'our people on Ø island'), indeterminate *one* ('live *one* missus there'); absence of morphologically encoded pluralization; absence of subject personal pronouns; *plenty* as a quantifier; absence of genitive -*s* with noun phrase constructions; absence of prepositions and the usage of locative, temporal and spatial attributives (-*side*, -*time*, etc.); absence of existentials or existential *it*; a very strong tendency to avoid morphological tense-marking (i.e. lack of -*s* or -*ed* suffixation) and reliance on preverbal markers instead (*done*, *been*, *used to*, etc.); *go* as a future marker ('you don't know what the weather *go be* like on the other side of the island'); completive *done*, *no* and *not* as negators ('you *no* eat *no* food'); bare root extension of irregular verbs (*ring*, *sing*, *sell*, *light*, *make* etc. as preterites and participles); copula absence; and serial verbs. Diagnostic and rare (possibly even endemic) features that may have arisen through independent developments on the island are: *they own* as a third person plural possessive pronoun; usage of *mussy* with VPs ('you *mussy* hear about that', cf. Wilson and Mesthrie 2004); preterites instead of bare infinitives with quasi-modals *used to* or in other contexts ('I like to *went* down Falklands', 'my daddy used *to got* the flax'); or the *was want* construction ('she *was want* one beer', 'the thing is they never *was wanna* do that').

All this suggests that the morphoyntax of StHE is characterized by mixing and diversity. It is not possible to single out one donor, and there is no doubt that StHE must have evolved out of contact between diverse varieties, drawing features from several co-existing dialects and/or languages and that it developed distinctive characteristics out of interaction between them.

4   Conclusion

StHE takes a special position among the varieties of English around the world. First of all, it is quite likely the oldest variety outside the British Isles, North America and the Caribbean, with a depth of time of three and a half centuries. Secondly, it has been continuously inhabited since 1671 and its social history is comparatively well recorded. This allows us to pinpoint its ancestral varieties, to reconstruct the feature pool out of which it emerged and to study the formation mechanisms that operated during its evolution. And thirdly, due to the community's unique settlement history and socio-ethnic make-up (particularly its strong component of slaves from Madagascar), StHE has few direct links with varieties of English in the Caribbean or elsewhere throughout the southern hemisphere (South Africa and Tristan da Cunha being the exceptions). Parallels with other varieties are thus an ideal testing ground for the analysis of founder effects (of British English) or independent, local language change under extensive contact situations. Research has only just begun (Schreier 2008) and will be continued.

As an LKVE, what does the future hold for StHE? It is very difficult to predict what will happen. As stated above, the 1999 governmental decision to restore full citizenship to the Saints has dealt quite a blow to the island. Reliable statistics are not available at the moment, but it is not an exaggeration to say that about one in four (mostly younger members of the community with their families) have left the island since then to resettle and look for work in England. Nobody knows whether this is a permanent movement; if it is, then the future of St Helena and StHE does not look good. If the exodus is compensated, that is to say when people from elsewhere relocate on the island, then the sociodemographic situation changes considerably. As a result, the traditional dialect may come under threat and be diluted. On the other hand, it is also possible that many of the recent emigrants return. When I was on the island in 2003 I was told that quite a few of them were dissatisfied with living in the UK and planning to return to St Helena. If this is the case, then the population is likely to restabilize, but it is not clear whether and to what extent features of British English picked up in the years abroad will be maintained, thus influencing the speech of younger St Helenians. In any case, the future of StHE depends to a large extent on the St Helenian emigrants to the UK.

References

Brooke, Thomas H. 1808. *A History of the Island of St Helena From Its Discovery by the Portuguese to the Year 1806.* London: Black, Parry and Kingsbury.

Gargen, Henry. 1665. 'A Description of the Island of St Helena to whom itt may concerne: By mee Henry Gargen from ye year 1661 to ye yeare of our Lord: 1665.' Ms.

Gosse, Philip. 1938. *St Helena, 1502–1938.* London: Cassell.

Janisch, Hudson Ralph. 1885. *Extracts from the St Helena Records.* St. Helena: Grant.

Kortmann, Bernd and Benedikt Szmrecsanyi. 2004. 'Global synopsis – morphological and syntactic variation in English.' In Bernd Kortmann, Edgar W. Schneider, Kate Burridge, Rajend Mesthrie, and Clive Upton, eds. *A Handbook of Varieties of English*, Vol. II: *Morphology and Syntax.* Berlin and New York: Mouton de Gruyter, 1122–82.

Melliss, John C. 1875. *St. Helena: A Physical, Historical, and Topographical Description of the Island, Including Its Geology, Fauna, Flora, and Meteorology.* London: Reeve and Co.

Mufwene, Salikoko S. 1996. 'The founder principle in creole genesis.' *Diachronica* 13: 83–134.

Schreier, Daniel. 2003. *Isolation and Language Change: Contemporary and Sociohistorical Evidence from Tristan da Cunha English.* Basingstoke: Houndmills; New York: Palgrave Macmillan.

2005. *Consonant Change in English Worldwide: Synchrony meets Diachrony*. Basingstoke: Houndmills; New York: Palgrave Macmillan.

2008. *St Helenian English: Origins, Evolution and Variation*. Amsterdam and Philadelphia: Benjamins.

Schreier, Daniel and Peter Trudgill. 2006. 'The segmental phonology of 19th century Tristan da Cunha English: Convergence and local innovation.' *English Language and Linguistics* 10: 119–41.

Strang, Barbara. 1970. *A History of English*. London: Methuen.

Trudgill, Peter, Daniel Schreier, Danny Long and Jeffrey P. Williams. 2004. 'On the reversibility of mergers: /w/, /v/ and evidence from lesser-known Englishes.' *Folia Linguistica Historica* 24/1–2: 23–45.

Wells, John C. 1982. *Accents of English*. Cambridge: Cambridge University Press.

Wilson, Sheila and Rajend Mesthrie. 2004. 'St. Helena English: morphology and syntax.' In Bernd Kortmann, Edgar W. Schneider, Rajend Mesthrie, Kate Burridge, and Clive Upton, eds. *A Handbook of Varieties of English*, Vol. II: *Morphology and Syntax*. Berlin and New York: Mouton de Gruyter, 1006–15.

13   Tristan da Cunha English

DANIEL SCHREIER

1   Introduction

Out of all the varieties presented and discussed in this book, Tristan da Cunha English is the smallest by a large measure: spoken by a tiny community of 278 speakers (as of June 2008), it is far from sociodemographically significant as a variety of English around the world. At the same time, it is the most isolated variety of all the LKVEs: Tristan is about 2,300 kilometres south of St Helena, 2,800 kilometres west of Cape Town (South Africa), and 3,400 kilometres east of Uruguay. The island is only accessible over the sea (there is no airport or air strip on Tristan) and the trip from Cape Town to the heart of the South Atlantic Ocean takes anywhere between five and fifteen days, depending on the weather conditions. To complicate matters even more, there are only eight to ten occasions to take such a trip a year (fishing trawlers, supply ships or cruise liners).

The variety that sprang up in this location, Tristan da Cunha English (TdCE), is unusual for a number of linguistic and sociolinguistic reasons. First of all, it is one of the youngest native-speaker varieties of English around the world: a bit older than Falklands Islands English (FIE; see Chapter 11) or New Zealand English, but a generation or so younger than South African or Australian English. It developed in the 1820s out of inputs brought to the island from various regions of the British Isles, the northeastern US, the South Africa Table Bay region and St Helena (cf. Chapter 12). It is a mixed dialect that drew distinctive features from various donors and that underwent considerable restructuring when it evolved (Schreier 2003). Second, the community is entirely anglophone and monolingual: languages other than English are not spoken on the island today (borrowing from other languages was limited, the exception being some Afrikaans words in the domain of fishing, picked up from South Africans aboard ship; see section 3.3 below).

Some of the findings presented here were published in 'The segmental phonology of Tristan da Cunha English' (*English Language and Linguistics* 10 (2006)), which I wrote jointly with Peter Trudgill. I would like to acknowledge his collaboration. Moreover, I thank Philip Baker and Karen Lavarello Schreier for their help with compiling and interpreting a brief lexicon of TdCE.

By the same token, there has never been prima facie language contact on the island: it was uninhabited when it was first settled and all the founders (in the sense of Mufwene 1996, 2001) spoke English (though some were bilingual, their native languages being Dutch, Italian, and quite likely early Afrikaans). Thirdly, the community resides in one village and there is no regional variation on the island. The capital and only settlement on Tristan is technically known as 'Edinburgh of the Seven Seas', locally simply referred to as 'the village'. This means that the Tristanians form compact social networks, characterized by high density and multiplexity. There are social differences on the island (the range of occupations is from factory manager to mechanic, from bank clerk to cleaning personnel; there is no unemployment) but peer pressure effects and group conformity eradicate any established form of social stratification (this means that two of the classic extralinguistic correlates of language variation, regionality and occupation/social status, are not operative). Fourthly, though the community has opened up over the last twenty years in particular (see section 2), their identity is very strongly that of a 'Tristanian' and their sense of orientation is focused on the island. Perhaps with the exception of some adolescents who wish for an 'overseas experience', all the islanders regard Tristan as their home and would not want to be anywhere else.

2   Sociolinguistic history and current status of the variety

The Portuguese were the first to venture into the South Atlantic, taking advantage of the favourable trade winds from South America to Table Bay. We know that admiral Tristão da Cunha discovered the island in 1506, charting it and naming it after himself, but the Portuguese did not pursue a concerted settlement policy. The English and Dutch became aware of the islands, the Dutch being the first to land (in 1643; Beintema 2000). Still, none of the colonial powers developed an interest in establishing a permanent colony since the island was too inaccessible and of no strategic value.

Things changed when, towards the end of the eighteenth century, the American fishing and whaling industry expanded to the South Atlantic Ocean and Tristan da Cunha served as an occasional resort to the sealers and whalers (Brander 1940). The growing economic interest, as well as the position of Tristan da Cunha along a major sea-route, soon attracted discoverers and adventurers as well. The island was officially settled in 1816, when the British admiralty formally annexed Ascension Island and Tristan da Cunha, apparently with the intention of blocking a possible escape route for Napoleon Bonaparte, who was exiled on St Helena (Schreier and Lavarello-Schreier 2003). A military garrison was dispatched to the island and withdrawn after a one-year stay. Some army personnel stayed and settled for good: two stonemasons from Plymouth (Samuel Burnell and John Nankivel), a non-commissioned officer from Kelso, Scotland, named William Glass, his wife, Maria Magdalena Leenders Glass, 'the daughter of a Boer Dutchman' (Evans 1994: 245), and their two small children.

The population increased when shipwrecked sailors and castaways arrived; some of them waited for the first ship and left at the first opportunity, whereas others remained and added to the permanent population. In 1824, apart from the Glass family, the settlers included Richard 'Old Dick' Riley (from Wapping, East London), Thomas Swain (born in Hastings, Sussex) and Alexander Cotton (from Hull/Yorkshire), all of whom had arrived in the early 1820s (Earle 1966 [1832]). The late 1820s and 1830s saw the arrival of a group of women from St Helena and three non-anglophone settlers (from Denmark and Holland), among them Pieter Willem Groen, who later changed his name to Peter Green and lived on the island until his death in 1902, at the age of 94. The population grew rapidly, and by 1832 there was a total of thirty-four people on the island, including twenty-two young children. The 1830s and 1840s saw a renaissance of the whaling industry and once again numerous ships called at Tristan da Cunha to barter for fresh water and supplies; this led to the arrival of a number of American whalers, some of whom settled permanently.

The second half of the nineteenth century was characterized by growing isolation, for a number of political and economic reasons. The American whale trade declined quickly, the increasing use of steam ships made bartering unnecessary, and the opening of the Suez Canal in 1869 reduced the number of ships in the South Atlantic Ocean. This affected the influx of settlers, and a weaver from Yorkshire (Crawford 1945) and two Italian sailors were the only new arrivals in the second half of the century (Crabb 1980). The sociocultural isolation of Tristan da Cunha peaked in the early twentieth century; at one stage, the community received no mail for more than ten years (Evans 1994) and a minister reported in the mid 1920s that the children had never seen a football (Rogers 1925). When the Second World War broke out, the Tristanians basically lived in non-industrialized conditions (Munch 1945). This situation ended abruptly when the British admiralty installed a naval station on Tristan da Cunha in April 1942. The arrival of the navy corps entailed far-reaching economic changes: for one, a South African company obtained exclusive rights to establish a permanent fishing industry on the island, employing practically the entire local workforce. The traditional subsistence economy was replaced by a paid labour force economy, and the traditional way of life was modified as a result of the creation of permanent jobs with regular working hours. Tristan da Cunha was an economic boomtown in the 1950s: the living conditions and housing standards improved and the changes brought about by the development scheme led to a complete transformation of the traditional Tristanian way of life within one generation (Schreier and Lavarello-Schreier 2003).

In October 1961, unforeseen volcanic activities forced a wholesale evacuation of the island. The Tristanians were transported to Cape Town and then on to England, but virtually all of them returned from their exile near Southampton to the South Atlantic in 1963. The dramatic evacuation and the two 'volcano years' in England affected the islanders more than any other single event in the history of the community. The community underwent quick modernization and adaptation to western culture as modern dress, dances and entertainment were adopted. A new fishing company provided all the households with electricity; this improved the living conditions considerably and the 1970s and 1980s were a period of economic prosperity again. Today, the population is stable and out-migration is practically nil; though the islanders spend more time abroad (for medical treatment, job training or simply for a holiday), nobody has left for good in the last few years.

3   Features of the variety

The settlement history has given rise to a distinctive local variety, which was formed via processes of feature selection from the inputs but underwent local innovation as well. The vowel realizations are as follows.

3.1   Segmental phonology

3.1.1   Short vowels

KIT /ɪ/

TdCE realizations of this vowel are typically default /ɪ/, with the exception of particularly close realizations before /ʃ/, as in *fish, dish, (par)tition*. Here we may in fact find FLEECE rather than KIT, so that the opposition between /ɪ/ and /iː/ seems neutralized in this environment. Moreover, DRESS words have KIT rather than /ɛ/ when the vowel is followed by an alveolar consonant, such as /t/ in *get* or *kettle*, /d/ in *head*, or /n/ in *engine*.

DRESS /ɛ/

TdCE DRESS is stable /ɛ/, with little raising or breaking. However, some speakers have a closer and/or longer vowel, sometimes accompanied by an off-glide [ɛ̝ ~ ɛ̝ə ~ eˑə ~ ɛë] before voiced consonants: *eggs* [hɛ̝ˑgs], *leg* [lɛ̝ˑg]. The word *catch* normally has DRESS.

TRAP /æ/

This vowel is mostly [æ ~ æˑ ~ æ̞ ~ æ̞ˑ]. Usually, TRAP is not raised though it is occasionally [ɛ ~ ɛ̝] in words like *bag*, which parallels the raising of DRESS in this particular environment.

FOOT /ʊ/

This vowel is unremarkable in TdCE: /ʊ/. As in many other parts of the world, speakers demonstrate some unrounding and centralization. Words such as *broom, room, groom, roof, hoof* have this vowel.

STRUT /ʌ/

The realization of STRUT in TdCE is fronted, but not as front as in London or South African English. The most usual quality is a vowel somewhat more front than [ɐ]. A large number of NURSE words have this vowel as well (see below). Moreover, STRUT can occur in open syllables: *fur* /fʌ/, which is unusual.

LOT /ɒ/

Unrounded [ɑ] variants are absent, and this vowel is very much as in southeastern England, e.g. [ɒ]. However, the incidence of this vowel is rather unusual, indicating a partial overlap with GOAT (see below). Words which have GOAT elsewhere may take LOT in TdCE: *rope, soak, soap, poke, smoke, hope, cope, broke, over* etc. To complicate matters, words which have THOUGHT in other varieties may have LOT in TdCE as well: *caught, taught, brought, thought,* but also *fork, short, pork, forty, fourteen*. There is also transfer in the other direction, so that words that have LOT in southeastern English English, e.g. *bottle, donkey,* have THOUGHT in TdCE. The *cloth* lexical set (*off, froth, across* etc.) has THOUGHT rather than LOT.

3.1.2 Rising/closing Diphthongs

FLEECE /iː/

This vowel is genuinely monophthongal [iː]; diphthongization to [ɪ̯] is not common, unlike in modern southeast of England accents and elsewhere in the southern hemisphere.

FACE /eː/

TdCE FACE generally has no *long mid diphthonging* (Wells 1982: 210–11). However, monophthongal [eː] is not tense and may have a very slight off-glide [e·ⁱ].

PRICE /ɑɪ/

PRICE in TdCE is a 'fast' diphthong [ɐɪ] before voiceless consonants, but a 'slow' diphthong [ɒ·ɛ] elsewhere (cf. Kurath 1964: 153), the latter demonstrating both *diphthong shift* (Wells 1982: 256) and *glide weakening*. This split allophony resembles the well-known *Canadian raising* pattern (Chambers 1973), which occurs 'in *nearly every* form of non-creolised, mixed, colonial English outside Australasia and South Africa' (Trudgill 1986: 160) and also in English Fens English (Britain 1991, 1997). It is unusual that TdCE does not have this pattern for MOUTH (see below).

CHOICE /oi/

This vowel has a rather close first element and is around [ɒɪ]. The archaic dialectal feature PRICE rather than CHOICE (Strang 1970: 112) e.g. 'bile' *boil*, may have been brought to the island initially. Evidence comes from local place names such *Tommy's oilhouse* (where Tommasso Corri, an Italian resident in the early years of colonization, stored whale blubber oil), which appears as 'Tommy's *eye-loose*' in Crawford's (1945) topographic map of the island. (If this is correct, then this would also be indicative of Scots *hoose* as opposed to English *house*, which is not found either).

GOOSE /uː/

GOOSE is genuinely monophthongal, and for older speakers GOOSE remains very back [uː].

GOAT /ou/

It is unusual in English accents around the world that there is no paralelism between GOAT and FACE. GOAT has *long mid diphthonging* while FACE does not (see above). TdCE speakers born before 1900 usually have a conservative realization [oˑʊ ∼ oʊ ∼ ɔʊ], those born in the early twentieth century and around the Second World War tend to have progressively more front realizations [ɵʊ ∼ øʊ ∼ øʉ].

MOUTH /aʊ/

The asymmetry between front and back vowel pairs is also apparent here in that there is no Canadian raising of MOUTH. The most usual pronunciation is around [æʉ ∼ ɛʉ].

3.1.3   *Long monophthongs and centring diphthongs*

NURSE /ɜː/

TdCE does not have /ɜː/. Rather, it has /aː/ from original /ɛr/, as is still the case in traditional East Anglian dialects (Trudgill 2004), but, unlike in East Anglia, the /aː/ in *earth*, *learnt* etc. is not the same vowel as the /ɑː/ in START. All other NURSE words, such as *bird* /bʌd/, have the STRUT vowel. However, and this is perhaps unique among the world's Englishes, the STRUT vowel also occurs in words which end in open syllables, such as *fur* /fʌ/. In all other varieties of English, STRUT occurs in closed syllables only, i.e. it is a checked vowel.

START /ɑː/

TdCE has this vowel in all the lexical sets where it occurs in the English of the southeast of England, e.g. *start, last, path.* This vowel is pronounced [ɑː], resembling South African English, and the START-backing innovation (dated to the early 1800s by Wells 1982: 234) is the norm. In pre-nasal environments, such as *dance, sample, demand, plant* etc., we occasionally find /ɑː/.

THOUGHT/FORCE/CLOTH/NORTH/POOR /ɒə/

This vowel is pronounced [ɒə]. It occurs in all five lexical sets, so both the *First* and the *Second force mergers* (Wells 1982) are complete. Moreover, [ɒə] is found in the CLOTH set (*dog, long, strong* etc.) as well. On the other hand, quite a few words have LOT instead of THOUGHT/FORCE/NORTH, which is suggestive of an overlap of lexical sets.

NEAR/SQUARE /ɪə/

Words from both these sets have a vowel around [ɪə] and are thus merged (Schreier 2003: 210).

3.1.4 Other vowel features

The weak vowel merger

TdCE resembles other SHemEs in that it commonly has /ə/ in unstressed syllables (what Wells 1982: 167 calls the 'weak vowel merger', which is to say that *trump it* and *trumpet* rhyme) whereas southeast England accents have /ɪ/ (where they are distinct).

happY-tensing

TdCE has happY-tensing (Wells 1982: 595, 616), i.e. words like *happy, money* have word-final /iː/ rather than /ɪ/.

3.1.5 Consonants

/p, k/

Intervocalic /p/ and /k/ are often glottalized: *people* [piːpʔɬ], *checkers* [tʃɛkʔəs]. Somewhat unusually, syllable-final /k/ is often uvular in the speech of older Tristanians, except after some close vowels: *clock* [klɒq], *work* [βʌq], *back* [bæ·q]. This feature is found in St Helena as well as in some Caribbean and Asian accents.

/t/

T-glottaling is common, particularly before syllabic /n/ and /l/ and in *button, bottle,* or *Nightingale* [nɒ·ɛʔŋge·ⁱl]. Intervocalic /t/ is usually a voiced flap; since intervocalic /d/ is also a flap, the contrast between the two phonemes in this position may be neutralized. TdCE also has 'preglottalization' (Wells 1982: 260), i.e. the use of a glottal stop before /p, t, k, tʃ/.

/θ/ and /ð/

The dental fricatives have complex realizations also. On the one hand, there is TH-fronting to /f/ and /v/ and TH-stopping to /t/ and /d/ (particularly in function words such as *the*, *that*, *then*). Moreover, TdCE has a (quite possibly unique feature of) 'TH sibilization' (Schreier 2003: 211), so that words like *thing*, *through* take /s/; *thing* and *sing* are homophonous.

/h/

TdCE is characterized not only by the presence of /h/ but also by very extensive 'H-insertion': /h/ occurs very regularly in words that begin with a vowel, such as *island*, *apple*, *after*. H-insertion is so common that it is one of the most salient characteristics of TdCE phonology. This is evidenced by the fact that outsiders frequently remark on it (Crawford 1945, for instance, writes that Tristanians say they live 'on a h'island' rather than an island).

/v, w, b/

TdCE, like a number of other colonial varieties of English and nineteenth century southeastern England (Trudgill et al. 2004), has a pre-stressed-syllable merger of /w/ and /v/. Phonetically, the single consonant is realized as [ß] or, less often, [ß] or [w], e.g. in *visit* [ßɪsɪt], *away* [əße:]. These pronunciations are best regarded as realizations of /w/ since TdCE also lacks /v/ in pre-unstressed-syllable and word-final position. Here, however, it is most often merged with /b/: *over* /hɒbə/, *canvas* /kænəbəs /, *live* /lɪb /, *living* /lɪbən /, *oven* /hʌbn/. (The word *twelve*, however, is also on occasion pronounced /twɛlf/). This merger is also apparent in the triphthong /ɑuə/ which in Tristan is presumably derived from */ɑuwə/ and is now pronounced /ʌbə/ e.g. *our* /hʌbə/, *flower* /flʌbə/. There is no contrast between /w/ and /ʍ/, e.g. *whale* is [ße·il].

/z, ʒ/

These consonants are uncommon in TdCE, /s/ and /ʃ/ occurring instead, e.g. *season* /siːsn/, *television* [tɛləßiʃn̩]. As /v/ and /ð/ are also both absent, the phonemic inventory of basilectal TdCE has no voiced fricatives.

/r/

TdCE is non-rhotic, and linking and intrusive /r/ are usual. The normal pronunciation of /r/ is, as in most of England, [ɹ] with retroflexion.

/l/

A clear /l/ is usual in prevocalic position and after front vowels, but dark /l/ after back vowels. There is no L-vocalization.

Consonant clusters

TdCE has a strong tendency to reduce word- or syllable-final consonant clusters (CCR). Where historical syllable-final consonant clusters consist of two voiced or two unvoiced consonants, the second is invariably lost (e.g. in *find*, *cask*, *first*). This deletion process is not context-dependent since the plural of *flask* /flɑːs/ is /flɑːsəs/, which is also reported elsewhere (for instance in African American English; Bailey and Thomas 1998). On the other hand, clusters that have both voiced and non-voiced consonants (/nk/ in *sink*, /lt/ in *melt*, /lp/ in *help*, etc.) can be variably reduced also, which is very uncommon (discussion in Schreier 2005).

3.1.6   The segmental phonology of TdCE: Some conclusions

The picture that emerges from a phonological analysis of TdCE is complex, both in terms of features traceable to specific input varieties and with respect to processes of dialect interaction. First of all, TdCE has a strong British pedigree, and it seems that accents from the English southeast were particularly influential in its formation phase: it is non-rhotic, it has six short vowels, slight STRUT-fronting, genuinely monophthongal FLEECE and GOOSE, a fully back START, T-glottalling, the merger of /w/ and /v/ before stressed syllables, and STRUT for NURSE. All of these features make (or made) an appearance in London and the surrounding counties (Essex, East Anglia etc.).

The segmental phonology of TdCE is characterized by the fact that GOAT and FACE behave differently in that only GOAT has undergone diphthongization (with a narrow diphthong and a fully back nucleus), FACE being more conservative in comparison. GOOSE and FLEECE are monophthongs and have no tendency towards shifting or off-gliding. PRICE, on the other hand, is innovative in that it has developed the 'Canadian raising' pattern, while MOUTH, which does not have this pattern, only shifted its nucleus as far as [æ ~ ɛ].

TdCE is untypical when compared with other varieties of SHemE in that the short front vowels KIT, DRESS and TRAP are not typically raised. On the other hand, as in other varieties of SHemE, PRICE has both 'diphthong shift' and 'glide weakening' and there are a number of mergers (NEAR / SQUARE; the weak (unstressed) vowels) as well. To complicate matters still, TdCE has a number of prototypical Creole features (extremely high amounts of CCR and the stopping of voiced bilabial fricatives) and quite a few independent (possibly even endemic) developments: 'TH-sibilization', /z, ʒ/, absence of voiced fricatives (/s/, /ʃ/, /v/ and /ð/) and the overlap of words from the lexical sets in GOAT, LOT and THOUGHT.

3.2   Morphosyntax

The most prominent morphosyntactic properties of TdCE can be summarized as follows.

3.2.1   Plural formation

The most common pattern of pluralization is a standard type of -*s* suffixation; nouns of measurement (*mile*, *pound* etc.) are typically not marked for plural:

(1)   that fish weigh over five pound

Agent nouns and animate subjects often take the so-called associative plural *dem/n' dem* (following plural NPs only):

(2)   Larry dem gone over the hill

3.2.2   Pronouns

The pronoun systems are fairly standard. The singular subject pronouns match the general patterns found in most varieties of English around the world (*I* for first person singular, *you* for second and *he/she/it* for third). The first and third person plurals are *we* and *they*. The second person plural pronoun is typically *you all/y'all*:

(3)   is y'all been up Nightingale yet?

The object pronouns are unremarkable, with *y'all* featuring here as well (*me, you, her/him/it, us, y'all, them*). Reflexive pronouns may be reinforced by *own self* (*my own self*, *they own self* etc.), which has also been reported in Bahamian English, e.g. on the Bahamas, in Earlier AAE (Schneider, p.c. 17 December 2007) and is very common on St Helena as well (Schreier 2008):

(4)   You's done see that you own self

3.2.3   Verb forms (principal parts, endings)

The inflectional morphology of TdCE has undergone considerable simplifi-cation, a tendency that is particularly noticeable in the verb forms. Affixation is nearly absent and there are virtually no present and past tense markers -*s* (third person present tense) and -*ed* (past tense for all grammatical persons in all weak verbs).

(5)   She sing real good

(6)   They walk out all the way to the patches last night

Moreover, TdCE has a strong tendency to extend bare roots so they feature in preterite and past tense contexts also:

(7)   We never eat much them days

Present- and past-tense forms of *be* are noteworthy in that there is no agree-ment with person and number. Instead, the present-tense paradigm invari-ably has *is* with all persons ('I's quite happy now, you know') and past *be* has *was* ('the cows was really wild then'). This means that *am*, *are* and *were* are not found at all, and this is not reported elsewhere.

3.2.4 *Adjective comparison*
Mono- and bisyllabic adjectives take affixation whereas adjectives with three and more syllables take *more* and *most*. However, there is a general trend for analytic techniques to be more common, so that *more/most* is used with monosyllabic adjectives as well. The two techniques may be combined, that is, *more* co-occurs with an adjective that is affixed:

(8)   I like that more better

3.2.5 *Negation*
TdCE has several negation types. On the one hand, there is a standard negation type that takes *do*-support, as in:

(9)   the fog was so thick they didn't see the island

(10)   we don't go round the island that often now

Though this is not common, *am not*, *is not* and *are not* are merged to *ain't*. *Ain't* may also occur in combination with preverbal tense markers like *done* (see below). Two alternative techniques are *never* and multiple negation:

(11)   we never had frying oil them days

(12)   but nobody never come out or nothing

3.2.6 *Interrogatives*
WH-question words are often monomorphemic, though compounds occur also. The former contain the classical WH-words (*who*, *what*, *where*, *which*, *how* and *why*), with no notable difference from their equivalents in BrE or SHemE generally, whereas the latter include *what-thing*, *what-time* etc. It is striking that TdCE does not have word-order inversion in WH-questions:

(13)   where they is?

As a result, syntactic complexity is reduced and the order of S and V remains as in declaratives (which reinforces the use of high-rise patterns in intonation to mark questions).

3.2.7 *Tense, aspect and modality*
As stated in section 3.2.3, the TdCE tense system has undergone heavy simplification: bare roots very commonly occur in preterite or past participle contexts and *-ed* suffixation for weak verbs is practically absent. The present tense copula is typically present (absent only in two environments: before *gonna* and *-ing* progressives):

(14)   that's the gang what Ø gonna hunt rats now

(15)   he's so lucky he Ø singin' all day

Preverbal *done* (with *be*-support, contracted to *'s*) marks completive aspect:

(16)   she's done gone and done it now

Unstressed *did* occurs with regular frequency, presumably to mark verbs for past tense that otherwise would not be:

(17)   we did like it very much in Cape Town you know

Future is invariably expressed with *gonna* or *will*. Deontic end epistemic modality are marked by *would* and *have to*, as is common elsewhere.

3.2.8 Complementation

Complementation is fairly standard insofar as *that* or *Ø* are the usual complementizers and *to* (or *for to*) is used with infinitival complements:

(18)   the coxswain know they was back on the island when the fog lift

(19)   they had to stay Sandy Point the rain was so bad

(20)   we use trays for to throw the crawfish in

3.3 Lexicon

The TdCE lexicon reflects the social history of the community and this is a domain where founder effects can be pinpointed fairly accurately. The majority of the word stock is of British origin, but loanwords were drawn from several other varieties, such as Dutch and/or Afrikaans, Italian and American English. For one, TdCE has maintained dialect words that are now considered obsolete or archaic in the UK, e.g. *quamish* 'sick in the stomach'. Similarly the word *chock*, a type of quantifier predominantly used in connection with the sea ('we caught so many crawfish, the sea was chockfull of them!'), may in origin be dialectal British English. We find word meanings in TdCE that ring familiar to English ears but that are unknown in the British Isles, such as the word *catfish*. Outsiders usually think of finfish when Tristanians talk about 'using catfish for bait' and are confused when they find out that a *catfish* refers to an octopus instead (the same meaning is reported on St Helena and in the speech of Cape Coloureds, which suggests that this word was adopted from several input varieties). Another interesting usage is the verb *to stop*, which does not mean 'come to a halt' but 'stay or live with somebody' (you stop in someone's home, instead of staying in it, and you stop in England, instead of living in England). On the other hand, distinctive words may also have been created on the island itself. One of the most common fish species in Tristan waters is called the *fivefinger*, a name that has not been reported anywhere else and may well have been made up by the islanders (it has dark stripes along the sides, as if five fingers had scratched it).

By contrast, some TdCE words are unknown in the British Isles, for instance *kooibietjie* which is from Afrikaans and means 'take a little nap', 'sleep a little while' (from Afrikaans *kooi* 'bed' and *bietjie* 'a little bit'), or *molly* or *mollyok*, which derives from 'mallemok', the Dutch word for 'albatross'. At the same time, technological inventions or newly imported products have led to the adoption of words from other languages (particularly from Afrikaans). For instance, recently imported goods from South Africa led to the borrowing of loanwords such as *braai* 'barbecue', *boerewors* 'sausage', and *bakkie* 'truck'. Dutch and Afrikaans (since both were brought to Tristan and are closely related, it is quite difficult to decide where the Tristan Slang adopted it from) also contributed words in the domains of cooking (*gherkin* 'cucumbers'), fishing terminology (*snoek*, *steenbrass* are local fish species) and everyday life (*kappi* 'bonnet', *lekker* 'good, delicious', *kraal* for 'sheep pen', perhaps also *kee-kee* 'ear' and *fardie* 'godfather'), and of course Italian contributed food and other terms to the local dialect as well (the ubiquitous *pasta* and *spaghetti*, but also terms like *buncatina* for 'bench'). South African English and Afrikaans had a considerable impact on TdCE as well, at least on a lexical level. An additional source for the lexicon of TdCE was American English, and distinctive words were picked up from Captain Hagan and his companions as well as from the American whalers who frequented the area in the 1840s and 1850s. An American heritage is found in words like *gulch*, the contracted form *tater* (for 'potato'), perhaps also the usage of *mad* for 'angry' and *I guess* for 'I reckon' and in the second person plural pronoun *y'all* ('y'all is watching too much out of the window').

Finally, we also find that English words are re-used for new terms in TdCE. The word *canary* is used to refer to the 'Tristan bunting' (*Nesospiza acunhae*), whose primary habitat now is Nightingale Island. Similarly, 'refrigerators' are called *coolers* on Tristan (which causes great confusion when they are ordered in Cape Town; South Africans have no idea what the order is). By the same token, only few Tristanians use the word 'ketchup'; instead, *mato sauce* (with a clipped first syllable, see above) is the common term. A special word in Tristan English is *canteen*, which is used to mean 'store' or 'supermarket', which can be explained historically: the Tristanians did not have a local shopping place until the soldiers arrived in 1942. They then built a small store for the patronage of the army personnel (which in military jargon is a *canteen*). When the naval station was withdrawn, the store remained for the local population, and with it stayed the name (Schreier and Lavarello-Schreier 2003).

Consequently, the lexicon attests to the contact scenario that gave rise to contemporary TdCE, in that we may directly trace lexical items to the varieties brought to the island. By the same token, TdCE has maintained British words that are now considered archaic or obsolete and creatively changed the meaning of existing words so as to meet the demands of an unknown flora and fauna.

4 Conclusion

Though demographically insignificant, TdCE represents an ideal showcase to investigate contact dynamics and processes of dialect interaction. Sociolinguistically speaking, it is a mixed dialect, the principal input variety being British English; other donors were St Helenian English, Afrikaans, South African English, Dutch, Italian and American English. Their input is evident on a lexical level but has affected other levels as well. TdCE morphosyntax in particular has undergone restructuring and regularization, which is most likely the legacy of a contact-derived form of Saint Helenian English (cf. Chapter 12). The dialect formed and stabilized in the nineteenth century, as speakers born before the First World War display comparatively little systemic variation.

The future of TdCE seems safe, at least for a generation or two. An increase in mobility reached a peak in the 1990s and at the time it looked like the out-migration of younger community members would seriously tip the sociodemographic balance of the population (about a dozen Tristanians left the island for good, a considerable blow for such a small village). The situation has changed since the turn of the millennium, however, and now the islanders remain on the island, despite the fact that they have the opportunity to receive a second degree in the UK for free. Nevertheless, a decrease in family size (families with three children or more are now rare) ultimately endangers any population of that size, so it is difficult to predict the long-term future of TdCE.

By the same token, more research needs to be done to find out how time in the 'outside world' affects the dialect right now. As said above, the Tristanians are more mobile now than they were some thirty years ago: every ship travelling to Cape Town is full of islanders who have to receive medical service, are leaving the island for short job training (mostly on St Helena or in the UK) or simply going for a holiday abroad. One can only speculate how this affects the rate of change in TdCE. Will the adoption and maintenance of supraregional features (of British or South African English) lead to a loss or disappearance of distinctive local features or not? In Schreier (2003), I speculated that younger members of the community show higher awareness and flexibility as to whether they should use non-local features with outsiders and I argued that they switch between a local TdCE with islanders and a more supralocal variety with outsiders. It is not clear for now whether this is incipient dedialectalization or the beginning of bidialectalism and context-related dialect-shifting. I would suspect the latter, but more research is clearly needed here.

References

Bailey, Guy and Erik Thomas. 1998. 'Some aspects of African-American vernacular English phonology.' In Salikoko S. Mufwene, John R. Rickford, Guy Bailey and John Baugh, eds. *African American English: Structure, History and Use*. New York: Routledge, 85–109.

Beintema, Albert. 2000. 'Early shipping in Tristan da Cunha waters.' http://home. planet.nl/~beintema/ships.htm

Brander, Jan. 1940. *Tristan da Cunha 1506–1902*. London: Allen and Unwin.

Britain, David. 1991. 'Dialect and space: A geolinguistic study of speech variables in the Fens.' Unpublished PhD dissertation, University of Essex.

   1997. 'Dialect contact and phonological reallocation: "Canadian raising" in the English Fens.' *Language in Society* 26: 15–46.

Chambers, J. K. 1973. 'Canadian Raising.' *Canadian Journal of Linguistics* 18: 113–35.

Crabb, George. 1980. 'The history and postal history of Tristan da Cunha.' Self-published manuscript.

Crawford, Allen. 1945. *I went to Tristan*. London: Allen and Unwin.

Earle, Augustus. 1966. *Narrative of a Residence on the Island of Tristan D'Acunha in the South Atlantic Ocean*. (1st edn 1832.) Oxford: Clarendon Press.

Evans, Dorothy. 1994. *Schooling in the South Atlantic Islands 1661–1992*. Oswestry: Anthony Nelson.

Kurath, Hans. 1964. 'British sources of selected features of American pronunciation: problems and methods.' In D. Abercrombie, D. B. Fry, P. A. D. MacCarthy, N. C. Scott and J. L. M. Trim, eds. *In Honour of Daniel Jones: Papers Contributed on the Occasion of his Eightieth Birthday*. London: Longman, 146–55.

Munch, Peter. 1945. *Sociology of Tristan da Cunha*. Oslo: Det Norske Videnskaps-Akademi.

Mufwene, Salikoko S. 1996. 'The founder principle in creole genesis.' *Diachronica* 13: 83–134.

   2001. 'The ecology of language evolution.' Cambridge: Cambridge University Press.

Rogers, Rose. 1925. *The Lonely Island*. London: Allen and Unwin.

Schreier, Daniel. 2003. *Isolation and Language Change: Contemporary and Sociohistorical Evidence from Tristan da Cunha English*. Basingstoke: Houndmills; New York: Palgrave Macmillan.

   2005. *Consonant Change in English Worldwide: Synchrony meets Diachrony*. Basingstoke: Houndmills; New York: Palgrave Macmillan.

   2008. *St Helenian English: Origins, Evolution and Variation*. Amsterdam and Philadelphia: Benjamins.

Schreier, Daniel and Karen Lavarello-Schreier. 2003. *Tristan da Cunha: History, People, Language*. London: Battlebridge.

Schreier, Daniel and Peter Trudgill. 2006. 'The segmental phonology of 19th century Tristan da Cunha English: Convergence and local innovation.' *English Language and Linguistics* 10: 119–41.

Strang, Barbara. 1970. *A History of English*. London: Methuen.

Trudgill, Peter. 1986. *Dialects in Contact*. Oxford: Blackwell.

   2004. 'The dialect of East Anglia: Phonology.' In Bernd Kortmann, Edgar W. Schneider, Kate Burridge, Rajend Mesthrie, and Clive Upton, eds. *A Handbook of Varieties of English*, Vol. 1: *Phonology*. Berlin and New York: Mouton de Gruyter, 163–77.

Trudgill, Peter, Daniel Schreier, Danny Long and Jeffrey P. Williams. 2004. 'On the reversibility of mergers: /w/, /v/ and evidence from lesser-known Englishes.' *Folia Linguistica Historica* 24/1–2: 23–45.

Wells, John C. (1982). *Accents of English*. Cambridge: Cambridge University Press.

Part IV

Africa

14   L1 Rhodesian English

SUSAN FITZMAURICE

1 Introduction

The variety that is the subject of this description is the L1 English spoken
mainly by descendants of European, principally British, settlers in Zimbabwe, a land-locked country in sub-Saharan Africa bordered by South
Africa to the south, Botswana to the west, Zambia to the northwest and
Mozambique to the east. Zimbabwean English (ZimE) might be grouped
with South African L1 varieties as well as New Zealand and Australian
Englishes as a southern hemisphere L1 variety of English descended from
British input dialects transported in the course of the nineteenth century. As
a southern hemisphere variety, Rhodesian English shares some phonological
and grammatical features with these varieties at the same time as exhibiting
some features, principally lexical, acquired through contact with L1 speakers of local, indigenous languages. A note on terminology: the L1 English
variety under examination will henceforth be referred to as *Rhodesian English*
(RhodE), spoken by white people who either settled in or who were born
before 1980 in the former British colony of Southern Rhodesia and who no
longer live in the country. RhodE is regarded as a fossil, non-productive
dialect.[1] Independence as a democratic republic under black majority rule in
1980 changed the social, economic and political conditions in which blacks
and whites interacted in Zimbabwe; in this environment, it is appropriate
to refer to the prevailing L1 English dialect in the country as *Zimbabwean
English* (ZimE) as it is a productive and changing variety.[2]

Postcolonial Zimbabwe is an ethnically diverse, multilingual country.
English is the official language. The literacy rate is 90 per cent, given an
operational definition as the ability of speakers over 15 years of age to read

---

[1] I am grateful to the Wells-West family for serving as informants for this essay and dedicate
this account to them. I salute the members of Zimdays, whose comments and descriptions of
RhodE provided an excellent way for me to verify the reliability of my linguistic judgements
as a native speaker and participant observer. I also acknowledge Roger Lass' expertise and
brilliant ear for authenticity. All errors are my own.

[2] See Fitzmaurice, chapter 4 ('The ideal of Standard English and the reality of regional
standards') in *Standardization in English* (forthcoming) for an extended treatment of these
questions and comparative description of RhodE and ZimE.

263

and write English. Of about 12 million people, 98 per cent are African, and whites and Asians make up the remaining 2 per cent.[3] The two principal ethnic groups are Bantu-speaking: the majority Shona (about 64 per cent of the population) and Ndebele (about 28 per cent).[4] Other significant Bantu ethnic groups make up the remaining 6 per cent: the Batonga in the Zambezi valley, the Venda in the Limpopo valley, and the Shangaan in the southeast of the country. The population is principally rural, with 30 per cent living in urban areas. The capital Harare has about 1.5 million people; the second city, Bulawayo, has nearly 1 million people, and Chitungwiza, the fastest-growing high-density town in the country, has about 400,000 dwellers. Most Zimbabweans are L1 speakers of various regional dialects of chiShona (for example, chiNdau, chiZezuru, chiKoreKore, chiManyika and chiKaranga). In addition, there are numerous urban lingua francas, including chiChewa (Makoni, Brutt-Griffler and Mashiri 2007). English remains the official medium in public domains such as government, broadcasting, education and the law courts.

Since about 2000, the country has experienced extraordinary difficulties. The AIDS pandemic has had devastating consequences for Zimbabweans, resulting in a significant AIDS orphan population. Additionally, the very high rate of unemployment, combined with very low rates of food production and raw materials export and the highest rates of inflation in the world at time of writing (150,000 per cent), have resulted in what the World Bank terms 'economic freefall'. Some of these phenomena have been attributed to the insularity and intransigence of the ruling ZANU party under the leadership of the president, Robert Mugabe, and the ruinous results of the latter's policy of land apportionment. One of the consequences of these circumstances has been the estimated departure of nearly 3 million people between 2002 and 2008; many now live in the more prosperous neighbouring states, principally South Africa. Many have moved farther afield, to the USA, to the UK, and to Australia and New Zealand.

This essay on one of the world's rapidly receding lesser-known varieties of English must thus be taken as a historical sociolinguistic account of the emergence and fossilization of the L1 variety of a small, minority community that no longer exists as a coherent fragment.

---

[3] The World Bank data and statistics website (http://devdata.worldbank.org/external/ CPProfile) provides the figure for 2006. Population growth for 2006 was 0.8 per cent per annum, and the life expectancy was 42 years owing to the fact that AIDS is a major cause of mortality: 1.8 million people are living with AIDS and the prevalence is 18 per cent. The figures vary to a small degree depending upon the source.

[4] The Northern Ndebele language, or isiNdebele, or Sindebele, is an African language belonging to the Nguni group of Bantu languages, and spoken by the Ndebele or Matabele people of Zimbabwe. It is commonly known as Sindebele. Sindebele is related to the Zulu language spoken in South Africa. This is because the Ndebele people of Zimbabwe descend from followers of the Zulu leader Mzilikazi, who left kwaZulu in the early nineteenth century during the Mfecane. (Source: Wikipedia.)

2   Methodology

This study of RhodE relies on a range of different methods of data collection and analysis. As a RhodE native speaker who has not lived in the country since 1977, I have witnessed the dialect's fossilization in expatriates in the United Kingdom and in the USA who have served as informants for the phonological and lexical descriptions. They include colleagues and friends as well as members of my extended family (see section 6). Extensive web resources and social networking groups of all ideologies and affiliations such as Zimdays, Rhodesians Worldwide, Rhodesia.net, Mr. Zims.net and Sok-wanele/Zvakwana have informed the sociolinguistic analysis of the variety under examination. I have also drawn upon published historical and political studies as well as personal memoirs, both published and unpublished, for cross reference and validation of authenticity. Finally, I have consulted with linguist colleagues who are familiar with the dialect to ensure reliability of the descriptions based on auditory analysis.

3   Historical background

The first Europeans to explore the territory north of the gold and diamond mines of the Rand were big game hunters, prospectors and missionaries. In 1888, the king of the Ndebele, Lobengula, granted agents of Cecil John Rhodes 'exclusive rights to mine for gold, with the stipulation that they should undertake to keep off all others [Germans, Boers, Americans] and should pay him a heavy subsidy in money and rifles' (Hole 1936: 39). Rhodes used the concession as a basis to persuade the British Government to give him a charter to exploit central south African territory that other European powers had not made bids for. The region was first occupied permanently in 1890, when the British South Africa Company (BSAC) dispatched a 'pioneer column' consisting of 200 white settlers, 150 blacks, backed by 500 paramilitary police, further north to Mashonaland, the northern province of present-day Zimbabwe. In 1893, Rhodes' administrator in Mashonaland, Dr. Jameson, used Company forces and white settlers to invade Matabeleland. The result was the destruction of the Ndebele kingdom and the appropriation of Ndebele cattle and lands, the occupation by the BSAC and white settlement. In 1895, the regions between the Limpopo and Zambezi rivers – Matabeleland and Mashonaland – were united as a single territory administered by the British South Africa Company, and named Rhodesia, after the Company's chief, Cecil Rhodes.

In 1896, Jameson used British South Africa Company police in an ill-advised raid into the Transvaal in an attempt to destabilize the Kruger government, depleting the colony's military force and precipitating an uprising by the Ndebele in March 1896. The 'rapaciousness of the settlers, who looted their cattle, ravished their women, and stole their land, and who were uncontrolled by the ramshackle government Rhodes had established', and 'the outbreak of the catastrophic cattle disease rinderpest', on top of their defeat in 1893, 'goaded the Ndebele beyond endurance' (Marks and Trapido 2006). Despite settler and military opposition, Rhodes decided to negotiate a peace directly with the Ndebele. The uprising had spread to the Shona, who continued to resist in the eastern province until 1898. One of the consequences of the first *Chimurenga / Umvukela*, as the uprisings are called, was direct British government intervention which included the appointment of a British resident commissioner in Bulawayo and the establishment of a legislative council in October 1898 in an attempt to mollify the settlers. As Marks and Trapido (2006) conclude, '"Native administration" was put on a more systematic footing and stripped of its more immediately coercive aspects. The age of adventurism was over; the era of settler domination was about to begin.'

The political recovery of the Afrikaners after the South African war (1899–1902) culminated in the unification of South Africa in 1910. When the BSAC's royal charter expired in 1922, the white Rhodesians were presented with a choice of joining the Union of South Africa as a fifth province or becoming a British colony. In a referendum on 'Responsible Government', they rejected the South African option and so in 1923 Southern Rhodesia became a self-governing British colony with a locally elected white government ('Responsible Government'). Britain thus fulfilled her policy of devolving authority and economic responsibility to settlers in an effort to maintain the Empire and maximize the financial dependability of the colonies from the perspective of British interests (Schutz 1973: 4–5).

Britain combined Southern Rhodesia with Northern Rhodesia (Zambia) and Nyasaland (Malawi) in a federation of south central African states in 1953. In 1960, in the midst of decolonization and struggles for majority rule elsewhere in Africa, Britain led constitutional talks to widen black participation in southern Rhodesia's electoral franchise, and to establish majority self-rule for Nyasaland and Northern Rhodesia. In 1964, a year after the break-up of the federation, these former British protectorates became the independent countries of Malawi and Zambia. In the same year, Southern Rhodesian whites elected a pro-republican, anti-British Rhodesian Front government and voted ten-to-one in a referendum in favour of independence from Britain. In November 1965, the Rhodesian Front government under Ian Smith issued a Unilateral Declaration of Independence (UDI) from Britain rather than submit to independence with African majority rule. Mounting black nationalist agitation marked by riots, strikes and local activism was met with the detention without trial of nationalist leaders and the declaration of a permanent state of emergency.

In December 1972, civil war broke out between the Rhodesian regime and armies sponsored by rival nationalist organizations ZANU, which operated out of Mozambique, and ZAPU, which was based in Zambia. In 1978, the government entered talks to bring the war to an end through a negotiated settlement, agreeing to elections for a transitional legislature to shared governance. The Patriotic Front – a coalition of ZANU and ZAPU – boycotted the elections and continued the war; the international community refused to recognize the transitional government headed by Bishop Abel Muzorewa. In 1979, the British government brokered new negotiations which marked the country's formal independence, guaranteed minority rights in a system of universal suffrage and ended the war. Britain supervised one-person-one-vote elections in 1980 in a renamed Zimbabwe. Robert Mugabe's ZANU party established a one-party state, eliminating ZAPU opposition in Matabeleland and the Midlands in a campaign of massacre known as *Gukurahundi* carried out by the North Korean-trained Fifth Brigade as well as the intelligence services.[5] Mugabe and ZAPU leader Joshua Nkomo signed a Unity Accord in December 1987 to combine the parties as ZANU-PF.

In a referendum in 2000, voters rejected proposed constitutional changes, which included an extensive programme of land reform. A narrow victory in parliamentary elections in 2000 gave Mugabe a mandate to embark on his land reform programme which transferred the land owned by 4,000 (out of 4,500) white farmers to blacks over five years. In this period, agricultural production declined dramatically owing to prolonged drought and the lack of expertise and training of new farmers. In 2002, the UN and the IMF cut aid to the country in response to the land reform programme, and the Commonwealth excluded Zimbabwe. By 2005, 3 million people were reliant on food aid.[6] In March 2008, parliamentary and presidential elections were held. Morgan Tsvangirai, leader of the Movement for Democratic Change (MDC) opposition party, narrowly beat Robert Mugabe, triggering a run-off presidential election. Amidst widespread escalating political violence, Tsvangirai withdrew from this election, leaving Robert Mugabe to stand for the presidency unopposed. The Southern African Development Community

---

[5] Godwin (1996: 343) notes:

> the word literally means 'the first rains of the wet season', that much-awaited down-pour which washes away all the accumulated dust and debris of the preceding year. *Gukurahundi* was also the unofficial name of the army's new Fifth Brigade. It was to be the force that would purge society of all the unacceptable debris of history.

The Legal Resources Foundation (LRF) and the Catholic Commission for Justice and Peace (CCJP) published a formal report (1997): *Gukurahundi in Zimbabwe: A report on the disturbances in Matabeleland and the Midlands 1980–1989*. www.hrforumzim.com/members_reports/matrep/matrepintro.htm.

[6] In 2005, Mugabe's government carried out a campaign code-named *Murambatsvina*, a Shona word meaning 'to drive out rubbish' or 'clean out the filth'. The other code name for this blitz is *Operation Restore Order*. The 'clean out' operation involved the destruction of informal residential settlements and informal trading markets and stalls in urban, peri-urban and semi-rural areas of towns and cities all around Zimbabwe. For a full description, see *Order out of Chaos, or Chaos out of Order? A Preliminary Report on Operation 'Murambatsvina'. A report by the Zimbabwe Human Rights NGO Forum, June 2005*. www.hrforumzim.com/special_hrru/order_out_of_chaos_or_chaos_out_of_order.htm.

Table 14.1 *White population growth in Rhodesia, 1891–1969*
(adapted from Schutz 1973 and Mlambo 1998)

Year	# Europeans	% Increase	Est. total population
1891	1,500	–	
1901	11,000	633	
1911	23,606	114	
1921	33,620	42	771,077
1931	49,910	48	1,118,000
1941	68,954	38	1,453,000
1946	82,386	19	
1956	177,124	53.5	
1961	221,000	19.8	
1969	228,000	3	4,858,000

(SADC) sponsored talks between the MDC and Zanu-PF in an attempt to resolve the political crisis and end the violence. After protracted negotiations, the MDC and Zanu-PF formed a coalition government. In this Government of National Unity, Mugabe continues as president and Tsvangirai is prime minister; the parties have divided the ministries between them.

4   Sociolinguistic history: source of input dialects

The settlement history of Zimbabwe as a British colony and as a neighbour of South Africa and Mozambique is important for understanding the socio-linguistic history and current fossil status of RhodE. Having rehearsed the country's history as a chartered territory, as a British colony, as a rebel state and as a postcolonial republic, let us examine its population history.

The European population in the territory in 1904 was estimated to be 12,596, just 1.4 per cent of the total. The 1921 Census Report published the total population of Southern Rhodesia as 771,077, of whom 33,620 were Europeans. The increase in the European population was accounted for by a surge of British South African farmers and 'smallworkers' who provided the socioeconomic class foundation in Rhodesian development (Arrighi 1967). The European population changed from a temporary, highly mobile one made up principally of single men between the ages of 20 and 44 who worked as miners and military policemen in a frontier environment (64 per cent in 1911), to a relatively settled farming and trading society characterized by married couples with children (Schutz 1973: 8). A good indication of the change in the nature of the population is the increase in the number of white women in the colony; in 1904 there were 406 women per 1,000 men; by 1926, this proportion had increased to 796 per 1,000 men (Mlambo 1998).

The Rhodesians sought English-speaking skilled lower-middle-class workers – people who would not compete with Africans for labouring jobs and thus drive up the cost of unskilled labour in a situation in which whites received preferential treatment. At the same time, they did not want to attract whites of leisured classes who would neither stay nor work, such as the whites who settled in Kenya. These inclinations and attitudes resulted in a persistently low rate of British immigration throughout the colony's history (Mlambo 1998). By 1921, the European population, overwhelmingly South African-born, English-speaking and pro-British, had increased to 33,620, up more than 200 per cent from 1901. Non-British European immigrants including Greeks, Russians and Italians made up 5 per cent of the white pop-ulation and Afrikaners, whites whose first language is Afrikaans and whose religion is Dutch Reformed Church, accounted for 19 per cent.

The results of the 'Responsible Government' referendum (8,774 for status as a self-governing British colony, 5,989 for union with South Africa) provide a symbolic expression of the values held dear by this small, white, English-speaking enclave in central southern Africa. Ethel Tawse Jollie commented in 1923 on the emergence of a self-centred Rhodesian national identity:

Young as the colony is, it has a strong sense of nationality, and not merely of British but of Rhodesian identity. Probably to people [in Britain] all South Africans (Rhodesians included) are alike. We do not recognize this, and if you ask, 'Where do you come from?' the answer will be 'From Natal', 'From Rhodesia', never 'From South Africa' . . . We do not find Newfound-land accused of a ridiculous particularism [because of its refusal to join Canada] . . . We believe in Rhodesia, we believe that she enshrines some-thing worth preserving, and we cling to our heritage not merely for its own sake but because of what it may mean to South Africa and the Empire later on. (Quoted by Lowry 1997: 159)

The 1930s saw the economy diversify beyond mining and tobacco farming to include wheat and maize production. Rhodesia experienced the Great Depression as 'the Slump', which made small farmers and artisans fear 'competition as much from white [European] refugees as from Africans' (Schutz 1973: 12). These fears expressed themselves in an official government immigration policy that encouraged British immigrants; at the same time the government discouraged the potential flood of Afrikaner trekkers from the south through tactics such as discriminatory loan strictures. In addition, worries about white unemployment in an economy that could resort to cheap black labour undermined further white settler immigration.

Significant in the construction of Rhodesian identity then was an antipa-thy towards non-English-speakers, particularly Afrikaners, and Europeans like the Portuguese, who settled neighbouring Mozambique. These attitudes engendered a strong affinity for British values, goods and culture as perceived from afar. The nature of their participation in the Second World War under-scored the sense of loyalty felt by white Rhodesians; the official literature eulogized the colony's contribution to the imperial war effort and all but ignored the hardships experienced by civilians in the country. Ideal weather conditions combined with distance from the principal theatre of war made Rhodesia an excellent training ground for the Royal Air Force as well as a safe location for prisoners of war and refugees. By 1940, there was sufficient capacity for the training of 1,800 pilots, 240 observers and 340 air gunners per year. The influx of military personnel and prisoners of war increased the white population by 20 per cent (Samasuwo 2003). As the colony's economy expanded to produce food and tobacco for military consumption abroad and at home, the state ordered white farmers to stay on the land for the duration of the war and passed legislation to conscript African men as farm labourers. The consequence was a great deal of contact between settlers and their descendants and British military personnel, although the latter were sojourners only for the war's duration. The end of the war brought a fresh influx of immigrants from the UK who sought a life of white privilege in Rhodesia by escaping the rigours of postwar Britain. Schutz (1973: 16) notes:

From the RAF trainees, word spread through the services that Rhodesia was a land of peace and comfort with a glorious climate as well. There was plenty of room; easy-going competition; flexible standards; plentiful and *cheap* servants; and none of the restrictions that were plaguing post-war Europe. . . . The new immigrants drifted to the towns, particularly Salisbury, while the myths of rural Rhodesia and the Pioneers justified their migration.

Urbanization increased after the war, with Salisbury attracting non-British-born Europeans, classified by the census-takers as 'aliens' and referred to by most 'British' Rhodesians as 'foreigners', to reach about 5.6 per cent of the white population. These included Greeks, Italians, Sephardic Jews from Rhodes and Ashkenazi Jews from Eastern Europe, who continued to be relatively culturally autonomous but whose political interests chimed with those of the Rhodesians. By 1956, the settler population had swollen to 177,000, and by 1969, the European population had grown to about 228,000 as against a total population of about 4,858,000; a ratio of about twenty Africans to one European (Schutz 1973: 20).

Britain responded to Rhodesia's UDI in 1965 by imposing economic and political sanctions. These included denying the rebel regime access to capital markets, terminating export credit guarantees, banning the import of tobacco and sugar, and then imposing an embargo on oil supplies. The United Nations Security Council followed with two resolutions specifying further restrictions to be placed on Rhodesia by its member states, creating increased isolation from the international community. These included the withdrawal of recognition of Rhodesian passport holders and the restriction on air travel by Rhodesians (McKinnell 1969: 561). Rhodesians thus relied increasingly on their neighbours, South Africa to the south and the Portuguese administration of Mozambique to the east, for passage to African coasts. Emigration of British-born Rhodesians to the UK increased during this period, while Rhodesian-born English-speaking and Afrikaans-speaking whites remained in a white enclave.

Between 1966 and 1972, Rhodesia became increasingly isolated, foreshadowing the fate of independent Zimbabwe after 2000. Smith's emergency legislation served the Rhodesia Front and later ZANU-PF equally in quashing opposition and objections to rigid methods of holding power. The advance of African political consciousness in the form of nationalism, the withdrawal of British power from elsewhere on the African continent and the emergence of a powerful Afrikaner state just to the south confronted Rhodesian whites with the spectre of dissolution.

Formal political and economic isolation led to the consolidation of the variety of English spoken by Rhodesian whites as an ethnic dialect. Its speakers experienced rapidly reduced exposure to contemporary British and other L1 varieties of English. The escalation of guerilla war led to the polarization and increased segregation of whites and blacks, and the development of parallel rather than hitherto intersecting cultural and linguistic practices. The regime adopted a range of measures to prevent the guerillas (*abafana* 'the boys' vs. *terrs* 'terrorists') from recruiting rural Africans or using their villages (*kraals*) as contact points for ambushes on the security forces. They set up so-called 'protected villages' which created rural concentration camps for women, children and old people, and created a growing, highly politicized urban black population as a result of flight from the countryside.

From 1974, compulsory national conscription for all white male school-leavers was instituted, which stretched into a two-year stint in 1976. Consequently, young English-speaking whites with educational opportunities, financial means and external contacts left the country for Britain or the US if possible, or South Africa if not. The steady stream of leavers marked the shrinking of the white population to those who supported the war or who were unable to leave, and generated a vocabulary for describing the exodus – *taking the gap, gapping it, joining the chicken run*. At the same time, those whites who remained were occupied by the war. Men who had completed their 'call-ups' remained liable for police reserve duty and were frequently away from home serving in various paramilitary capacities. Although women were not conscripted, they were able to serve in the police force and in this capacity were directly engaged in the civil war. Official estimates of war-related deaths in Rhodesia between December 1972 and December 1979 give the figure of 20,000-plus: 468 white civilians, 1,311 members of the security forces (about half of them white), 10,450 guerillas, and 7,790 black civilians.

Although the permanent white population did not increase appreciably after 1961, the security forces attracted professional soldiers and mercenaries of all nationalities. This temporary swell echoed the influx of RAF personnel to the country for training during the Second World War. However, this later group tended to join the country's security forces: the completely white Rhodesian Light Infantry, the mounted Selous Scouts commando unit, and the Rhodesian Special Air Services (SAS). They brought experienced soldiers as well as adventurers from Australia, the USA, South Africa and the UK.

5 Rhodesian English: Current status

The variety is a fossilized dialect in that it does not characterize the speech of a settled or permanent speech community. However, it might be regarded as a coherent or intact variety as it constitutes the vernacular of a speech community that can be identified with a specific historical period, namely, 1901 through to the date of independence, 1980. This period marks the beginning of the steady exodus of white, L1 English-speaking Zimbabwean/Rhodesians for other English-speaking communities. In the first year after independence alone, 40,000 Rhodesians (or 'ex-Rhodesians') emigrated to South Africa (Simon 1988: 53).

Whites who have remained in Zimbabwe after independence experience considerable contact with blacks on a daily basis in all settings, from the school playground to the workplace, from the sports field to the store. From 1978, institutional segregation based on race diminished rapidly and dramatically, creating social conditions for dialect-mixing and code-switching. Makoni et al. (2007) provide an extensive analysis of the urban linguistic behaviour of Africans who negotiate their everyday lives in as many as three languages, including a Bantu vernacular variety of chiShona or Sindebele; English; and an urban patois, such as chiChewa.

We distinguish between the Rhodesian English spoken by whites born before 1980 and those who no longer live in Zimbabwe, and the variety spoken by Zimbabwean whites, born after 1980, who have remained in the country. Their dialect is inflected through contact with African English speakers whose phonology is marked by Bantu vowels and prosody. In contrast, RhodE is a recessive minority dialect. In Zimbabwe there are fewer than 25,000 RhodE speakers and they are mainly elderly. However, RhodE is the vernacular of about 60,000 self-identified ex-Rhodesians or Zimbabwean whites who emigrated from Rhodesia between 1965 and 2000. These people resettled in South Africa, the US, Britain, Australia and New Zealand.

6 Case history

The case history of an extended white family in Rhodesia illustrates various sociolinguistic influences on the fossil dialect described below.

Frederick West was born into a farming family in the small coastal north Norfolk town of Sheringham in 1906. He joined the Royal Navy and saw action in the First World War. Finding few opportunities after the war, he responded to the recruitment drive for the British South Africa Company police force, and sailed for Durban, with his destination Bulawayo, in 1920.

He was the first member of his family to leave Norfolk to settle elsewhere. He was posted almost immediately to a rural police station, a British South African Police Camp on the banks of the Limpopo River. The closest social centre was Messina, a border mining settlement on the Transvaal side, where Fred met Margaret Rutherford, the daughter of a Canadian copper miner, a veteran of the South African War of 1899–1902, and an Afrikaner woman. Margaret spoke English as her first language. Fred and Margaret married and set up home at Limpopo Drift. In Margaret's words, he was 'Immigration, Customs and Pass Officer and sometimes acting Cattle Inspector. Also he was responsible for the policing of about 5,000 square miles' (West 1957: 1). Their son John was born in the nearest town of Bulawayo in 1928 and their daughter Anita was born eighteen months later. Frederick West spent thirty years in the district police force, and was stationed at a number of rural posts, and then provincial towns. Anita had married into a prominent Rhodesian livestock and land auctioneering family; her husband's British South African father and Scottish nurse mother had met in Rhodesia. John West attended REPS (Rhodes Estate Preparatory School) and Plumtree in Matabeleland, boarding schools modelled on nineteenth-century English public schools, and which recruited British-educated teachers and housemasters in the first half of the century.[7] John is a speaker of a conservative, prestige variety of Rhodesian English, which is influenced by southern standard British English, with mostly RP accents, spoken by the British staff. He also learned isiNdebele at Plumtree and, like many of his fellow graduates, joined the Native Affairs Department after school. He was assigned to the rural outpost Tjolotjo but soon left the civil service to seek his fortune in tobacco as an assistant on a farm in Umvukwes until his father told him to join the police or the army. In 1952, John joined the Rhodesian African Rifles, a regiment with white officers and African troops. In 1959, he married Bridget Fitzwilliam, a school teacher who was born in Salisbury in 1935. Bridget's parents were George (b. 1909), an upper-middle-class London bank clerk who was recruited into the BSAP in London and came out to Southern Rhodesia in 1928, and Mary Osborne, the South African-born daughter of Scottish settler farmers from the Orange Free State district of Koffiefontein. Mary and her sister Norah came to Rhodesia for teacher training in Bulawayo. Mary met George during her first year of teaching at Rusape. Married in 1934, George and Mary had two other daughters and a son. George Fitzwilliam rose through the ranks to become senior assistant commissioner before retiring to Natal in 1963. Bridget's dialect is a prestige variety of Rhodesian English; her accent is very

---

[7] REPS and Plumtree were based on the English public school system. Robert Hammond, the Peterhouse, Cambridge-educated headmaster of Plumtree from 1906 to 1936, shaped the school's emphasis on religious and moral principles, gentlemanly conduct, intellectual pursuits and the house and dormitory system (http://oldprunitian.rhodesiana.com/op11-004.html#top).

close to the RP encountered in British films of the 1940s, except for the centralized close vowel in *bit*, which identifies her as Rhodesian.

This case history illustrates the sources of the input dialects to Rhodesian English. Bridget Fitzwilliam was not exposed to anything other than a variety of southern British English before 1946, when she encountered working-class London (Cockney), and non-standard northern English dialects spoken by child migrants whose passage to and educations in Rhodesia were sponsored by the Fairbridge Memorial Scholarship scheme.[8] The immigrants to Rhodesia after the war were different in demographic and socioeconomic background from those who settled before 1940: predominantly working-class families from cities like London, Manchester and Birmingham, they settled in newly built government-sponsored economic housing developments in Salisbury, contributing to the capital's expansion. Many of these immigrants did not stay; according to R. S. Roberts (1979: 61), 'for every hundred migrants arriving, between sixty and eighty were always leaving.'

Thus far, we have exemplars of the population history elaborated in the section above. British-born men settled the colony in the first quarter of the century, marrying British South African women who came to the colony as brides (in the case of Margaret Rutherford) or as school teachers (in the case of Mary Osborne). Their children were born in Rhodesia and married other Rhodesians of British backgrounds or indeed British-born men who were recruited for the civil service or the forces in England.

The first-generation Rhodesians of this family exemplify an early conservative RhodE dialect that they perceive has more affinity with southern standard British English than South African (more explicitly Afrikaner) English. In fact, the British English to which they were exposed was tied to a particular historical and social milieu; their respective fathers' accents and their teachers' accents were fixed as early-twentieth-century sociolects. Their mothers, speakers of South African English acquired in rural settings, were censorious of Akrikaners and Afrikaner L2 English as socially inferior, and these prejudices were instilled in their children. Accordingly, families like these aspired to speak an English that could be identified discernibly with the Rhodesians' notion of what a prestigious English accent was.

The second generation, now in their forties, and all living abroad, are speakers of the spectrum of RhodE. It could be argued that from the moment RhodE speakers began to leave their birthplace permanently to live in other English-speaking communities, the variety ceased to be productive. Children born in Zimbabwe who emigrated at an early age rapidly replace their

---

[8] The first eighteen boys sailed from Southampton on 18 November 1946, on the *Carnarvon Castle*, and disembarked at Cape Town, South Africa, on 4 December 1946 on their way to start new lives at Rhodesia Fairbridge Memorial College in Bulawayo. The council manifesto introduced the scheme in the following terms: 'It is the object of this Scheme to select children from Great Britain, who wish to emigrate, to enable them to receive a sound education in the sunshine of Southern Rhodesia in order to become permanent settlers there.' (www.fairbridge-worldwide.com/)

vernacular with the one that is dominant in the new domicile. In our case study, John West's grandchildren (aged 8 and 10), who settled in Britain with their parents in 2000, had acquired the prosodic characteristics of the dialect dominant in their new home within six months, and the most salient vowels within eight months. In contrast, their second- and third-generation Rhodesian-born parents, John junior, aged 37, and Janet, aged 35 at the time, still have intact Rhodesian accents (ten years later).

7 Features of the variety

7.1 Phonology: General remarks

The main characteristics of RhodE phonology are shared with SAE (cf. Lass 2004) as a southern-hemisphere extraterritorial English of similar age and genealogy. However, RhodE exhibits only indirect influence of Afrikaner English, specifically in the pronunciation of consonants. Like SAE, RhodE exhibits variation that is socially salient. Specifically, more advanced varieties of RhodE share features with Lass' Type 3 ('Extreme') SAE (2004: 384). In contrast, more prestigious conservative RhodE varieties exhibit resistance to the influence of local features (see details below).

7.2 Vowels

7.2.1 Short vowels
The short vowels in the KIT, DRESS, TRAP word classes participated in a raising-and-centralizing shift (Lass and Wright 1985, 1986; Lass 2004) so that the DRESS and TRAP vowels are considerably higher than in other varieties.

KIT [ï] (diacritic indicating centralization approaching /ə/)

This vowel distinguishes RhodE as a southern hemisphere extraterritorial variety of English, along with New Zealand English and South African English. It is definitive of the dialect and is socially unmarked.

DRESS [e]

Raised front vowel, participant in the chain shift. Wells (1982: 128) comments on the presence of closer variants of the vowel in old-fashioned RP and Cockney; it is possible that the stability of the raised front vowel in all generations of RhodE is a legacy of the colonial inputs together with their reinforcement through isolation and lack of later exposure to the reflexes of older prestige varieties. This feature is a traditional shibboleth for Rhodesians. Bridget West reports being corrected as a child and told to say 'yes not yis'.

TRAP [ε – ɛ̝] (raised front vowel)

This word class participates in the raising-and-centralizing chain shift discussed above. However, Gordon et al. (2004: 102ff.) discuss the evidence for the vowel's raised variants in the British input dialects for NZE, as evidenced by Ellis (1889), Wright (1905), and Gimson (1962). In RhodE, the reflexes of a conservative RP clash with the stigmatized raised variants associated with SAE, resulting in a fairly stable realization as /ε/. However, hypercorrection to avoid identification with SAE results in a markedly lowered /æ̝/ (rare).

LOT [ɒ – ɑ]

Weakly rounded and not fully open, sometimes advanced and occasionally slightly lengthened, in words like *god* which rhymes with *guard*. There is also a variant that is much closer and rounded, influenced very likely by Afrikaans: [gɔd]. This pronunciation is socially stigmatized as extreme; it is thus avoided in most varieties of RhodE.

FOOT [ʊ]

A fully rounded short, half-close back vowel. There is some variation in its realization; younger speakers may exhibit less rounding and more fronting, as in [ʉ].

STRUT [ɐ̝]

Typically a raised mid vowel with no lip-rounding, occasionally further fronted to approach [ä].

7.2.2   Long monophthongs

FLEECE [i̝].

No gliding or diphthongization. The vowel is very close and fronted; if anything, in some varieties, the vowel is shortened and tensed.

GOOSE [ʉ:]

Close, fronted vowel with very open rounding or lip-contraction, associated specifically with younger white speakers. Coloured speakers who may code-switch English, Afrikaans and Shona ('goffal') have a fully rounded back realization.

SQUARE [e:]

This vowel is close, long and glideless. Hypercorrection produces a monophthong that is opener and retracted: /a:/; this quality is also a feature of conservative varieties.

NURSE [ö:]

The most common realization of this vowel is as a rounded tense vowel. Hypercorrect and conservative versions are unrounded /ɜ:/ but these are associated with older speakers.

THOUGHT [o:]

This vowel is raised in comparison with most other varieties of English. A shorter realization is found in words that would be expected to be part of the LOT/CLOTH class, such as *off* [of]. The latter realization is lexicalized for many speakers.

BATH [ɑ: – ɒ:]

This vowel has variable rounding with typical realizations back and more rounded. The more back and more rounded the variant, the more stigmatized it is. Conservative RhodE speakers produce less rounded but lower variants.

7.2.3 Diphthongs

MOUTH [aʊ – a: – eɐ̯]

There is considerable variation in the pronunciation of this vowel, all socially and partly ethnically marked. This glide has an onset that is half-open and front. The second element is the locus of most variation; the more back, close quality is associated with prestige speakers; the monophthong and more open qualities are stigmatized variants.

PRICE [aɪ – a:]

A monophthongized glide is typical of speakers under 30 years of age, and is associated with upwardly mobile women in Harare.

FACE [ai]

Lowered onset with upward front glide is typical. There is considerable variation in the realization of the onset: the higher the vowel, the higher the speaker's social status.

GOAT [ɜʉ – ɐ]

The first element is quite central with a glide front. Some realizations have the slightest glide only and are unrounded.

CHOICE [oi]

The first element is typically close and always rounded in quality.

NEAR [iɐ]

For some speakers, the first element is markedly palatal with a distinct glide. A widespread variation is monophthongization of the glide without any palatal first element: [eː].

CURE [iø – iɔ]

The second element varies from a front rounded quality to a backed quality.

7.3 Consonants

In general, the consonant set is not markedly different from other extraterritorial Englishes. Some local realizations may be shared with South African English (Lass 2004), and some are identified as non-standard characteristics of other varieties (Hickey 2004: Appendix 1).

Realization of /r/

There are a number of different realizations of /r/, many of them socially marked. The oldest speakers exhibit an intervocalic alveolar tap in words like *very* [ˈverɪ], identified as markedly posh colonial, but an alveolar approximant in all other positions. Lower-middle-class speakers with Afrikaner connections tend to show a tap in most positions, including prevocalic positions, as in *three* [θri], *precisely* [pri'saːsli]. The majority of speakers have an alveolar approximant in all places [ɹ]. There is no rhoticity in L1 RhodE.

Word-initial /h/

Word-initial /h/ has different variants depending on the following vowel. Before a palatal glide and close vowel, /h/ is pronounced as a voiceless alveolar fricative. Accordingly, *here* occurs as a palatal fricative and glide plus high front vowel /i/ thus: [çjiə]; while *hue* is realized as a palatal fricative followed by a palatal glide and close fronted rounded vowel [çjʉ]. When followed phonologically by a non-close vowel, /h/ may not be pronounced at all. For example, *hell* may be realized as [>eɫ] with no glottal onset, as in [əˈeləvəˈsɐːt] 'a hell of a sight'.

Tapping of voiceless alveolar stops

A characteristic feature of connected speech is the tapping of word-final and intervocalic voiceless alveolar stops. The stop /t/ in *better*, *out of* is realized as a tap: [ˈberɐ] [ˈaːrɐ].

Alveolarization of velar nasals

The realization of this feature in *-ing* endings is a compensatory lengthening and raising of the final vowel as in the following phrase: *rioting stoning burning*

/'ra:ti:n 'stɐːniːn 'böːniːn/. This feature is prevalent in strong Rhodesian accents.[9]

Distinction between <W> and <WH>

The most conservative speakers of all (exemplified by professional women over 65) have minimal pairs such as *where : wear; what : watt*. For these speakers, the contrast symbolizes a socially marked feature. However, the vast majority of speakers do not show the contrast.

7.3.1   *Phonotactic features*

Absence of linking /r/

As in South African English, linking /r/ is quite rare. Instead, speakers exhibit the use of glottal stops in vowel-initial words. Quite frequently, /r/ is substituted by a glottal stop. An extreme example occurs word-internally, as in *wherever* [we'ʔevɐ], *moreover* [mo'ʔəʊvə]. More typical examples include the common string, *for example* [fo ʔeg'zɑmpɫ]. One of the consequences is the lack of vowel reduction in connected speech, so that the vowel in *for* above is unchanged from a half-close rounded back vowel. 'Intrusive' /r/ does not occur as the use of the glottal stop is so well established. In such cases, word-citation vowel quality persists in connected speech, as for example, in the sequence *the answer is* [ðə 'ʔansə 'ʔz] (instead of BrE [ðijɑnsəɹɪz]). Elocution lessons and drama training in Rhodesia included exercises designed to train the speaker to 'soften' word-initial glottal stops to avoid hiatus. Interestingly, these exercises also involved teaching the avoidance of linking /r/ as a solution to hiatus.

Non-reduction of vowels

In many non-conservative RhodE varieties, there is little or no vowel reduction of the close front vowel in the initial unstressed syllable in words such as *remove* [ɹiˈmʉːv], *precise* [pɹiˈsɐːs], *enough* [iˈnɐf], *concern* [kɒnˈsøn] in connected speech.

7.4   *Voice quality*

Commentators characterize the sound of RhodE, particularly in the mouths of women, as whining. Simon Hoggart, writing for the *Guardian* on the eve of Zimbabwe's independence in 1980, comments:

Rhodesian women, black and white, tend to be remarkably good looking. The Shona women have high cheekbones and fine features which make

---

[9] This feature is associated with the accent of UDI prime minister Ian Smith, and is a stereotypical feature used to characterize 'Rhodies'.

them exceedingly pretty, to European eyes at any rate. The whites have golden hair, lovely toast-coloured skin, and because of the weather, few clothes. There is something particularly disconcerting about hearing those famous racist views expressed in that shrill mounting whine, coming from someone whose rounded figure is straining out of a thin nylon dress. (Hoggart 1980)

Hoggart is referring to a nasal voice quality that was associated particularly with women speakers. For women under 30, the nasality accompanies a rising pitch in tone-unit final position and is marked in open final syllables, so words such as *better* may be rendered as [berẽ], with a tapped /t/ followed by an open nasalized unstressed vowel in place of schwa. Secondary nasality contributes to Hoggart's 'whine', while initial glottalization yields an impression of a clipped, staccato enunciation associated with men.

7.5   Morphosyntax

The morphosyntax of this variety is unremarkable. It shares some features with SAE, including the temporal adverbials *just now* and (less commonly) *now now* (Wright 1987), and the aspectual *busy* V-*ing* (Lass and Wright 1986), as in 'She's busy waiting for a call'.

7.6   Lexicon

As with a number of colonial varieties of L1 English, the core lexicon of RhodE is British English. The principal influences on RhodE lexis are Afrikaans and Bantu (mainly chiShona and isiNdebele). The more informal the situation, the more likely it is to encounter local expressions; at the same time, the more local and the lower the speaker's socioeconomic status, the more likely it is for the variety to be strongly inflected with Afrikaans and Bantu lexis. The domains marked by these influences include those that appear in any colonial setting in which the indigenous languages are quite different from the settler language, namely flora, fauna and topography.[10] Some domains result from conditions peculiar to the Rhodesian situation, on the one hand, typical settler activities (farming, mining), and on the other, the bush war (1972–1980).

7.6.1   Flora, fauna and topography

Afrikaans borrowings: *kopje* ['kɒpi] 'rocky outcrop, hill'; *veld* ['fɛɫt] 'savanna grassland'; *vlei* ['flɛi] 'marshland'; *spruit* ['sprɛit] 'stream'.

---

[10] Edgar Schneider (2007) discusses this phenomenon in postcolonial varieties of English extensively.

IsiNdebele and chiShona borrowings: *gomo* < Shona *ngomo* 'hill, mountain'; *gwasha* 'thick vegetation in a canyon'; *donga* 'ravine or riverbed in a depression' (<Nguni) attested in the OED; *chongololo* < *tsongololo* (IsiNdebele) 'millipede'; *mopani/mopane* worm: the large edible caterpillar of the Empire moth (*Gonimbrasia belina*), named for the tree that it is found in, the mopane tree (*Colophospermum mopane*).

7.6.2   Farming and mining

Terms for implements: *badza* 'hoe'; *simbi* 'metal', specialized as metal disc beaten as a cymbal, also a bicycle. *Kraal* < Afrikaans, adapted from Portuguese *curral*, in farming refers to a cattle pen (cf. OED), but its earliest Rhodesian use was to refer to the collection of huts that formed the village of a tribal headman or chief. Selous uses the term in both senses in his memoir of life in Matabeleland:

[*Cattle pen*:] we found that owing to the scarcity of grass for cattle near the chief town, Lo Bengula had trekked away and built a temporary *kraal* near Amachi Mashlopay. (Selous 1893: 290)

[*Village*:] About this time the Amandebele, under their warlike chief, Umziligazi, being unable to hold their own against the Dutch Boers, who were then commencing to settle in the Transvaal, crossed the Limpopo, and traveling northwards, destroying as they went, finally halted, and built permanent kraals in the country now known as Matabeleland. (Selous 1893: 318–19)

Dagga [dɑːɡə]: mud, clay combined with cow-dung and occasionally blood to make a mortar used in the construction of houses. Early houses were made of 'pole and dagga'. Cf. OED.

7.6.3   General lifestyle

Afrikaans borrowings: *lekker* 'nice, good, pleasant'; *lightie* < *laaitie* 'small child, kid'; *footsack* < *voetsek* 'go away'; *mal* (edj.) [mʌɫ] 'crazy'; *skinner* (v. n.) 'gossip'; *braai* < *braaivleis* 'barbecue'; *boerewors* 'rough, farmer sausage'; *naartjie* [nɑːtʃiː] 'mandarin orange'; *vellies/fellies/veldskoens* < *veldskoene* 'suede shoes covering ankles'; *stoep* 'verandah'; *mealies* < *mielies* 'maize', also *mealiemeal* 'maizemeal, polenta'.

Bantu borrowings: *gortcha* [ɡɔtʃɐ] 'barbeque/braai (v.)' < Shona; *mbanje* 'cannabis' (Shona); *moosh* [mʊʃ(i)] 'nice, good, pleasant'(< Shona); *fundi* < *mfundisa* 'teacher' (Shona) 'expert'; *amaxlatula* (< Ndebele) 'sandals made of tyre rubber'; *patapata* ' flip flops'; *chia* 'play, go and do' (e.g. *chia golf*); *a mangwana* 'until tomorrow'; *kaya* 'African dwelling'; *lapa* 'there': *lapa side* 'over there'; *nganga* (Shona) 'traditional healer, witch doctor'; *muti* 'medicine'; *tokalosh* 'mischievous spirit'; *kutundu* 'baggage, luggage, kit'; *umzingwari* 'over the top'.

RhodE (and ZimE) is characterized by local innovations and lexical items not easily traced to a specific influence, e.g. *stay in a place* = 'live' ('where do you stay?' 'In Bulawayo.'; transliteration of Afrikaans); *takkies* = 'sneakers, trainers'; *robots* = traffic lights; *scoff* = eat (v.), *scoff up* = finish (food), *scoff* (n.) = food, *scoff box*; *cooldrink* = soda/pop as well as fruit squash. Brandnames are commonly recruited to denote the object they label, e.g. mazoe < Mazoe orange crush = orange squash; colgate < Colgate toothpaste = toothpaste; neos/neomagics < Neomagic felt-tip colour pens = coloured felt-tip pens; lifeboy < Lifebuoy bar soap = carbolic bar soap; palmolive < Palmolive cosmetic soap = tablet toilet soap; fray bentos < Fray Bentos beef extract = beef extract spread.

7.6.4 People

Language in Rhodesia is oriented around race, both as a category and as a means of evaluation. Given its history as a rebel colony that resisted political developments to try to remain a 'white man's country' at the expense of morality, peace and African advancement, it should not be surprising that much of the vocabulary specific to RhodE reflects the central place of race and racial conflict in people's lives. The vocabulary for racial slurs is regrettably both large and explicit in nature. An enduring, typical term used by whites to refer to Africans is the diminutive *Af* < *African*. A term derived from Shona for similar reference is *munt(s)* (< *umuntu* 'people'), but unlike the preceding term, is a clear racial slur as it is never used for any purpose other than denigration. The most extreme racial slur is traditionally associated with Afrikaner use, namely, *kaffir*, but in fact was widely used among English-speaking Rhodesians.

The bush war (1972–1980) generated parallel discourses oriented to opposing ideologies and political persuasions (see above). Local, widespread jargon emerging during the civil war to refer specifically to the war situation but now generalized includes: *hot up* 'escalate'; *take the gap, gap it* 'leave Rhodesia ≫ leave any place'. Many terms leaked into general use during the war: *mujiba* 'young insurgent supporter'; *hondo* 'war' (Shona); *povo* 'proletariat, poor people' < Portuguese, now commonly Shona 'poor people'; *chimurenga* 'war'; *stonks* 'mortar attacks'; *eggs* 'landmines'. These terms occur in the following context:

Seated beneath a portrait of Churchill, Gresham opened a bottle of Rhodesian red and complained that life now was just 'hassles', what with the terrorist 'stonks', 'eggs' and the 'freddies' making trouble over the border. (Caute 1983: 79)

So-called 'troopie' talk marked the trooper (private) ranks of the Rhodesian Light Infantry (RLI) and similar forces. Soldiers were recruited from uneducated, lower socioeconomic strata of Rhodesian white and mixed-race communities. The principal linguistic source is Afrikaans; this vocabulary includes items imported from other wars and adapted for use in Rhodesia.

> *tune me in the ages, dad, I'm ticker shy.* ('I don't have a watch')
> *gook* 'enemy' (This term is a common racial slur in American English, used in the Korean and Vietnam wars.)
> *Charlie Tango* ('ct') 'Communist Terrorist'
> *doppie* 'spent cartridge'
> *dumpie* 'small bottled beer'
> *Ek sê* (< Afrikaans) 'I say'
> *Freds/freddies* 'frelimo troops'
> *mukka* [mɐkɐ] = 'friend' (unknown source)

The principal inputs of the RhodE lexicon are British English, chiShona, isiNdebele, Afrikaans, and finally, a jargon that served as a lingua franca, mainly in the exchange between whites and Africans in domestic settings, variously called Fanagalo, kitchen kaffir, chiLapalapa.

8   Conclusion

As an LKVE, the variety treated in this essay has no future. As the dialect of a community that has largely dispersed throughout the English-speaking world and whose offspring will speak the dialect prevalent in their place of settlement, it has ceased to be productive. However, it is important to reiterate that the non-native-speaker dialect of English prevalent in Zimbabwe continues to change because it is the principal official language and medium of instruction. RhodE is rapidly diminishing as an L1 variety as the L1 English-speaking population continues to shrink.

References

Arrighi, Giovanni. 1967. *The Political Economy of Rhodesia*. The Hague: Mouton.
Caute, David. 1983. *Under the Skin: The Death of White Rhodesia*. London: Allen Lane.
Ellis, Alexander J. 1889. *On Early English Pronunciation*, Vol. v. London: Trübner and Co.
Gimson, Alan C. 1962. *An Introduction to the Pronunciation of English*. London: Arnold.
Godwin, Peter. 1996. *Mukiwa: A White Boy in Africa*. New York: The Atlantic Monthly Press.
Gordon, Elizabeth, Lyle Campbell, Jennifer Hay, Margaret Maclagan, Andrea Sudbury and Peter Trudgill. 2004. *New Zealand English: Its Origins and Evolution*. Cambridge: Cambridge University Press.

Hickey, Raymond. 2004, ed. *Legacies of Colonial English: Studies in Transported Dialects*. Cambridge: Cambridge University Press.

Hole, H. Marshall. 1936. 'Pioneer days in Southern Rhodesia.' *Journal of the Royal African Society* 35(138): 37–47.

Hoggart, Simon. 1980. 'Ironing the lawn in Salisbury, Rhodesia'. *Guardian*, Saturday 9 February 1980. *Guardian Unlimited*: www.guardian.co.uk.

Lass, Roger. 2004. 'South African English.' In R. Hickey, ed. *Legacies of Colonial English: Studies in Transported Dialects*. Cambridge: Cambridge University Press, 363–86.

Lass, Roger and Susan Wright. 1985. 'The South African chain shift: order out of chaos?' In Roger Eaton, Olga Fischer, Willem Koopman and Frederike van der Leek, eds. *Papers from the 4th International Conference on English Historical Linguistics*. Current Issues in Linguistic Theory 41. Amsterdam: John Benjamins, 137–62.

1986. 'Contact vs. Endogeny: "Afrikaans influence" on South African English.' *English Worldwide* 7(2): 201–23.

Lowry, Donal 1997. ' "White Woman's country": Ethel Tawse Jollie and the making of white Rhodesia.' *Journal of Southern African Studies* 23(2) (Special Issue for Terry Ranger): 259–81.

Makoni, Sinfree, Janine Brutt-Griffler and Pedzisai Mashiri. 2007. 'The use of "indigenous" urban vernaculars in Zimbabwe.' *Language in Society* 36: 25–49.

Marks, Shula and Stanley Trapido. 2006. 'Rhodes, Cecil John (1853–1902).' *Oxford Dictionary of National Biography*, Oxford University Press, September 2004; online edn, May 2006 (www.oxforddnb.com/view/article/35731, accessed 23 April 2008).

McKinnell, Robert. 1969. 'Sanctions and the Rhodesian Economy.' *Journal of Modern African Studies* 9/1: 559–81.

Mlambo, Alois S. 1998. 'Building a white man's country: Aspects of white immigration into Rhodesia until World War II.' *Zambezia* 25/2: 123–46.

Roberts, R. S. 1979. 'The Settlers.' *Rhodesiana* 29: 55–61.

Samasuwo, Nhamo. 2003. 'Food production and war supplies: Rhodesia's beef industry during the Second World War 1939–1945.' *Journal of Southern African Studies* 29/2: 487–502.

Schneider, Edgar. 2007. *Postcolonial English: Varieties around the World*. Cambridge: Cambridge University Press.

Schutz, Barry M. 1973. 'European population patterns, cultural persistence, and political change in Rhodesia.' *Canadian Journal of African Studies/Revue Canadienne des Etudes Africaines* 7/1: 3–25.

Selous, F. C. 1893. 'Twenty years in Zambezia.' *The Geographical Journal* 1/4: 289–322.

Simon, Alan. 1988. 'Rhodesian immigrants in South Africa: Government, media and a lesson for South Africa.' *African Affairs* 87(346): 53–68.

Tawse Jollie, Ethel. 1923. 'Britain's new colony.' *United Empire* 14: 41.

Tawse Jollie, Ethel. 1927. 'Southern Rhodesia: A white man's country in the Tropics.' *Geographical Review* 17/1: 89–106.

Webster, Wendy 2001. ' "There'll always be an England": Representations of colonial wars and immigration, 1948–1968.' *Journal of British Studies* 40/4 ('At Home in the Empire'): 557–84.

Wells, John C. 1982. *Accents of English*. Cambridge: Cambridge University Press.

West, Margaret. 1957. 'Reminiscences of a policeman's wife.' Unpublished manuscript.

Wright, Joseph. 1905. *The English Dialect Grammar*. Oxford: Oxford University Press.

Wright, Susan. 1987. '"*now now* not *just now*": the interpretation of temporal deictic expressions in South African English.' *African Studies* 46/2: 163–78.

15 White Kenyan English

THOMAS HOFFMANN

1 Introduction

> White African English [. . .] is relatively insignificant in East Africa today.
>
> (Schmied 2004: 919)

Schmied's claim that the English spoken by the white population in East Africa is insignificant is at least correct in that up to now no linguistic studies on that variety have been carried out. Considering that over forty years after independence the number of white speakers of English in Kenya is estimated to range between 30,000 and 40,000, however, this is somewhat surprising. After South Africa, Kenya thus has one of the largest white communities on the African continent whose mother tongue is English. Due to this it seems high time for this variety to receive some linguistic attention.

This paper is a first attempt at a linguistic description of the variety of English spoken by the whites in Kenya, which will be referred to as White Kenyan English (WhKE). In the following I will first give an introduction to the sociolinguistic history and current status of the variety. Since WhKE is clearly a postcolonial English, I will frame my analysis in terms of Schneider's (2007) dynamic model, which has explicitly been designed for such varieties and has already been applied to Black Kenyan English (BlKE; Schneider 2007: 189–97). In addition to this, I will explore the role of dialect contact

There are several people without whom this article would never have been written. First I would like to thank Edgar W. Schneider for his continuing support and trust. It was he who pointed out to me that WhKE was a lesser-known variety and that it might be worth a try to collect data on it during my fieldwork in Kenya. I am also deeply indebted to Alfred Buregeya from the University of Nairobi for his friendship and assistance during my time in Kenya. Next I very much have to thank Mary-Ann and David Nicholas for their hospitality and for introducing me to the Gilgil community. Furthermore my thanks go to the headmaster and pupils of Pembroke House school in Giligil for allowing me to collect data. I am also extremely grateful to Oliver Keeble, Philip Coulson and the other Pembrokeans for letting me attend their meeting at the Muthaiga club, Nairobi, and for providing me with adult informants. Last but not least I would like to express my gratitude to Tim Hutchinson for inviting me to his home for a nice cup of tea and a chat and always being willing to reply to my many emails. Finally I would like to acknowledge that the fieldwork in Kenya for this study was partly financed by the German Academic Exchange Programme DAAD (PhD fieldwork grant D/06/42348/).

in the emergence of WhKE by drawing on Trudgill's (2004) model of new-dialect formation. Finally I will present an acoustic phonetic analysis of the vowel system of WhKE. The data for this analysis consists of four adults and eighteen children reading an extended version of the IPA's *The North Wind and the Sun* passage and was collected during a field trip to Kenya in September 2006. Due to the limited nature of the data set, base, the analysis will focus on the variety's monophthong set. This, of course, can only be considered a first pilot study on WhKE, but like all other contributions in this volume it is hoped that it will at least help to elevate the status of the variety from a lesser- to a slightly-better-known one.

2   Sociolinguistic history and current status of the variety

The dynamic model describes the evolution of postcolonial Englishes by five phases (foundation, exonormative stabilization, nativization, endonormative stabilization and differentiation), each of which is characterized by a particular combination of several extralinguistic and (socio-)linguistic parameters. A major assumption of the model is that all stages and parameters can best be explained by investigating the developments in the colonizer/settler (STL) strand and the colonized/indigenous (IDG) population strand, with both strands 'getting more closely intertwined and their linguistic correlates, in an ongoing process of mutual linguistic accommodation, approximating each other in the course of time' (Schneider 2007: 33). In his discussion of Kenya Schneider (2007: 189–97) suggests that the variety of English there has already passed through the stages of foundation (1860s–1920) and exonormative stabilization (1920-late 1940) and since the late 1940s is undergoing nativization, a phase which is characterized by e.g. phonological innovations. It is important to point out, however, that the claim concerning nativization is only made for the IDG strand, i.e. BlKE, since up to now there had been no data available for the WhKE STL strand.

While the dynamic model mainly focuses on the interaction of white settlers and indigenous people, Trudgill (2004) emphasizes that in many cases it was not a single variety of a language that the original white settlers brought to their new homes. Instead, people from different accent and dialect backgrounds had to interact and accommodate to each other in the colonial settlements, which ultimately lead to 'dialect contact, dialect mixture and new-dialect formation' (Trudgill 2004: 13). Another important question is therefore in how far features of present-day WhKE can be explained by the dialect ecology of the original white settler community in Kenya.

Next I will give a detailed account of the history of the WhKE strand in order to see how the English of the settlers has evolved up until today. In particular I shall pay attention to the potential role of input dialects of WhKE as well as the relationship between settlers and indigenous people.

2.1   Foundation (1860s–1920)

While the first British ships arrived at the East African coast in the late sixteenth century (Hancock and Angogo 1982: 309), it was not until the end of the nineteenth century that the British became seriously interested in East Africa (Schneider 2007: 189). From the 1860s onwards the British began to use the East African coast as a stepping stone to India (Schneider 2007: 189). In addition to that, '[n]ow occupying Egypt, the British saw the River Nile as crucial to their strategy to control the Suez Canal' (Nicholls 2005: 1). Therefore, when white explorers and Christian missionaries had found a way from the East African coast to Lake Viktoria, the source of the River Nile (Nicholls 2005: 1), the East African inland also became the object of British imperial interests. Originally there had been some German competition, but this was resolved by the 1884/5 Berlin conference, which established British authority in the region. From 1887 a commercial venture called the British East Africa Association (which in 1888 became the Imperial British East Africa Company (IBEAC)) was granted 'full judicial and political authority over [. . . the area] from the Umba river in the south to Kipini in the north' (Nicholls 2005: 2–3) by the Sultan of Zanzibar. The major aim of the IBEAC was 'to develop commercial opportunities in Uganda and along the East African coast' (Nicholls 2005: 3). In 1895, when the IBEAC had run into financial problems, the British Government officially took over East Africa, which from then was known as the East African Protectorate. One of the first decisions by the British Government was to build a railway from the coast to Lake Victoria. Once the railway was completed in 1902/3 it was decided to make the investment profitable by inviting settlers to the region. As a result, a 'large number of settlers established a plantation system in the highlands north and west of Nairobi, forming one of Africa's few large-scale European settlements' (Schneider 2007: 189). The majority of these early settlers had an upper-class background (including many aristocrats and Brigadier-Generals; Duder 1991: 427) and acquired vast acreages of land (Nicholls 2005: 57; cf. also Duder 1992 for a failed attempt at establishing a settlement of middle-class disabled ex-officers after the First World War). In fact, the East African Protectorate is claimed to have attracted more peers and members of the upper classes than other colonies (Nicholls 2005: 57). In addition to these, after the Boer War a considerable number of settlers came from South Africa, which according to Hancock and Angogo allegedly explains a 'more or less discernible substratum of South African phonology' (1982: 312; more on this below).

The settlement history of Kenya has two important linguistic consequences: first of all, compared to other southern-hemisphere varieties the English language was transplanted to Kenya fairly late. As Trudgill (2004: 23–5) points out, dialects of English were brought to, e.g., New Zealand or South Africa in the early nineteenth century and then started to develop

Table 15.1 *European birthplaces: Kenya 1911–1931 (Kennedy 1987: 200)*[a]

Birthplaces	1911		1921		1926		1931	
	N	%	N	%	N	%	N	%
Kenya	–	–	1,140	11.7	2,063	16.5	2,910	18.2
England	1,472	46.6	5,175	53.0	6,335	50.5	8,473	53.1
Scotland	118	3.7						
Ireland	42	1.3						
Wales	–							
South Africa	642	20.3	1,878	19.3	2,083	16.6	2,910	18.2
Europe	332	10.5	467	4.8	792	6.3	1,149	7.2
Asia	95	3.0	329	3.4	540	4.3	56?	0.4
America	100	3.2	238	2.4	258	2.1	228	1.4
Australasia	72	2.8	217	2.2	259	2.1	220	1.4
Other	284	9.0	311	3.2	207	1.7	?	–
Total	3,157		9,755		12,537		15,956	

[a] As Kennedy notes, 'the Asian figure for 1931 appears to be in error' (1987: 200).

independently of the British source dialects. Consequently, these varieties did not participate in changes in the source dialects that occurred in the late nineteenth and twentieth centuries (such as short front vowel lowering; cf. Trudgill 2004: 31 and below). Due to the late settlement of Kenya, however, such changes will already have affected the dialects of the settlers in the East African Protectorate to a certain degree. Secondly, the largely upper-(middle-)class background of the first settlers means that in contrast to other southern hemisphere varieties, early twentieth-century standard RP must have been the major input dialect in Kenya.

2.2   Exonormative stabilization (1920–late 1940s)

In 1920 the East African Protectorate was formally established as a colony named Kenya, which resulted in a steady influx of settlers and by and by also led to a considerable number of children being born in the colony. Table 15.1 illustrates this development by giving an overview of the European population demography in Kenya between 1911 and 1931.

The figures in Table 15.1 are based on the European population census data of the years in question. Since these data are only estimates of the actual population, it is not unusual to find slightly different figures in other sources.[1] Nevertheless, some general trends can be observed in all of the official documents: first of all there is a steady increase of Europeans (in

[1] A report on the non-native population in 1931, e.g., gives the total number of Kenyan-born Europeans as 3,175 (Kenya Colony and Protectorate 1932: 8), while the population census of 1962 claims 3,167 resident Kenyan-born Europeans for the same year (Directorate of Economic Planning 1964: 41).

1911 only 3,157 Europeans had lived in the East African Protectorate, but by 1931 already 15,956 Europeans resided in the colony). Even more interestingly, the number of children born in Kenya also steadily increased: in 1921 only 11.7 per cent of the Europeans (1,140 out of 9,755) had been born in the colony, while in 1931 the percentage had risen to 18.2 (2,910 out of 15,956).

With respect to the input dialects it is interesting to note that the majority of speakers came from England (accounting for 40.6 per cent of the population in 1911). In addition to that, a substantial number of settlers from South Africa made up between 18.2 and 20.3 per cent of the entire European population. In contrast to this, speakers of Irish or Welsh English only constituted a negligible minority. In accordance with Mufwene's 'founder principle' (1996, 2001), this would imply that the main input variety of WhKE was an 'English English' dialect (Trudgill 2004), which, as we have seen above, was probably an early twentieth-century form of upper-(middle-)class RP. On top of that, the early influx of a significant number of South African farmers might also have lead to a White South African English (WhSAE) contribution to the original feature pool.

Most of the British white settlers in Kenya 'felt British on foreign soil, maintained strong ties with the homeland, and refrained from socializing with Africans' (Schneider 2007: 191). Trying to maintain the social distance between the STL and the IDG strand, the British Government decided that only a handful of the indigenous population who were selected as administrators should receive English language lessons. The settlers in particular seem to have had no interest in the indigenous population learning English. Yet since they still needed to communicate with them, they had to acquire a reduced form of Swahili (labelled 'kiSettla' (Schneider 2007: 191) or 'kitchen Swahili' (Nicholls 2005: 162)). Thus, unsurprisingly, the impact of the IDG strand on the English language at this stage is limited to a small number of terms describing indigenous fauna (e.g. *simba* 'lion'), objects and customs (e.g. *shamba* 'cultivated plot of land', *matatu* 'collective taxi' and *ugali* 'maize dish'; cf. Schmied 2004: 939–40; Schneider 2007: 192; Zuengler 1982: 116). Besides, this lack of contact obviously means that during its formation WhKE was not greatly affected by settlers accommodating to the indigenous population. Instead, dialect contact will have had a greater influence on the development of the settlers' English.

2.3   Nativization (late 1940s–)

After the Second World War, the British Empire started to fall apart. The role-model colony India became independent, and shortly afterwards the Africans started demanding political rights as well. In Kenya this resulted in violent uprisings known as the Mau Mau rebellion (1952–9). Finally, in 1963 – under its first president Jomo Kenyatta – Kenya became independent.

Table 15.2 *Population statistics in Kenya, 1962–1969 ('ooos) (Statistical Abstract 1969: 13)*

Ethnic group	1962	1963	1964	1965	1966	1967	1968	1969
African	8,325	8,575	8,832	9,097	9,370	9,651	9,941	10,239
Asian	176	180	183	185	188	192	182	182
European	56	53	49	42	43	42	42	40
Arab	34	35	36	37	38	39	40	41
Other	4	4	4	4	4	4	4	4
Total	8,595	8,847	9,104	9,365	9,643	9,928	10,209	10,506

Consequently, the white population was faced with the decision of whether to stay or leave the country. Usually it is claimed that 'there was a great exodus of whites from the continent' (Nicholls 2005: 277) and that 'the majority of settlers, who apparently felt more English than African or simply did not feel safe any longer, decided to leave the country' (Schneider 2007: 192). In order to assess the validity of this claim it is insightful to take a closer look at the available census data.

Table 15.2 summarizes the demographic development of the European population in Kenya from 1962, the year before independence, to 1969. The table shows that in 1962 over 55,000 Europeans lived in Kenya, over three times as many as in 1931. As the post-independence census data in Table 15.2 reveal, there was then indeed a steady decline in the number of Europeans. At first it seems as if this cannot be described as a large-scale exodus of the majority of the white population: in the first three years after independence (1963–5), the number of Europeans dropped by over 14,000 to about 42,000 in 1965, but by 1968 40,000 Europeans were apparently still living in Kenya. This figure, however, not only comprises Europeans who remained in Kenya after independence but also includes people who immigrated to Kenya in the 1960s: as Rothchild (1973: 373) has shown, almost 45,000 Europeans actually emigrated between 1962 and 1969, while at the same time over 30,000 new Europeans immigrated into Kenya. In essence this means that only a core of about 10,000 to 15,000 of the original WhKE population stayed in Kenya.[2]

The precise linguistic effects of this gradual exchange of large parts of the white population are difficult to assess, especially since we have no information on the place of origin of the new immigrants (and accordingly of their dialects). What we know is that most of them were apparently British and seem to have integrated fairly well into the white Kenyan society. It is thus very well possible that the dialects spoken by these newcomers lead to an influx of features of mid-twentieth-century British English. On the other hand, in accordance with Mufwene's founder principle (1996, 2001) it might also be that the features of the original settlers persisted (Trudgill 2004: 163).

[2] It is impossible to give precise figures for this since some of the new immigrants might have emigrated from Kenya again after a short time, while a few emigrants seem to have returned.

If so many original settlers left Kenya, then why was there a considerable minority that decided to stay? One major reason for this probably lay in president Kenyatta's conciliatory approach: the whites who remained in Kenya were treated well and unlike in other African ex-colonies there were no atrocities or large-scale farm invasions (Nicholls 2005: 277). White people were even offered the chance to integrate into the new nation by adopting Kenyan citizenship, and by 1969 3,889 of the 40,000 Europeans had already decided to do so (*Statistical Abstract 1969*: 69).[3] Another reason for the peaceful co-existence of the whites and the indigenous population lay in the fact that 'under a willing-buyer-willing-seller scheme'[4] the majority of settlers sold their land. The scheme was subsidized with 25 million by the British government (Nicholls 2005: 274), which meant that those who decided to sell received considerable financial compensation. Besides, this large-scale land redistribution led to large areas of land being returned to African families, thus reducing the unequal land ownership across different ethnicities. This obviously also contributed to the stable and peaceful relationship between Europeans and Africans in Kenya.

Precise demographic data on the European population after 1969 are somewhat difficult to come by since later surveys often collapse the numbers for all non-African groups (i.e. Indians, Arabs and Europeans). The CIA *World Factbook 2008*, for example, estimates that 1 per cent of the almost 38 million Kenyans are non-African by descent (Asian, European and Arab; CIA 2008). What is important, however, is that the number of WhKE speakers never seems to have fallen below 30,000. In 1979 there were still at least 35,500 Europeans living in Kenya (*Länderbericht Kenia 1989*: 28),[5] and estimates for the present numbers range between 30,000[6] and up to 40,000 (Skandera 2003:16). Over forty years after independence, a considerable WhKE community is therefore still living in Kenya. This raises the question whether their variety of English in this postcolonial setting is showing signs of what Schneider (2007) calls nativization.

The first parameter that characterizes nativization in the dynamic model is weakening political ties with Britain, often culminating in the independence of the former colony (though some type of cultural association remains; Schneider 2007: 40–1). In addition to that, from an identity construction

---

[3] At first surrendering their (mainly) British passports and taking on Kenyan citizenship seems to have been a prerequisite for the whites being allowed to stay. Yet this government policy appears to have been relaxed rather quickly (Nicholls 2005: 277).

[4] Source: http://en.wikipedia.org/wiki/Whites_in_Kenya (accessed 18 June 2008). Note that for several farmers the term 'willing seller' will probably have been a euphemism since due to the changing political situation they might have felt forced to sell.

[5] Note that this source gives 36,700 as the number of Europeans in 1969 (*Länderbericht Kenia 1989*: 28), which means that the decrease in numbers between 1969 and 1979 would be even less dramatic.

[6] Sources: www.guardian.co.uk/world/2006/oct/26/kenya.chrismcgreal and http://en.wikipedia.org/wiki/Whites_in_Kenya.

point of view, during the nativization stage the STL strand comes to see itself as permanent residents of British origin (Schneider 2007: 41). Both parameters apply to the WhKE strand in modern Kenya: politically the country has been independent for over forty years now, and those WhKE speakers who decided to stay largely identify themselves as permanent Kenyan residents of British origin (though a certain insecurity seems to exist among older speakers as to whether their children will also live in Kenya;[7] more on this below).

The next feature of the nativization stage, namely sociolinguistic conditions leading to 'widespread and regular contacts' and 'accommodation' (Schneider 2007: 56), however, does not seem to describe the Kenyan situation adequately. Kenya is home to over forty different ethnic groups (Michieka 2005: 173). Yet while the various groups have lived together mostly peacefully since independence (with occasional but basically rare exceptions such as the violent uprisings after the 2007 elections), they have also tended to keep themselves to themselves. This is true for the indigenous tribes such as the Kikuyu or the Luo, and even more so for the WhKE speakers. The majority of White Kenyans live together, for example in the small suburbs of Nairobi such as Langata or Karen or in smaller communities in the Highlands such as Naivasha or Gilgil (Parkinson, Philips and Gourlay 2006: 96, 124, 233, 252). Only a minority is still farming, while the others are working in the tertiary sector (e.g. the wildlife industry, finance, importing, air transport) or 'are on short-term commercial contracts from other countries' (Nicholls 2005: 281).[8] In a lot of these cases the STL strand will have more contact with other White Kenyans or foreign investors and tourists than with indigenous countrymen. In addition to this, children are mostly sent to expat schools for primary and secondary schooling. A considerable number of parents even send their children to England or (since the end of the apartheid era) to South Africa for secondary and tertiary education. The main contact with the indigenous population is thus probably the interaction with employees: manual labour is comparatively cheap in Kenya, so most middle-class households – the White Kenyans being no exception – are able to afford servants and *askaris* (i.e. watchmen). This contact, however, is obviously limited with respect to the topics discussed (mostly focusing on the daily chores) and will often be carried out by code-switching between kitchen Swahili and English. Finally, with the exception of a few individuals such as the palaeoanthropologist Richard Leakey, the WhkE population has always tried to stay out of Kenyan politics in order to keep a low profile and avoid attracting unwanted resentment.[9]

---

[7] www.guardian.co.uk/world/2006/oct/26/kenya.chrismcgreal. One of my informants expressed her doubts, saying 'I think it's getting harder and harder, you know, to get a job here. I don't think there's much of a future for my kids in this country, really.'

[8] Cf. also http://en.wikipedia.org/wiki/Whites_in_Kenya.

[9] www.guardian.co.uk/world/2006/oct/26/kenya.chrismcgreal.

In light of these facts it might be surprising to hear that '[t]o many Kenyans, the whites are just another tribe – one with its own strange codes and rituals, but an African tribe nonetheless'.[10] Yet it has to be kept in mind that, for example, 'white farmers are widely considered to be good employers, and are respected by black Kenyans'.[11] Also, despite the relatively limited amount of interethnic contact they do get along well with their black fellow countrymen.[12] Besides, the WhKE speakers do feel – especially those who decided to return after having received secondary or tertiary education in Britain or South Africa – that Kenya is their home. One of the female WhKE speakers I talked to in Gilgil put it like this: 'because I was brought up here, you know, it really gets under your skin, this place. And so many kids, you know, they're sent off for university or whatever, and they all come back.' She herself had been sent to secondary school near Bristol and after her A-levels she returned to Kenya because she had 'had enough of England by then'. Another of my male informants praised the British education system but later added that he felt that the men there had gone soft (since they, e.g., were not able to carry out minor car repairs on their own). On the one hand, there is clearly a close cultural association with Britain ('we have always looked north', as another male informant said). On the other hand, there is something about Kenya, whether it is the countryside, the community or perhaps even the challenges that life presents there, which brings back many WhKE-speakers who received education abroad.

Returning to the issue of nativization, the lack of close contacts between WhKE speakers and indigenous people obviously prevents the expected linguistic nativization effect of '[t]he difference between the STL and IDG strands [. . . being] reduced to a sociolinguistic distinction' (Schneider 2007: 45). While English is still only a second language for a majority of the indigenous people, WhKE is a first-language variety that shows a strong influence of the exonormative British norm. From my own impressionistic experience I would argue that in contrast to other postcolonial varieties undergoing nativization, structural IDG innovations (such as the insertion and omission of particles as in *pick* 'pick up' or *cope up with* 'cope with'; Schneider 2007: 196) are not spreading to the WhKE STL variety. Yet this is obviously a hypothesis that will have to be tested by further empirical studies.

The data that I collected during my fieldwork only allow a first investigation of the vowel system of WhKE, which in the light of the above

---

[10] www.guardian.co.uk/world/2004/feb/03/worlddispatch.kenya.

[11] www.guardian.co.uk/world/2004/feb/03/worlddispatch.kenya.

[12] The only ones giving the white population a bad reputation are the small number of '"Kenyan cowboys", young men who race around in cars and give whites a bad name' (Nicholls 2005: 281). A great number of my informants indicated that these Kenyan cowboys have their own special accent. Unfortunately, however, I was not able to sample any data from these speakers.

unsurprisingly also differs significantly from the IDG system (for which cf. Schmied 2004). The main question will therefore not be whether there has been any IDG influence. Instead, it will have to be seen how far the language ecology and dialect contact during the early settlement of Kenya (cf. Mufwene 1996, 2001; Trudgill 2004) might have shaped the variety. Furthermore, the prominent role of direct exposure to the exonormative British model should not be underestimated: due to the large number of children attending secondary schools and universities in Britain it is to be expected that present-day standard British English (i.e. Received Pronunciation RP) still exerts a considerable influence on adolescent and adult WhKE. Finally, the possibility of phonological innovations should also be taken into account: the first settlers arrived in Kenya over one hundred years ago, so it is very possible that the variety has also developed its own linguistic innovations.

3   Features of the variety: An acoustic phonetic pilot study

3.1   Data and methodology

The data of the present study were collected during a field trip to Kenya in September 2006. They consist of four WhKE adults (a 45-year-old female, a 30-year-old male, a 52-year-old female and a 67-year-old male) and eighteen WhKE children (nine female, nine male, all between 12 and 13 years old) reading a version of the IPA's *The North Wind and the Sun* passage which was extended by the *Bad*-passage (Salbrina Haji Sharbawi 2006: 250; cf. below). The informants were supplied with a USB headset and all readings were directly recorded onto a notebook with a sampling frequency of 22,050Hz using *Praat* for Windows (www.praat.org). The four adult speakers were recorded in the Muthaiga Club, Nairobi. They were all either born in Kenya before independence or came from long-term resident families (the 30-year-old informant is a third-generation White Kenyan). Thus, despite the limited size of this data set it should nevertheless provide a window on the WhKE of those speakers who decided to stay in Kenya after independence (and not of the immigrants that arrived later). The children were all pupils of the Pembroke House school in Gilgil (www.pembrokehouse.sc.ke) and were interviewed in the headmaster's office. The decision to collect data from children stemmed from the fact that all adult informants had left Kenya for up to twelve years for secondary/tertiary schooling or because of work. In contrast to this, with the children it was ensured that they had never left Kenya up to the time of the interview. The data from the children should therefore better reflect a WhKE vowel system uncontaminated by large-scale, first-hand exposure to the British exonormative model abroad. On the other hand, the children are growing up in a society into which the post-independence immigrants of the 1960s have completely been assimilated. Therefore if the post-independence immigrants had any linguistic influence on WhKE, effects of this should surface in the children's data. Both data type (text reading) as well as recording setting (at school), however, will strongly favour more formal registers so that the present study cannot hope to be a description of the most vernacular WhKE variety.

The full text presented to the informants was the following:

The North Wind and the Sun were disputing which was the stronger, when a traveller came along wrapped in a warm cloak. They agreed that the one who first succeeded in making the traveller take his cloak off should be considered stronger than the other. Then the North Wind blew as hard as he could, but the more he blew the more closely did the traveller fold his cloak around him; and at last the North Wind gave up the attempt. Then the Sun shone out warmly, and immediately the traveller took off his cloak. And so the North Wind was obliged to confess that the Sun was the stronger of the two. (IPA 1999: 39)

I am a bad traveler. When I fly, I get mad as soon as the captain takes off, and I feel like a cat trapped in a small cage. (Salbrina Haji Sharbawi 2006: 250)

In the selection of tokens for the acoustic analysis, I followed Salbrina Haji Sharbawi (2006): all tokens whose formants could be suspected to be affected by following approximants /j, w, r/ and preceding the velar nasal /ŋ/ and dark /l/ were excluded. This made it necessary to add the *Bad*-passage since the *The North Wind and the Sun* text contains only instances of the TRAP-vowel which are preceded by [r], a sound which is well known to lower the values of adjacent vowel formant frequencies (Hagiwara 1995: 15; Salbrina Haji Sharbawi 2006). Both my impressionistic observations and the auditory analysis of the recorded data showed that WhKE is a non-rhotic variety. Accordingly, words with an orthographic postvocalic *r* did not have to be excluded. Finally, all function words were ignored since these are prone to phonetic reduction. Table 15.3 gives an overview of the remaining tokens investigated by the present study, providing the individual tokens as well as the corresponding RP phonemes and the classification of the vowel according to Wells' (1982) lexical set.

The recordings were annotated and analysed using the *Praat* software. The tokens in Table 15.3 were first manually identified and labelled. Then the Linear Prediction Coding (LPC) formant tracks of the vowels under investigation in the spectrogram were checked. After that the mean first two formants (F_1 and F_2) were measured at a section of the vowel (ranging from 0.015 to 0.02 seconds) which exhibited steady formant values and no transition effects.

3.2   Adult WhKE results

Figure 15.1 presents the mean results for the adult WhKE speakers presented in the form of Bark-scale plots of F_1 against F_2 (following Deterding 1997,

Table 15.3 *Kenyan English monophthongs measured from each subject (adapted from Salbrina Haji Sharbawi 2006: 250)*

RP phoneme	Lexical set label				
iː	FLEECE	*immediately*	*succeeded*		
ɪ	KIT	*considered*	*did*		
e	DRESS	*then (x2)*	*attempt*	*confess*	
æ	TRAP	*bad*	*mad*	*captain*	*cat*
ʌ	STRUT	*sun (x3)*	*other*	*up*	
ɑː	START	*hard*			
ɑː	BATH	*last*			
ɒ	CLOTH	*off (x2)*			
ɔː	NORTH	*north (x4)*			
ɔː	FORCE	*more (x2)*			
ʊ	FOOT	*could*	*took*		
uː	GOOSE	*two*	*blew (x2)*		
ɜː	NURSE	*first*			

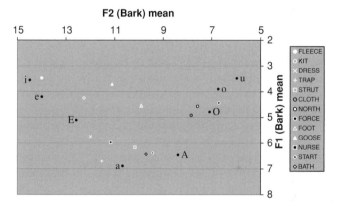

Figure 15.1 Formant plot of the average adult WhkE monophthongs (including Whitley's cardinal vowel as reference points)

2003). In order to better assess the precise vowel position, the IPA cardinal vowels as measured by M. Stanley Whitley[13] are also plotted as black spots together with their IPA symbol.

Figure 15.1 only gives the means of the formant values. For an exact phonetic description of the range of vowel pronunciations it will also be necessary to investigate the variance in the data (cf. the ellipses plots in Figures 15.2–6). The most important results of Figure 15.1, however, can already be seen: there is considerable *u*-fronting in GOOSE [ʉ:] (and to a lesser degree in FOOT). CLOTH appears to have a half-open pronunciation [ɔ]

---

[13] These measurements are included in the Speech Analyzer 2.7 software of the SIL Speech Tools 2.2 www.sil.org/computing/speechtools.

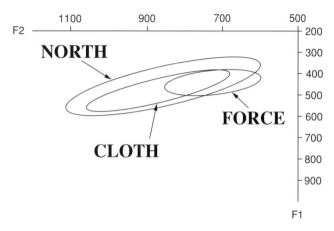

Figure 15.2 CLOTH-NORTH-FORCE merger in WhKE

approaching NORTH and FORCE [ɔː], and the NURSE vowel shows a fairly fronted realization (yet cf. Figure 15.5 below).

In addition to this, the short front vowel set is remarkable in that while KIT appears slightly centralized [ï], both DRESS and TRAP are not raised but even more open than in RP (being realized as [ɛ̞] and [æ], respectively). FLEECE, on the other hand, is unremarkable in exhibiting a high front vowel [iː]. Furthermore, STRUT is realized as a centralized [ë] and BATH and START seem to be merged in [ɐ].

It is important to remember that the claims above are based on a small number of tokens from only four speakers. Nevertheless, even the variance in such a small sample can yield interesting insights into the range of pronunciations of a vowel. Next I will therefore discuss the realizations of selected vowels employing plots created by the *JPlotFormants v1.4*[14] software, which presents the spread of data with ellipses encompassing all data points.

Figure 15.2, for example, illustrates how a closer look at the spread of data points indicates a merger of the vowel qualities of CLOTH, NORTH and FORCE (with the position of the mean value being occupied by the name of the vowel).

Since for the adult data we have Whitley's measurements of the IPA cardinal vowels' formants as reference points, the graphs in Figure 15.3 allow us to investigate the precise phonetic realization in even more detail (with 'o' representing cardinal vowel [ɔ] and 'O' standing for [o]).[15]

As Figure 15.3 shows, NORTH has the widest range of pronunciations from [ɒ̝] to [o] (though the variation can in part be explained by the fact that the text contains two times more tokens of NORTH than of CLOTH and FORCE). The mean values for both CLOTH and NORTH are

[14] Source: www.linguistics.ucla.edu/people/grads/billerey/PlotFrog.htm.
[15] Unfortunately, *JPlotFormants* does not support IPA characters.

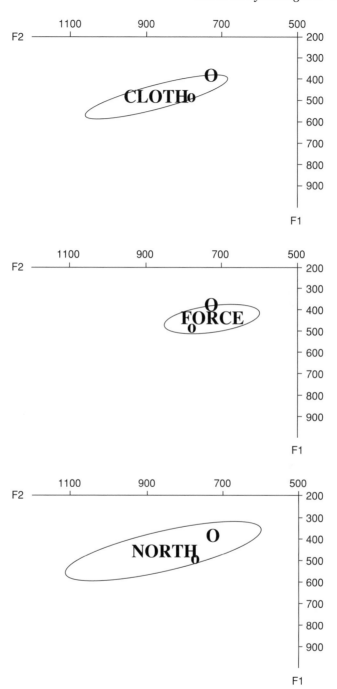

Figure 15.3 CLOTH, NORTH and FORCE compared to the cardinal vowels 'o' [ɔ] and 'O' [o]

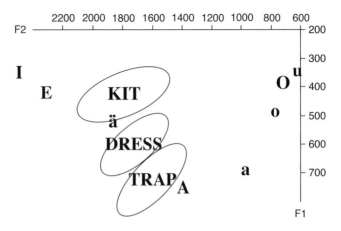

Figure 15.4 The short front vowel set in WhKE

both close to cardinal vowel [ɔ], while FORCE has a mean realization halfway between [ɔ] and [o] (i.e. between [ɔ̞] and [o̞]). The most striking result of this set, however, is that in the adult WhKE data, CLOTH does not exhibit the low open pronunciation expected by present-day RP. Instead the observed half-close vowel can be seen as a conservative realisation which mirrors more closely the vowel quality of CLOTH in RP up to the Second World War (Wells 1982; Upton 2008: 244). Note furthermore that this realization can also be found in present-day Broad WhSAE (cf. Bowerman 2004: 938).

Next, Figure 15.4 focuses on the short front vowel set (here and in the following formant plots the cardinal vowels are represented as follows: [i] = I, [e] = E, [ɛ] = ä, [a] = A, [u] = u, [o] = O, [ɔ] = o, and [ɑ] = a):

As can be seen in Figure 15.4, despite the lowering and slight centralization of KIT (ranging from [ɛ̞] to [ë]) all three short front vowels are kept maximally distinct, with no overlapping realizations. In fact, in order to maintain the difference in vowel quality the lowered KIT might even have ensured that both DRESS and TRAP do not exhibit raising as in other southern–hemisphere varieties such as New Zealand English (Bauer and Warren 2004) or some varieties of WhSAE (Bowerman 2004). Instead, DRESS is realized as [ɛ̞] and TRAP as [æ], which would also be in line with recent trends of short front vowel lowering in RP (Upton 2008: 242).

The above results now make it possible to take a closer look at *u*-fronting in WhKE: As Figure 15.5 illustrates, the mean pronunciation of GOOSE is fairly centralized [ʉː], though realizations range from [ʏː] to [ʊː]. FOOT, on the other hand, is also fronted but possesses a slightly lower quality (although the apparent [ə]-like quality seems to be largely due to the fact that the subjects tended to pronounce the two tokens *could* and *took* with relatively weak stress). *U*-fronting could be argued to be an indication of WhSAE influence

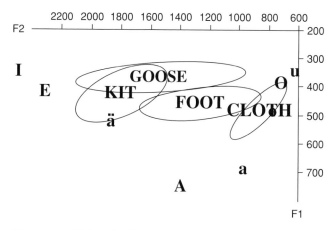

Figure 15.5 U-fronting in context

since the phenomenon can also be found in that variety (Bowerman 2004). Yet, *u*-fronting has been observed in many other varieties as well, including RP. As Harrington (2007) points out, the widespread nature of this change can also be attributed to coarticulatory pressure effects: as the CELEX database (Baayen, Dijkstra and Schreuder 1997) shows, over 70 per cent of instances of /u/ in English occur in contexts where the vowel follows a /j/ (e.g. *few*) or an alveolar (e.g. *soon*). Both of these consonant types have high F2-loci, and *u*-fronting in these cases can be seen as a kind of assimilation process. *U*-fronting is therefore an example of 'drift' (Trudgill 2004), i.e. the emergence of a shared feature of geographically separated varieties due to common linguistic properties and not because of a completed sound change of a single input dialect. Consequently, *u*-fronting is only a weak diagnostic feature for the identification of potential input dialects.

The final set of graphs in Figure 15.6 deals with other interesting phenomena concerning the BATH, START, STRUT and NURSE vowels.

The left graph in Figure 15.6 shows that just as in RP the BATH and START merger is practically complete and in WhKE has [ɐ] as its dominant realization. STRUT, on the other hand, is slightly more centralized and fronted [ɐ̈]. Finally, just like WhSAE (Bowerman 2004), the realization of NURSE ranges from [œː] (more on this below) to [ɜː].

3.3 Child WhKE results

The above results for the adult informants indicated several interesting features of WhKE pronunciation. In the following it will be necessary to see whether the data from the children corroborate these findings. Figure 15.7 presents the results of the mean F1 × F2 values for the children data (again on the Bark scale).

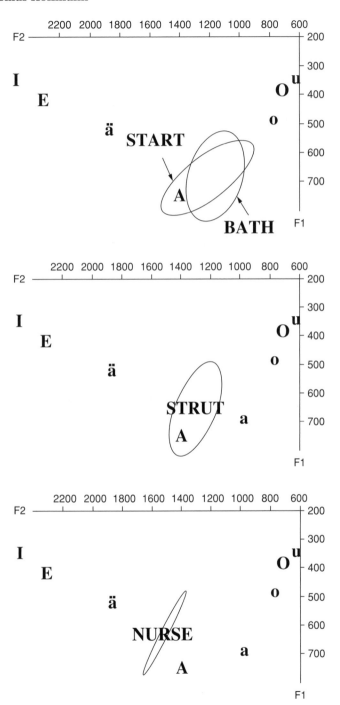

Figure 15.6 Other phenomena: BATH–START merger/STRUT/NURSE

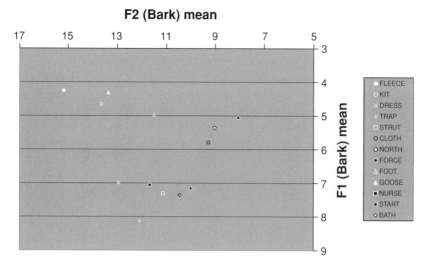

Figure 15.7 Mean formant values for monophthongs of child informants

Due to shorter vocal tracts, children have significantly higher formant frequencies than adults (Hillenbrand et al. 1995), so simply plotting Whitley's cardinal vowel formants as reference points in Figure 15.7 would yield a distorted picture. Unfortunately, there are no reference formant values for cardinal vowels produced by children. It is, however, possible to at least extrapolate predicted formant values for the cardinal vowels from Hillenbrand et al.'s (1995) data: Hillenbrand and colleagues measured the formant frequencies of American English vowels produced by children only slightly younger than the ones recruited for the present study (age range 10–12). In addition to that they also collected the formant frequencies of male and female adult speakers. Calculating the F1 and F2 formant differences between the children and the male adult speakers shows that on average the children's F1 values are 1.01 Bark steps higher than the adults', and their F2 Bark values exceed the adults' ones by 1.59. While this is certainly a crude way of adjusting Whitley's data, Figure 15.8 nevertheless illustrates that correcting the cardinal vowel formants by these figures (i.e. adding 1.01 Bark steps to the F1 values and 1.59 Bark steps to the F2 values) considerably improves the interpretability of the children's results.

Figure 15.8 indicates several findings corroborated by the auditory analysis of the data:

1. CLOTH has a half-close [O] realization (patterning with NORTH and FORCE in the mid back area).

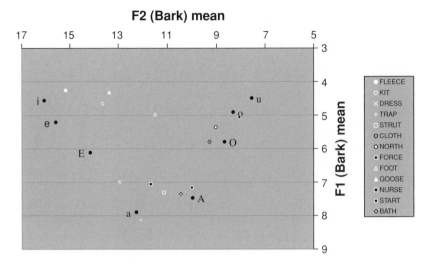

Figure 15.8 Mean formant values for monophthongs of child informants with adjusted cardinal vowels

2. *u*-fronting in GOOSE is even more advanced in the children's speech, with FOOT seemingly lagging behind (though cf. below for the discussion of the vowels' exact quality).
3. KIT is not as heavily lowered and centralized as in the adult data, but has a half-close pronunciation [ɪ] similar to RP. In addition to that, comparable to the adult informants, DRESS and TRAP show no signs of southern-hemisphere raising, but are very open instead ([ɛ̞] and [æ̞], respectively);[16]
4. START and BATH are merged and have a more RP-like back [ɑː]-quality;
5. STRUT is realized as [ɐ] and NURSE as [ɜ̝ː] (or as rounded [ɵ]).

A more detailed phonetic description of these vowels can again be gained by investigating the spread of data points. Figure 15.9, for example, gives the distribution of CLOTH, NORTH and FORCE.

Just like in the adult data, the children exhibit realizations of the NORTH-FORCE-CLOTH set that mirror the early-twentieth-century RP input dialect: NORTH ranges from [ɔ̝] to [o], CLOTH has a slightly more open realization [ɔ], and FORCE has a mean realization halfway between [ɔ̝] and [o̞]).

Next, Figure 15.10 illustrates that *u*-fronting of GOOSE and FOOT is more advanced in the children's speech. The children's mean for GOOSE is closer to [ʏ], with the most advanced realizations overlapping with high front FLEECE, indicating a [yː] pronunciation. FOOT, on the

---

[16] The fact that TRAP appears to have an even more open pronunciation than the cardinal vowel [a] in Figure 15.8 is obviously an artefact of the extrapolated formant adjustments. The auditory analysis clearly supports the analysis of TRAP as [æ].

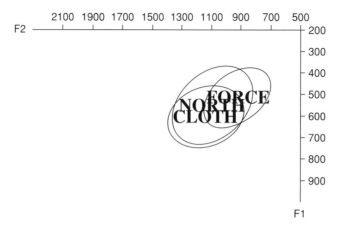

Figure 15.9 CLOTH-NORTH-FORCE merger in WhKE

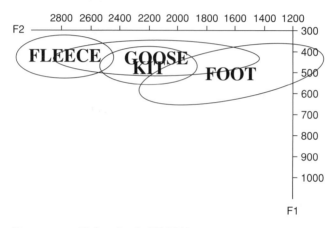

Figure 15.10 U-fronting in WhKE in context

other hand, also has a fairly high and fronted pronunciation [ʉ], which occasionally approaches [ʏ].

As pointed out above, another observable trend is that the children's front vowels do not exhibit raising but lowering (a trend that has recently also been observed in RP; Upton 2008: 242). As can furthermore be seen in Figure 15.11, the three vowels are maximally distinct, with only a minor overlap of the DRESS–TRAP sets.

Finally, Figure 15.12 presents two cases of strongly overlapping distributions, only one of which represents an actual merger. The left graph illustrates the merger of START and BATH in a vowel that in accordance with Figure 15.8 was identified as corresponding to RP [ɑː]. The apparent merger in the right graph, however, is only due to the fact that information

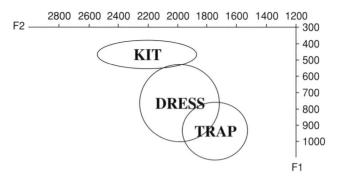

Figure 15.11 The short front vowel set in WhKE

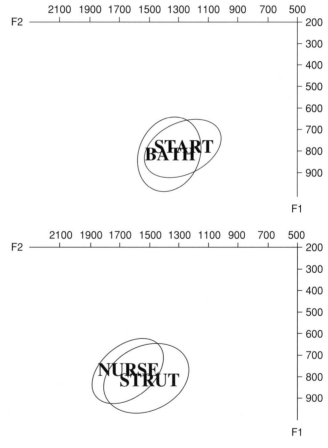

Figure 15.12 START–BATH merger and apparent NURSE–STRUT merger

on lip-rounding is only indirectly encoded in F1 and F2 (with lip-rounding lowering both formants, particularly F2; Stevens 1998: 290–4): while STRUT is an unrounded [ɐ], NURSE has realizations ranging from unrounded [ɜ̃] to rounded [ɞ]. The rounding of NURSE in WhKE is another instance of drift that can be observed in several southern-hemisphere Englishes (e.g. Australian English or South African English; Trudgill 2004: 143–4). Margaret Maclagan (cited in Trudgill 2004: 144) suggests that rounding in NURSE words can actually be seen as an acoustic compensation strategy for the loss of /r/: while the /r/ was still pronounced in NURSE it led to the lowering of all formants of the vowel, especially F2 and F3 (cf. above). After the loss of rhoticity, 'lip-rounding largely compensated for the loss of /r/ and preserved the formant structure of the NURSE vowel' (Trudgill 2004: 144) because it also leads to formant lowering.

3.4 Dialect input and nativization revisited

BlKE tends towards a reduced five-vowel system (Schmied 2004). As the above discussion has shown, WhKE employs a much more complicated vowel system. Besides the different status of the two varieties (i.e. second vs. first language), the accent differences can also be explained by a lack of large-scale social contacts between the STL and the IDG strand in Kenya. Socio-politically this situation has so far been mostly unproblematic, since the white and black tribes of Kenya generally appear to respect each other. Yet from a linguistic point of view the limited nature of contact between the white and black speakers seems to prevent large-scale accommodation and consequently the nativization effect of reducing the difference between the two groups to a mere sociolinguistic distinction (Schneider 2007: 45). Nevertheless, in order to assess the full degree to which nativization effects do or do not operate within WhKE, further studies, e.g. on potential structural BlKE innovations spreading into WhKE, are needed.

Returning to the WhKE vowel system, its most striking feature is its resistance to short front vowel-raising – a widespread phenomenon in southern-hemisphere varieties (including WhSAE). The main reasons for this phenomenon seem to be the input dialect of the original settlers and the continuing strong, direct exonormative influence of RP. Kenya was settled considerably later than other southern-hemisphere colonies. As a result, the English transplanted to Kenya was already affected by short front vowel-lowering, though it could be argued that the initial upper-class settlers might have preferred more conservative close pronunciations. Besides this, a majority of WhKE speakers consider Kenya their home and feel more comfortable there than in Europe, but they nonetheless keep strong affiliations with Britain, which is reflected in their accents. By this I do not suggest that the prestige of RP as such plays any significant role (there are good reasons arguing against such an influence; Trudgill 2004: 151–3). There is, however, a considerable number of speakers who still receive secondary and/or tertiary education in Britain. These speakers thus have direct contact with RP speakers (and, of course, other English regional and social dialects) and have to accommodate to them. Upon their return to Kenya, these speakers then become models for the Kenyan-born WhKE children. In the twentieth century this might have led to short front vowel-lowering receiving further input from such speakers. WhKE appears to have continued this change, yielding more open vowels than the corresponding RP ones.

Furthermore, the highly conservative RP realization of CLOTH as [O] can, of course, be interpreted as a sign of the founder effect since the early, largely upper-(middle-)class, settlers probably used this variant. In addition to this, *u*-fronting in GOOSE and FOOT could be attributed to WhSAE influence, but then again this feature is surfacing in English varieties world-wide (including the idiolect of RP's most prominent speaker, the Queen; Harrington 2007). As discussed above, the main factor favouring this sound change appears to be a coarticulatory assimilation effect (together with the fact that there is no vowel in the high mid area which might block the fronting of *u*; Harrington 2007).

In general it can therefore be said that the input dialects, the strong affiliation with the exonormative British model and local innovations can account for most of the features discussed.

4   Conclusion

Despite that the fact that a majority of the 56,000 whites residing in Kenya in 1962 left after independence, a steady number of at least 30,000 whites[17] has remained there up to the present day. Most of these WhKE-speakers consider Kenya their home and many who leave the country for schooling or work decide to return. Yet, there exists a certain insecurity as to whether future generations of whites will continue to live in Kenya.[18] As I pointed out throughout this article, generally the white and black tribes of Kenya get along well. As in all societies, however, crime is a problem in Kenya, and over the years there have been a few isolated killings of white Kenyans. In addition to that, the court case of Tom Cholmondeley, the son of one of the biggest white landowners, Lord Delamere, generated some publicity and for some time it was not clear how this would affect the relationship of black and white Kenyans: after having been acquitted of murdering a black Kenyan in 2005, Cholmondeley was accused of shooting a black poacher on his property in 2006. Both shooting incidents apparently generated some hostility against whites (Parkinson, Phillips and Gourlay 2006: 233), but in general the trial

---

[17] Though this number obviously also includes expats who moved to Kenya after 1963.
[18] www.guardian.co.uk/world/2006/oct/26/kenya.chrismcgreal.

(which is still in progress at the time of writing) does not seem to have greatly affected the relationship between the white and black communities.

Predictions about the future are always difficult to make (and often wrong). Nevertheless, at present it appears as if the future of the WhKE-speakers in Kenya does not so much hinge on the relationship of blacks and whites but rather on the general political stability of the country. Since its independence in 1963, Kenya has been one of the most stable African democracies. All the same, as the 2007 post-election riots revealed, there are also tensions between all tribes in Kenya which seem to be mainly fuelled by large-scale poverty. Only if this issue together with others that are associated with it (namely tribalism and corruption) is successfully addressed by the government can long-term political stability be ensured. In such a case, it is very possible that a significant white community will continue living in Kenya. Whether their variety of English, however, will undergo further nativization effects will strongly depend on the sociolinguistic contact situation of the WhKE and BlKE strands.

References

Baayen, R., T. Dijkstra and R. Schreuder. 1997. *The CELEX Lexical Database*. (CD-ROM). Philadelphia: Linguistic Data Consortium, University of Pennsylvania.

Bauer, Laurie and Paul Warren. 2004. 'New Zealand English: Phonology.' In Kortmann *et al.*, eds. 580–602.

Bowerman, Sean. 2004. 'White South African English: Phonology.' In Kortmann *et al.*, eds. 931–42.

CIA. 2008. *"Kenya". The World Factbook 2008*. <*https://www.cia.gov/library/publications/the-world-factbook/geos/ke.html*>

Deterding, David. 1997. 'The formants of monophthong vowels in Standard Southern British English pronunciation.' *Journal of the International Phonetics Association* 27: 47–55.

———. 2003. 'An instrumental study of the monophthong vowels of Singapore English.' *English World-Wide* 24: 1–16.

Directorate of Economic Planning. 1964. *Kenya Population Census 1962. Nairobi, Kenya: Ministry of Finance and Economic Planning*.

Duder, C. J. D. 1991. 'Love and the lions: The image of white settlement in Kenya in popular fiction, 1919–1939.' *African Affairs* 90: 427–38.

———. 1992. 'Beadoc – the British East Africa Disabled Officers' Colony and the white frontier in Kenya.' *The Agricultural History Review* 40.2: 142–50.

Hagiwara, Robert. 1995. 'Acoustic realization of American /r/ as produced by men and women.' *UCLA Working Papers in Phonetics* 90: 2–187.

Hancock, Ian F. and Rachel Angogo. 1982. 'English in East Africa.' In Richard W. Bailey and Manfred Görlach, eds. *English as a World Language*. Ann Arbor: The University of Michigan Press, 306–23.

Harrington, Jonathan. 2007. 'Evidence for a relationship between synchronic variability and diachronic change in the Queen's annual Christmas broadcasts.' In

Jennifer Cole and José I. Hualde, eds. *Laboratory Phonology 9*. Berlin: Mouton de Gruyter, 125–44.

Hillenbrand, James, Laura A. Getty, Michael J. Clark and Kimberlee Wheeler. 1995. 'Acoustic characteristics of American English vowels.' *Journal of the Acoustical Society of America* 97.5: 3099–111.

IPA (International Phonetic Association). 1999. *Handbook of the International Phonetic Association*. Cambridge: Cambridge University Press.

Kennedy, Dane. 1987. *Islands of White: Settler Society and Culture in Kenya and Southern Rhodesia, 1890–1939*. Durham: Duke University Press.

Kenya Colony and Protectorate. 1932. *Report on the Non-native Census Enumeration made in the Colony and Protectorate of Kenya on the night of the 6th March 1931*. Nairobi: Government Printer.

Kortmann, Bernd, Edgar W. Schneider, Kate Burridge, Rajend Mesthrie and Clive Upton, eds. 2004. *A Handbook of Varieties of English*, Vol 1: *Phonology*. Berlin and New York: Mouton de Gruyter.

Länderbericht Kenia 1989. (Statistisches Bundesamt der Bundesrepublik Deutschland.) Stuttgart: Metzler-Poeschel.

Michieka, Martha Moraa. 2005. 'English in Kenya: A sociolinguistic profile.' *Word Englishes* 24.2: 173–86.

Mufwene, Salikoko S. 1996. 'The Founder Principle in creole genesis.' *Diachronia* 13: 84–134.

2001. *The Ecology of Language Evolution*. Cambridge: Cambridge University Press.

Nicholls, C. S. 2005. *Red Strangers: The White Tribe of Kenya*. London: Timewell.

Parkinson, Tom, Matt Philips and Will Gourlay. 2006. *Lonely Planet Kenya*. London: Lonely Planet Publications.

Rothchild, Donald. 1973. *Racial Bargaining in Independent Kenya: A Study of Minorities and Decolonization*. London: Oxfod University Press.

Salbrina Haji Sharbawi. 2006. 'The vowels of Brunei English: An acoustic investigation.' *English World Wide* 27: 247–64.

Schmied, Josef. 2004. 'East African English phonology.' In Kortmann *et al.*, eds. 918–30.

Schneider, Edgar W. 2007. *Postcolonial English: Varieties of English Around the World*. Cambridge: Cambridge University Press.

Skandera, Paul. 2003. *Drawing a Map of Africa: Idiom in Kenyan English*. Tübingen: Gunter Narr.

Statistical Abstract 1969. Nairobi, Kenya: Ministry of Economic Planning and Development, Statistics Division.

Stevens, Kenneth N. 1998. *Acoustic Phonetics*. Cambridge, Mass.: MIT Press.

Trudgill, Peter. 2004. *New-Dialect Formation: The Inevitability of Colonial Englishes*. Edinburgh: Edinburgh University Press.

Upton, Clive. 2008. 'Received Pronunciation.' In Bernd Kortmann and Clive Upton, eds. *Varieties of English*, Vol. 1: *The British Isles*. Berlin and New York: Mouton de Gruyter, 237–52.

Wells, John C. 1982. *Accents of English* (3 vols.). Cambridge: Cambridge University Press.

Zuengler, Jane E. 1982. 'Kenyan English.' In Braj B. Kachru, ed. *The Other Tongue: English Across Cultures*. Urbana, Ill.: University of Illinios Press, 112–24.

Part V

Australasia and the Pacific

16   Eurasian Singapore English

LIONEL WEE

1 Introduction

Singapore is an ethnically diverse society, and the state is guided by the principle of multiracialism, where respect and equal treatment must be accorded each ethnic community (Benjamin 1976). This commitment to multiracialism stems from the state's belief that the desire to maintain ethnic and cultural distinctiveness is a primordial fact, and any policy that tries to force different 'tribes' to submerge their differences can only lead to insurgency. We see this in the following statement by Singapore's first Prime Minister and currently Minister Mentor, Lee Kuan Yew (in Han, Fernandez and Tan 1998: 163–5):

The Indians have their own method. So do the Malays. The Malays: Islam and kinship ties . . . I don't think you can erase all that. That's for hundreds of years, or thousands of years . . . In every culture, there is a desire to preserve your distinctiveness. And I think if you go against that, you will create unnecessary problems, whether it is with the Indians and their caste or with the Chinese and their clans.

To facilitate the management of this diversity, the state divides the population into four ethnically based categories. As a result, a population of about 3.2 million is effectively seen as being made up of 76.8 per cent Chinese, 13.9 per cent Malays, 7.9 per cent Indians, and 1.4 per cent Others (2000 Census of Population). Each of the three major ethnic groups is assigned an official mother tongue (a language assigned by the state as representative of a community's ethnic identity): Mandarin for the Chinese, Malay for the Malays and Tamil for the Indians. There is no official mother tongue for the Others category since this group does not really constitute a specific ethnic community; rather, it is a residual category where various minority groups are classified, including at times the Eurasians, who make up about 0.43 per cent of the population.

Against this backdrop of state emphasis on maintaining ethnic distinctiveness, the Eurasian community occupies an uneasy position. Together with the Chinese, Malays and Indians, the Eurasians are considered among the 'founding races' of Singapore (Hill and Lian 1995: 103). This is perhaps one reason why, in some circumstances, the Eurasians are recognized as a category on their own, distinct from the Others. For example, the state introduced an ethnic self-help scheme in the 1980s, establishing four self-help groups, which are public institutions to which it gives dollar-for-dollar matching for funds that are raised. These groups are the Chinese Development Assistance Council (CDAC), Mendaki (for the Malays), the Singapore Indian Development Association (SINDA), and the Eurasian Association (EA). Though the EA was originally established in 1919 as a sports and social club for Eurasians, it was co-opted into the self-help scheme when this was introduced. As another example, Singapore's National Registration Identity Card system, which applies to citizens and permanent residents, lists an individual's gender, blood type, address, religion and 'race'. The options for 'race' are Chinese, Malay, Indian, Eurasian or Other (Rappa and Wee 2006: 86). In these cases, Eurasians are treated as a distinct category.

But the state has also sometimes suggested that their small number makes it more administratively expedient to absorb them under the Others category. In the case of language, this is highly consequential, since it denies the Eurasians their own official mother tongue alongside the other major ethnic groups. As a result, there have been anxieties about the place of Eurasians in Singapore society. As Benjamin (1976: 127) pointed out sometime ago:

the more that Singapore's national culture demands that each 'race' should have a respectably ancient and distinctive exogenous culture as well as a 'mother tongue' to serve as the second element of a bilingual education, the more will the Eurasians come to feel that there is no proper place for them.

However, the lack of a specific mother tongue for the Eurasians is not just a matter of numbers: the choice of language is also problematic because the Eurasians generally feel that English should be their official mother tongue (Wee 2002). This is in no small part due to the fact that, since the time of British colonial rule, many Eurasians have grown up with English as the home language (Gupta 1994: 19; Rappa 2000: 168). But although the language policy of Singapore recognizes English as an official language, it is not acceptable by the state as a mother tongue on the grounds that it needs to remain ethnically neutral for various reasons. One, it serves as an interethnic lingua franca. Two, as the major language of socioeconomic mobility, its ethnic neutrality ensures that the distribution of economic advantages is not seen as being unduly associated with a specific ethnic group, which would otherwise raise the danger of interethnic tension. And three, English is treated as a language that essentially marks a non-Asian identity while Singapore's political ideology insists on constructing itself as an Asian society (Rappa and Wee 2006).

The language policy of Singapore therefore recognizes a total of four official languages, English and the three official mother tongues, and it expects each Singaporean to be bilingual in both English and the mother tongue. Knowledge of English is necessary for the reasons outlined above, and knowledge of the mother tongue is essential for maintaining a connection to one's ethnic heritage. In the school system, English is the medium of education and students are expected to study their official mother tongue as a second language subject.[1] This has resulted in a situation where many Eurasians grow up speaking English, but upon entering school, are required to take on a second language simply to meet the state's bilingual requirement, even though this second language bears no ethnic or heritage affiliation for them. Most of them end up choosing Mandarin (because of its perceived economic advantage in relation to China's development) or Malay (because it is supposed to be relatively easy to learn) (Braga-Blake 1992: 11, 19). For many Eurasian parents, there still remains the anxiety that their children are being 'handicapped' in comparison with their Chinese, Malay or Indian counterparts since, for the latter, the second language is also the official mother tongue (Wee 2002: 290).[2] And in fact, in the 1970s, many Eurasian families emigrated from Singapore, most of them citing the 'high pressure' education system as the main reason for their departure (Rappa 2000: 158). Patricia Monkman (personal communication, 2007), a senior manager with the Eurasian Association, suggests that the mother tongue policy was a major contributing factor, because many Eurasian families feared that their children would be unduly burdened in an education system that demanded they learn what was for them effectively a foreign language.

2   The Eurasians

The category 'Eurasian' was originally created by the British colonial bureaucracy to 'signify colonial subjects who were offspring of European fathers and Asian mothers' (Rappa 2000: 157, 162). Gupta (1994: 37) notes that the 'European component of a majority of Eurasians had been Portuguese, British or Dutch, and they were mostly English-speaking'. Citing Braga-Blake (1992), Gupta (ibid.) also states that:

Families with Portuguese, British, and Dutch surnames, and Indian, Macao, Malacca, Bencoolen, Burmese, Siamese and Ceylon origins intermarried . . . so that from disparate origins a unified, Christian, English-speaking community had emerged before the end of the nineteenth century.

The intrinsically hybridized nature of the Eurasian identity has, not surprisingly, led to a number of attempts to clarify, both for the community itself and

---

[1] The exceptions are the Special Assistance Plan (SAP) schools, where an elite minority studies both English and Mandarin as first languages.

[2] While this is a perception with some truth, it is also the case that an increasing number of children from the other ethnic groups are also coming from English-speaking homes. Thus, even children with an official mother tongue are often faced with learning what is for all intents and purposes simply another second language (see below).

for outsiders, what it actually means to be a Eurasian. In 1997, the Eurasian Association proposed the following definition (intended to supersede the earlier definitions of 1989 and 1993) (Rappa 2000: 159):

A Eurasian for the purpose of these Rules only is a person: –

(i)   Who is of mixed European and Asian ancestry and who has shown a desire to be identified as a Eurasian; OR
(ii) Whose family has been accepted as Eurasian by custom and tradition, and who has shown the desire to be identified as a member of the Eurasian community.

The primary advantage of this definition seems to be that it allows individuals to be accepted as Eurasians as long as these individuals wish to be so identified, and the community is itself willing to accept these individuals. This effectively leads to a more inclusive definition and makes it much easier for this small community to accept newer members, thus helping to increase its numbers. Despite this, there is still a strong perception that the prototypical Eurasian is Catholic and has some degree of Portuguese ancestry.

Contentions over religion and ethnic mixing notwithstanding, there has always been a close historical association between the Eurasians and the English language.[3] This can be seen from the fact that 'the oldest Eurasian enclave was in the very central area of Waterloo Street and Queen Street, which was also the area where the principal English-medium schools were located' (Clarke 1992: 51, cited in Gupta 1994: 33). Eurasians were prominently represented in the early English-medium schools, both as students and as teachers. For example (Gupta 1994: 38–9):

The superior standard of English in the girls' schools is often commented on in the Reports on Education. This was because the girls' schools had a much higher proportion of European/Eurasian pupils than the boys' schools, as the European and Eurasian families were more likely than other communities to educate both their sons and their daughters. . . . Until the early 1920s, the largest single racial group among the teachers was Eurasians.

In addition to teaching, a large number of Eurasians, especially Eurasian women, were also very well represented as nurses, stewardesses, secretaries, clerks, telephone operators, journalists and broadcasters (Asiapac 2003: 20–1). It is no accident that many of these professions required a fair degree of proficiency in English. This proficiency, however, did not necessarily mean occupational mobility to the highest levels of an institution or organization, which tended to be reserved for the colonizers themselves (Rappa 2000: 168).

---

[3] Another group that was strongly associated with the English language in Singapore's early history was the Peranakans or Straits-born Chinese (Ansaldo 2004: 143; see also Lim's contribution to this volume).

In fact, the English spoken by the Eurasians appears to have been grudgingly tolerated by the colonial rulers. It was considered by them to be far from the ideal 'proper' or 'correct' variety that they (that is, the colonialists) spoke. Thus, an 1895 report by J. B. Elcum, director of education (1895–1915) stated that:

At many schools the lower standards are taught by Eurasian Masters or Mistresses who have anything but a correct knowledge of English, do not even speak it correctly and are absolutely incapable of explaining niceties of meaning to their pupils. (quoted in Gupta 1994: 44)

There is no doubt that in comparison with many of the other ethnic communities at the time, English was also far more common among the Eurasians as a home language. But not surprisingly, the negative attitudes that the British held towards the variety of English spoken by the Eurasians extended from the public domain of education to the private domain of the home. Thus, in a 1915 report, H. W. Firmstone (quoted in Gupta 1994: 39) reminded his readers that 'the home language of the [Eurasians]... even where it professes to be English, is distinguished by a peculiar accent and idiom, and in many respects must be classed as a different language'.

It is difficult to obtain details of this 'peculiar accent and idiom', but in order to provide some sense of the kind of English that may have been spoken by the Eurasians, I include below extracts from an oral history interview conducted by Daniel Chew (DC) in 1984.[4] The person being interviewed is Mrs Mabel Martin (MM), a Eurasian who was born on 4 August 1905. Mrs Martin finished her Senior Cambridge Examination in 1921 and worked intermittently as a stenographer until she retired in 1969. Admittedly, the interview creates a rather formal context, but in the later parts of the interview, the interviewee does seem to become more relaxed. And though the general use of English appears to be quite standard throughout, there are a number of constructions that are more colloquial in nature, and that appear to indicate grammatical idiosyncrasies, especially in relation to number agreement.

In dialogues D1 and D2, MM is describing her youth. Note in D1 the phrases 'there were a certain time limits' and 'if there were anything that we didn't like'. All of these show problems with number agreement. In D2, MM's use of 'Oh, I dare say' and 'to have a cuddle and a kiss' seem quite distinctly British. While perhaps more a matter of pragmatics than grammar,

---

[4] 'Communities of Singapore (Eurasians)' project, from the National Heritage Board, National Archives of Singapore. The interview was transcribed by a Mrs Wong-Yong Lee Yoong, and it is not possible to determine if any non-standard usages in the transcripts are attributable to the interviewee or to errors in the transcription process. Nevertheless, aside from occasional non-standard constructions, it seems quite clear that the interviewee spoke what could be considered fairly good English.

MM's use of 'no problems here' in D1 and 'no problem there' in D2 shows an interesting variation in deixis. One might have expected the same distal deictic 'there' to be used on both occasions. But 'here' seems to be motivated by the fact that MM is placing her narrative in the specific context of her home and family. 'There', in contrast, may be motivated by the fact that she is speaking about a general social practice amongst young Eurasians.

D1

DC: Can you tell us what it was like to grow up as a young Eurasian girl in Singapore?

MM: . . . In those days, there were a certain time limits set for engagements. You got engaged first. And then there you have your courtship days. And then you fixed them . . your dates for your marriage. And happily we were not restricted like . . . I would say the Chinese girls would have to be always accompanied and then marriages arranged for them.

Well, we had quite enough amount of freedom. The Eurasian girls can't complain that they were restricted . . . We were allowed to discuss points with our family . . . anyway my family. My father always said that if there were anything that we didn't like, we sat down and discussed things. We had no problems here.

D2

DC: What about mixing with members of the opposite sex?

MM: . . . Most of us, I think, listened then to our parents where that was concerned. Oh, I dare say . . . in those days the girls and the boys did find a quiet spot somewhere to have a cuddle and a kiss. No problem there.

In D3, MM is describing the movement of the Eurasian community to different parts of Singapore. Note the phrase 'all the Bukit Timah district', which, again, points to some confusion over number agreement between determiner and head noun. MM's final sentence ('got some very nice big bungalows there') is particularly interesting. Her use of 'got' as an existential is a commonly noted property of colloquial Singapore English (see below).

D3

MM: Then quite a number of Eurasians also moved out to all the Bukit Timah district. Pasir Panjang, very few I recall . . . Then quite a number of them, I would say, rich or affluent Eurasians had houses in Orchard Road or they called the Tanglin district. . . . Actually we would call it Chatsworth Road and all these places, got some very nice big bungalows there.

Thus, aside from the issue of number agreement (either between subject and verb or between determiner and head noun), most of the constructions used by MM appear to show a good command of English, the views of the British colonialists notwithstanding.

3   Variation in Singapore English today

Since English has been fast gaining currency amongst the general population such that there is a fair amount of interethnic interaction involving the use of this language, it is largely the case that the English spoken by the Eurasians is not particularly distinct in modern-day Singapore. The description of 'Eurasian English' in a cultural guidebook (Asiapac 2003: 42) lists just a small number of 'colorful expressions' such as those in (1).

(1) a.   *To close one eye* 'To ignore something'

   b.   *Easier to get the Queen* 'Hard to reach the person in question'

   c.   *Face like the back of a bus* 'An unpleasant countenance/facial expression'

   d.   *Teach your grandmother to suck eggs* 'Don't tell an elder what to do'

It is not clear that these are distinctively Eurasian expressions. (4a) and (4d), for example, appear to be quite common among other Singaporeans. Because the existence of linguistic features particular to ethnic groups is more unstable and harder to identify, it is common for most scholarly discussions to focus on 'the more stable and characteristic pan-Singaporean features' (Lim 2004: 19). Current discussions of Singapore English typically make a distinction between colloquial and standard varieties, although other scholars prefer to treat the variation involved as more of a continuum (Lim and Foley 2004: 19). Ansaldo (2004), for example, prefers to speak in terms of a lectal cline, where the colloquial variety roughly corresponds to the mesolect. This appeal to a lectal cline is not to be confused with the earlier work by Platt and Weber (1980), which tended to equate particular lects with speakers' socioeconomic status. Without taking a position on these complex issues, it seems reasonable to hypothesize that, as 'early adopters' of English in Singapore's history, most Eurasians, whatever their socioeconomic background, tend to speak a variety of Singapore English that is, even under fairly informal circumstances, more acrolectal in nature or closer to the standard.

In what follows, then, I provide a brief description of Singapore English phonology and morphosyntax (for details, see the papers in Lim 2004 and Wee 2004a, b), drawing attention to the major differences between the colloquial and standard varieties. I then illustrate how these phonological and morphosyntactic properties are manifested in the speech of a Eurasian informant, Jill.

Table 16.1 *Singapore English vowel chart*

	Front	Central	Back
Close	i		u
Close-mid	e	ə	o
Open-mid	ɛ		ɔ
Open	æ		ɑ

4   Singapore English phonology and morphosyntax

The following is the list of vowels in colloquial Singapore English, according to Wells' lexical sets.

KIT	i	FLEECE	i	NEAR	iə
DRESS	æ	FACE	e	SQUARE	æ
TRAP	ɛ	PALM	ɑ	START	ɑ
LOT	ɔ	THOUGHT	ɔ	NORTH	ɔ
STRUT	ɑ	GOAT	o	FORCE	ɔ
FOOT	u	GOOSE	u	CURE	ɔ
BATH	ɑ	PRICE	ai	happY	i
CLOTH	ɔ	CHOICE	ɔi	lettER	ə
NURSE	ə	MOUTH	au	commA	ə
horsES	ə	POOR	uə		

(POOR is not part of the standard lexical set, but it is included here because the diphthong /uə/ appears in words like *poor*, *sure* and *tour*.)

The vowel chart is shown in Table 16.1. The colloquial variety makes a smaller number of vowel distinctions than the standard version. In particular, length or tense-lax distinctions are not present in the colloquial variety so that words like *seat* and *sit* are homophonous, as are *cart* and *cut*, whereas such distinctions tend to be maintained in the standard variety (Lim 2004: 21–2). Also, the colloquial variety often maintains full vowel quality where some reduction to schwa might be expected with the standard, especially in unstressed syllables (Lim 2004: 23). For example, the word *connect* might be pronounced as [kənɛkt] in the standard variety, but [kɔnɛk] in the colloquial; note also that the colloquial variety also shows a simplification of the consonant cluster in the coda, where the final [t] has been omitted.

The inventory of consonants is similar to that of a better-known variety such as RP. This is not surprising, since accents of English do not tend to differ very much in their consonant inventories. There are two points worth noting (Wee 2004a: 1025). The colloquial variety does not usually aspirate voiceless plosives or affricates, so that /p/, for example, tends to be realized the same way in words like *pin* and *spin*. Also, the interdental fricatives tend to be realized as [t, d] when prevocalic and [f] when at the end of a word. So, *thin* is realized as [tin] and *then* [den], but in word-final position, we get [brɛf] and [brif] for *breath* and *breathe* respectively. In contrast, the standard variety tends to aspirate voiceless plosives or affricates. It also maintains the distinction between the interdental fricatives, on the one hand, and the alveolar stops and labial fricative, on the other.

To get a sense of the morphosyntax of colloquial Singapore English (sometimes known as Singlish), here are some sample Singlish utterances, showing how it is characterized by a productive use of reduplication (2) and discourse particles (3: the particle *lor* indicates a sense of resignation, and *meh* scepticism). See Fong 2004; Wee and Ansaldo 2004; Wee 2004c for further discussion).

(2) a.   I like hot-hot curries. 'I like very hot curries.'

   b.   I walk-walk-walk then I fall down.
         'I was walking and then I fell down'

(3) a.   I won't get married, lor. 'I have no choice but to not get married.'

   b.   You really did your homework, meh?
         'Did you really do your homework?'

Other notable features of colloquial Singapore English include the absence of number agreement and the copular *be*, as well as the use of *got* as a perfective, possessive or existential marker (*He got go to Japan* 'He has been to Japan', *The car got problem* 'There is a problem with the car'). Within the noun phrase, articles tend not to be used (*She got car or not?* 'Does she have a car?'). Zero pluralization is common in count nouns (*She buy ticket for us already* 'She has already bought us the tickets'). Colloquial Singapore English is also characterized by pro-drop (*Always late!* 'You are always late!'), object-preposing (*The car don't know whether expensive or not* 'I don't know whether the car is expensive'), question formation with an invariant tag (*He watch television, is it?* 'He's watching television, is he?'), and the use of the Malay word *kena* in the passive voice (*The thief kena caught by the police* 'The thief was caught by the police').

5   Jill

This brief discussion of colloquial and standard Singapore English will suffice to situate our appreciation of the English used by the Eurasians, as illustrated by Jill.[5] Jill is a Eurasian woman, very proud of her heritage and

---

[5] The Eurasian Association put me in touch with Jill (a pseudonym) after I asked for volunteers who might be willing to carry a small recorder for about a week or so. My original

actively involved with the Eurasian Association. Jill is 40 years old. She has 'O'-levels and is presently a full-time homemaker, married with two young boys. The elder boy is 8 years old and the younger is 4 years old. Her parents are both in their 70s, and both have primary school education. Her father was a technician in the telephone service and her mother worked as a telephone operator. She has a lot of pride in her own use of English, and is also very conscious of ensuring that her children speak good English.

The data presented here are taken from two different situations.[6] In the first, Jill is conversing with her parents. This takes place in Jill's car. Jill is driving, and the conversation involves various topics, including home repairs, the children in Jill's neighbourhood, and hiring a domestic helper. In the second, Jill is having dinner with a visitor as well as her two young sons, Joseph and Alan. She is trying to maintain a conversation with the visitor, whilst disciplining her sons who are fighting amongst themselves and refusing to finish their food.

I want to draw attention to the fact that there is clearly some degree of style-shifting involved between the two situations, as Jill first converses with her own parents, and then is involved in an interaction where she now assumes the role of parent. When she is talking to her own parents, Jill's speech is more colloquial, but when talking to her children, it moves closer to the standard. The shift from a more colloquial to a more standard English is less evident in her pronunciation features than in her morphosyntax. However, even her more colloquial use of English is significantly more standard than general descriptions of colloquial Singapore English would lead us to expect. In other words, even on the occasions when Jill style-shifts 'downwards' towards the colloquial variety, she still stays relatively close to the standard.

---

intention was to have volunteers who were in their 70s (the age of Jill's parents), since I was hoping to focus on the use of English among the older generation. However, in the recordings, Jill's speech was clearest since she was often closer to the recorder than the other interlocutors. Furthermore, her father was not in good health at the time, and spoke only infrequently and with some difficulty. As a result, I decided to shift the focus to Jill herself, as an example of contemporary use of English. The fact that Jill was involved in two different situations, one showing her interaction with the previous generation (her parents) and one showing her interaction with the younger generation (her children) is an unexpected bonus that allows for some interesting comparisons. Funding for this research project came from the National University of Singapore FASS Research Support Scheme (FY 2007).

[6] Transcription key:

Brackets with three dots { . . . }: indecipherable speech
Hash sign #: pause
Brackets within a turn [ ]: interruption
J: Jill; JF: Jill's father; JM: Jill's mother; Jo: Joseph; Al: Alan; V: Visitor

5.1   *Jill with her parents*

D4

1	J:	But the problem is that, as you say, lah, because there's no tiles so that round the area will be white cement correct? . . . Toh gave me one # six hundred over so
2	JF:	Around there, lah.
3	J:	But I, I mean, I can't
4	JF:	[You're, you're converting from the { . . . }]
5	J:	[Yah, this I know . . . you know, not me, lah, but he has to pay a bit more . . .]
		. . .
6	J:	Yesterday both fighting for the toilet, alamak!
7	JM:	Who?
8	J:	Joe and Alan, lah! Both got. One wants to pee, one wants to go and loo.
9	JF:	Both got?
10	J:	Yah, but they forget there's one bathroom in my house . . .
		. . .
11	JF:	Oh, look at the rain there [. . .] main road [. . .]
12	J:	Actually I'm quite happy it's raining. I said I'm quite happy it's raining because, I tell you, it's so hot.
		. . .
13	J:	My doorbell, five o'clock always will ring . . . and they all run out and they're playing . . .

Jill's pronunciation is generally quite close to the standard. For example, she aspirates the voiceless plosives in *tiles* (turn 1) and *tell* (turn 12), and maintains the distinction between interdental fricatives and alveolar stops. Elsewhere though (not shown in the above extract), she pronounces *cul-de-sac* as [kʰuːl di suk].

Jill uses various Singapore English colloquialisms, including the highly versatile pragmatic particle *lah* (which indicates the speaker's mood/attitude and appeals to the addressee to accommodate that mood/attitude) (turns 1, 5, 8), and the Malay interjection *alamak* (which is an expression of shock/dismay) (turn 6). Note that *lah* initially appears in her father's speech (turn 2). Other colloquial features are the omission of the auxiliary verb (*both fighting*) (turn 6) and the use of *got* as a perfective (turn 8), which is echoed in the father's question (turn 9). A less elliptical use of *got* would be *Both got fight*. Finally, Jill's use of *loo* as a verb (turn 8) is rather uncommon in colloquial Singapore English, and could be fairly specific to her own family. Despite these colloquialisms, Jill's speech still is fairly standard. Most of her utterances show number agreement: *one wants to* (turn 8), *he has to pay* (turn 5), and *they're playing* (turn 13).

5.2   *Jill with her sons*

D5

1   A: I think school is fun# it has a lot of great stuff . . .
                Actually at school, at my school we we run a lot of programs like
                # Food From The Heart and next time, it's going t-going to be
                Toys From The Heart?

2   V: Toys, oh yes.
                . . .

3   A: He's got my glasses case!

4   J: Put it down, I will smack you! Put it back where you found it #
                one # two # put food in your mouth, Alan, lets go.
                . . .

5   Jo: He keeps hitting my knee!

6   J: I will send you to the kitchen # ok, I will # Pick up your fork
                and spoon and # eat nicely!
                . . .

7   J: Joseph, Alan, I'm talking about something else. I'm not gonna
                talk about spelling right now. You just listen. I'm trying to have
                a conversation with { . . . } it cannot be that you interrupt and
                interrupt all the time. It's very rude. Alan, you eat now.
                . . .

8   J: See, again! # Eat your food. The mere fact that you can talk
                means your mouth is not full. Put food in your mouth. Joseph, I
                already have a hard time with Alan, please.

The colloquialisms that were noted in D4, such as the use of *lah* and *alamak*,
are absent. This is especially noteworthy given that, in D5, Jill is scolding
her boys, and one could reasonably expect various particles and interjections
to be used – but none are. Jill's utterances consistently show attention to
number and tense, except in the case of imperatives. We see this in *I will send
you to the kitchen* (turn 6), *I'm trying to have a conversation* (turn 7), and the
various imperatives found in turns 4, 6, 7 and 8. Even Jill's children speak
English that is more standard than colloquial, both when speaking to a visitor
(turn 1) – which might be expected – and when speaking to Jill herself (turns
3 and 5).

It is possible that the presence of Jill's visitor is a key factor that induces
both Jill and her children to avoid the more colloquial features, so that in the
absence of the visitor, we might actually see more colloquialisms emerging.
This cannot be ruled out entirely, of course – but it is worth noting that
the interaction between Jill and her children seems to be fairly informal
and unconstrained by the visitor's presence. Also, there are parts of the
conversation (omitted here because of the material's sensitivity) when Jill is
discussing fairly salacious aspects of her family history with the visitor. This
suggests that the visitor is in fact a close family friend.

6   Concluding remarks

In Singapore's early colonial history, the Eurasians were able to distinguish themselves from the other ethnic groups and in the process acquire a fair degree of socioeconomic benefits, due in no small part to their familiarity with the English language. However, in modern-day Singapore, the state's positioning of English as an interethnic lingua franca and its insistence that all Singaporeans be proficient in the language have led to a massive language shift over the last thirty years or so (Li Wei, Saravanan and Ng Lee Hoon 1997: 368). The result has been a dramatic increase in the number of Singaporeans growing up with English as a home language across all ethnic groups (Kwan-Terry and Luke 1997: 296; Pakir 1993: 75). This means that the Eurasians' claim for English as their mother tongue (on the basis that this is the language they grew up with) is increasingly also applicable to Singaporeans of all ethnicities.[7]

The English spoken amongst the Eurasians has therefore become significantly less distinct as the language continues to be increasingly spoken by Singaporeans of various ethnicities, and as these different ethnicities continue to interact. The Eurasians can, however, be justifiably proud of their role as 'early adopters' of English, with many Eurasian families tracing a history of English proficiency back many generations. It is this sense of historical pride that motivates contemporary Eurasians like Jill to speak English well, and also to ensure that the next generation of Eurasians does the same.

References

Ansaldo, Umberto. 2004. 'The evolution of Singapore English.' In Lisa Lim, ed. *Singapore English: A Grammatical Description*. Amsterdam: John Benjamins, 127–49.

Asiapac Editorial. 2003. *Gateway to Eurasian culture*. Singapore: Asiapac Books.

Benjamin, Geoffrey. 1976. 'The cultural logic of Singapore's "multiracialism".' In Riaz Hassan, ed. *Singapore: Society in Transition*. Kuala Lumpur: Oxford University Press, 115–33.

Braga-Blake, Myrna. 1992. 'Eurasians in Singapore: An overview.' In Myrna Braga-Blake, ed., with Ann Ebert-Oehlers. *Singapore Eurasians*. Singapore: Eurasian Association/Times Editions, 11–23.

Clarke, Louise. 1992. 'Within a stone's throw: Eurasian enclaves.' In Myrna Braga-Blake, ed., with Ann Ebert-Oehlers. *Singapore Eurasians*. Singapore: Eurasian Association/Times Editions, 51–65.

Gupta, Anthea Fraser. 1994. *The Step-tongue: Children's English in Singapore*. Clevedon: Multilingual Matters.

---

[7] Rather than seeing this as a reason to reconsider the position that English is not acceptable as an official mother tongue, the state has decided to continue with its policy of recognizing only Mandarin, Malay and Tamil. The main concession has been a re-examination and simplification of the mother tongue syllabus so that students who come from English-speaking homes have a more realistic chance of passing their language exams.

Han, Fook Kwang, Warren Fernandez, and Sumiko Tan. 1998. *Lee Kuan Yew: The Man and his Ideas*. Singapore: Times.

Hill, Michael, and Lian Kwen Fee. 1995. *The Politics of Nation Building and Citizenship in Singapore*. London: Routledge.

Kwan-Terry, Ann, and Luke Kwan Kwong. 1997. 'Tradition, trial and error: Standard and vernacular literacy in China, Hong Kong, Singapore and Malaysia.' In Andrée Tabouret-Keller, Robert B. Le Page, Penelope Gardner-Chloros and Gabriella Varro, eds. *Vernacular Literacy: A Re-evaluation*. Oxford: Clarendon Press, 271–315.

Lim, Lisa, ed. 2004. *Singapore English: A Grammatical Description*. Amsterdam: John Benjamins.

Lim, Lisa and Joseph A. Foley. 2004. 'English in Singapore and Singapore English.' In Lisa Lim, ed. *Singapore English: A Grammatical Description*. Amsterdam: John Benjamins, 1–18.

Li Wei, Vanithamani Saravanan and Julia Ng Lee Hoon. 1997. 'Language shift in the Teochew community in Singapore: A family domain analysis.' *Journal of Multilingual and Multicultural Development* 18/5: 364–84.

Pakir, Anne. 1993. 'Two tongue-tied: Bilingualism in Singapore.' *Journal of Multilingual and Multicultural Development* 14/1–2: 73–90.

Platt, John and Heidi Weber. 1980. *English in Singapore and Malaysia: Status, Features, Functions*. Kuala Lumpur: Oxford University Press.

Rappa, Antonio L. 2000. 'Surviving the Politics of Late Modernity: The Eurasian Fringe Community.' *Southeast Asian Journal of Social Science* 28/2: 153–80.

Rappa, Antonio and Lionel Wee. 2006. *Language Policy and Modernity in Southeast Asia: Malaysia, Philippines, Singapore, Thailand*. New York: Springer.

Wee, Lionel. 2002. 'When English is not a mother tongue: Linguistic ownership and the Eurasian community in Singapore.' *Journal of Multilingual and Multicultural Development* 23/4: 282–95.

   2004a. 'Singapore English: Phonology.' In Bernd Kortmann, Edgar W. Schneider, Kate Burridge, Rajend Mesthrie and Clive Upton, eds. *A Handbook of Varieties of English*, vol. II: *Morphology and Syntax*. Berlin: Mouton de Gruyter, 1017–33.

   2004b. 'Singapore English: Morphology and syntax.' In Bernd Kortmann, Edgar W. Schneider, Kate Burridge, Rajend Mesthrie and Clive Upton, eds. *A Handbook of Varieties of English*, vol II: *Morphology and Syntax*. Berlin: Mouton de Gruyter, 1058–72.

   2004c. 'Reduplication and discourse particles.' In Lisa Lim, ed. *Singapore English: A Grammatical Description*. Amsterdam: John Benjamins, 105–26.

Wee, Lionel and Umberto Ansaldo. 2004. 'Nouns and noun phrases.' In Lisa Lim, ed. *Singapore English: A Grammatical Description*. Amsterdam: John Benjamins, 57–74.

17   Peranakan English in Singapore

LISA LIM

1   Introduction

> We Peranakans have our own way or style of speaking that has become our
> trademark, which those outside the community recognise instantly, be it in
> English, Malay or Chinese. One Nyonya, for instance, tells me she is never
> surprised when people she meets for the first time straightaway say 'Ah,
> you are Peranakan, right?'
>
> Anthony Oei and Peter Lee, editorial, *The Peranakan*, Jul/Sep 2002

The Peranakans – also known as Peranakan Chinese, Babas or Straits (-born)
Chinese, and even the 'King's Chinese' – are the descendants of Southern
Chinese traders who settled in Southeast Asia and local Malay/Indonesian
women. An introduction such as this already provides a titillating idea of both
the origins of the community and the input that would have gone into the
formation not only of their vernacular, Baba Malay, for which they are most
well known, but also of their variety of English. While the word *Peranakan*
(pronounced [pranakán]), derived from the Malay root *anak* 'child', meaning
a locally born person, is also used to refer to other mixed communities in
Malaysia and Indonesia,[1] this chapter describes the English spoken by the
Peranakan Chinese community in Singapore.

These days, there is of course a much more recognizable and well-known
variety of English which has developed in this island city-state, namely

I thank Umberto Ansaldo for our constant discussions on the Peranakan community and
its languages, as well as for his suggestions regarding how to construe the variation in
Peranakan English. I also acknowledge Salikoko Mufwene for his view of the Peranakans
being the founder population in the evolution of SE (though this is not developed here),
as well as the individuals betul-baba?, bunga-telang, wonjyunyun, Emeric and helen who
responded to my query on the Peranakan Association's website forum regarding numbers of
Peranakans and the notion of Peranakan English. Above all, my heartfelt appreciation goes
to my consultants, who have, all these years, gladly put up with being scrutinized, recorded,
and interrogated, even during the most intimate of family gatherings: I hope this article does
justice to our heritage.
[1] For example, the Jawi Peranakan in Penang and Singapore are offspring of mixed unions
between South Indian Muslims and Malay women (Tan 1988a: 26); the Chitty Melaka
(Tamil *chitty* 'merchant') or Peranakan Indians of Malacca and later Singapore are the result
of contact between early South Indian settlers and indigenous Malay, Javanese or Nyonya
women (Dhoraisingam 2006: xi).

Singapore English (see e.g. Lim 2004a), which a critical mass – and a rapidly growing number – of Singaporeans now speak natively. This was not however always the case. During the early days of Singapore's existence, from pre-colonial times through to the first years after independence from Britain (for an account of the different eras, see Lim 2007, in press), English was a language in the repertoire of a very small minority. Up to the 1970s and early 1980s, English would have been increasingly acquired by the majority of the local population as a school language, but not to a high level of proficiency, and would not be considered a dominant language for them (see e.g. Platt, Weber and Ho 1983, whose 'Singapore English' speakers had English education ranging from a few years in primary school to the four years in secondary school). It is only from around the late 1980s that we can recognize a country that is English-speaking and English-dominant with a growing body of native (Singapore) English speakers (see Lim and Foley 2004 for details).

Nonetheless, even before the emergence of Singapore English, there were a number of communities in Singapore for whom (a variety of) English was a mother tongue or at least a dominant (home) language in a multilingual repertoire (Lim in press). It was naturally the language of the Europeans who were residing in the British colony at the time, namely the British, Americans and others. It was also the language of other communities such as the Armenians, and some Indians and Ceylonese (Bloom 1986), many of the latter two groups recruited from then-Ceylon (Sri Lanka) and India during colonial times for the teaching profession (Ho and Platt 1993: 6), in particular before the late 1920s when Chinese teachers started outnumbering all other ethnic groups. Crucially, it was also the dominant language of two indigenous communities. Many of the Eurasians, a mixed community of local and Portuguese or Dutch extraction had English as a mother tongue (Braga-Blake 1992: 12–13), and theirs would be a particular Eurasian English (Gupta 1994: 37, 44; Wee, this volume). An English-dominant repertoire was also increasingly the case for the Peranakans in Singapore, who were one of the earliest groups in Singapore to have held a high regard for English-medium education and sent their children to English-medium schools. The variety that evolved may be considered Peranakan English, which, as the opening quote shows, while perhaps lesser-known in the wider world, is certainly well known and instantly recognized in the local context.

2   Sociolinguistic history and current status

2.1   Sociolinguistic history of the Peranakans

In order to appreciate the status and features of Peranakan English (PE), an account of the origins of the community is necessary[2] – this is not only

---

[2] The account here is necessarily distilled, and more comprehensive coverage may be found in Ansaldo, Lim and Mufwene (2007) and Ansaldo (2009). While this chapter is about

fascinating from a sociohistorical point of view, but also vital for understanding the evolution of PE and its features, as well as the status it had and still has as a variety of English.

2.1.1 'Locally born' origins and acculturation

The Chinese had been an important maritime and trade power in Southeast Asia from as early as the twelfth century, with one of the most prominent figures being Zheng He, who, in command of an extensive fleet, and leading expeditions to Southeast and South Asia more than eight times in the early fifteenth century, apparently established small communities along the route (Pan 2000). It is believed that the earliest Chinese stable trade colonies date back to this period, though it should also be noted that Chinese settlers in Malacca were already reported to be found during their expeditions (Tan 1988a: 28–9). A longer-lasting Chinese maritime empire developed in the sixteenth and seventeenth centuries, led particularly by Fujian-based traders (Pan 2000: 49), who are said to be among the earliest to actually settle down in Southeast Asian ports and establish local communities (Norman 1988). By the time the Europeans, led by the Portuguese, started trade colonies in the sixteenth century in the 'East Indies' – the region extending either from India or from Malaysia to New Guinea – they found several Chinese-based communities already established; in Malacca, in particular, they encountered the demographically most important Peranakan colonies. Later, once Singapore was established as a British trading post in 1819 (to later become a Crown Colony of Britain in 1867, forming together with Malacca and Penang the Straits Settlements), many Malacca Babas moved there in the early nineteenth century, attracted by the trading opportunities which arose there (Pakir 1986). Additionally, there was a great influx of immigrants from southern China, South Asia, Malaysia and the Indonesian archipelago; as a result, Singapore's population increased dramatically from a few hundred to over half a million by 1931, the largest and most swiftly growing proportion of this being the Chinese.

   Quite typical of the time, the Chinese traders consisted of men, the women staying behind to take care of their households and to observe filial piety and ancestor worship (Lim 1967: 63–5), female emigration being strongly discouraged by the Manchu regime (Tan 1988a: 34). The women who did get brought over to the Straits Settlements were there for the purpose of prostitution, and by the nineteenth century they comprised a significant proportion of the Chinese women there (Tan 1988a: 35). Nonetheless, in Malaya, Chinese women were still greatly outnumbered by Chinese men – by four to one in 1881 in Malaya, and by fifteen to one in 1864 in Singapore (Liu 1999: 85) – an imbalance which unsurprisingly led to frequent interethnic

---

the Peranakan Chinese in Singapore, history requires much mention of Malacca, as the Singapore Peranakans came from Malacca in the first instance.

marriages involving local women. Marriages to non-Muslim women, often slaves of Balinese, Bugis or Javanese origin, required no religious conversion (Tan 1988a: 40–1; Pan 2000), while those marriages which involved Muslim Malay women entailed conversion of the males to Islam in only a subset, and in general, such conversion was clearly nominal: this can be seen in the fact that the Chinese generally continued observance of Chinese folk religion and brought up their children as Chinese (Skinner 1960: 96–7; Tan 1988a: 38f). The first description of such a community seems to be by Crawfurd (1856: 96, in Tan 1988a: 44), who wrote that 'the settlers, whenever it is in their power, form connections with the native women of the country; and hence has arisen a mixed race, numerous in the older settlements, known to the Malays under name of Paranakan China [*cina* 'Chinese']'. Gradually, especially once the community attained a critical mass, marriages between Baba men, Nyonya women and locals was discouraged, and an endogamous practice established (Lim 1917: 876–877, in Tan 1988a: 37, 47).

The new hybrid culture that emerged in this context shows unique traits that set the Peranakans apart from other Chinese, the more indigenous local populations, and other ethnically mixed groups (Rudolph 1998; Tan 1988b). Non-linguistic examples include a mixed Nyonya cuisine largely influenced by Malay traditions, and the wearing of Malay/Indonesian sarong and kebaya (instead of the Chinese dress) by the women. These contrast with the retention of Chinese rituals, such as religious practices mentioned above and traditional wedding customs involving imperial-era wedding costumes (Tan 1988b: 299). According to some observers, the Peranakans had 'lost touch with China in every respect, except that they continued to uphold Chinese customs, and to practice, in variously modified forms, the social and religious practices of the forefathers' (Lim 1917, in Kwok 2000: 202 and Tan 1988a: 47).

Linguistically, a new variety known as Baba Malay (BM) developed as the mother tongue of the community, distinct from other Malay varieties due partly to the large amount of Chinese influence on it, particularly from Hokkien, Teochew and Cantonese.[3] By around the nineteenth century, the Peranakans had shifted to BM as their only vernacular: Song (1923: 3) refers to this period in his observation that 'in Malacca, however, where the Chinese had formed a continuous colony for about six centuries, the women-folk had entirely dropped the use of Chinese, while the Malacca-born Chinese males only acquired the Hokkien dialect colloquially for the purpose of trade'.

---

[3] While Ansaldo and Matthews (1999) note several grammatical similarities between Hokkien and BM which can be attributed to Hokkien substrate influence or the congruence of the latter and non-standard Malay varieties, they also acknowledge the presence and potential influence of other southern Chinese groups and languages, such as Teochew and Hakka.

2.1.2 British affiliations

The majority of the non-Peranakan Chinese in nineteenth-century Singapore continued harbouring plans to return to China: statistics from 1881 up to the 1960s show not only a continuous stream of Chinese immigration but also return emigration (Kwok 2000: 200). Where the Peranakans were concerned, however, while the early Chinese males may have returned regularly to China to ship more goods, and the sons of the wealthier ones (a minority) to receive education[4] (Lim 1917: 876), they always returned to the Straits; in fact, the Peranakans considered Malacca and Singapore their home. Until as recently as the 1950s, only the Straits Chinese could be considered 'permanent', 'native', or indigenized Chinese communities in the region (Song 1923, in Kwok 2000: 205).

It may be surmised that it is due in no small part to the fact that they had been in the region longer, more continuously and more permanently than the other Chinese immigrants that the Peranakans formed the larger proportion of the influential class of Chinese capitalists in the Straits Settlements, as a result of the mining of gold and tin, the large-scale commercial agriculture business (in gambier, pepper, tapioca, and especially rubber), import-export business, and other economic enterprises that had been drawing Chinese to Malacca for years (Tan 1988a: 48). By the time of the European exploitation and colonization of the region in the nineteenth century, most Babas of Malacca had accumulated much wealth and become prestigious subgroups in the region, forming separate communities of their own and distinguishing themselves from later Chinese immigrants, referring to them derogatorily as *sinkeh* 'new guests' = 'new arrivals', considered poor and with low social status (Tan 1988a: 45). In Malacca, the well-off Baba were able to take over the houses of the great Dutch merchants in Heeren Street which then became 'the fashionable and aristocratic resort of the Chinese' (Braddell 1853: 74). In Penang, it was also noted that the Chinese, 'who have long been settled in the place, and who have wedded native wives, dwell in large and elegant houses environed with fruit and flower-gardens' (Thomson 1875: 13, in Tan 1988a: 51).

In Singapore as well, it is widely agreed (see e.g. Kwok 2000: 202) that the Babas were a class apart from the other ethnic groups. Although small in number ('Malacca men' comprised only 2.5 per cent of the Chinese population in 1848, growing to just 9.5 per cent in 1881), their social and economic influence was disproportionately strong in comparison, and they formed an important sector of the local elite (Kwok 2000: 202–4). The Peranakans were seen, for instance, to be the 'more enlightened, and better merchants' (Earl 1837: 363). Singapore-born Peranakan Lim Nee Soon, for example,

---

[4] This is supported by a study of emigrant communities in South China, according to which there were in the emigrant villages and especially in the schools supported by the emigrants in southeast Asia 'many boys of partly Malay blood' (Chen 1939: 143).

by the 1920s controlled most of the rubber which was cultivated, at one time more than 8,000 hectares in Singapore as well as in Malaya – this together with tin drove Singapore's prosperity in the late nineteenth to twentieth centuries (Liu 1999: 98); he was also the 'Pineapple King' of the major pineapple industry (Liu 1999: 152). Another Peranakan, Tan Jiak Kim, was one of the founders of the Straits Steamship Company (Liu 1999: 162). But it was not only in business that they excelled. Peranakans Lim Boon Keng and Tan Keong Saik were early advocates of education for girls (Liu 1999:162), and the latter's daughter Tan Teck Neo was indeed tutored in English, and later founded the Chinese Women's Association. She and her husband Lee Choon Guan were also well known for Mandalay Villa, their home by the sea which was one of the great houses of pre-war Singapore (Liu 1999: 225). This was not an uncommon phenomenon, as the Peranakans were wealthy enough to afford weekend retreats or second homes in the form of seaside bungalows, some of which even boasted swimming enclosures, in the east coast of the island, which had become increasingly attractive as a residential area from the end of the nineteenth century (Liu 1999: 148). The Peranakans were certainly seen as the best educated, the wealthiest, and the most intelligent section of the Chinese community (Nathan 1922: 77).

What is also significant is the kind of education they received. Since the early nineteenth century, English had become an increasingly important language in southeast Asia, and the Peranakans were among the privileged few who acquired and benefited from it (Pan 2000: 172). They held a high regard for English-medium education and sent their children to English-medium schools. The establishment by members of the community of four early educational institutions – the Anglo-Chinese College of Malacca (1818), Penang Free School (1816), Singapore Institution (1823; later, renamed the Raffles Institution, 1868), and Malacca Free School (1826, Malacca High School since 1878) – was especially important to the development of the community (Tan 1988a: 52). While in earlier days they were noted to have spoken English 'tolerably well' (Earl 1837, in Tan 1988a: 50), by the mid nineteenth century their ability to converse in this colonial language had strengthened their prominent socioeconomic position within other local communities in relation to the British, to the point where they were in fact sometimes referred to as the 'King's Chinese' (Tan 1988a: 53), in reference to the King of England. The establishment of the Queen's Scholarship in 1885 for British subjects in the Straits Settlements further enabled a few Peranakans to be educated in higher institutions in Britain, producing scholars and leaders such as Song Ong Siang and Lim Boon Keng (Tan 1988a: 65, 82). Many of them worked for the Dutch and British East India Companies (Tan 1988a: 51f.). Their closer contact with British administrators and merchants due to their command of the English language, together with their predominance in the commercial sectors, and their knowledge of Malay and the local ways, afforded them a significant role as intermediaries between Europeans, locals and Asian newcomers (Tan 1988a; Kwok 2000).

They additionally distinguished themselves from the continuously increasing population of China-oriented immigrants by their local (Malayan) orientation and their pro-British sentiments (Tan 1988a: 54f.). Not an uncommon observation then was for Peranakans 'on being asked if they were Chinamen [to] bristle up and say in an offended tone "I am not a Chinaman, I am a British subject"' (Vaughan 1879). In their social clubs, 'to which they will admit no native of China . . . they play billiards, bowls, and other European games, and drink brandy and soda ad libitum' (ibid.). Identifying politically with the British (Kwok 2000: 205), they formed the Straits Chinese British Association (SCBA) in August 1900,[5] with an admitted aim to promote trade with, and foster loyalty to, the British Empire (Song 1923: 319), and – significantly – with the language of the association being exclusively English. The first volume of *The Straits Chinese Magazine*, published in 1897, is, naturally, in English.

The growing importance of English among them as a lingua franca, as a vernacular and as an identity marker can be clearly seen in the debates that arose during the mid twentieth century regarding the increasing shift around this period to English as the only vernacular, even while there is no doubt that most Peranakans identified themselves with BM (Tan 1988b). While BM had competed fairly well with English as a lingua franca until the early twentieth century, by the end of the 1960s English had almost completely prevailed de facto as the means of interethnic communication par excellence (Rudolph 1998: 335).

Today English is certainly the Singapore Peranakan's language: even if, in the BM revitalization thrust of recent decades, the material which is deliberately produced for the purposes of maintenance, revitalization and the display of cultural expression centres around BM (e.g. Peranakan plays, musical performances, the production of a Baba Malay dictionary and the collection of Baba Malay idioms), when language is used more instrumentally, in the dissemination of information via the association's newsletter and website, at association meetings, in speeches at events, it is English that is used.

2.2   Current status of Peranakan English

It is difficult to establish the number of Peranakan English speakers today simply because it is a challenge estimating numbers of Peranakans in the first place, for two main reasons. To begin with, the Peranakans are not officially

---

[5] The Malacca branch of SCBA was formed in October of the same year (1900), and the Penang branch was founded later in 1920. The Associations are all still extremely active to date, the Singapore one renamed The Peranakan Association.

recognized as a separate ethnic group in Singapore, but are counted within that of 'Chinese', thus no official census figures are available (cf. the Eurasians who are considered one of the founding races of Singapore and in some circumstances are recognized as a category on their own, distinct from the 'Others'; see Wee, this volume). Nor does the Peranakan Association, to my knowledge, have any figures either. Furthermore, the increase in marriages in recent decades between Peranakans and non-Peranakans poses problems for identification: is someone who is half- or quarter-Peranakan still considered a Peranakan? We can nonetheless attempt a rough approximation. The number of Baba Malay-speakers in Singapore two decades ago is estimated at some 5,000 fluent and semi-fluent speakers (Pakir 1986: 9). We can safely assume that these would by and large be Peranakans of about 35 to 40 years and above (the younger generations not speaking BM). Some of the oldest of these would possibly not speak English, and in any case, would not be alive now. We may perhaps also exclude the younger generations, since it is quite likely that their variety of English, at least for the most part or in most domains, is more Singapore English rather than Peranakan English (though see the analysis in section 3). Given the above considerations, we may perhaps estimate there to be fewer than 5,000 PE speakers today.

As suggested in the opening quote, the English spoken by the Peranakans has always been considered 'good English', not only because the community was one of the earliest indigenous groups to be educated in the language and to have it as a native language, but possibly also in no small part due to the status that the community itself has had in Singapore.

3   Features of Peranakan English

3.1   The Peranakan English corpora

There is no research to date on the English of the Peranakans, all attention having been paid to what is considered their vernacular, Baba Malay. The description sketched here has been put together for the purpose of this chapter, and is based on the following: (a) an audio recording in a Peranakan household in May 2003, comprising 75 minutes, and involving three generations of Peranakans; and (b) the corpus of newsletters published by the Peranakan Association, dating from 1994 to the present, with an average of three to four issues per year (Peranakan Association 1994–2008). Together they afford us insights into characteristics of PE in both spoken and written form.

Because the assumption made in this chapter is that the English of younger generations (below c. 40 years of age) may already show levelling towards Singapore English, in general, data from Peranakans of the middle and older generation (c. 40 years of age and above) are considered more representative of Peranakan English. The ability to select appropriate material in the written corpus is possible due to the author's familiarity with the community and consequently the writers of articles or editorials in the newsletters. In the analysis of the spoken corpus, however, a comparison with the younger generation's PE is also made as it allows highlighting of certain characteristics of the older generations' speech.

3.2 Spoken Peranakan English

Observations of features of spoken PE are based on a typical conversation in a three-generation family that regularly gathers on Sunday for family lunch. A brief account of the participants in this conversation is necessary for establishing their repertoires; it also provides further and more specific details of the sociolinguistic situation of the community already sketched in section 2.[6]

CKT (b. 1921), second daughter of an eminent Peranakan compradore and philanthropist,[7] grew up speaking BM and English with her parents and husband[8] when they were alive, but primarily English with her siblings, as well as some BM; she also spoke Cantonese with the live-in Cantonese maid, and Hokkien at the market. She attended the Methodist Girls' School, as did the other three sisters, where the majority of the teachers were American missionaries, and where the language medium was English, with Latin being taught as a subject. She studied there up until she was 16 years old, completing her Senior Cambridge examinations, after which she went to the Teachers' Training College. Note that only those who obtained the highest level of

---

[6] This is based on interviews conducted in September 2002.

[7] Cheong Keong Tuan (CKT)'s family's settlement in the region can be traced along her paternal line to her great-great-grandfather, Cheong Joo Keng, who sailed from China to Malacca in the early 1800s. Three generations on, her father, Cheong Koon Seng (b. 1880), educated, like many other Babas then, at the Anglo-Chinese School where the teachers were American missionaries, was a renowned auctioneer, philanthropist (making donations particularly to schools such as his alma mater), and founder President of the Chinese Swimming Club. Her mother, Chia Siew Tin (b. 1896) went to the Singapore Chinese Girls' School, where the teachers were English missionaries. She studied there up until Standard 5 when she turned about 12. She could read and write, and sign her name, and is remembered for having won a prize for reading *Little Lord Fauntleroy*. As can be seen, the Peranakans were certainly in command of English, at a time (late 1800s and early 1900s) when it would have been rare for non-Peranakans, especially girls, to be given formal education, in particular English education. Cheong Keong Tuan's grandfather on the maternal side, Chia Hood Theam, was a third-generation Peranakan, and was a one-time compradore of the Mercantile Bank in Singapore

[8] CKT's husband, Koh Kong Hai (b. 1910), spoke Baba Malay to his parents. His father Koh Sek Lim, originally from Malacca, owned a large stretch of coastal land at the eastern end of Singapore, on which estate the family grew up fishing, sailing and hunting. With his siblings, while Baba Malay was predominant, English was also used. He attended St Andrew's School until Secondary 3 when he was about 15 years of age; there the teachers were English missionaries. Because he was proficient in English, he became a foreman in a government office, which raised his social status in relation to Asians, as he worked directly under the British, in charge of distributing the weekly salary to the Singaporean civil servants.

Grade 1 in English could go on to train to become teachers, and the only ones who could do this at that time were the Eurasians and the Peranakans, those who typically were proficient and fluent in English.

MK (b. 1942), eldest daughter of CKT, grew up speaking English with her parents and her siblings and the rest of the extended family, along with a certain amount of Baba Malay, and has no Chinese languages in her repertoire. She attended a convent school where the teachers were Irish nuns as well as Eurasians and Peranakans. As a young girl in school, in an essay on herself, MK started off writing 'I am an English girl' – a telling sign of how anglicized the Peranakans had become.[9] LKL (b. 1939) is MK's husband, whose mother tongue is Hokkien, but with his mother being Peranakan (but who died when he was young) he also has BM in his repertoire. He learnt English in school and eventually went to English-medium St Joseph's Institution where many of the teachers were priests from Britain.

LL (b. 1969) and JL (b. 1972) are MK's daughters, who grew up with English as their first and dominant language. Exposed to BM passively when in the company of their grandparents' generation, they speak it minimally. Both studied Mandarin in school as a second language (in line with Singapore's bilingual education system, since they are considered 'Chinese' and must have a Chinese 'Mother Tongue'), but use it in very limited domains for basic functional purposes.

Dialogue D1[10] illustrates CKT's PE speech, representative of the oldest generation. Prompted by a discussion of foetal alcohol syndrome, she passes comments on the effects that drinking and other factors can have on a foetus. Her commentary continues over a span of some two minutes, alongside the description by MK of the story, interspersed with comments or responses from other participants; for our analysis, only CKT's turns are presented in this extract.

D1

1   CKT   When you think of having babies, don[t] drink! . . . For one year! . . . Abstinence. Really clean . . . your system. You never know what you get.

2   CKT   Like drugs you know when you're under drugs . . . The babies come out crying crying. *Apa dia mo? mo?* Drugs. *Nanti* alcohol the same. They get into their system.

3   CKT   *Kita semua tak drin[k]* . . . Keep yourself clean and healthy. Don[t] drin[k] don[t] drin[k]. Don[t] say oh it's only beer never min[d]. beer also has alcohol!

9   Such anecdotes are not uncommon. A similar one is related by D. Lee (b. 1958), a prominent figure of the Baba community who, as a boy with a father who was 'more English than the English', grew up believing he was English. It was only on his arrival in England to continue his education that he was disillusioned in his discovery that he was a Chinese Singaporean.
10   In the extracts, the following transcription conventions are used: . . . pause; *** indecipherable speech; { overlapping speech; [ ] segment not realized; *italics* Baba Malay.

4	CKT	Before you get the child, you mus[t] already tell yourself, if you're going to have children, you very well keep your blood clean.
5	CKT	And don[t] don[t] have furry animals also. You never know, you breathe the thing, it's carried in your blood system. . . . Go and get stuck somewhere in the chil[d] . . . also . . .
6	CKT	Animals! Animals also can affect . . . Very fine fur. Don't keep animals. And *chium-chium* them. Ee uh. Enough!
7	CKT	You want to have babies, you don't *ah*. One year you give yourself cleansing. . . . No alcohol.

Dialogue D2 illustrates an exchange between the various family members which, occurring over lunch, pertains to LL being encouraged to finish up a dish, the spicy chilli in the dish she is eating and the use of chilli sambal in a fish dish.

D2

8	LL	I can't finish this.
9	JL	{Yes you can . . . It's nothing!
10	LKL	{No lah you *** No need to finish.
11	JL	Just eat a fishball.
12	LL	I have had a fishball.
13	CKT	The fishball is nice. {It's mixed with meat. Isn't it?
14	MK	{Come on, Lisa! Sl- Plod along!
15	LL	Oh! This is so hot, this chilli!
16	MK	{Don[t] eat the chilli *lah*! Eat that nice long thing.
17	CKT	{Take the . . . Peel it out *lah*!
18	LL	Take out the this part?
19	CKT	{But already seedless . . . seedless.
20	LL	{There's no seeds anyway, they took the seed out, but it's really soaked through the–.
21	LKL	No, red, red chilli some of them are hot.
22	MK	Why you eat chilli? I never eat.
23	LL	Nice . . .
24	MK:	I always tell Daddy I dowan the chili . . . I only take the other things.
25	LL	Nice . . . if you–.
26	JL	This one can cook fish or what . . . Mama was saying . . . *ikan* . . .
27	LL	Huh?
28	JL	The chilli {can make fish.
29	CKT	{Ya can fry-fry . . . fish.

The first point to note about the spoken data is that PE speakers demonstrate variation between more acrolectal features approximating Standard British

Table 17.1 *Standard lexical sets for StdBrE, SSE, CSE and PE*

set number	keyword	StdBrE	SSE	CSE	PE
1	KIT	ɪ	ɪ	i	ɪ
2	DRESS	ɛ	ɛ	ɛ	ɛ
3	TRAP	æ	æ	ɛ	æ
4	LOT	ɒ	ɒ	ɒ	ɒ
5	STRUT	ʌ	ʌ	a	ʌ
6	FOOT	ʊ	ʊ	u	ʊ
7	BATH	ɑː	ɑː	a	ɑː
8	CLOTH	ɒ	ɒ	ɒ	ɒ
9	NURSE	ɜː	ɜː	ə	ɜː
10	FLEECE	Iː	iː	i	iː
11	FACE	eɪ	eɪ	e	eː
12	PALM	ɑː	ɑː	a	aː
13	THOUGHT	ɔː	ɔː	ɔ	ɔː
14	GOAT	əʊ	oʊ	o	oː
15	GOOSE	uː	uː	u	uː
16	PRICE	aɪ	aɪ	ai	aɪ
17	CHOICE	ɔɪ	ɔɪ	ɔi	ɔɪ
18	MOUTH	aʊ	aʊ	a	aʊ
19	NEAR	ɪə	ɪə	iə	ɪə
20	SQUARE	eə	ɛ	ɛ	ɛː
21	START	ɑː	ɑː	a	ɑː
22	NORTH	ɔː	ɔː	ɔ	ɔː
23	FORCE	ɔː	ɔː	ɔ	ɔː
24	POOR/CURE	ʊə	ʊə	uə	ʊə
25	happY	ɪ	i	i	I
26	lettER	ə	ə	ə	ə
27	commA	ə	ə	ə	ə

English, and more basilectal or vernacular (i.e. Baba Malay) features.[11] Such variation is observed in PE speakers of all generations, who readily display both acrolectal and vernacular features in a single conversation, and at times within a single turn or utterance.[12] In what follows, a brief description of characteristic features of PE, both acrolectal and vernacular, is made (in separate subsections, for systematicity and clarity), with reference to the data in Extracts (1) and (2).

3.2.1   Acrolectal Peranakan English features

The vowel system of PE is quite consistent, and is summarized in Table 17.1, using Wells' (1982) lexical sets, also showing Standard British English (StdBrE), Standard Singapore English (SSE) and Colloquial Singapore

---

[11]   As has been observed, English in Singapore can be spoken along a continuum of varieties (e.g. Platt and Weber 1980) and this surely applies to the English of the Peranakans.

[12]   Gupta (2001), in observing a similar pattern of variation in Singapore English speakers, considers this 'leaky diglossia', where a distinction between the use of Standard SE and colloquial SE is not maintained. I, however, find it more appropriate to view this as the unmarked pattern, and as a single code in its own right.

Table 17.2 *Consonants of PE*

	Bilabial	Labio-dental	Dental	Alveolar	Palato-alveolar	Palatal	Velar	Glottal
Plosive	p b			t d			k g	
Nasal	m			n			ŋ	
Fricative		f v	θ ð	s z	ʃ ʒ			h
Affricate					ʧ ʤ			
Approximant	(w)			r		j	w	
Lateral approximant				l				

English (CSE) for comparison (from Lim 2004b: 21; the comparisons with CSE in this section are based on Lim 2004b).

Vowel contrasts between the various lexical sets are as in StdBrE; in other words, PE has the same vowel phonemes as StdBrE, without the neutralization, in terms of quality and length, between sets as found in CSE such as those of KIT/FLEECE, DRESS/TRAP, and COT/CAUGHT, amongst others.

The consonants of PE, shown in Table 17.2, are also as in StdBrE. Some of their actual realizations differ depending on variation, and are described in the following sections.

Acrolectal PE features are observed in the oldest generation in Turns 1 and 4. Initial voiceless plosives in *clean* and *tell* are aspirated (though perhaps with shorter VOT than in StdBrE), and there is no TH-stopping in initial dental fricatives as in *think*; in final position these are also fully realized, as in *breathe* in Turn 5, unlike in CSE where they may also be realized as labiodental fricatives. Final plosives are not reinforced by or realized as glottal stops, but are maintained and often fully released, as in *drink* and *get* in Turn 1, and final voiced obstruents are not completely devoiced as they are in CSE. Intervocalic /r/ is realized as a tap, as seen in *very* and *furry* in Turns 4 and 5 respectively. Word stress patterns are also as in StdBrE: for example, in Turn 1, *abstinence* and *system* have primary stress on the initial syllable and a reduced vowel in the final. At the level of the sentence too, patterns of rhythmic and nuclear stress are quite standard. Morphosyntax and lexis need no particular comment, following standard patterns. In Turn 4, for example, standard usage of subordination is observed, in *If you're going to have children, you very well keep your blood clean.* And in Turn 13, CKT uses the question tag *isn't it?* to the utterance *The fishball is nice*; this contrasts with the typical CSE general purpose tag *is it?* used regardless of verb and polarity of the main clause. In lexis choice, the use of the phrase *Plod along!* by middle-generation speaker MK can also be seen to be very British.

As younger-generation Singaporeans, LL and JL may for the most part be considered SE speakers (see Lim and Foley 2004), and, especially in LL's case, usually display many CSE features in their speech. It is notable that, in contexts involving other PE speakers as in this conversation, their speech then tends to diverge from colloquial SE. In phonology, acrolectal features, as those noted for CKT above, are noted in Turns 8, 9, 11 and 12. Acrolectal features are also clearly seen in their prosodic patterns in the exchange in Turns 8 to 12 where focus on new or contrastive information is clearly marked by pitch prominence as follows: ‖ *I* ↗ *can't finish this.* ‖ ↗ *Yes you* ↗ *can.* | *It's* ↘ *nothing.* ‖ *Just* ′*eat a* ↘ *fishball.* ‖ *I* ↘ *have had a fishball.* ‖ This is in contrast to utterance-final prominence patterns (as opposed to focus) and the use of other phonetic cues of loudness and length noted for CSE.

In sum, the features outlined above, observed in all generations, already set PE apart from those of CSE, with acrolectal PE seen to approximate StdBrE. This is not unexpected, given the sociohistorical factors of the origins of PE. As outlined in sections 2.1.2 and 3.2, the Peranakans would have received education in mission schools where the variety of English imparted would have followed StdBrE norms (even if some teachers may have been Irish or American), and in some cases would have been educated in England. Furthermore, given their pro-British tendencies, as highlighted in section 2.1.2, the attitude towards adopting a variety as close to StdBrE as possible and keeping it highly focused would have been (and still is) a strongly positive act of identity (after Le Page and Tabouret-Keller 1986). This may be contrasted with the evolution of SE, where political independence and the developing of a new Singaporean identity would support the appropriation and nativization of English on a more endonormative basis. At the same time, as mentioned at the outset, PE exhibits variation such that more basilectal or vernacular features may also be noted in PE, as described in the next section. Brief reference to the influence from the input variety Baba Malay (BM) is also made.

3.2.2   Vernacular Peranakan English features

Where vernacular features of PE phonology are concerned, reduced aspiration of initial voiceless plosives is observed, as in *crying* and *keep* in Turns 2 and 6 respectively. This reflects BM phonology where voiceless plosives are not aspirated (Lim 2004b: 34–7). Consonant cluster simplification observed in *don't* and *drink* in Turns 1, 3 and 5, while possibly considered normal connected speech processes, may also be viewed as the result of substrate influence, particularly in the light of the BM utterance in Turn 3, *kita semua tak drin(k)*, where the realization of *drink* here without final [k] may be seen as following BM phonotactics where the coda only has one consonant. In the actual realization of vowels, small differences from StdBrE are noted, reflecting (B)M phonology (see Lim 2004b: 25–7). In general, the monophthongs are found in less extreme positions in vowel space; the BATH / PALM vowel, in particular, is much more low central than low back. The FACE, GOAT and SQUARE diphthongs are realized as monophthongs.

Characteristically vernacular prosodic patterns are also observed. In the final word of the phrases *The babies come out crying crying* (Turn 2), *Beer also has alcohol* (Turn 3), *No alcohol* (Turn 7), *Animals. Animals also can affect* (Turn 6) and *you give yourself cleansing* (Turn 7), while equal stress is noted on initial and final syllables, the pitch peak is located on the final syllable – a pattern that is distinct from that of sustained level steps noted for CSE (Lim 2004b) – which can be traced to the input variety. Similar patterns are noted in BM (Wee 2000) and in other varieties of Malay where the accent is found on the final word of the focused phrasal category, with the focal information unit tending to come at the end of an utterance (Deterding and Poedjosoedarmo 1998, noted in Lim 2004b; see also Lim 2009).

A vernacular feature of syntax is seen in *Nanti alcohol the same* 'in future (=wait and see), (the effect of) alcohol is similar' (Turn 2), where we note the absence of a copular – this is consistent with BM where, because no syntactic distinction is made between 'verb' and 'adjective', an 'adjective', when in predicate position, occurs without a copula (Lim 1988: 29). Topic–Comment structure is observed as well, also a characteristic of BM (Lim 1988: 39f.). In Turns 26 and 28, possibly prompted by the topic of a local dish, such influence from the input variety is also noticeable in younger generation JL's speech: *This one [sambal] can cook fish or what* '(as for) this one [the chilli sambal], you can cook fish with it', and *The chilli can make fish* '(as for) the chilli, you can make fish with it'. Topic–Comment is also noted at the level of the sentence, where in Turn 7, CKT produces utterances such as *You want to have babies* [Topic] *you don't ah* [Comment 'you don't (have and kiss animals)'], and *One year* [Topic] *you give yourself cleansing* [Comment]. This contrasts with the use of subordinating conjunctions as seen earlier in more standard utterances in Turn 4, but such structure is perfectly consistent with the semantically connected Topic–Comment structure of BM (Lim 1988: 41). The use of reduplication in PE is seen in Turn 29 when CKT reduplicates *fry-fry* for attenuation 'to fry a little' – this can be seen to be the influence of BM, where verb reduplication has the function of attenuation (Ansaldo 2004); an instance in BM itself is also described below.

What is also worthy of note is the presence of certain discourse particles and the absence of others. We see the use of *lah* and *ah* in Turns 16 and 17 and Turn 7 respectively. While common in SE, these two particles have been shown to have come into SE in an earlier era (by the 1970s), from Bazaar/ Baba Malay and/or Hokkien (Lim 2007), and in fact, *lah* is clearly documented in BM, originating in Hokkien (Lim 1988: 24f.). It is thus quite expected that they be found in PE, for reasons of timeframe and substrate typology. What is interesting is that the particles which were acquired into SE at a later stage (late 1980s) and shown to come from Cantonese, such as *lor*, *hor* and *meh*, do not figure in PE.

Up until now, discussion has centred on the English of the Peranakans, but in fact, what must be striking is the presence of instances of Baba Malay in the data – whether single words, phrases or utterances.[13] Younger-generation JL reiterates her reference to 'fish' using the BM term *ikan* in Turn 26. Oldest-generation CKT also switches to BM in Turn 6 for the lexical item *chium* 'to kiss', reduplicated as *chium-chium* for attentuation to mean 'to kiss a little'. The very common *nanti* 'in future (= wait and see)' is used in Turn 2 in a largely English utterance *Nanti alcohol the same*, while Turn 3 starts with *Kita semua tak drin(k)* 'All of us didn't drink' in BM with English verb, and then continues in English. Entire BM utterances are also found: speaking of babies, born of drug-addict mothers, who cry constantly, CKT in Turn 2 presents the question 'What do they want?' in BM *Apa dia mo*?

This, I would say, is a hallmark of Peranakan English. While there is extensive code-switching in Singapore English, this (in contemporary SE) involves Mandarin, Hokkien, Cantonese and Malay,[14] whereas in PE, code-switching involves Baba Malay (BM in turn would involve Hokkien[15] loanwords for address practices, food, certain cultural and religious practices, and terms of emotive import and value judgement). Further, while traditionally this may be viewed as English–BM code-switching, I venture the suggestion that this be seen instead from a monolectal view (see e.g. Meeuwis and Blommaert 1998); in other words, the alternate use of English and BM in PE should be viewed as a single English-BM code in its own right, one that defines Peranakan English.

3.3   Written Peranakan English

Observations of features of written Peranakan English are, as mentioned above, based on articles and editorials of *The Peranakan*, the newsletter published by the Peranakan Association, written by Peranakans for Peranakans.

One striking characteristic noted in this genre may be seen as evidence for the Peranakans' being early acquirers of English during the British colonial period: the use of typically English lexis or phrases (1, 2), classic English idioms and archaic turns of phrase (3 to 10), and literary references (10). In the examples that follow, the feature in question is highlighted in bold.

(1)   **a jolly time** at chili padi [name of a restaurant]

(2)   But **hopes** of *chope*-ing [reserving] any jewelled heirlooms are soon **dashed**.

---

[13] These extracts happen to be English-dominant, but in interactions between Peranakans in whom BM is more active, a greater amount of English–BM code-switching occurs.

[14] Naturally, in intra-ethnic exchanges with Malays, Tamil Indians and Chinese, there is English–Malay, English–Tamil and English–Mandarin (or other Chinese language) code-switching respectively.

[15] Tone, as in Hokkien, is not transferred to BM, nor is it realized in PE (cf. Sinitic tone being acquired in SE, Lim 2009).

(3)   I am afraid I have gone into areas **'where even angels fear to tread'** but someone has to say something even at the risk of **'being hung, drawn and quartered'**

(4)   It is said that **'Manners maketh the Man'**.

(5)   I greeted the spritely Mr Tan Beng Tee, the birthday boy smartly **dressed in his Sunday best**, with 'panjang panjang umor' [very long life (a traditional birthday wish)]

(6)   **If only the walls could speak**, how much more would they have told of the other beautiful events that had graced this splendid house in the years gone by.

(7)   . . . and whom we should gather into our fold by inviting them to our functions and convincing them that there is **still life in the old grey mare** although 'she ain't what she used to be!'

(8)   . . . those who are not Peranakans – who have displayed greater zeal for our cause than **our own kith or kin**.

(9)   Is the Peranakan Community an already vanished breed, **as dead as the dodo** . . .

(10)   Those who fit into the **dyed in the wool** mould of the true-blue Peranakan – the descendants of Hokkien immigrants from Malacca who still speak impeccable Baba patois and English only – are over 50 years of age and belong to a vanishing breed. They are **the last of the Mohicans** who proudly cling on to their traditions and to whom all tribute must be paid for successfully keeping the flag flying for so long.

The other feature of note is, as already seen in the spoken genre, code-switching with BM (which includes Hokkien loans). In contrast with the patterns described earlier, code-switching in written PE is more constrained, and tends to be restricted to a few categories of borrowed lexical items: terms and phrases for cultural practices (*ronggeng, dondang sayang* [Malay]), food (*tong poon lady* [Hokkien]; *biji sagar seeds, rempah* [Malay]), naming and address practices (*kimpoh choh* [Hokkien 'maternal great-great-aunt'], exclamations (*kus semangat!* [Malay]), greetings, wishes and thanks (*apa khabar* [Malay 'how are you']; *May we extend to all readers a Selamat Tahun Baru* [Malay 'happy new year'] *and may you all enjoy panjang panjang umor* [Malay 'very long life'] *in the year of the Goat; The Main Wayang Company would like to say a big KAMSIAH* [Hokkien 'thank you']) are sprinkled throughout the English editorials and articles.

4   Reflections on Peranakan English

4.1   On Peranakan English features

As mentioned at the start, this is the first description of the variety known as Peranakan English, which, based on a small corpus and given the scope of the chapter, comprises a modest account of the variety, but one which already hopefully lends some insights into its evolution. The recognition of variation showing vernacular and acrolectal features is also a reflection not only of the influence of the community's original vernacular BM on the emergent English, but also of identity and alignment practices of the community as subjects in a particular ecology.

4.2   On the future vitality of Peranakan English

The Peranakans, along with other communities such as the Eurasians and Anglo-Indians, were groups which saw their formation and evolution in a particular sociohistorical context. Bloom (1986: 360) recognizes this fact, pinpointing 'the amalgam of Asian cultural traits and the English language in groups such as the Straits Chinese, Anglo Indian groups and Portuguese Eurasians, in particular in the Straits Chinese, unique to the Straits Settlements, which made them an indigenous culture in a palpable sense'. The ecology in which these groups were formed has however certainly changed; as a consequence, some even predict 'the dying out of the Peranakans' (Kwan-Terry 2000: 96). Their ethnolinguistic vitality is nonetheless still very high in the present day – perhaps even seeing a boost in the past decade. This is not only because of their very active and dedicated association, whose membership grows annually, and which organizes well-attended activities throughout the year including food festivals, talks, annual conventions, and their annual dinner and dance, as well as individual members who have published on various cultural aspects. The community has also very recently received increased recognition and/or support from the state, for example in the form of a restored traditional Baba House, costing €2 million, and the dedicated boutique Peranakan museum costing €6 million, both having opened in 2008, a successful drama serial on a Peranakan family in Singapore, *The Little Nyonya*, which crucially was produced for the Chinese channel and above all being recognized as an important cultural group in the country. All this certainly contributes to the revival and maintainance of Peranakan culture. The question is whether from the linguistic point of view the prognosis is different.

On the one hand, given Singapore's rapidly changing linguistic ecology, driven to a large extent by language policies (Lim in press), the positioning of English has led to the evolution and establishment of SE as the mother tongue of most young Singaporeans. Young Peranakans, classified as 'Chinese', have studied Mandarin as a second language in school, and have little or no exposure to Baba Malay, due to the move from extended to nuclear family units and the demise of the BM-speaking older generation, as well as the general shift already in place from BM to English in the community at large. Such a decrease in (speakers of) BM means a reduction in their presence in the ecology, and consequently a reduction in their influence on English in Singapore, even if we only consider the community of Peranakans. All these circumstances suggest that the conditions which were vital for the formation of PE are no longer applicable, and thus a natural disappearance of PE may be expected, in particular in the face of the extremely vital Singapore English.

On the other hand, the high vitality of the community that is undeniably in existence may well go some distance in the maintenance of PE. For one thing, even if BM is gradually disappearing as a widely used vernacular, there are clearly conscious efforts being made in its maintenance and revitalization: publications such as the Baba Malay dictionary (Gwee 2006) and a collection of Baba Malay idioms (Gwee 1993) have appeared recently, plays are written and performed regularly in BM, and churches in traditional Peranakan districts have started to hold services in BM. For a while, at least, the presence of BM in the ecology of the Peranakans may still be assured, even if only passively in the younger generation. Just as crucial is the socio-psychological dimension, and this perhaps is promising. With the revival of interest in all things Peranakan comes the recognition, especially amongst the younger generation, that the culture is not obsolete but relevant: there is a Peranakan presence in the virtual world of Second Life, for example, and the association's youth group has regular gatherings which involve not only engaging in Peranakan cultural activities but also revitalizing BM and using it in popular culture such as hiphop and rap. Such identification with and reinforcement of the culture may well lead to a focusing (in Le Page and Tabouret-Keller's 1986 sense) and maintenance of features that mark this particular variety of English as Peranakan.

References

Ansaldo, Umberto. 2004. 'The evolution of Singapore English: Finding the matrix.' In L. Lim, ed. *Singapore English: A grammatical description* (Varieties of English Around the World G33). Amsterdam/Philadelphia: John Benjamins, 127–49.

    2009. *Contact Languages: Ecology and Evolution in Asia*. Cambridge: Cambridge University Press.

Ansaldo, Umberto, Lisa Lim and Salikoko S. Mufwene. 2007. 'The sociolinguistic history of the Peranakans: What it tells us about "creolization".' In Umberto Ansaldo, Stephen Matthews and Lisa Lim, eds. *Deconstructing Creole*. Typological Studies in Language 73. Amsterdam and Philadelphia: John Benjamins, 203–26.

Ansaldo, Umberto and Stephen J. Matthews. 1999. 'The Minnan substrate and creolization in Baba Malay.' *Journal of Chinese Linguistics* 27(1): 38–68.

Bloom, David. 1986. 'The English language in Singapore: A critical survey.' In Basant K. Kapur, ed. *Singapore Studies*. Singapore: Singapore University Press, 337–458.

Braddell, T. 1853. 'Notes of a trip to the interior from Malacca.' *Journal of the Indian Archipelago and Eastern Asia* 7: 73–104.

Braga-Blake, Myrna. 1992. 'Eurasians in Singapore: An overview.' In Myrna Braga-Blake, ed. *Singapore Eurasians*. Singapore: Eurasian Association/ Times Editions, 11–23.

Chen, Ta. 1939. *Emigrant Communities in South China: A Study of Overseas Migration and its Influence on Standards of Living and Social Change*. Shanghai: Kelly & Walsh Ltd.

Crawfurd, J. 1856. *A Descriptive Dictionary of the Indian Island and Adjacent Countries*. London: Bradbury & Evans.

Deterding, David and Gloria R. Poedjosoedarmo. 1998. *The Sounds of Singapore English: Phonetics and Phonology for English Teachers in Southeast Asia*. Singapore: Simon and Schuster (Asia) Pte Ltd.

Dhoraisingam, Samuel S. 2006. *Peranakan Indians of Singapore and Melaka: Indian Babas and Nonyas – Chitty Melaka*. Singapore: Institute of Southeast Asian Studies.

Earl, George Windsor. 1837. *The Eastern Seas or Voyages and Adventures in the Indian Archipelago in 1832–33–34*. London: Allen & Co.

Gupta, Anthea Fraser. 1994. *The Step-Tongue: Children's English in Singapore*. Clevedon/Philadelphia/Adelaide: Multilingual Matters Ltd.

2001. 'English in the Linguistic Ecology of Singapore. The Cultural Politics of English as a World Language.' GNEL/MALVEN conference, Freiburg, 2001.

Gwee, Thian Hock William. 1993. *Mas Sepuloh: Baba Conversational Gems*. Singapore: Armour Publishing Pte Ltd.

2006. *A Baba Malay Dictionary*. Singapore: The Peranakan Association; Tuttle Publishing.

Ho, Mian Lian and John Platt. 1993. *Dynamics of a Contact Continuum: Singaporean English*. Oxford: Claredon Press.

Kwan-Terry, Anna. 2000. 'Language shift, mother tongue, and identity in Singapore.' *International Journal of the Sociology of Language* 143: 85–106.

Kwok, Kian Woon. 2000. 'Singapore.' In Lynn Pan, ed. *The Encyclopedia of the Chinese Overseas*. Singapore: Chinese Heritage Centre; Cambridge, Mass.: Harvard University Press, 200–17.

Le Page, Robert and Andrea Tabouret-Keller. 1986. *Acts of Identity*. Cambridge: Cambridge University Press.

Lim, Boon Keng. 1917. 'The Chinese in Malaya.' In W. Feldwisk, ed. *Present Days' Impressions of the Far East and Prominent and Progressive Chinese at Home and Abroad: The History, People, Commerce, Industries and Resources of China, Hong Kong, Indo-China, Malaya and Netherlands India*. London: Globe Encyclopedia Co.

Lim, Joo Hock. 1967. 'Chinese female immigration into the Straits Settlements 1860–1901.' *Journal of the South Seas Society* 22: 58–110.

Lim, Lisa, ed. 2004a. *Singapore English: A Grammatical Description*. Varieties of English Around the World G33. Amsterdam and Philadelphia: John Benjamins.

2004b. 'Sounding Singaporean.' In Lim 2004a, 19–56.

2007. 'Mergers and acquisitions: On the ages and origins of Singapore English particles.' *World Englishes* 27(4): 446–73.

2009. 'Revisiting English prosody: (Some) New Englishes as tone languages?' In Lisa Lim and Nikolas Gisborne, eds. *The Typology of Asian Englishes*. Special issue, *English World-Wide* 30: 21–39.

in press. 'Migrants and "mother tongues": Extralinguistic forces in the ecology of English in Singapore.' In Lisa Lim, Anne Pakir and Lionel Wee, eds. *English in Singapore: World Language and Lingua Franca*. (Asian Englishes Today.) Hong Kong University Press.

Lim, Lisa and Joseph A. Foley. 2004. 'English in Singapore and Singapore English.' In Lim 2004a, 1–18.

Lim, Sonny. 1988. 'Baba Malay: The language of the "Straits-born" Chinese.' In Hein Steinhauer, ed. *Papers in Western Austronesian Linguistics* No. 3. Pacific Linguistics Series A, No. 78. Department of Linguistics, Research School of Pacific Studies, The Australian National University, 1–61.

Liu, Gretchen. 1999. *Singapore: A Pictorial History 1819–2000*. Singapore: National Heritage Board and Editions Didier Miller.

Meeuwis, Michael and Jan Blommaert. 1998. 'A monolectal view of code-switching: Layered code-switching among Zairians in Belgium.' In Peter Auer, ed. *Code-switching in Conversation: Language, Interaction and Identity*. London: Routledge, 76–98.

Nathan, J. 1922. *The Census of British Malaysia, 1921*. London: Waterloo & Sons.

Norman, J. 1988. *Chinese*. Cambridge: Cambridge University Press.

Pakir, Anne. 1986. 'A linguistic investigation of Baba Malay.' PhD dissertation, University of Hawai'i.

Pan, Lynn, ed. 2000. *The Encyclopedia of the Chinese Overseas*. Singapore: Chinese Heritage Centre; Cambridge, MA: Harvard University Press.

Peranakan Association Singapore. 1994–2008. *The Peranakan*. (newsletter) Singapore: The Peranakan Association.

Platt, John and Heidi Weber. 1980. *English in Singapore and Malaysia*. Kuala Lumpur: Oxford University Press.

Platt, John, Heidi Weber and Ho Mian Lian. 1983. *Singapore and Malaysia*. Varieties of English Around the World T4. Amsterdam and Philadelphia: John Benjamins.

Png, Poh Seng. 1969. 'The Straits Chinese in Singapore: A case of local identity and socio-cultural accommodation.' *Journal of Southeast Asia History* 10(1): 95–114.

Rudolph, Jurgen. 1998. *Reconstructing Identities: A Social History of the Babas in Singapore*. Aldershot, Vermont: Ashgate Publishing Co.

Skinner, G. William. 1960. 'Change and persistence in Chinese culture overseas: A comparison of Thailand and Java.' *Journal of the South Seas Society* 16(1–2): 86–100.

Song, Ong Siang. 1923. *One Hundred Years' History of the Chinese in Singapore*. London: John Murray. Reprinted 1967, Singapore: University of Malaya Press.

Tan, Chee Beng. 1988a. *The Baba of Malacca: Culture and Identity of a Peranakan Community in Malaysia*. Petaling Jaya, Selangor: Pelanduk Publications.

1988b. 'Structure and change, cultural identity of the Baba of Melaka.' *Bijdragen tot de Taal, Land- en Volkenkunde* 144: 297–314.

Thomson, J. T. 1875. *The Straits of Malacca, Indo-China and China, or Ten Years' Travels, Adventures and Residence Abroad*. London: Sampson Low; Marston: Low & Searle.

Vaughan, J. D. 1879. *Manners and Customs of the Chinese in the Straits Settlements*. Singapore: The Mission Press. (Reprinted by Oxford University Press 1971, 1992.)

Wee, Kim Soon Gabriel. 2000. 'Intonation of the Babas: An auditory and instrumental approach.' BA Hons thesis, National University of Singapore.

Wells, John C. 1982. *Accents of English*. Cambridge: Cambridge University Press.

18   Norfolk Island and Pitcairn varieties

PETER MÜHLHÄUSLER

1   Introduction

Lesser-known varieties of English are predominately those spoken by racially mixed or non-European speakers in remote locations and having small speaker numbers. Pitkern and Norf'k, spoken on Pitcairn Island and Norfolk Island respectively, meet all three criteria. That Pitkern–Norf'k (P/N) was deemed a language not worth describing can be seen from the fact that during ten years' work as the resident linguist at the Melanesian Mission Boarding School on Norfolk Island, the Oxford philologist Codrington never bothered to discuss or describe the Norf'k language; and that it was not a language worth knowing was the ideological position of the school teachers that were sent to Norfolk Island from Australia. When Reinecke et al. published their bibliography of pidgin creole languages in (1975), they emphasized that 'Pitcairn Island English with its offshoot on Norfolk Island is of extraordinary interest because it offers as near a laboratory case of creole dialect formation as we are ever likely to have' (p. 590).

The two pages of bibliographic resources they list at the time stood in stark contrast with the perceived keystone role of the language. There has been some serious research on P/N in subsequent years by Harrison (1972), Laycock (1982, 1989, 1990) and Källgård (1998), and for the last ten years I have carried out fieldwork on Norfolk Island and archival work around the world. What has contributed to the fact that the language remains among the lesser-known varieties is that it is an esoteric language, with outsiders not expected to speak it or find out about it. It certainly does not lend itself to Blitzkrieg fieldwork and its study requires diplomacy, persistence and much time.

The speakers of P/N are the descendants of the British mutineers of the *Bounty* and their Tahitian consorts who settled on the uninhabited Pitcairn Island in 1789, where they founded a mixed British-Polynesian society and developed distinct customs and a language referred to variously as Pitcairnese, Pitcairn English and Pitkern. Three additional British males came to Pitcairn in the first half of the nineteenth century to provide educational and spiritual guidance to the community. The population had outgrown the natural resources of Pitcairn by about 1850, and in 1856 the entire population was relocated to Norfolk Island, situated about 1,500 kilometres east of the Australian mainland. Norfolk had ceased to be a penal settlement around 1850, and the island was uninhabited when the Pitcairners arrived in 1856. In the following years a small number of Pitcairners migrated back to Pitcairn Island, where about fifty of their descendants still reside. On Norfolk Island there are about 900 Pitcairn descendants, outnumbered by 'mainlanders' from Australia and New Zealand.

The inhabitants of Pitcairn and Norfolk Islands have always been bilingual in English and P/N, with most speakers competent in both languages, and with P/N often being the first and dominant language until 1950. Since then, English has taken over most of the domains previously reserved to P/N (children's plays, family and workplace), and the language in its traditional form is passed on to only a very small number of children. More recently on Norfolk Island, the government, school and museum in cooperation with the University of Adelaide have embarked on a project to reverse the decline of the language. Details about this can be found in Mühlhäusler (2007).

The focus of the present paper is the question of whether P/N is indeed the canonical case of a creole and whether its structures reflect the factors commonly appealed to by creolists to describe such languages in terms of either substratum influence or universals of creolization. More precisely, I would like to focus on those lesser-known aspects in the history and structure of the P/N language that would need to be better understood before the question of creolization can be really fully addressed.

2   Some lesser-known facts of P/N

2.1   Origins

Most accounts of the language begin with the Mutiny of the *Bounty* on 28 April 1789, or the landing of the *Bounty* mutineers and their Tahitian consorts on the uninhabited Pitcairn Island on 15 January 1790. Between October 1788 and April 1789, when the *Bounty* was anchored in Tahiti, some pidgin form of communication appears to have arisen between the Tahitians, in particular Tahitian women, and the *Bounty* crew. Whilst we do not have any written records of this language, we know that it was a mixed Tahitian-English form of speech, and importantly that it was not only used as a pidgin but also as an anti-language to antagonize Captain Bligh, who took a dim view of mixing English and Tahitian and adopting Tahitian customs such as tattoos (Dening 1992). The use of the language to taunt has remained one of its functions to date.

2.2   Languages involved in the creation of P/N

Most writers (though not Flint n.d., or Ross and Moverley 1964) assume that speakers of only two languages, English and Tahitian, were present in its founding years (1789–1807). They ignore or underestimate the importance of Midshipman Edward Young, who was born in St Kitts (in all likelihood as the son of an English nobleman and a slave girl), and who was looked after by his black mother. He received some education and could read and write and, in the last years before his death, he taught John Adams, as well as the children, to read and write. He was reputed to be a good storyteller and well liked by the women and children.

There are a number of lexical items of West Indian origin in P/N, among them *morla*[1] 'tomorrow', *morga* 'thin', *santaped* 'starfish', *cherimoya* 'custard apple', *bastard* in expressions referring to the 'inferior or inedible variant of a plant species', as well as possible phonological processes such as 't' becomes 'k' in *lekl* 'little', *kekl* 'kettle'; but further research needs to be carried out. Norfolk Islanders who have visited the West Indies have commented that they were struck by the similarity between their languages and West Indian Creole English.

2.3   American influence

One of the mutineers, Isaac Martin, was born in Philadelphia. During most of the nineteenth century, both Pitcairn Island and Norfolk were called on by numerous American vessels. At times captains' wives stayed on Pitcairn Island for long periods whilst their husbands went on whaling expeditions – and in the words of Shapiro (1928: 3) 'many of the young men shipped on long cruises, returning with Yankee tricks of speech and customs', and there were contacts with American whalers on Norfolk Island as well. Thanksgiving is celebrated on Norfolk Island, and there are a number of words of American origin, such as *skunk* 'to fail to catch a fish or fail to score in a card game'.

2.4   The Melanesian Mission on Norfolk Island

From 1860 to 1920 there was a boarding school for Melanesian Islanders on Norfolk Island, and there were numerous contacts between the mission community and the Norfolk Islanders. Words of Melanesian origin include *walkstil* 'to creep', *mekies* 'to hurry, rush, make haste', and possibly *setau* 'settle, perch from, sit down', as well as other possible items.

2.5   Family differences and the role of individuals

P/N to date has remained an unfocused language in the sense that there are relatively few agreed social norms, either with regard to its use or to its

---

[1]   The Norfolk Islanders have no agreed standard spelling and I do not wish to take sides in the ongoing dispute whether and how the language should be written. There is also no standard pronunciation (see Ingram and Mühlhäusler 2004).

lexicon and grammar. Different families have adopted very different family language policies. In some families English only has been spoken from the 1820s; in many mixed families in more recent times children grew up as English monolinguals; whereas in others, both English and P/N are spoken. Because of the small size of the community, individuals can have a significant influence on the language. Inventors of new words or ways of speaking are often known by name in their inventions (*dar thing fe* + name of the person), and the use of their inventions can be restricted to their own family. Such differences are used deliberately as markers of separate identity.

The role of individuals in adapting to and changing the natural environment of Pitcairn and Norfolk is often signalled by prefixing the individual's name to the name of the life form referred to. Thus, there are forms like:

Austin grass 'a tall grass introduced to Pitcairn by Austin Young'
Edmond plun 'a cooking banana introduced by Edmond McCoy'
Hannah 'first fruit associated with Hannah Adams'
Saias baekboen 'an endemic tree on Norfolk Island after "saia" who believed
it was ideal for the keel of a locally built ship'

2.6 Deliberate language-making

P/N being an esoteric language and being used as an additional language contains a considerable number of lexical items that appear to have been deliberately made up, additional to the 'mysterious' words *bishe* 'she-goat' and *kutshe-kutshe* 'kind of fish' commented on by Ross and Moverley (1964: 169):

tampali 'friendly greeting'
stochi 'exclamation of admiration'
solan, sorlan 'empty'
smiej 'masturbate'
slogos 'hastily whipped up scones'
bolos 'cold'
shika 'intoxicated'
rutus, rotus 'nonsense'
pala puch 'cheeky, friendly greeting'
nitho 'absolutely nothing'
lambutiet 'to remove swiftly'
gildagara 'accumulation of grime'
mumu 'beast'
duruch 'grime'
chuchu 'exclamation of admiration'
baabahulas 'shake aggressively'
tirij 'totally exhausted, beyond repair'

2.7   Anthroponyms

A particularly striking type of word in Norf'k derives from the names of individuals whose striking characteristics or predispositions have become words of the language. It appears that many of them started as taunts between different families and, as many speakers remember who is referred to, they are dangerous words to use. They include:

> *saia* 'to invite oneself' (from 'Josiah')
> *snell* 'to cater insufficiently' (from a family named Snell)
> *luusi* 'to whimper or cry in public' (like a woman named Lucy)
> *toebi* 'to help oneself to other people's vegetables' (like Toby)
> *breman* 'very thin' (from a visitor Mr Bremen)
> *aata* 'to be proud of, to look at with admiration' (from a man called Arthur)
> *sor fe ankel felaps* 'malinger' (sickness of Uncle Phillip)

2.8   Tahitian substratum

The influence of Tahitian was reduced by the fact that all Tahitian men on Pitcairn were murdered within a few years of their arrival, and only mixed marriages occurred. Tahitian culture and language was held in contempt until very recently, and compulsory teaching of English was initiated on Pitcairn Island in the 1820s. There are some interesting traces of the pervasive racism of early Pitcairn society, including the fact that no children were given Polynesian names, that many life forms were named after Europeans who discovered them (as mentioned in section 2.5) but not after Tahitians who may have known them; and the fact that the majority of lexical items referring to undesirable, unnatural or dangerous situations or objects are typically of Tahitian origin, as well as words with taboo connotations.

2.9   Access to the acrolect

Creolization is often associated with access to the acrolect or target language, but as Baker (1990) has pointed out, the notion 'target' is a problematic one. It should be noted that many *bona fide* creoles developed in situations where English was formally taught, including Hawaiian Pidgin which, according to Reinecke (1969), originated in the school grounds, rather than in isolated plantations.

Similarly, Australian Northern Territory Kriol developed in the English Medium Boarding School at Bamyili; Unserdeutsch, from German New Guinea, developed in an orphanage school run by German priests (1993); and New Caledonian Tayo came into being in an orphanage on New Caledonia (Ehrhart 1993). Input and access to the acrolect does not prevent creolization, which is strongly associated with the creation of a new identity, often in opposition to the dominant dialect or society.

Table 18.1 *Semantically marked words of Tahitian origin*

Tahitian word	Meaning
ama'ula	awkward, ungainly or clumsy
eeyulla	adolescent, immature, not dry behind the ears
hawa	excrement, faeces
hoowi-hoowi	filthy, extremely dirty
howa-howa	to soil one's pants from a bowel movement
iwi	stunted, undersized
laha *(also* lu-hu*)*	dandruff
mutty-mutty	dead, died
nanu	jealous
ootatow	youth who has reached maturity but is still very small in stature
po-o	barren or infertile soil
poo-oo	unripe or green fruit
tarpou	stains on the hands caused from peeling some fruit or vegetables
toohi	to curse, blaspheme or swear
tye-tye	tasteless food
unna-unna	to lack self-confidence
wa-haloo	dilapidated, ramshackle
whawhaha	conceited, full of self-importance

Varieties of English were used by the British sailors who settled on Pitcairn in 1789, and the children received informal lessons in English literacy even before an English teacher John Buffet set up a school in Pitcairn in 1823.

From this date, English literacy has been compulsory for all children. There have been sustained and intense contacts with English speakers on both islands. The emergence of P/N as an additional language thus is not due merely to communicative requirements; rather, it reflects the strong wish to preserve a separate identity in the face of pervasive pressure to assimilate to the dominant society and language.

2.10   Phases of fluency

The status and use of P/N vis-à-vis English is not one of stable diglossia (Flint 1979) but one of constant change. Indeed, there are many intriguing observations in the history of the language that suggests the waxing and waning of P/N as a response to external circumstances.

Laycock (1990: 622) takes the view that by 1831, when the entire population of Pitcairn Island briefly relocated to Tahiti, an experience which left them traumatized, the mixed Tahitian English of Pitcairn was moribund, and it was revived and consolidated as a communal act of identity:

I am not suggesting that this was done with the deliberateness of a modern linguistic planning committee. Although there is little literature on the subject, there is no doubt that small communities can carry out what I call *naïve linguistic engineering.* [More details on this concept can be found in Laycock and Mühlhäusler 1990: 864–5.] . . .

The process in this instance would have been carried on in conversations like the following:

Do you remember what old X used to say?
Wouldn't it be a pity if we forgot the old words?
When we say things the old way the others can't understand us.
We've got a special way of saying that in our family
Such statements reinforce the use of the variety, and set the standards for group acceptance. Similar statements are still made by Norfolk Islanders, as: *yu main watawieh oel Chaali bin yuus a' tal et?* 'Do you remember how old Charley used to say it?'. (Laycock 1989: 626)

Shortly before their relocation to Norfolk Island, we find a comment by 'Metoixos' (1850) that the English of the Pitcairners was 'fast degenerating into a dialect', and Cook (1938: 9) remarks:

The tendency to use a Pitcairnese dialect is very pronounced both in the home and in the school. It is difficult to understand this dialect, which is spoken with a peculiar drone and words are continually 'clipt' or distorted. Its use is spreading. The older inhabitants speak purer English than the rising generation.

Similarly, for Norfolk Island we have a number of reports to the effect that the language is a recent innovation. Thus, in an unpublished manuscript titled *Norfolk Island* written by the headmaster of the Government school, Passmore (written around 1916 – privately held by the late Mrs Merval Hoare, Norfolk Island), we read:

The dialect is of comparative recent growth. Very little of it came from Tahiti. Most of the words are corruptions of English. Sullen for children – Larn to tell. Larn a little sullen no do da. (Tell the little children not to do that.) If you pretend not to understand the lingo as most English people do in self-defence you will hear one say sneeringly "He's agamonin he car was it!!" 'Car' is the negative of 'to do' and 'to know'. It means 'I cannot' or 'I do not know' and is the same for all persons. (p. 24)

Such observations by outsiders may reflect either genuine reinvention or changing patterns of the public visibility of the language. There appears to be a strong pattern of recurring acts of linguistic identity in times of conflict with the colonial powers. Recent difficulties between Pitcairn Islanders and Great Britian, and Norfolk Islanders and Australia, have promoted greater use of the language in both private and public domains.

3   Diagnostic features of pidgins and creoles

3.1   Structural typology of pidgins and creoles

Diagnostic or salient (Samarin 1971) features in pidgin/creole studies are widely used for determining:

the pidgin/creole status of a given variety
the affiliation with or relationship to other pidgin and creole languages.

Features most commonly used are a mix between universals of simplification (multifunctionality, absence of copula, absence of relativizers, lack of number distinctions), putative bioprogram features (biomorphemic interrogatives, existential 'got', specific-non-specific rather than definite-indefinite), substratum features (distinction between inclusive/non-inclusive first person plural pronouns, predicate markers) and salient lexical items (*picinnini* 'child', *kalabus* 'prison', *boy* 'adult male employee' in Pidgin English). Suggested feature batteries in the past were often ad hoc but have become increasingly sophisticated. An important consideration in more recent research is negative features (the absence of constructions such as passives, discontinuous phrasal verbs or consonant clusters).

There have been recent attempts to determine either the status of Pitkern-Norf'k as a creole or its relationship to other English pidgins and creoles, beginning with Harrison (1972) and continuing down to the most recent attempts by Baker and Huber (2001) and Kortmann and Szmrecsanyi (2004). Both Laycock (1989) and Mühlhäusler (1998), in discussing their findings of earlier work, have pointed to their inconclusiveness and contradictions. There would seem to be a number of principled deficiencies in all of the attempts to date:

lack of justification for the selection of particular diagnostic feature batteries;
lack of attention to the changing nature of all languages, including creoles (features present in later stages may not have occurred in the formative period);
lack of detail due to an impoverished database.

Lack of space and time prevents from me from providing a full answer, but I would like to show, with a few relevant examples, that the languages to be compared need to be far better known before conclusions can be drawn. I have chosen the following constructions to illustrate this:

- multiple word class membership
- adverbial clauses
- reduplication.

Table 18.2 *Introducers of adverbial clauses in Norf'k*

Time	*aafta* 'after', *wail* 'while', *wen* 'when', *wenaewa* 'whenever', *biifor* 'before', *tal* 'until', *suunes* 'as soon as', *lornges* 'as long as', *faastaim* 'when first'
Cause and effect	*ko(s)* 'because', *sait* 'because', *miek* 'because'
Opposition	*orlthoe* 'although', *domain* 'although'
Conditional	*(s)ef* 'if', *wedha* 'whether', *swaeda* 'whether', *spoesen* 'if', suppose', *watef* 'what if', *anles* 'unless'
Manner	*semes(wieh)* 'like', *sef* 'like if'
Place	*said* 'where'
Purpose and result	*soe* 'so that', *bembeya* 'lest'

And, as negative features:

- consonant clusters
- phrasal verbs.

In his comparison of Norf'k with Jamaican Creole and Hawaiian Pidgin, Harrison (1972: 73) appeals to the shared property 'some word forms pass fairly freely from one class to another'. Prior to this, Ross and Moverley (1964: 158) had commented that the lack of distinction between word clusters in Tahitian 'has been carried over into Pitcairnese', giving examples such as *mard* 'to play tricks', *sof* 'to become soft', and a few others. In Mühlhäusler (2008) I have shown, after examining the categorial multifunctionality of all words of P/N, that earlier findings were a consequence of generalizations from a problematic selection of examples. In actual fact:

Categorial multifunctionality in P/N is far less productive than in English
It is essentially a subset of English plus a small number of analogous innovations
It behaves differently from Tahitian
It differs from multifunctionality in other Pacific pidgins and creoles such as Tok Pisin, with which it has been proposed to group together. (Kortmann and Szmrecsanyi 2004)

3.2   Adverbial clauses

Lack of embedding and lack of formal introducers of embedded constructions have often been used as an indicator of creoleness. There is no shortage of adverbial clauses in P/N, and the majority of introducers of adverbial phrases come from English, as can be seen from Table 18.2.

Unfortunately, there is little diachronic evidence, but it is noted that the conditional *suppose* is documented in 1821 by Captain Raine in the sentence 'suppose he bad man strike me, I no strike him'. It is also noted that many of the forms listed are found both in the Pitcairn and Norfolk Island varieties, which suggests that they had emerged by the early 1860s when the community split.

This is certainly the case for the three possible local innovations, *bembeya* 'lest', *said* 'because', and *miek* 'the reason why'. In adversative clauses, *bembaya* (from 'by and by') is similar in form to Melanesian Pidgin English *baimbai* but different in function and meaning. Ross and Moverley (1964: 221) suggest that a meaning documented in the OED (1631) 'therefore, as a consequence' is the likely source, though this is not necessarily so. They note that 'by-and-by' is also found in an adversative sense in some English dialects. The causative *said* from P/N *said* 'place', and *miek* from the verb *miek* 'to make', appear to be examples of reanalysis.

The development of *said* from a location to a causative probably originated in ambiguous sentences such as:

(1)   *Ai se ban f' san said ai bin in aa san*
        'I got sunburnt because of (where) I was in the sun'

(2)   *Mais lieg stil sor said ai step orn a wana*
        'My foot is sore because (where) I stepped on a sea urchin'

And that *said* was reinterpreted subsequently as a causal conjunction:

(3)   *Ai se fatu said ai bin work tuu haad*
        'I am tired because I worked too hard'

In the case of *miek*, the reanalysis involved a change of grammatical category rather than a semantic shift as is illustrated by:

(4)   *Ai gat a lef miek ai erli es dieh*
        'I got a lift that's why I am early'

The difference between *miek* and *said* is illustrated in the following sentence:

(5)   *Miek hii klai isse es said dem yus' roht'net*
        'The reason why he cries easily is because they used to spoil him'

Ross and Moverley (1964: 257) argue that *said* in the meanings of 'because' and 'where' 'probably originate from English besides, beside respectively', which still suggests reinterpretation by the speakers of P/N.

3.3   Reduplication

That reduplication and repetition are central to the linguistic characterization of pidgins and creoles is a view that has been superseded, only as a result of detailed work with pidgin and creole data. Bakker (1994: 33) summarizes such research:

The morphological process of reduplication is common (but not universal) in creole languages, but, strangely enough, rare in Pidgins as a productive process, even where one of the contributing languages is rich in reduplication.

A few pages later (p. 39), Bakker refers to the process of reduplication in creoles as 'almost universal'. Holm (1988: 85) again states that reduplication suggests 'the influence of language universals'.

For P/N, Tahitian substratum influence rather than universalist explanation have been proposed by both Ross and Moverley (1964: 15a) and Harrison (1972: 28–9). Whereas most Tahitian words may be said to exist in three phrases – simple, partially reduplicated and fully reduplicated (Ross and Moverley 1964: 158) – P/N words of Tahitian origin rarely appear in the latter two phases, and I have found fewer than forty reduplicated words. Nor is it the case that English words are often 'reduplicated under Tahitian influence' (ibid.: 158), and I have not been able to add many new examples to the two given by Ross and Moverley:

break-break 'broke, carelessly grated'
pick-pick 'kind of fish whose flesh when cooked is easy to pry from the bones'

The only additional ones are:

tea tea 'tear into many little bits'
bony bony 'full of bones'
hilly hilly 'choppy, very hilly'
make make 'fiddle about'

Given the lack of productivity, reduplication must be dismissed as a potential distinguisher for the creole status or substratum influence. The absence of typological properties of Polynesian languages and Tahitian in particular is very much in evidence.

3.4 Complex consonant clusters

Norf'k does not have a simple phonology. Flint (n.d.) distinguished seven vowel phonemes, twelve-plus diphthongs, three triphthongs and twenty-seven consonants – all in all more than the sometimes-mentioned figure of forty phonemes for English, and far more than 25 for Tahitian. A comprehensive phonological analysis of the language is still to be done. But, as a number of observers have mentioned, e.g. Ross and Moverley (1964: 143), 'there is no aversion to, rather an abundance of consonant groups' in all parts of the P/N word.

Table 18.3 *Consonant clusters in P/N*

Initial	Final
black 'black'	*apkuks* 'non-committal'
breken 'broken'	*behnk* 'bank'
tʃerimoya 'custard apple'	*britʃ* 'jump up'
drain 'water course'	*faens* 'paddock'
stig 'pierce'	*smedj* 'masturbate'
spail 'spoil'	*shaenks* 'thank you'
slush 'wash hurriedly'	*ritch* 'reach'
skrep 'scrape'	*johlops* 'insert a laxative into a fruit'
	neks 'next'

There is some simplification of word-final clusters, not just in pronunciation but also at the underlying level. Most final *-t* of English *-ct* has become *-c##*, as in:

'must' *mus*
'first' *fuss*
'most' *moos*

The continuous ending *-en* or the object passive ending *-et*, does not change this, thus:

laembies < *lambaste*

gives:

laembiesen   *laembieset*

However, in more recent loans, the *-t* is retained, as in:

kolek   *kolekten* 'collect'

Similarly, the *-d* in final *-nd* is variably realized when the endings are added:

staan 'stand'
staan up 'stand up'
ben 'to bend'
benet 'to be bent'

But:

raun 'round'
raundas 'a particular board game'
ailan 'island'
ailanda 'islander'
laen 'to land'
laenden 'to be landing'

It is not clear whether final -*d* is a recent phenomenon under the influence of English, as historical sources are scarce. It is noted, however, that present-day *aklan* 'we insiders' was recorded as *akland* in a number of earlier sources.

The phonology of P/N as discussed here certainly does not lend support to the notion that P/N is a creole.

3.5   Phrasal verbs

Laycock (1989) drew attention to the fact that P/N, like English, but unlike many pidgin and creole Englishes, has distinctive phrasal verbs. The behaviour of this particular construction is more or less as in English. With pronoun subjects, the particle typically follows the pronoun:

(6)   *ai gwen tek yu aut* 'I'm going to take you out'

With short noun phrases, it can occur directly after the verb, or after the object NP (Buffett and Laycock 1988: 68), as in:

(7) a.   *pat orn wan cardigan* 'put on a cardigan'

    b.   *pat wan kardigan orn* 'put a cardigan on'

With longer NP objects, it follows the verb:

(8)   *tek aut orl dem puu plan* 'take out all the green bananas'

But:

(9)   *pat orl dem things insaid* 'put everything inside'

3.6   Other matters

There are many other areas of P/N grammar that await close attention, including the distinction between a distributive and non-distributive plural (the *orl* and *dem* plurals in the example in the previous paragraph); the tendency in traditional P/N to distinguish specific/non-specific rather than definite/indefinite; a likely residual distinction between alienable and inalienable possession (*mais* 'my' vs. *fe mi* 'my'), which may reflect Tahitian grammar; its TMA system; an absolute spatial orientation system, briefly discussed by Mühlhäusler (2003); and numerous others. At this point observationally adequate accounts of these are not available, and many more years of painstaking recording and analysis are required.

An aspect of P/N, in particular the Norf'k variety, that has escaped most linguists is that not only do its lexicon and grammar differ significantly from English, there are also conventions for its use that differ. As yet no complete ethnography of speaking P/N is available, and what I shall say here is based on fieldwork and preliminary observations on Norfolk Island.

One way of finding out about language use is a scrutiny of the metalinguistic lexicon of P/N. This lexicon would seem to reflect the role of P/N in a small, isolated, dense multiplex communicative network (Milroy 1980) with a potential for conflict and violence. This is reflected in the need to avoid threatening people's face directly and to encourage other forms – more indirect ones – of social control, notably: *dem taal* 'rumour', *dem yuse taal* 'rumour', and teasing: *saawenout* 'tease, provoke', *migiem* 'make a fool of' and its counterpart *graabet* 'appear to have taken unwanted offence'.

Buffett (1999: 30) in connection with the expression *estoley/estole* 'it is not true' writes: 'the word "lie", as in "not tell the truth", was regarded as "not civil talk" by the forebears of the Norfolk Islanders from Pitcairn, so rather than say "you are lying", they would say in a more courteous way, "it is a story"'.

The obligation to share information is rather attenuated on Norfolk, and there are several words and expressions signalling one's unwillingness or inability to share information:

kaa laan 'can't divulge'
kaawa 'don't know'
nor taalen 'not telling'
nor laanen 'not telling'
ai se slai 'I'm not going to tell'
apkuks 'non-committal answer'

Dissimilation is another way of dealing with the community's requirement of a low-information society. Norfolk has two words for pretend:

miekaut
duubaagen

and several expressions to refute such practice, including:

fer 'expression of disagreement'
burus/boros 'talk rubbish'.

Norfolk Islanders distinguish information for insiders from information suitable for outsiders. Direct questioning about language use or knowledge of language can be very counterproductive. Rules for the use of language emphasize that the language is not for outsiders, with the consequence (disastrous for the well-being of the language) that in mixed households English only is spoken; a rule not to use Norf'k when talking about religion or official contexts or written documents; and others, which again and again have created intercultural difficulties in dealings with outsiders. I have started collecting ethnographic information of language use both from written sources and observations in the field. It appears that the comments made by observers in the nineteenth century for Pitcairn Island continue to exist on Norf'k Island, and they persist even in the English spoken by Norfolk Islanders.

4 Conclusions

Having worked with Norf'k language for more than a decade, I am becoming increasingly aware how much still needs to be found out about this language, and how this is becoming more difficult as time passes. Unless drastic measures are taken, Norf'k and Pitkern may, together with other lesser-known varieties of English, disappear and remain underdocumented. Fortunately there is an almost universal wish among Norfolk Islanders to see their language preserved. All parents who returned a questionnaire distributed by the school in 2007, for instance, expressed a wish to see more Norf'k language in the primary school, and there is a cooperative project between the school, museum and government and the University of Adelaide to preserve and strengthen the language. There are still many fluent speakers of traditional Norf'k, as the majority of children that entered school were dominant speakers of Norf'k until about 1960. After this date, English-dominant or English-only has become the norm. Because of the small size of the population and the participation of older speakers in the project, there is a good chance that the shift to English can be reversed.

References

Baker, Philip. 1990. 'Off target.' In *Journal of Pidgin and Creole Languages* 5(1): 107–19.

Baker, Philip and Magnus Huber. 2001. 'Atlantic, Pacific and world-wide features in English-lexicon contact languages.' In *English World-Wide: A Journal of Varieties of English* 22(2): 157–208.

Bakker, Peter. 1994. 'Pidgins.' In Jacques Arends, Pieter Muysken and Norval Smith, eds. *Pidgins and Creoles: An Introduction*. Amsterdam and Philadelphia: John Benjamins Publishing Company, 25–9.

Buffett, Alice. 1999. *Speak Norfolk Today: An Encyclopaedia of the Norfolk Island Language*. Norfolk Island: Himii Publishing Company.

Buffett, Alice and Donald Laycock. 1988. *Speak Norfolk Today*. Norfolk Island: Himii Publishing.

Cook, Duncan. 1938. *Pitcairn Island Medical Report*. London: His Majesty's Stationery Office.

Dening, Greg. 1992. *Mr Bligh's Bad Language*. Cambridge: Cambridge University Press.

Ehrhart, Sabine. 1993. *Le Créole Francais de St-Louis (le Tayo) en Nouvelle-Calédonie*. Hamburg: Helmut Buske Verlag.

Flint, E. H. n.d. 'Form-meaning correspondences.' Unpublished typescript, located in Flint papers, Fryer Collection, University of Queensland.

    1979. 'Stable societal diglossia in Norfolk Island.' In William Francis Mackey and Jacob Ornstein, eds. *Sociolinguistic Studies in Language Contact: Methods and Cases*. The Hague/Paris/New York: Mouton Publishers, 295–333.

Harrison, S. 1972. 'The Language of Norfolk Island.' M.A. Hons. Diss., School of English Studies, Macquarie University, Sydney.

Holm, John. 1988. *Pidgins and Creoles*. Cambridge: Cambridge University Press.

Ingram, John and Peter Mühlhäusler. 2004. 'Norfolk Island-Pitcairn English: phonetics and phonology.' In Bernd Kortmann, Edgar W. Schneider, Kate Burridge, Rajend Mesthrie and Clive Upton, eds. *A Handbook of Varieties of English*, vol. I: *Phonology*, 781–802. Berlin and New York: Mouton de Gruyter.

Källgård, Ånders. 1998. 'Fut yoli noo bin laane aklen – A Pitcairn Island word list.' In Peter Mühlhäusler, ed. *Papers in Pidgin and Creole Linguistics*. No. 5. Canberra: Pacific Linguistics, 107–71.

Kortmann, Bernd and Benedikt Szmrecsanyi. 2004. 'Global synopsis: Morphological and syntactic variation in English.' In Kortmann et al., 1142–1202.

Kortmann, Bernd, Edgar W. Schneider, Kate Burridge, Rajend Mesthrie and Clive Upton (eds.). 2004. *A Handbook of Varieties of English*, vol. II: *Morphology and Syntax*. Berlin and New York: Mouton de Gruyter.

Laycock, Donald. 1982. 'Melanesian linguistic diversity: A Melanesian choice.' In R. J. May and H. N. Nelson, eds. *Melanesia: Beyond Diversity*. Canberra: Research School of Pacific Studies, Australian National University, 263–72.

   1989. 'The status of Pitcairn-Norfolk: Creole, dialect or cant?' In U. Ammon, ed. *Status and Function of Languages and Language Varieties*. Berlin/New York: Walter de Gruyter, 608–29.

   1990. 'The interpretation of variation in Pitcairn-Norfolk.' In Jerold A. Edmondson, Crawford Feagin and Peter Mühlhäusler, eds. *Development and Diversity: Linguistic Variation across Time and Space. A Festschrift for Charles-James N. Bailey*. Texas: Summer Institute of Linguistics and the University of Texas at Arlington, 621–7.

Laycock, Donald and Peter Mühlhäusler. 1990. 'Language engineering: special languages.' In N. E. Collinge, ed. *An Encyclopedia of Language*. London/New York: Routledge, 843–75.

'Metoixos' [Hugh Carleton]. 1850. 'Pitcairn's Island, The Shipping Gazette and Sydney general'. *Trade List*, vii, pp. 272–277. Cited in H. E. Maude. 1964. 'Some quotations about the Pitcairnese language.' In A. S. Ross and A. W. Moverley, eds. *The Pitcairnese Language*. New York: Oxford University Press, 45–101.

Milroy, Lesley. 1980. *Language and Social Networks*. Oxford: Basil Blackwell.

Mühlhäusler, Peter. 1998. 'How creoloid can you get?' *Journal of Pidgin and Creole Languages* 13: 355–72.

   1999. 'On the origins of Pitcairn-Norfolk.' *Stellenbosch Papers in Linguistics, Language Genesis* 32: 67–84.

   2003. 'A note on reduplication in Pitkern-Norfolk.' In Silvia Kouwenberg, ed. *Twice Meaningful: Morphological Reduplication in Contact Languages*. London: Battlebridge, 239–43.

   2007. 'How can dominated languages be marketed? With special reference to Norf'k (Norfolk Island, South Pacific).' Presented at Babel in Reverse? Language Ideology in the 21st Century – Duisburg Essen Conference, February 2007.

   2008. 'Multifunctionality in Pitkern-Norf'k and Tok Pisin.' *Journal of Pidgin and Creole Languages* 23: 75–113.

Raine, Captain. 1821. 'Captain Raine's narrative of a visit to Pitcairn's Island in the ship Surrey, 1821.' In *Australian Magazine*, 1: 80–84, 109–114.

Reinecke, John E. 1969. *Language and Dialect in Hawaii: A Sociolinguistic History to 1935*, ed. Stanley M. Tsuzaki. Honolulu: University of Hawaii Press.

Reinecke, John E., Stanley M. Tsuzaki, David DeCamp, I. F. Hancock and R. E. Wood. 1975. *A Bibliography of Pidgin and Creole Languages*. Honolulu: The University Press of Hawaii.

Ross, A. S. and A. W. Moverley. 1964. *The Pitcairnese Language*. New York: Oxford University Press.

Samarin, William J. 1971. 'Salient and substantive pidginization.' In Dell Hymes, ed. *Pidginization and Creolization of Languages: Proceedings of a conference held at the University of the West Indies Mona, Jamaica, April 1968*. Cambridge: Cambridge University Press, 117–400.

Shapiro, H. L. 1928. 'Robinson Crusoe's children. Pick from the past.' In *Natural History*, May–June. www.naturalhistorymag.com/editors_pick/1928_05_06pick.html-24k (accessed 6 July 2007).

Index